P. 46
64 93,98
91
136
249
257
264
273 287
285
303

Prince of Players

EDWIN BOOTH

Prince of Players

EDWIN BOOTH

BY

ELEANOR RUGGLES

W · W · NORTON & COMPANY · INC ·

NEW YORK

PRINTED IN THE UNITED STATES OF AMERICA
BY H. WOLFF, NEW YORK

For Katherine Coldwell

Contents

vii

PART SEVEN

Illustrations

ix

Author's Note

EDWIN BOOTH made two recordings in 1890, but for some time I was half afraid to hear them—afraid that Booth's voice and style might not measure up to the enthusiastic descriptions I had at second hand.

It seemed my plain duty to listen, however, and so I did, at the Harvard Theatre Collection in Cambridge, Massachusetts, not three miles away from where Booth lies buried in Mount Auburn Cemetery. I listened while Booth's voice sounded, faint but distinct, out of the crackling surface noise in Othello's address to the senators:

> Most potent, grave, and reverend signiors.

I had expected rant, but these were quiet tones. The diction was exquisite, the delivery formal and grand but stirring and unstilted. A few reminders of an older method had to be got used to: the elocutionary use of "me" for "my" of "oll" for "all," and—a definite flaw to a modern ear—an occasional singsong cadence, as "my *boy*ish days." The voice itself, though, was the most beautiful speaking voice I had ever heard, with great poetry and feeling, yet with no straining for effect, and I suddenly understood the ecstatic, nostalgic praises of the men and women, my own grandparents, for example, who had heard Booth in life.

The second record was of Hamlet's "To be, or not to be." The surface noise was much more obstructive this time, with fearful sputterings and banshee wails. I tried playing the disc over and over, following the words of the speech on a printed copy until by degrees they became clear. It was a moving revelation. Booth had been for more than fifty years a dweller in that country of which he was speaking so softly and intimately:

> The undiscover'd country from whose bourn
> No traveller returns.

Yet through the screeches and burrs of that ancient record penetrated a voice that was saturated with the magnetism of the living man and an emotion that seemed to breathe itself out of a whole lifetime's "acquaintance with grief."

I have heard Hamlet's famous lines given by twentieth-century actors less conventionally, and, perhaps, from an intellectual point of view, more interestingly than Booth delivered them. But not from anyone else have I heard a rendering that so touched and thrilled with that overwhelming, mysterious quality of "something more"; that extraordinarily poignant and yet robust appeal, which, I suppose, is genius, and which sweeps away reservations in the listener, making the mere originality and intellect so much cultivated by our contemporaries seem superficial and insipid.

To judge by these fragments of his art, Edwin Booth really was an actor whose greatness would tower over the talents of today. We should all have more faith in the claims of our grandparents.

PART ONE

CHAPTER 1

Mr. Booth

My father, in his habit as he liv'd.
Hamlet, *Act III, scene 4*

 LATE IN the 1840's a middle-aged man and a boy, the one obviously in the care of the other, could be seen occasionally weaving through the streets of one of the eastern cities, New York or Philadelphia or Richmond. It was the boy who led; the lurching, grizzled man who followed. This, combined with the man's look of being *somebody* and the exceptional beauty of the dark-haired, anxious-eyed child, made passers-by stare. One would ask another: "Who's that?"

"Don't you recognize him? It's Mr. Booth. Junius Brutus Booth. He's drunk again."

"And the boy?"

"That's his son Edwin."

More than twenty years earlier Junius Brutus Booth had made his home in the wooded country north of Baltimore. He was in pursuit of solitude. First he bought his land, or rather, leased it for a thousand years (which would last his time!), having made sure that it included a spring of sweet water. Then he

3

bought the log cabin some way off in which he was already living, and with the help of every man, horse, and ox in the vicinity rolled it across the fields to his new property and set it down far back from the highroad in a clearing among the giant oak and beech treees on the skirts of the dense forest. He had the bare logs plastered and whitewashed, and the window frames, shutters, and door painted bright red.

There he settled in 1824 with the young girl he called his wife, their two tiny children, little Junius and Rosalie, two loaded blunderbusses, and two fierce watchdogs. As more children were born (Henry, Mary Ann, Frederick, Elizabeth, Edwin, Asia, John Wilkes, and Joseph), he added more rooms; he built quarters for the Negroes, a barn, and stables, and planted an orchard and a vineyard. His place was three miles from the nearest neighbor, three miles in another direction from the town of Belair. Booth called it "the Farm," and through Harford County he was known familiarly as "Farmer Booth."

Often in winter the snow fell so deep that the white cabin lay muffled with only the upper windowpanes visible and the red door from which a path had been shoveled. A plume of smoke, curling from the immense stone chimney, melted a spot of snow on the roof just under it. Everywhere else the empire of the snow was absolute. The woods cast blue shadows over an arctic wasteland across which sharp gusts of wind threw up jets of sparkling snow dust. The house lamps twinkled through the early twilight. The country around lay perfectly hushed, and the only sound from civilization was heard once a week when the postboy's horn wound eerily from the road a quarter of a mile away, as a bag of letters was tossed over the fence.

This was the winter. But with the spring the nipping air gradually turned balmy, and the sun, growing stronger at each rising, coaxed the frozen land back to life. The Judas tree put out its pink blossoms. The woods began to hum like a tuning orchestra. Every door was thrown open; distances grew shorter. From adjacent farms the neighbors arrived in their carryalls to pay visits, but often as not they found Booth gone. In pursuit of solitude he had stepped over the snake fence that bounded his acres, crossed the lane beyond, and entered the forest.

Here along the sweet, spicy-smelling aisles, dappled with beads of light and patches of shadow that swayed with the stirring branches, he would follow paths at first clearly defined. The trail grew fainter as he pressed on through bowers of wild grape and tangled creepers. Still, on he went, across sunny glades gay with butterflies; past the "dismal swamp" flaming with scarlet lobelias; deeper and deeper into thickets where the sun hardly penetrated, secret haunts of the raccoon and opossum. And as he walked his eyes took in these sights with a woodsman's keen interest; his thoughts were content and strayed no further.

But there were times when he neither saw nor heard what lay all around him, for his mind, nourished on the philosophers and poets of every century, retreated inward to dwell on unanswerable questions: Whence do I come? Who am I? Whither am I going? Sometimes he half guessed the answers, saw into his heart, and knowing himself, understood the inmost hearts of others. His body responded with a thrill of sympathy, and just as he was, tramping ahead with hands clasped hard together behind him or groping to thrust aside the interfering branches, which rocked under his grasp, he would cry aloud into the murmuring forest King Lear's mighty invocation to wind and torrent, or one of Richard Crookback's satanic challenges. While his voice explored, his ear weighed critically the sense of each word, each fall of emphasis. Sometimes he stood still, the better to listen. He was a man at work, creative and tentative. For Farmer Booth was called a farmer only by courtesy of his neighbors. He was better known along the whole eastern seaboard as "Mr. Booth," and Mr. Booth was an actor.

His peaceful days at the farm and solitary forest walks were brief respites from a life of strain and travel. Up and down the coast he ranged, from Boston to Charleston, west to Pittsburgh and Nashville, south to Natchez and New Orleans. He played the tragic roles for which he was famous: Richard III, Lear,

Iago, Sir Edward Mortimer in *The Iron Chest*, and Pescara in *The Apostate*. His audiences cheered the small, muscular figure whose face and hands showed healthily sunburned under the theater lamps and whose powerful voice shook the scenery.

Between engagements he hurried home. In the forest silence the bustle of the theater seemed like a dream; it was hard to believe he would ever return to it. At sunrise he sprang out of bed to dig in his garden, barefoot, whistling cheerfully. On summer evenings, when full moonlight swept all Maryland and far out in the country the cry of whippoorwills topped the bass accompaniment of the swamp frogs, he sat beside his wife on the doorstep and watched their daughters and the girls of the neighborhood "tread the green grass." Joining hands and tripping in a circle around one of the trees, while their black, elongated shadows flickered across the moon-drenched clearing, the children sang old English ballads. Many of the songs were acted out and these had a special charm for Booth. Raising his head, he would whistle two low notes, the signal for his youngest daughter, Asia, to run over and hear him request his favorite, which was "Oats, Peas, Beans, and Barley Grow."

His two worlds seldom touched. One winter day, though, as he was on his way to Baltimore with some other actors, the coach broke down. The nearest shelter for the night was his farm, so they all plodded back along the highroad, then in through the trees to the remote cabin.

Booth ushered them inside past the servants and children staring shyly, and as their complete isolation came home to these theater folk one of them exclaimed, shuddering: "Booth, how can you exist in such a wilderness?"

II

Booth was born in London in 1796, and the London he grew up in was a rowdy, gaudy city of coffeehouses and bear gardens, cockfights and daring cardplay: the city of Castlereagh, Beau Brummel, and Fanny Burney. His father was Richard Booth, a lawyer; his grandfather was John Booth, a Jewish silversmith whose forebears had been driven out of Portugal.

Mingling with this Oriental strain in young Junius was a trace of Welsh blood from his mother's side, and through his father's mother he was related to John Wilkes, the parliamentary reformer.

Richard Booth, tall, swarthy, dandified, was an ardent republican. At twenty he had tried idealistically to fly to America to fight alongside the revolutionists but had been caught in mid-flight and haled back to his tyrannical homeland; since that time the ideal of his youth had become the crotchet of his middle age. He was no longer so ready to fight for liberty, but was forever irascibly arguing for it. He held everything American in peculiar honor, hung a portrait of General Washington in his drawing room, and forced his guests to uncover when they looked at it, then to make a respectful bow.

He had married Miss Elizabeth Game, who, after giving him two sons, named Junius Brutus for the Roman republican and Algernon Sydney for the English Roundhead, had died at the birth of her third child, a daughter, Jane.

Junius Brutus Booth was thirteen when a neighbor's servant girl accused him of having got her "in the family way" and was hurriedly paid off. He was seventeen and had enlisted as a midshipman on the brig *Boxer* when he was kept from sailing by a court summons to answer the same charge made by another servant girl, employed in the Booths' own house. Richard Booth went into court himself to be Junius' lawyer and defended him hotly, but the father and son lost their case and the father was compelled to pay up again.

Richard Booth, who had given each of his sons an excellent classical education, now ensconced Junius as a clerk in his law office. The law bored Junius. He lightheartedly detached himself from it and experimentally attached himself to a troupe of "strollers." This was one of the countless bands of wandering players who tramped through the country, eluding the sheriff, sleeping by the road, often reduced to eating the vegetables thrown at them onstage, but perking up bravely as they entered each new town to the beating of a drum from the baggage wagon. The Kembles, founders of a great stage dynasty,

had begun as strollers. So had Edmund Kean, now the lion
of London audiences. Prosperous actors who had climbed the
ladder could always detect the stroller by his seedy look and a
certain strut.

The gypsy life of the stage suited young Booth. He played
farce and tragedy, a clown one night, a king the next; and all
the while he learned to act by getting onstage and acting. What
to do with his hands, how to pitch his voice so it would be heard
in the gallery, were problems he must solve himself. The audience was his faithful teacher. "Speak louder!" "Don't fall
asleep!" roared the spectators, and if a player were incorrigible:
"Get off the stage!" followed by boos and a rain of apples.

"Lord, what legs to stop a pig with at the end of a lane!"
someone bawled at Booth, who was definitely bowlegged.

It was the year 1814 when he crossed the English Channel
along with his troupe to play in the Low Countries. A fellow
traveler saw him on shipboard: "A handsome youth . . .
seated astride a barrel eating a meat pie and shouting: 'By Holy
Paul, I will not dine until his head be brought before me!' "

In Amsterdam Booth watched history in the person of the
Emperor Alexander, who arrived from Russia to take a hand
in the coalition against Napoleon. The young actor, who already had worn the pasteboard crowns of many monarchs,
was disappointed in the Emperor's bearing. "He lacked that
majesty," Booth wrote, "that look above the world, I thought
to see in a sovereign."

In Brussels Booth was quartered at the house of a Madame
Delannoy, whose sprightly daughter Adelaide was twenty-
two, no longer quite young. When he left Brussels Adelaide
eloped with him. Some months later the pair, still unwed,
turned up at his father's house in London. On May 8, 1815,
they were married, and after an interval a baby girl was born
to them.

Booth's acting in the provinces had begun to be noticed. He
was a magnetic little man. Although very short, with stumpy
legs, he carried himself imperiously; his blue-gray eyes looked

black by gaslight; his commanding, delicately formed nose was faintly Oriental; his ears, pierced for earrings, were curiously pointed—"I'm a real satyr!" he liked to boast.

Early in 1817 he received the accolade of the provincial player, an invitation to star in London. He appeared at Covent Garden Theatre as King Richard III in Colley Cibber's blood-and-thunder version of Shakespeare's play, which was immensely more popular than the original.

It was no more than forty years since David Garrick's last performance; there were men living who remembered Garrick. Just seven years before Garrick's birth Thomas Betterton had died, the foremost tragedian during the reign of Charles II. Sixteen years before Betterton was born Richard Burbage had died, for whom it was supposed that his fellow player Shakespeare had written *Hamlet*. So from Burbage to Betterton to Garrick to George Frederick Cooke, who had only departed this life in 1811, the noble traditions of English stagecraft had been handed down. The latest to inherit them was Edmund Kean.

Now Kean, the star of Drury Lane Theatre, considered the part of Richard III virtually his own property. Diminutive and dark as a gypsy, with a sharp, resolute face, Kean was a brutally realistic actor. His King Richard died fighting like a trapped highwayman, staving off sword thrusts with his bare hands, and in this Kean broke away from the inhumanly dignified, reposeful style of acting of which John Philip Kemble was still the great exemplar. Members of the Kemble school portrayed the crudest emotions with fastidious taste. Caught up in the whirlwind of passion, they were careful to keep their dress orderly. In a stage battle (the byword went) "they parried like schoolboys and dropped like gentlemen."

Kean, on the other hand, and now young Booth, were bumptious, bustling little professionals who portrayed naked emotions nakedly. "God renounce me!" growled one old actor, " 'tis only necessary nowadays to be under four feet high, have bandy legs and a hoarseness, and mince my liver! but you'll be thought a great tragedian."

That Booth should have chosen *Richard III* for his London
debut seemed to Kean a clear-cut challenge, which he accepted
by craftily inviting Booth to make a guest appearance on the
same stage with him at Drury Lane playing Iago to Kean's
Othello. Booth foolishly agreed. On their entrance together
down the broad apron the rival actors, both such small men,
looked like two pygmies even through the spyglasses focused on
them by the London beaux. But when they began to act it
was a battle of giants. "He is terribly in earnest," was the su-
percilious Kemble's grudging tribute on first seeing Kean act.
Kean was terribly in earnest now. He used every trick known
to the seasoned star to embarrass a green rival; and as the performance stormed on to its climax the figure of Othello seemed
to grow and to tower over a diminished Iago.

When it was over, Booth scurried back to Covent Garden,
where there was no jealous senior to crowd him out. The reign
of Kean as king of the London stage continued, but in the next
three years Booth's powers wonderfully developed, and by
1820 he was heir apparent.

His and Adelaide's baby girl had died in infancy. Adelaide
had since borne him a son called Richard Junius. Thus happily tethered, Booth and Adelaide seemed the very model of
a devoted couple, but Booth was a hard man for anyone to
tether. He left his family and traveled back briefly to Amsterdam, where he failed to appear for a command performance
before the Prince of Orange; his friend the comedian Tom
Flynn unearthed him in a saloon, his lap full of Dutch girls.

Yet Booth had a capacity for true, deep feeling and singular
faithfulness that had not been tapped. He was in London again
when he met a black-haired flower girl who kept her stall in
the Bow Street Market outside Covent Garden. Mary Ann
Holmes was from Reading in Berkshire. She had a creamy skin
and full bosom, was remarkably voluptuous looking for an
English girl, and she was eighteen, ten years younger than
Adelaide. She had seen Booth onstage in the part of King Lear.
Meeting him offstage, she could hardly believe her liquid
brown eyes and asked softly: "Are you really that poor little
old man?"

Booth persuaded her that he was. He was very persuasive. Since she could read, he gave her a tiny, exquisitely bound set of Byron's poems and soon induced her to take a little trip with him to Calais and Boulogne. On his return Adelaide and his father were none the wiser. But this double life had its disadvantages, the main one being that he was becoming seriously smitten. Appeasing his wife with another false story of a theatrical engagement, he slipped off with Mary Ann to the port of Deal. This second ecstatic holiday was not nearly long enough, and before going home he extended it by a short sea voyage to the Island of Madeira.

Booth was by now hopelessly in love, his passion worked on by the potent native wines; the blue and green landscape, romantic and fantastic as the drop scene for an opera; the hot, whispering nights. The yielding Mary Ann was already with child by him. With hardly a glance back at the wife and son he was abandoning and the career he was cutting short, Booth made his choice. In May, 1821, he engaged passage for himself and his gentle, fruitful sweetheart on the sailing ship *Two Brothers,* bound out of Madeira for America.

III

Charles Gilfert, manager of the theater in Richmond, Virginia, where Booth first applied for an engagement in the New World, seriously doubted whether this boyish stranger really was the famous Booth whose reputation had preceded him across the Atlantic. He offered him a trial as Richard III. It was a triumph, and a few weeks later Booth played the same part in Petersburg. He was late for rehearsal, having missed the coach and walked twenty-five miles in the July heat from Richmond. The Petersburg company waited, and, finally, "a small man," recalls one of the actors, "that I took to be a well-grown boy of about sixteen . . . came running up the stairs, wearing a roundabout jacket and a cheap straw hat, both covered with dust, and inquired for the stage manager. . . . I do not think any man was ever more astonished than I was. . . . Is it possible this can be the great Mr. Booth? . . . I began to think the manager was trying to put off some joke upon us all."

That evening the whole company gathered in the wings of the little country theater, curious to see how the star from London would acquit himself. Booth, handsome and debonair, the nodding white plumes that sprang from his headdress adding a foot to his height, walked casually out onstage and recited Richard's opening soliloquy in a bored, tired voice with an English accent. He made his exit to an eloquent lack of applause. The players in the wings exchanged glances. "It may be very good," whispered one old trouper, the King Henry of the performance, "but I don't fancy it."

Exhausted after his morning's walk, Booth was saving himself for the finale. Not until Act IV, by which time the audience was rattling the playbills and coughing irritably, did he give the first inkling of his powers. Richard darkly hints to the Duke of Buckingham his plan to murder the two little princes:

> I tell thee, coz, I've lately had two spiders
> Crawling upon my startled hopes . . .

As Booth spoke these lines, making his final "g" sing metallically, he plucked at his breast as though something prickled there, and instantly everyone in the theater felt spiders crawling on his own flesh.

The actor's spell had begun to work. His greatest effect occurred in the tent scene, when, to the blue-burning of the lamp and the muffled tap of the drum outside, the King wakes from his nightmare. On the words

> Give me a horse—bind up my wounds!
> Have mercy, Heaven!

Booth started from his couch and dashed down the sharply raked stage to the footlights.

> Ha! soft! 'twas but a dream;
> But then so terrible, it shakes my soul.

In the beams cast upward by the row of candles the whites of

Booth's eyes flashed. His face had turned ashen; it poured so with sweat that the dark ringlets of his wig clung to it.

O tyrant Conscience; how dost thou afflict me?

Again the lack of applause was eloquent. This time it had a different meaning. Five hundred sinners searched their consciences; the awed silence was broken only by their prototype's gasps for breath. But after the last scene, when Richard, as played by Booth in the Kean tradition, had fought tigerishly and died writhing, a long-drawn, involuntary sigh rose out of the audience. Its members returned to themselves and burst into wave on wave of hysterical bravos. So did the actors onstage who stood around Booth's prostrate figure. Booth sprang to his feet and bowed, smiling.

He traveled north to play in New York at the Park Theater, verging on the Bowery, where the streets were loud by day with pedlars' cries: "Sweep-ho!" "Mend your pots and pans!" and by night with the scrape of fiddles, thump of feet in the square dance, and clink of mugs from the sailors' dance halls out of whose doors, invitingly open, streamed the light of whale-oil lamps.

The theaters were noisy as Bedlam. The all-powerful pit whistled and stamped, sending up a stench of onions and whisky to the boxes where the gentlemen sat—in their shirt-sleeves, dangling their legs over the rails and signaling with their fingers to the painted "fancy women" who jammed the third tier reserved for them. In the gallery babies whined until their mothers nursed them, and onstage the actors shouted over the crackle of peanut shells and the kwa-aw-pt of hawking and spitting.

Booth had an ovation in New York and on the Southern circuit where he played next: Baltimore, Norfolk, Charleston (here Mary Ann's child was born in December, 1821), New Orleans, and Savannah. His simple republican manner endeared him to the touchy Americans, notoriously anti-English. Suddenly, impulsively, in a spasm of revulsion from the theater, he determined to leave it. He was only twenty-six but he was disillusioned. He felt he was wasting away his life in the theater, where "nothing is but what is not." His soul was dry with the tumult, the glitter; it thirsted for quiet and reality. He applied for the position of keeper of the desolate Cape Hatteras lighthouse, thinking to bury himself there. A number of managers, worried at this threat to a good investment, made it their business to prevent his getting the post.

Booth had five mouths to feed now, counting the two in England. He was forced to go on acting. But his need of a refuge—a practical need as well as a spiritual, for he must keep Mary Ann under cover—drove him to leave his lodgings in Baltimore and move his mistress and baby son Junius to a log cabin on the lonely property of a Maryland farmer. Here a daughter was born. It was a year later, in 1824, that he leased his own acres and had the cabin rolled across to them, to a still more remote spot on the very edge of the woods. Booth himself was seldom at his farm, but his mind found rest in dwelling on it.

Richard Booth came to America and managed the farm when his son was on tour. The old republican was distinctly surprised at the primitive condition of the republic he had dreamed of so gloriously. He called Belair "Beggarsburg" and the isolated farm "Robinson Crusoe's Island."

In the crude love nest in which Booth had deposited her, a place lonely and strange, peopled by the bronze and ebony faces of the Negro servants, Mary Ann bore her husband eight more children. He was her husband; she was his wife. So they were known in the country around. Booth's father accepted the situation with the better grace as it became clear that this girl from the London flower market, who had aroused his son's passion and who might have been anything, was actually (more than Booth deserved) a stanch and tender helpmate, as devoted to her lover as he to her.

Booth could hardly bear their separations. "The Time seems long while away from you," he wrote from the road. "Let me hear from you by return and believe me ever and affectionately to be Your husband and worshipper, Junius."

To the Booth children every article of rough-hewn furniture inside the cabin was a landmark, solid and dependable, in the dreamlike world of childhood. Each piece stood for a function of life. Their mother's spinning wheel clothed them. The cavernous stone fireplace was the household god before which they worshiped, lying dozing in wicker cradles woven during the winter evenings by Joe, the black boy. And at each waking the sun and moon, painted as human faces on the upper half of the looking glass, beamed down on them; and mysterious objects later identified as an inkhorn, a bunch of quills, and little bags of seed swinging from hooks set around the glass lured their sleep-filled eyes. Bread was taken out of the round Dutch oven and fed to them smoking on pewter platters with a silver spoon worn thin with age. Their great-grandfather, a silversmith in England, had made the spoon. In the corner cupboard was some painted china, which they were not allowed to handle: this was art. And for education, three gawky engravings hung on the walls—"Timon of Athens," "The Death of Bonaparte," and "The Roman Matron Showing Her Husband How To Die."

Booth was acting during most of the winter but in summer he was home for long periods, and to prove he was a farmer in earnest would harness Fanny the plowhorse and Peacock the piebald pony to the carryall, which was loaded with home-grown vegetables, then jog into Baltimore to sell his produce. He advertised for bones to use as fertilizer; a great stack of them bleaching in the sun by the barn door gave the farmyard a grisly look. He subscribed to a weekly farm journal and filed it away with his playbills.

Yet there was a side to Booth that the simple life could not satisfy. The life of the mind also attracted him. The farmer's living room was also the scholar's library. His books, small calf-bound editions, were in several languages. Here were the English poets, Burton's *Anatomy*, Locke's *Essay*, Paley's *The-*

ology, Dante, Tasso, Terence, Plutarch, Racine, Lope de Vega, the Koran, the Talmud, *The Imitation of Christ*, and the Bible. Booth was deeply spiritual; he found truth everywhere—in the pages of the Talmud, in synagogues where he talked with the rabbis in Hebrew, in Catholic cathedrals where he sank to his knees and crossed himself. He loved animals and believed with Pythagoras that men's souls are born again in animals' bodies. In his pocket he carried a piece of human skin, would pull it out, ask people to say what creature it came from, and when they guessed wrong would cry triumphantly: "That's a man's hide, tanned! We animals are all alike."

For several years he forbade his family to eat meat or fish. No stock was killed on his farm, no opossums were hunted, no rabbits trapped. Even the poisonous copperheads went unmolested. When one of them sunning in a furrow was hurt by the plow, Booth tossed Mary Ann's bonnet out of the only bandbox in the house, lined the box with wadding and bedded the snake inside until it was well enough to crawl away. "For nearly *three days*," Mary Ann told her neighbors plaintively, "that fearful reptile occupied my band-box and our parlor!"

Master and arbiter of his little community, Booth was often its doctor, sometimes its clergyman. If a death occurred and no minister was near, it was Booth who read, most beautifully, the service in the tiny family burying ground where the black servants (he had no slaves) were buried too, outside the rails. His comings and goings were the erratic pendulum that regulated the life of the farm. Whenever he returned, travel-weary, and set eyes once again on the white-washed cabin, guarded by trees and with the body of the forest looming up behind it, his nerves relaxed, his step quickened and his heart leaped with affection for his own fireside. Away from home he sent busy instructions: "Joe must fit up the Garden Paling so as to prevent the fowls getting in, & it is time now to sow Radishes and Carrots."

His two chief cares were for his animals: the dog Boatswain "should have a run once or twice every Day & his Tub of Water always supplied (a thing very likely to be forgot as of no importance when in fact it is). . . ." And for his children: "Pay all attention to the regularity of their diet & *motions*."

To his father he wrote: "I'm sick of acting—much rather would I be home. Have the stray Hogs returned?"

And to Mary Ann: "My love for you is still undiminished. Take care of your Health & don't be dull or fretting there's my own soul. God bless you dear Wife."

IV

Booth went back twice to England, re-entering briefly the brilliant arena of the London theater with its satiety of talent and cut-throat rivalries.

In 1825, with unbelievable boldness, he spirited Mary Ann to England with him and with unbelievable adroitness kept his two wives safely apart. Mary Ann was packed off to visit her mother in Reading, while Booth rejoined Adelaide and his son Richard, now six years old, in London. He had sent them money during the past four years and Adelaide, still in blissful ignorance of his other household, welcomed him gratefully.

But soon he slipped off with Mary Ann for the continent and sailed from Rotterdam for New York, leaving his legitimate wife and son alone again to shift for themselves. His stage appearances in London and the provinces had not been entirely successful, and he came back thankfully to the warmer embrace of the uncouth, friendly country that had made him one of its brightest stars.

The name MR. BOOTH on a playbill could fill any theater in America. Booth was often paid a hundred dollars a night. But he was not happy; he was a man against himself. When he was young, fame was his spur. Now he had fame, and the spur was wanting.

He took to reviving himself after the play with a pint of porter or a glass of brandy. From there it was only a step to drinking beforehand to brace himself. Then he began to act when drunk, though this was nothing singular. All too frequently an actor, his stomach whirling, whisked offstage for a moment to heave-ho, then tottered back, or wholly fuddled, fell plunk to the floor and was hauled off by the elbows and heels, after which the harassed manager sidled from the wing to read the delinquent's part out of the promptbook.

Richard Booth drank too, neglecting his duties as overseer and sneaking off to the nearest saloon. He and Junius had it back and forth. "Sir," Booth wrote home furiously to his father during one of his own absences from the farm, "Argument with you is out of the Question, but I beg you for *your own Sake*, to refrain from that destructive and Sense-depriving Custom."

Alas, the same craving that could transform the father from a dignified gentleman in formal clothes, with hair neatly powdered, into a disheveled figure muttering and stalking through the house, his hair in strings, his bare feet showing long, uncut toenails—this same craving had increasing dominion over the son. And then: "Ah, Junius, Junius," the old man whimpered when it was his son's turn for a debauch.

But Junius Booth's drinking was only one symptom of something more serious, more alarming. He began to show signs of derangement. His drinking brought to the surface a deep-seated disturbance of mind.

His sorrows helped to unhinge him. He was playing in Richmond when word arrived that his four-year-old son Frederick was desperately ill. He made all haste home, but the child died. Dangerously despondent, Booth was returning to Richmond when news of the illness of his little daughter Elizabeth caught up with him. He reached home to see her die.

At this second loss Booth went out of his mind completely. Mary Ann nursed him back to health. He was up and off again when a third child, another daughter named after her mother, died suddenly. Booth hurled himself back across the snowy miles that separated them, had the little girl's body disinterred and carried into the warm house where he hung over it, beseeching God for a miracle. Recently he had broken his rule and eaten "dead flesh." He was sure this had caused his afflictions. Guilt oppressed him and he did penance, filling his shoes with dried peas, then fitting leaden soles to them and trudging all the way from Baltimore to Washington.

"Father's calamity" was what Booth's children called his spells of madness. They learned from their courageous mother to treat him during these periods with tact and patience mingled with reverence. The general public was not so forebearing, and Booth was often blamed for being drunk when he was really ill.

"I can't read! I'm a charity boy! I can't read! Take me to the lunatic asylum!" he shouted in the middle of a performance at the Tremont Theater in Boston. The manager hustled him offstage while he simpered and screeched with laughter. Then he gave his captors the slip, shucked off most of his clothes and walked in his stocking feet from Boston to Providence. The driver of the Providence coach going the other way saw him in his underwear striding along the road between Dedham and Walpole, shaking his head and gesticulating.

Once, for no good reason except that he felt like it, he played Cassius in *Julius Caesar* walking on tiptoe and Pierre in *Venice Preserved* speaking in a whisper. Often he bolted from his dressing room before the curtain rose. He was a favorite, so the audience usually stayed seated, venting its impatience in brays from the pit of "H'ist dat rag!" while one of the actors and perhaps a gentleman or two from the boxes hurried out to find him. They tried the taverns first, but Booth was not always in them. During *The Merchant of Venice* in New York they discovered him dressed as Shylock slaving at the pumps to put out a fire many blocks away. In Providence a hotel clerk climbed through a window into the tragedian's locked room and peeped under the bed. There almost in his face were Booth's bright eyes staring at him.

"He had some very odd ways at times," one old actress recollected fondly. This was Mrs. John Drew, who remembered a performance of *Hamlet* in Natchez. Ophelia was giving her all in the mad scene when a voice offstage began to crow like a rooster and the manager, glaring up into the flies, saw Booth, who was doing the crowing, perched on top of a ladder.

"The manager," Mrs. Drew recalls, "ascended the ladder and had quite a lengthy discussion with Mr. Booth, who at last consented to come down on condition that he should resume his high position after the play, and remain there until Jackson was re-elected President." Booth knew Jackson, whom he had visited at The Hermitage, near Nashville.

And sometimes Booth was normally drunk. Again in Boston an audience waited for his King Lear. Backstage the exhilarated star was being helped to his dressing room when he heard the growling and stamping of the crowd. He shook off the puny arms holding him, pushed his red, hilarious face between the curtains, and waved his clenched fist.

"Shut up, shut up!" he yelled. "Keep quiet! You just keep still and in ten minutes I'll give you the God damnedest Lear you ever saw in your lives."

He kept his promise.

Even those who knew him well couldn't always be sure if he were drunk or raving. "I must cut somebody's throat today. Whom shall I take?" he demanded at rehearsal one morning. Next minute, whipping out a dagger, he made a rush for James Wallack, the English actor, who in his panic stumbled and fell so that the blade passed harmlessly over him.

Booth arrived by sloop at Annapolis and failed to show up at the theater where his name was billed. Tom Flynn, his old friend from England, discovered him still on board ship in the captain's cabin pointing a pistol at the captain, who cowered in a corner hugging a bowl of Epsom salts.

"Drink, sir, drink!" boomed the little actor in the giant's voice that astonished his audiences. "You're bilious and need physic. I know it by your eyes! I know it by your skin! Drink, sir, or I'll send you to another and a better world!"

"Pray let me off. Think of my wife and children. I've drunk six bowls full already," the victim was sniveling as Flynn burst in.

It was becoming fashionable to allow stage plays on Sunday, but many actors primly refused to perform. Booth was in Philadelphia. The first Sunday morning of his engagement there he jumped into his Hamlet costume, borrowed a horse, and clattered through the streets alongside the church-bound Philadelphians.

"Ladies and gentlemen," he called into the Sunday hush, "I intend to perform *Hamlet* tonight and a good play is worth forty sermons." Then he broke into a Lincolnshire drinking song called "The Poachers":

> Oh, 'tis my delight
> Of a shiny night. . . .

He hadn't troubled to saddle or bridle his horse. Without warning it bolted and Booth, who had twisted halfway around, lurched forward onto its rump. He clutched the streaming tail with both hands, locked his legs around the animal's neck, and was borne as though on the wind's back out of sight of the amazed citizens. This ended his Philadelphia engagement. His friends returned him to the farm in Maryland, where his family closed its ranks around him and the country life soon soothed his mind.

In 1836 Booth visited England again, taking Mary Ann and the children. Adelaide and young Richard were in Brussels visiting her family. Somehow Adelaide still believed him, as he assured her by letter through the years that he would return one day to be with her permanently.

In London little Henry—Henry Byron Booth, named for Lord Byron—died of smallpox. He was eleven. Edwin, who was three, and the baby Asia came down with the plague but only lightly, having been vaccinated, and soon were well. Of all the children Henry was the dearest to his father. On the stone raised over his son's grave in the yard of the Pentonville chapel Booth had carved the beautiful lines by Southey:

> Oh, even in spite of death, yet still my choice,
> Oft with the inward, all-beholding eye
> I think I see thee, and I hear thy voice.

The old sense of guilt overhung him as he herded his family back to America. He had other cares. His sister Jane had married a fellow named Jimmy Mitchell, who had been a kitchen boy in her father's London house. While Booth was in London Mitchell blackmailed him—Booth was open to blackmail, as his brother-in-law well knew. Home again in Maryland, Booth sent his sister the wherewithal to leave her husband and join him at the farm with her eight children. But all ten Mitchells including Jimmy came, and the unsavory tribe of Mitchell children, one of whom was "not right," scuffled and snapped like scabby puppies over Booth's chosen refuge. Their father bullied their mother, wouldn't work, was constantly in liquor, and courtly old Richard Booth found his own solace in another bottle and declined to address a word to any of them.

Booth's health was usually better at the farm, where he seldom drank. Even here the cloud sometimes settled over him. His pony Peacock died. Booth wrapped the body in a bed sheet and invited his neighbors to the funeral. His feeling for animals had become a mania. He loved each dog, each horse, belonging to him with a personal love, and in their devoted eyes he saw every virtue that man has not. He was playing in Louisville when he wrote to a Unitarian clergyman there, the Reverend James Freeman Clarke, requesting a burial place for his "friends." Clarke, misreading the word as "friend," for he had never been required to bury more than one friend at a time, called on the actor at his hotel.

"Was the death sudden?" he asked sympathetically.

"Very," said Booth.

"Was he a relative?"

"Distant," answered Booth laconically, then offered wine and cigars, which were refused.

"Well," Booth said, "let me try to entertain you in another way. Perhaps you'd like to hear me read?"

He opened a book and the incantatory stanzas of *The Rime of the Ancient Mariner* began to beat forth. They held Clarke hypnotized. "I have listened," he writes, "to Edmund Kean, to Rachel, to Jenny Lind, to Fanny Kemble, to Daniel Webster, to Dr. Channing, to Emerson, to Victor Hugo; but none of them affected me as I was affected by this reading. Booth actually thought himself the mariner. *I was* the wedding-guest, listening to his story."

At last the reading ended and "again I found myself sitting in the little hotel parlor, by the side of a man with glittering eye. I drew a long breath."

Booth asked: "Would you like to look at the remains?" and snatching up a candle led his guest into the bedroom. Laid out on a sheet were about a bushel of dead pigeons, which had been shot flying over Louisville and offered for sale on the street corner. Booth knelt and gathered up an armful of the little, limp bodies. Tears streamed down his cheeks as he railed at the massacre. Clarke was really touched, but he flatly rejected Booth's request for a coffin, hearse, Christian service, and plot in the churchyard for his pigeons.

"Why not help me?" Booth pleaded. "Do you fear the laugh of man?"

"No," said Clarke sincerely, "but I don't look at it as you do."

Booth bought a plot in a cemetery outside the city and buried his friends there. At the theater during the next few days he acted his parts with such savage abandon that the other players were terrified of him. Soon his fit reached its climax. He disappeared from his hotel and was found wandering through the snow in some woods beyond Louisville.

Booth's family never did learn just what happened in Charleston on the famous occasion when Booth broke his nose. He and Tom Flynn were bound for Charleston with a theatrical troupe when their ship reached the spot off the city harbor where a discouraged actor named William Conway had drowned himself. Booth cried: "I'm just going to see Conway!" and jumped overboard. A couple of sailors helped Flynn lower a boat and Booth was hoisted into it.

But this was only a preliminary. According to one story, as Booth and Flynn sat drinking in Truesdale's saloon after their

Charleston opening, Booth suddenly imagined he was Othello and Flynn was Iago, and shrieking

"Villain, be sure thou prove my love a whore,"

he flew at Flynn and hurled him under the table. Flynn seized a poker and landed a blow that broke Booth's nose.

Another version had it that Booth crawled through a window into the room in the Planters' Hotel where Flynn lay sleeping, swung an iron firedog up from the fireplace and brought it down over Flynn's right eye. Flynn leaped out of bed, and the two men grappled and crashed to the floor. Flynn, twice the larger, finally pinned Booth down, but in the struggle Booth's nose was broken.

Even before this accident Booth's disorder had changed him. He was in the prime of life but his face was ravaged, clawed by dissipation and sorrow. His once clear eyes were bloodshot, they had pouches under them. He came back to his family from Charleston with his remaining good feature, his aquiline nose, bashed in and ruined. The damage to his nose had injured his voice and his head tones emerged weak and disagreeably nasal. "The last time we saw Mr. Booth in *Hamlet*," declared a member of his audience, "we could not but dwell on the appositeness of Ophelia's remark:

O! what a noble mind is here o'erthrown."

Yet even now in his inspired moments—battered and disreputable, known over the land as "crazy Booth, the mad tragedian"—he could enter a lagging scene and instantly animate it. He carried himself still like a handsome man. His person bristled with charm and intellect. He continued to act. After the first shock his audiences forgot the broken nose and in time his voice grew strong again.

So Booth went on his way from theater to theater. The brown-bearded Walt Whitman saw him as Richard. The first thing one saw was his lifted foot passing the wing, then the quiet entrance from the side, "as with head bent," writes Whit-

man, "he slowly walks down the stage to the footlights with
that peculiar and abstracted gesture, musingly kicking his
sword which he holds off from him by its sash. Though fifty
years have passed since then, I can hear the clank and feel the
perfect following hush of perhaps three thousand people waiting."

Booth went on his way, dazzling the public and driving managers distracted, borrowing playscripts from barkeepers who
kept them under the counter for him, spouting Shakespeare
from table tops, bawling out "The Poachers" ("Oh, 'tis my
delight . . ."), and smashing tavern furniture. "Praise be to
Allah!" he began a letter to a friend. The letter was headed:
"Exterior of Louisville Jail."

"Your loving communication has been just delivered after
my third incarceration in the above for carrying on solely an
unprofitable and disgraceful business: namely—telling the
Truth to Scoundrels."

Booth had been jailed for disorderly conduct. His letter con-
tinues: "I hear you intend making money by sale of Hog's
blood—in which is the life. It is none of my business—only
be sure blood calls for blood. . . . The Hindoo religion is the
only one I believe to be at all like Truth—were this my last
moment & Death hanging over me I would declare myself
Hindoo versus quasidum.—Had there been no fish there would
have been no Crucifixion—do you take? Excuse bad pen, hurry
—dirty hands torn papers and Steamboat about to go."

Between these adventures there were halcyon days at the
farm, where communion with nature usually restored Booth's
balance. Then back on the road he went, to the turbulent life
that most undid him. But as his drinking became more determined and his outbreaks more dangerous, he could no longer
be trusted to go alone. In his last years a companion traveled
with him whose duty it was to divert and tranquilize his excited mind and to coax the glass from his hand when possible.
His son Edwin was the companion.

CHAPTER 2

Father and Son

Come on, my boy. How dost, my boy?
. . . I have one part in my heart
That's sorry yet for thee.
                    King Lear, *Act III, scene 2*

 ON THE night of November 13, 1833, a shower of meteors, fiery spearheads trailing clouds of brightness, shot across the sky over the Booth farm. Below in the cabin candles were burning. A son had just been born. He was born with a caul. In the servants' quarters the wise old Negroes cackled delightedly while the huge shadows of their turbaned heads and corncob pipes wagged in chorus on the walls behind them. Consulting the weird lore of their African ancestors, they peered into the child's future and predicted that because of the star-shower and the caul he would be lucky and "gifted to see sperrits."

Booth named this son Edwin for the American tragedian Edwin Forrest and Thomas for Tom Flynn. Edwin Thomas was the seventh child, another good omen. After him was born a daughter, named Asia by her father in remembrance of that pleasant continent where God walked with man after the creation; and next came John Wilkes, who bore the proudest name in the family. Tenth and last was Joseph Adrian.

The little Booths were lovely to look at. Edwin, Asia, and John looked much alike, having their mother's dark hair and her glorious eyes with irises of such an intense brown as to seem black, the whites very white, the lids fringed with long, up-curling lashes. From their father they had all three inherited a nervous instability, a feeling for beauty, and, underlying everything else, a capacity for melancholy never to be out-grown.

Edwin was a quiet boy. Sturdy Junius had his father's asser-tiveness, and Johnny was a born charmer. But visitors to the house who met Edwin often overlooked his own charm, which was not assertive. He was as full of fun and charged with en-thusiasms as his boisterous brothers, but much less eager than they were to challenge. His motions were very quick and graceful, like a small cat's. In moments of excitement his vel-vety eyes grew enormous, but only an occasional expression—when the black eyebrows arched, the lashes swept upward, and the deep pupils flashed—gave promise of his father's fire.

Asia was passionate and sensitive. She shut herself in her room to weep and write poems. The give and take of life in a large family came hard to her, and she passed whole days glowering with resentment over imagined slights. "Missy's long sulks," the servants called these moods.

Johnny stormed through the woods on horseback, scream-ing his throat dry at invisible enemies and whirling a Mexican War saber over his head. He loved the grim old ballads like *Lord Randall* and *Barbara Allen,* and could detect the sadness in the music of the Negroes' jew's-harps twanging tunelessly out of the dim kitchen on a summer evening. He had the Booth love of animals. Once his darling horse Cola di Rienzi bit him and he cried. Once he caught a katydid and kissed it before letting it go. Johnny took the place in his father's heart of little dead Henry, and his adoring mother saw in his escapades the germ of heroic deeds. A hundred times she had told how one night when he was six months old, as she sat nursing him beside the warm chimney place, she had prayed to know his future. And as if in answer, the dying flames blazed up, taking the shape of an arm, then distinctly forming the word "country," and finally in fiery letters her son's name: JOHN WILKES BOOTH. The vision suggested glory.

One of Edwin's earliest glints of memory was of riding out with his father and reaching the farm very late. The midnight forest swarmed with horrors. As they pulled up at the edge of the farm Booth swung Teddy, trembling, down from the horse and over the snake fence and set him firmly on the ground. "Your foot is on your native heath!" he cried masterfully, and his voice banished the unseen evil things and cast a charmed, safe circle around themselves. In the now friendly darkness they waited, listening to the clopping of hoofs until the man who had come with them to take back the hired horses had galloped out of hearing.

Old Richard Booth died and was buried in Baltimore. A Hebrew inscription was cut into his gravestone. Young Junius, called "June"—a rather heavy but handsome youngster, with his father's strong profile before the nose was broken—left home to go on the stage and soon married into the profession. His bride was an actress eleven years older than he, named Clementine De Bar. At home Rosalie, the eldest daughter, who was painfully shy and had the reputation locally of being somewhat odd, helped her mother in the kitchen and dairy.

The younger children grew taller. Joseph, the baby, began to grow into the dark good looks of the three ahead of him; and, along with them all, a cherry shoot their father had planted by his cabin door sprang up until from the crotch five branches separated like fingers. On summer afternoons the tree babbled aloud with many young voices as the Booths and their Mitchell cousins crouched in the branches and ranted Shakespeare. Away in the forest they searched for elf-shot, the tiny flint arrowheads, and on the smooth grass they traced the fairy rings trodden by invisible dancers. Asia strummed her guitar beside the brook while little brown frogs slipped out of the water to listen to her. A great green bullfrog that lived in the well popped to the surface and bellowed as loud as a bull; the neighbors could hear him a mile away and the children, knowing he was very old, wondered for how long his terrifying roar had sounded in the forest before any Booth set foot there. In the evenings the Negroes told ghost stories, their eyes rolling with the relish of horror. Far out in the darkness the wind wailed and the long howl of a dog made the children's flesh crawl.

Mr. Booth was forever urging his sons to work with their hands. He had wanted Junius to study surgery and June had done so for a few months, then defaulted to become an actor. Edwin his father seriously advised to be a cabinetmaker. By this time they were living in Baltimore on Exeter Street, staying at the farm only in summer. The Mitchells had been got rid of, though they were in Baltimore, too. The boy who "wasn't right" peddled papers. One of the girls sold refreshments in a theater. Their father lived by himself in an attic and occasionally climbed out through a trap door down a ladder and slouched along the streets, sneering at the young Booths when he ran across them that they were "too fine for him, begad."

All the Booth children had fair educations except Edwin, who was still of school age when the great change occurred in his life. He had gone first to a class in Baltimore taught by Susan Hyde, a maiden lady. There he learned the three R's, and from there his father sent him to be tutored by a retired French naval officer, Monsieur Louis Dugas, who more than anything improved Edwin's fencing. June, an expert, had already taught him the rudiments of swordsmanship. Still later he went at erratic intervals to a Baltimore school whose principal, a Mr. Kearny, emphasized elocution and dramatic readings —this was accident, and not design on his father's part; Booth did not wish his sons to be actors. From an Italian, Signor Picioli, Edwin learned a little of the violin, and a friendly Negro taught him to sing plantation songs and thrum the banjo like a professional, making it give out a bell-like bass resonance.

But this was all. He was thirteen when he was sent on the road to watch over his father.

When they were young, Booth and Mary Ann had often traveled together and even acted together for a few performances, though Mary Ann was no real actress. Sometimes they had taken Teddy with them to be put to bed in a chest of drawers in the dressing room, and when Booth rushed in between scenes, he would toss the rudely awakened infant into the air with a, "Why, that's my dainty Ariel!"

Later Mary Ann dropped out, and for a time Booth traveled alone. His drinking grew worse and June was dispatched with him to be his chaperon. Then June, having acquired a taste for the theater, married into it and struck out on his own. Booth's next companion was none other than his legitimate son Richard, called over from London, where he had been scraping a paltry living teaching Latin and Greek. Booth forwarded him the funds to sail to America, then took him on the road. But this was tempting fate too far. When Richard discovered that another woman passed as Booth's wife and that Booth had six children who carried his name with no legal right to it, he left his father's service. In 1847 it was Edwin, one of the base-born sons, who became Booth's last and most faithful guardian.

At first when his father wasn't acting, Edwin went back to Mr. Kearny's classes. Sometimes Booth would start out by himself, but sooner or later the word came: "I need Ted!"

When his son appeared, "Did you bring your books?" was Booth's greeting, for they kept up the fiction that while Booth was behind the footlights Edwin sat studying in the dressing room. Then father and son would sally forth together on the grinding theater circuit by coach and rail and river steamer. Booth's engagement over, Edwin dropped from his high place as a man among men and became a schoolboy again until the next summons. His schoolmates envied him wildly, never realizing how gladly he would have stayed among them. A vagabond life soon lost its charm.

At home and in his right mind, Booth largely ignored Ed-

win. His other children, Johnny especially, being more vivacious, amused him more and were the children of his happy
hours. But away from home he needed a quiet presence. It
steadied him to re-enter his dressing room after a performance
and find Edwin there, wan, heavy-eyed, rather taciturn, but
instantly and silently solicitous of his father's comfort. And
Edwin alone of the children was able to persuade Booth when
he was in drink or madness. Just as once it had been the father's
powerful voice that dispelled the horrors of the night from a
little son's imagination, so now it was this son's voice, a quiet
voice, that could recall the father when Booth was wound
about in melancholy or lost in frenzy. Soon Edwin did not go
back to school. His manhood had been thrust upon him.

II

Edwin went with his father behind the scenes, across the
stage, vast and bare by daylight, through wings cluttered with
the raw material of the night's illusion, into the snug greenroom where the players gathered to peruse the call board, re-
volve before the long mirror, and discourse oracularly. Their
simplest speeches were pontifical with quotations, racy with
anecdotes.

Second in interest only to the supreme subject of themselves
as actors ("How they loved me, m'boy!") was the comparison
of different readings of the famous roles. Respective merits of
"a Macready," "a Wallack," or "a Forrest" were hotly dis-
puted.

While the rest watched critically, some English-born veteran
would stiffly rise and demonstrate one of the great points—
tremendous, special effects—of the stars he had supported: fall
into the attitude of George Frederick Cooke when, as Sir Giles
Overreach, Cooke had menaced with his eloquent forefinger
(the finger Edmund Kean filched from his skeleton to keep
as a talisman) and launched the curse at the climax of *A New
Way To Pay Old Debts*. He might reproduce Kean's poignant

Farewell! Othello's occupation's gone,

in which the throbs and hesitations were as coolly calculated as the crescendo and diminuendo of a musical score. He might screech ear-piercingly like Macready as Werner, roar like Forrest, when as Lucius Brutus he turned on Tarquin, or let drop Booth's bland utterance of Richard's

> Off with his head! so much for Buckingham!

And his solemn, fanatical manner gave the younger listeners, including Edwin, a sense of the tradition to which they were heirs and the richness of the art in which they were apprentices.

Yet for all their proud tradition and lordly bearing these poor players were lonely people. The profession they loved was still considered violently disreputable. Tradesfolk never trusted them. Gentlefolk despised them, referred to them as "persons" even while they wined, dined, and made love to them, as they often did. The law imposed scornful penalties. In Booth's young days a strolling player in England could be jailed as a vagrant if caught on the road without an actor's license. David Garrick, born a gentleman, sustained the illusion that he had not lost caste by cultivating men of rank who received him as an equal—almost. "He loves to loll with lords," his enemies sneered.

But Edmund Kean, born a vagabond, had no illusions. Invited to play at a private house before the Duke of Wellington, he refused rudely: "I'm not invited as a guest but as a wild beast to be stared at."

Even in democratic America the line was drawn. One day as Edwin and his father were walking to rehearsal from their hotel Edwin noticed that nearly every man they passed greeted Booth and was greeted by him.

"Father, who was that?" he asked the first time.

"Don't know," said Booth.

Another gentleman nodded discreetly. "Who was that, Father?"

"Don't know."

The greetings persisted and so did Edwin until, "My child," said Booth wearily, "I don't know these people. But everybody knows Tom Fool."

Everywhere Booth was announced the company soon learned to expect Edwin with him. Mr. Booth, short and thickset, his gray hair cropped, and wearing his usual pepper-and-salt suit unfashionably cut, would bustle into the green-room to pump hands vigorously with the new members, "Delighted, sir, to form your acquaintance"; and slap the backs of the old ones, "I hope I see you well, my boy." A few paces behind glided his young keeper, who wore his black hair long and was wrapped in a Spanish cape. There would be more introductions.

The older actresses' hearts warmed to the boy; their faded cheeks dimpled as they held his hand. Twenty-year-old Joseph Jefferson never forgot his first sight of Edwin at sixteen. Edwin looked tired and uncared for; his face was strained and anxious. But Jefferson, with a painter's eye (acting was his trade and painting his enthusiasm), recognized the swan in the unkempt fledgling whom he thought the handsomest lad he had ever come across, "with his dark hair and deep eyes he was like one of Murillo's Italian peasant boys."

Edwin walked with his father to and from the theater. He ate with him at the long tables of theatrical boardinghouses. He slept beside him on mattresses often infested with creatures that Booth refused to drown (were not their little lives dear to them?) and on springs that jangled as Booth rolled over in his sleep. And if Booth couldn't sleep, neither should his son. While Booth prowled the room, Edwin dragged out his banjo and perched on the edge of the crumpled bed, chanting soft melodies.

Sometimes Booth favored something lively. At the theater one day Edwin was picking out "Old Zip Coon" between the acts when the door banged open and Edwin Forrest, most celebrated tragedian of the American stage, all dressed up and wearing a tall gray hat, strode into the dressing room. Edwin was hustling the banjo out of sight but Forrest cried to his namesake: "My boy, I like music! Give us some more."

As Edwin began again, Forrest kept time with his cane, then started rocking on his heels and swaying. And then Mr. Booth, dressed for *Richard III*, jumped up and began to sway and twitch. Edwin warmed to his work. The music got hotter. Forrest and Booth put in every step they could think of: jig, double shuffle, turn and twist, round and round the center, and all the fancy heel-and-toe touches they remembered. Finally they sank panting into chairs. "Well," gasped Forrest, "this is fun, ain't it? It don't remind me of Shakespeare but it does of the Bible. 'Whatsoever thy hand findeth to do, do it with thy might!' "

Edwin protected his father from intrusions. In Boston at the Albion, a dingy public house over an apothecary's on the north corner of Beacon and Tremont streets, he was resting in their room when his father dashed in, whispered hoarsely, "Gould! Coming up! Say I'm out!" and dived under the bed.

Thomas Gould was a Boston sculptor. He worshiped Booth, of whom he had done a fine bust, but Booth thought him tiresome. Now Gould seemed astonished not to find his idol, whom he had seen sprinting upstairs. He and Edwin talked lamely until there fell a pause, which Booth misinterpreted.

"Is that damned bore gone yet?" he sang out from under the bed.

Like every star Booth was a specialist in a few favorite roles in which the players in the stock companies along his route were trained to support him. All he asked for was to be fed his cues and given center stage. Let him do the acting! When a greenhorn once apologized for blundering into a scene from the wrong wing—"Young man," Booth barked at him, "it makes no difference to me. Only *come on!* I'll find you!"

All through the morning and afternoon he lived the character he was to play that night. Somebody once offered him a pork sandwich on a Shylock day. He snatched the meat out and threw it on the floor: "Infidel dog!"

When evening approached, and if he were sober (it was Edwin's business to keep him so), he would bounce into the dressing room a bare quarter hour before the curtain rose, paint his face, press powder onto it, brush off the surplus, lift and fit on his wig with rapt concentration, then stretch out his feet to Edwin to be shod. By the time the gaslights in front had been lowered and the orchestra swinging into "Hail, Columbia" or "Yankee Doodle" had wound up the audience to a thrilled expectancy, Booth would be frowning beside the door while Edwin—nervously silent, for his father brooked no chatter at this moment, or speaking, if he had to speak, in a colorless voice—still hovered around, clasping Booth's belt, holding open his cloak and adjusting his headdress, sometimes mounting a chair to do it. If Booth were playing Richard, Edwin took care that his padded hump was firmly fastened. Once it had fallen off in mid-scene, and Booth, glancing down and seeing it lying there, had kicked it viciously into the wing. Between them they made sure he had somewhere on him one of his good-luck charms: Moorish coins for Othello, an antique dagger for Richard, an old purse for Sir Giles Overreach, a breast ornament worn by rabbis for Shylock.

The callboy would knock. "Overture, Mr. Booth." And Booth would sail out of the dressing room and stump up the stairs into the wing.

But just before his entrance he seemed to relax and joked and gossiped with the other actors who stood all around, some of them even at this eleventh hour memorizing their lines—this was called "winging" a part. One night Joseph Jefferson was waiting with him between scenes of *The Iron Chest*, in which Jefferson played Samson Rawbold to Booth's Sir Edward, when Booth began dreamily to recall how Jefferson's grandfather had acted Samson many years back.

"He used," said Booth, "to sing the original song. It ran thus:

> A traveler stopped at a widow's gate.
> She kept an inn, and he wanted to bait,"

and screwing up his face comically Booth sang the first verse in a low tone, while keeping his ear cocked for his cue. Suddenly the cue was spoken and he rushed onstage to discover the actor who played Wilford opening the mysterious iron chest. In that instant the whole man changed. Sir Edward had been betrayed and ruined, and so had Booth. The veins of his corded neck swelled, his tremendous voice hit the audience like a hammer stroke. Then the scene was over and he rejoined Jefferson.

> "He paid like a prince, gave the widow a smack,
>   Then flopped on his horse at the door like a sack,"

sang Booth, a little louder this time so as to be heard over the crash of applause.

Sometimes Edwin waited in the wing, ready with half a glass of brandy and water. If a scene were particularly strenuous his father would escape from it for one split second to drain down the toddy, which Edwin literally threw into his mouth. When Booth played Sir Giles, the margin of time between cues was especially slim, and Edwin always trembled. Midway in Sir Giles' fit of madness Booth would charge into the wing, take one gulp—his head bent back—then with his long hair and short cloak flying almost straight out behind him would gallop onstage again screaming as he ran: "Are you pale? Are you pale?"

More often Edwin stayed below. But as he sat with head in hands and elbows straddling his open schoolbook, he could hear the voices from onstage ring through the floors and along the corridors. The ovation that welcomed the entrance of the star would thunder down to him. Abandoning his book, he would crouch by the door, his ear to the keyhole, shivering with anticipation of the clarion lines that every few minutes topped the others: King Lear's

> O Regan! Goneril!

or King Richard's

> A horse! a horse!

Edwin drank them all in. This was the theater. This crowning moment was the motive and excuse for an actor's being. Even the short pauses were electric with excitement.

Turn, hell-hound, turn!

Macduff would roar, and the house would fall silent expectantly while the pursued and pursuer ran to opposite wings and each snatched the hilt of a sword held out by a stage-hand.

Up and down, backward and forward, the fighters pressed each other. Sparks rolled from their blades. The hard-pounding feet, the singing clash of steel made the building quiver. Macbeth staggered up after every tumble and launched himself, snarling, straight at Macduff, who was in real danger of his life, the pit believed delightedly.

This was what the pit had waited for. The kid-glove element of the audience found Booth's performances too violent, but not the pit, whose applause was bare-handed and iron-throated. Men leaped onto the benches beside themselves with elation and cheered on the fight with wild, joyous whoops: "Hi-hi! Hi-hi! Hi-hi!"

For the last time that evening the door would be thrown wide and Booth would surge into the dressing room, rip off his helmet and wig, pull a worsted nightcap over his heated head and drop heavily into a chair, breathing as though to burst his chest open.

"I acted *well* tonight!"

Edwin would spring up, instantly apprehensive. His own night's work was just beginning. Now was his father's dangerous hour, and if Edwin with a sinking heart tried to separate him from the raffish hangers-on who lurked outside the stage door, Booth would begin to saw the air beside his head with his right hand in a dismissing gesture and to threaten Edwin: "Go away, young man, go away! Or by God, sir, I'll put you aboard a man-o'-war, sir!"

And yet it was his wish that Edwin be present. It was to his son's vigilance that the father committed himself. Having done so, he tried to escape this vigilance with all a drunkard's and a madman's cunning. Locked into his hotel room from the outside, he bribed a passing bellboy to bring him mint juleps, which he sucked through the keyhole with a straw.

One night in Louisville after a savage performance of Richard III, Booth's blood was aroused; the night called to him as to a tomcat. He tossed over his shoulder to his son that he "wanted to walk," and darted off into the darkness with Edwin hard after him. They came to a long, roofed-over market. Booth bounded inside and began to pace up and down. Speaking never a word, he scowled, then chuckled maliciously. Sometimes he ran a short way, glancing back at Edwin. The city clocks struck midnight. Edwin and his father were still alternately walking and running up and down the market when a faint, cold dawn-breeze touched their faces. As the eastern sky turned rosy, Booth silently conceded defeat and allowed a silent Edwin, stumbling with exhaustion, to lead the way home.

Again they were in Boston at the Pemberton House on Howard Street in a ground-floor bedroom. Between the bedroom and the hotel stables was a closet that reeked with the smells of straw and horse manure. Booth was fond of thrusting his head in and inhaling deeply; he considered the fumes healthful. Back from the theater one night he announced he "wasn't sleepy." Edwin immediately offered to sing, to play the banjo.

"I'm going out," said Booth.

Edwin beat his father to the door and set his back against it. He was taller than Booth, but slighter and frailer.

"You shall NOT go out!" he commanded, and into the words he put the whole force of the moral ascendancy he knew himself to hold over his father.

Mr. Booth gave his son a long, penetrating, defiant stare of the kind he was famous for in his performances. He gave vent to the slow, stertorous sniff with which onstage he prefaced his important speeches. He had drawn himself up for an exit and an exit must be made somewhere. Quick as thought he opened the closet and shut himself inside.

Minutes passed. Edwin began to coax his father to come out. He implored him. He threatened him. There was no answer. At this point his brother, the stolid Junius, would have shrugged and walked off, but Edwin, completely unnerved, began to tug and strain at the locked door. Suppose his father were smothering to death? He sobbed with terror and had just turned away desperately to run for help when the latch clicked. Booth let himself out of the closet, breathing normally, and without so much as the flicker of one hooded eye in Edwin's direction, stalked regally across the room. If there is a quality that still distinguishes the king from the commoner when the king undresses and climbs into bed, Booth had it. His trembling subject put out the light and crept into bed beside him.

Edwin told these stories later. There were other stories, which he only hinted at. He could not always keep his father out of the gutter. Booth claimed to despise the life of the theater for its make-believe. Yet it was this make-believe that gave beauty to his own life, and it was the reality that was ugly.

Edwin grew used to the contrast. Often after a performance he hunted for his father through midnight streets in which he was the only moving figure, down among the low-lying buildings of the waterfront where the wet sea-wind whistled after him around the corners and up the lanes, or out along the edge of town where the dark, open fields encroached on the few mean houses, to discover Booth at last, throned in some fire-lit tavern like a prince of vagabonds in the middle of a court of weaving revelers whose oaths were murderous and whose breaths were vomit-laden.

Booth would offer to embrace the nearest cutthroat, call him "a learned Theban, a sage philosopher." And the actor's face, which an hour before under the stage lamps had shone sublimely with the passions of heroes, had become the face of a satyr, with a loose, sly smile and sodden, bloodshot eyes. When he saw his son, he would begin to slash the air beside his head with his right hand in the demented gesture that had become terrible to Edwin, and his voice would be coarse and unfriendly. "Go 'way, young man, go 'way."

There were times also when Booth was not drunk, but when his mind wandered through frightful regions from which only Edwin could call him back. And there were times when he raved and struggled, shrieked the lines of Lear,

> Arms, arms, sword, fire! Corruption in the place!

tore at his clothes, shook off his slender son like a fly from his coat sleeve, and sent him reeling into the corner.

When Edwin went with his father into the theater, he became acquainted not only with the isolation of an actor's life but also with a special loneliness. He was his father's only companion in Booth's tragic, private world. Although Booth demanded and endured Edwin's presence, he almost never spoke to him affectionately or praised him. Yet the bond was strong between them, never defined but mutually recognized, nourished by the father's need and the son's devotion. And as the years passed, with every journey and every somber crisis surmounted, the two grew closer together. Edwin lived in and for his father.

III

They were in Boston rehearsing *Richard III* when the stage manager, who played several small parts, turned to Edwin and muttered glumly: "This is too much work altogether for one man. *You* ought to play Tressel."

Edwin was willing. His brother Junius had made his debut in this tiny role inserted by Colley Cibber into the Cibber version of *Richard*. Accordingly,

Duke of Gloster, afterwards, King .... Mr. Booth
Tressel, (his 1st appearance on any stage) .. Edwin T. Booth

ran the notice in the playbill.

Strictly, this was not Edwin's first appearance. At fourteen he had begged the manager of the Holliday Street Theater in Baltimore to give him a chance and had wavered onstage in a part in *The Spectre Bridegroom.* He was mortifyingly bad, hitched and stuttered, and was sick with stage fright; perhaps for this reason he preferred to forget the whole thing and always said afterward that his debut had been made as Tressel on September 10, 1849. On this great night he shared his father's dressing room at the old Boston Museum. Mr. Booth lounged with his feet on the table while Edwin stood up for inspection draped in rusty black—Tressel is wearing mourning. Edwin was just short of sixteen. "I was a sight," he recalled later. "I wore my hair down to my shoulders like a woman. I had a sallow complexion and a thin face."

He also remembered how his father looked: a dazzling outsider in the kennel of a dressing room. Booth had on a belted purple velvet tunic sparkling with paste gems; his huge puffed sleeves were slashed with bright gold; so were his puffed breeches. His armhole cloak of a flaunting crimson was trimmed with gold and bordered with ermine. On his head was the traditional dark, curled wig of the tragedian; one corkscrew curl fell in front of each ear, and at the back a bunch of longer curls streamed down over his ample ermine collar. His crown, to be worn in Act III, lay ready near him, winking and glittering with the jewels given him long ago by a lady admirer in London. Now he snapped at Edwin: "Who was Tressel?"

"A messenger from the field of Tewksbury."

"What was his mission?"

"To bear the news of the defeat of the king's party."

"How did he make the journey?"

"On horseback."

"Where are your spurs?"

Edwin faltered. "I hadn't thought of them."

The gorgeous figure unbent a little. "Forgot them, did you? Here, take mine."

Edwin unbuckled his father's spurs and shifted them to his own boots. He departed and a few minutes later a boyish, breaking voice, which faded out beyond the first rows, could be heard conveying bad news from the field of Tewksbury.

"It's a great pity that eminent men should have such mediocre children," whispered former senator Rufus Choate, who sat out in front.

His scene over, Edwin raced back to the dressing room, where the villain of the play stood making absorbed preparations for his own entrance.

"Have you done well?" asked Booth curtly.

"I think so."

"Then give me my spurs." And Booth departed for the stage in his turn, though not before he had pressed on Edwin's head his own worsted nightcap and invited him to take a sup of the warm gruel that he drank to soothe his nerves when acting. Something in his manner, even crustier than usual, made Edwin wonder if his father hadn't been watching from the wing and reached the dressing room a minute in advance.

This was the beginning. On September 27 Edwin played Cassio to his father's Iago in Providence and two days later Wilford to Booth's Sir Edward. He began to be billed variously, in type only a little smaller than used for his father's name, as MASTER EDWIN BOOTH; MR. E. BOOTH (first appearance of); MR. BOOTH, JR. In New York the pair stopped on Broadway to greet an old actor, who asked Booth solemnly: "Upon which of your sons do you intend to confer your mantle?"

Without speaking, Booth laid his hand on Edwin's head. "He had to reach up," Edwin remembered.

Yet when managers begged for more of these joint appearances Mr. Booth was often reluctant. He had had other plans for this son. And he fended off at least one request by growling that Ted played the banjo well and to "let him do a solo between the acts."

But at the farm next summer he gleefully said Yes when Edwin pleaded permission for himself and his best friend, who was visiting him, to give a dramatic reading at the courthouse in Belair. The stage-struck friend was "Sleepy" (John Sleeper) Clarke, Edwin's fellow pupil at Mr. Kearny's in Baltimore.

Old Joe, the family's most trusted retainer, was sent out into the country to post the playbills. He trudged for miles ringing a dinner bell and bawling: "O yes, O yes, O yes, tonight great tragedy."

As Edwin and Sleepy rode into Belair that evening they saw their playbills smeared on every fencepost and outhouse.

GRAND DRAMATIC FESTIVAL
AT THE COURT-HOUSE IN BELAIR

the bills proclaimed. Old Joe, who couldn't read, had pasted them all upside down.

On one side of the packed courtroom sat all the men, Mr. Booth, looking pleased, among them; on the other side were the women. The dinner bell clanged, sheets borrowed from the farm flew apart, and the countryfolk were treated to eight classical readings including "Is this a dagger?" from *Macbeth* done by Edwin and the quarrel of Brutus and Cassius from *Julius Caesar*. As a finale the two boys blacked their faces, cake-walked, and sang "coon songs"; Ted stroked his banjo and Sleepy clacked the bones.

By the next year Mr. Booth was advertised generally as being "supported by his son EDWIN BOOTH." Edwin acted Laertes, Macduff, Gratiano in *The Merchant of Venice*, Edgar in *King Lear*, Hemeya in *The Apostate*. He began to get the feel of an audience. They were doing *Brutus* by John Howard Payne one night in Richmond. In the part of the doughty old Roman for whom he was named Mr. Booth had just ordered his son Titus beheaded for treason. He clasped Edwin as Titus in a last embrace. "Farewell," he murmured, "eternally farewell!" and his passionately sad tones, investing the few words with the whole terrible conflict between father and patriot, brought tears to the eyes of everyone watching, even of the supers dressed as Romans lictors—to all eyes except those of a drunken man in the gallery who sniggered.

A laugh in the wrong place, shattering the delicate structure of emotional tension so painstakingly wrought, often made the cheeks of veteran tragedians flush crimson, and their lips tremble. Booth was made of sterner material. He stared deliberately up in the direction of the rude noise, and improvising a line not in the text but perfectly in keeping with his role, said in a voice that suddenly filled the theater: "Beware, I am the headsman! I am the executioner!"

Edwin, at the time rigid in his father's arms, recalled afterward that the words fell "like a thunder-shock. . . . All in front and on the stage seemed paralyzed, until the thunders of applause that followed broke the spell."

In April, 1851, they were playing at the National in New York when Booth woke up from his nap one afternoon and announced that he "didn't feel like acting." It was a *Richard* night. Edwin reminded his father how vigorously he had rehearsed that day. Mr. Booth only smiled slyly. The hired carriage, with a wicker champagne basket full of the star's costumes strapped on the back, waited at the door.

"What will they do without you, Father?" screamed Edwin.

"Go act it yourself," said Booth.

The first person Edwin met at the theater was John R. Scott, the manager, who played Richmond. "No matter," Scott answered coolly after Edwin had breathlessly told his news. "*You* play Richard. Or else we'll have to close the house."

Huddled willy-nilly into his father's tunic and cloak, which were much too wide, while one of the company holding the promptbook heard him repeat Richard's first soliloquy, Edwin was led into the wing like a lamb to the sacrifice. No explanation had been given the audience, and as he stepped onstage he was greeted with the usual clapping. The applause hadn't wholly died down when an inquiring buzz filled the house, and there was a general turning of the playbill to the light to see the name printed there. Then silence fell and striking out into it Edwin forced his light voice into an approximation of his father's measured, chesty tones:

> And all the clouds that lowered upon our house
> In the deep bo͞osom of the o-ce-an buried.

Mr. Booth gave the word "ocean" three syllables, painting the rise, the swoop forward, and sliding crash of massy waves, and on the word "buried" his deep, hollow tone dropped a plummet to the sea bottom. Edwin did this too. The receptive audience caught the picture from his voice as it was trained to do, and when he limped forward, twisting his features into his father's expression of bitter malignancy, he felt the house warm to his earnestness. He was launched.

As the scenes flashed past, a wave of friendliness swept toward him across the footlights and from the wings where all the actors not onstage were crowded three deep. The greenroom was deserted. John Scott hovered protectively close. In the part of Richmond he bore down on his young Richard, sword in hand, with a mingling of triumph and tenderness. It was all over surprisingly soon, and then like music came the longed-for ovation.

Scott hugged Edwin, gripped him by the arm to draw him before the curtain, and the two stood there bowing and bowing with the traditional humility of the entertainer. "You see before you," shouted Scott, "the worthy scion of a noble stock!" and to Edwin out of the side of his mouth, "I'll bet they don't know what *that* means."

The applause, which seemed to be produced by one pair of hands, blazed up again, making the boards under them tingle and vibrate. It was this night's applause that Edwin heard for the rest of his life. Until this night he might have been happier as a cabinetmaker—or as a lawyer, his father's most recent dream for him because Richard Booth had been a lawyer. Now it was too late. Retreat where he might, the compulsion of this applause faintly roaring in his memory's ear would draw him back again. A capricious destiny had unfitted him for any life but one.

"Well," demanded Destiny coldly when Edwin arrived back at their dingy quarters, "how did it go?"

Booth was still precisely as Edwin had left him. Yet Edwin always suspected his father had gone out, had been in the theater, and moving fast, had got home just ahead of him.

Later this spring Edwin was engaged independently of his

father by the manager of the company in Baltimore in which he had made his flop in *The Spectre Bridegroom*. "Let him try it," said Booth damply.

So for six dollars a week Edwin played utility, and while his soul yearned for Hamlet and Othello, most of his parts were in farces like *The Dumb Belle* or *The Valet de Sham*, which, crude as they were, called for a quick professional pace and shrewd timing. The unlicked boy who had played Richard to applause blundered through these trifles, killing his laughs, and what was unforgivable, the laughs of the stars he supported. His voice was feeble. His handling of stage business was maddeningly clumsy. It began to get about that he hadn't inherited his father's talent, let alone his genius.

Mr. Booth did nothing to help. Out of his reservoir of experience he offered his son neither advice nor praise. He hardly ever spoke to him of acting or to any of his children, who remembered only that on two unforgettable evenings at home he had read aloud to them Shakespeare's *Coriolanus* and *King John*, read all the parts, including the women's, so convincingly that little Asia asked without thinking: "Do you ever play Constance, Father?"

"I should not look queenly," her father answered.

Another night, alone with Edwin, Booth musingly recalled his youth in England and the marvelous acting of Edmund Kean. "He had doubtless resolved," writes Edwin loyally, "to make me work my way unaided; and though his seeming indifference was painful then, it compelled me to exercise my callow wits. It made me *think*."

IV

In spite of Booth's drinking and fits of madness, his family adored him. The younger children did not see him drunk, and when he was deranged their mother protected his authority. So, although their father was a despised player and subject to a "calamity" that was never spoken of, the shelter and discipline of the family circle had given the younger Booths a sense of security, of being like other children. But about the time Edwin left home to go with his father, the surface of this family life had begun to tremble and crack, exposing for the first time the ugly secret hidden under it.

In November, 1846, Booth's real wife, Adelaide, had arrived in Baltimore. Their son Richard had written to his mother that a great wrong was being put on her and on him, the legitimate heir. Adelaide sailed from Liverpool as soon as she could. On reaching Baltimore she looked up Exeter Street, "where the Holmes live," as she wrote to her sister Thérèse. She would not dignify the members of this family by a name they had no right to. Booth was off on tour but she saw his house—"it has not a very grand appearance." Then Booth came home, and her lawyer "fell on his back like a bomb." It was all no good for him to rage and threaten. The case against him was unassailable.

Adelaide had established residence in Baltimore, taking rooms with her son, and sometimes confronting Booth when he was selling his vegetables in a stall at the market. The air was blue with her maledictions. Once she penetrated as far as the farm and railed at Mary Ann. Not until March, 1851, did she give up hope of winning Booth back and file suit for divorce.

Booth attempted no defense. The divorce was granted, and on May 10, 1851 (he had turned fifty-five on the first of May) he married his Mary Ann.

The Booth children bore the knowledge of their parents' adultery and their own bastardy by shutting their eyes to it. Like their father's calamity, it was driven underground; the scars it left on them were kept bravely hidden. Asia, who later wrote her father's life, airily dismissed his first marriage as "a boyish *mésalliance*," and Edwin, writing to the newspapers some years after Mr. Booth's death, simply denied that his father had ever been married except to Edwin's mother. As for Adelaide Booth, she took to drink and died broken-hearted in Baltimore in 1858. Her only mourner was her devoted son Richard.

When his parents were married, <u>Edwin</u> was playing in stock in Baltimore. A month later his brother <u>Junius</u> sailed for San Francisco, and with June went Harriet Mace, a pretty actress from Boston, to whom he was no more married than his father had been, until very recently, to Mary Ann Holmes. Junius had deserted his wife Clementine and their small daughter Blanche and set up housekeeping with Harriet. He was showing himself a much better manager than an actor and had been hired to run the Jenny Lind Theater in San Francisco. He and Hattie were gone eleven months. In May, 1852, having made the long trip back east across the Isthmus of Panama, he turned up at the farm bringing his mistress with him. Neither of his parents was in a position to object.

Junius came out of the West like Lochinvar, and described to his family the land of gold beyond the Sierras. It was four years since gold had been discovered in California, but the caravans of the fortune hunters still toiled westward to the strains of "Oh! Susannah."

I'm off for Californy with my washbowl on my knee,

ran the forty-niners' version.

The profiteers had soon followed the pioneers. There were easier ways to make a fortune than to delve it out of the river beds with pick and shovel. Already the gold dust from the diggers' pannikins was being exchanged by the handful and hatful for expensive French wines, Cuban cigars, and Dickens' novels in paper covers. And the actors had come, for above all else the miners loved a show and raced down in coaches from their mountain camps. Junius offered his father an engagement at the Jenny Lind. All the world was going west. Why not his father? The West would welcome him.

It was not so much the gold that attracted Booth as the new horizon. He was tired of travel and cold to fame, or so he considered. He was growing old, yet there was time for one more adventure, a last world to conquer, and the thought tempted him.

Late in the spring of 1852 Booth said good-by to his family.

He set off with Junius and Harriet for New York to catch the steamer for the Isthmus. But Junius was out of the habit of chaperoning his father. In New York Booth suddenly "fell ill"; this was the family version. What really happened was that he gave Junius the slip and danced off on a spree with one of his seedy chums, an actor named George Spear, making them all miss the boat. While they were waiting for another ship, Booth drove back to Baltimore to collect his indispensable son, and when he left for New York a second time, Edwin left with him. He, too, was headed for the land where the tumbling rivers tossed up precious particles, the golden land at the end of the rainbow—California. He was eighteen.

PART TWO

CHAPTER 3

Seeing the Elephant

Such wind as scatters young men through the world,
To seek their fortunes further than at home,
Where small experience grows.
The Taming of the Shrew, *Act I, scene 2*

 CRANING over the rail of the ship *Illinois* as she steamed past Mexico and drew near Colón, the passengers babbled of the conquistadors, of Ponce de León, De Soto, and Cortés. The sodden George Spear, otherwise known as "Old Spudge," was still very much with the Booths. There was no getting rid of him; he had insisted on coming.

From Colón they were all poled up the Chagres River in flat-bottomed *bungas* by Indian boatmen who sang "Oh! Susannah." The water was bright green with the reflected foliage. The heavy air smelled like a hothouse. From a mile or so off could be heard the thump of native drums and the whimpered *ña, ña, ña* of natives announcing a festival.

At Gorgona the party climbed on muleback for the journey through the jungle across the Isthmus. They spent the night in a hut by the trail. Harriet was given the only hammock. The men curled uncomfortably on trunks and wine barrels, each with his loaded pistol beside him. Edwin lay awake, nervously listening to the mad-sounding jungle cries and the muttering of the dark-skinned guides inside the hut as they sat on their haunches in a circle sharpening their machetes. Somewhere on him he carried a shrunken, withered remnant, a precious talisman against danger and accidents—his caul.

Next morning they were up and away at daybreak, and soon a salt breeze from the Pacific freshened the jungle air. In the grass-grown plazas and ruined cloisters of Panama City the street boys whistled "Yankee Doodle" and the señoritas twanged their guitars from balconies and caroled "Old Black Joe" and "Swing Low, Sweet Chariot." The city was choked with fortune hunters killing time until the next ship to San Francisco. Hundreds had been stricken with cholera and mysterious, shaking fevers, and the church bells chimed continually for those whose wives would never see them again; the chimes were gay and silvery. Below in the harbor rocked a fleet of native canoes, and white pelicans rode the Pacific waters.

The Booths boarded ship and sailed north. As they left the tropics, cool northwest trade winds began to blow. They sighted the sails of clippers on the horizon; now and then they heard strong voices singing chanteys from whalers far out to sea. On July 28 they entered the Golden Gate and next the broad harbor of San Francisco, which was a forest of masts flying the flags of all nations. On Telegraph Hill the black wooden "arm" was raised to signal their arrival.

Out swarmed the bumboats to ferry ashore the passengers. Edwin stepped nimbly after his father, who strode onto the dock, a pioneer carrying a carpetbag. All the actors in San Francisco were on Long Wharf to meet them. Tom Maguire, gambler and owner of the Jenny Lind Theater, had sent a brass band, which crashed into the inevitable but still stirring "Oh! Susannah."

Junius and Harriet, whom their western friends called "the handsomest couple in Frisco," waved back greetings at the shouts of, "Welcome home, June!"

But most of the attention was on the rough, travel-worn, somehow gallant figure of Mr. Booth, who met the crowd's interest with the level gaze of a man well used to it as he shouldered his way to the waiting carriage with his two sons flanking him, Junius on one side pointing out landmarks and Edwin on the other staring hungry-eyed.

Rows of tindery frame houses with wooden scallops across their fronts bordered the street that wound steeply and crookedly up from Long Wharf. Through gaps between the hills the dusty winds blew and blew, making movement everywhere. Many-colored tents pitched above town billowed and tugged at their pegs. The harbor was ruffled with whitecaps, and the gas in the street lamps flared restlessly.

The pulsing heart of the city was Portsmouth Square. Along its four sides bearded settlers in blue jackets and black trousers cut on Spanish lines, high-booted miners whose shoulder-length hair showed they were just down from the diggings, gamblers wearing starched shirt bosoms and diamond studs as big as peas, shoved their way or strolled, and every so often darted out of the paths of fine carriages or from under the hoofs of caracoling horses ridden by native Californians in serapes, sombreros, and spurs.

The Jenny Lind Theater, which had been built by the sleepy-eyed gambler Maguire, stood at a corner of the square near the Bella Union, most notorious of the gambling hells. Its company included June Booth and Harriet, who passed as man and wife, and featured the Chapmans, William and Caroline, who were brother and sister and had been brought up on their father's showboat, the first to ply the Mississippi.

Every playhouse and gambling house had its bar. The windows lined with bright bottles caught Mr. Booth's eye on his way from the wharf, and he and Old Spudge romped off together. They were gone all night, Booth's first night in San Francisco. But it was Edwin who was late next morning for the opening rehearsal and languid when he got there. His father screamed with annoyance. "That won't do! Come, come, come!"

Edwin started over, in Richmond's speech beginning

The weary sun hath made a golden set.

"For God's sake!" barked Booth. "Where does the sun set? Well, show it then! Point to it! Nod your head! Damn it, DO SOMETHING!"

Booth played for two weeks to packed houses. He was supported by Junius and Edwin. At the end of his fortnight the whole company was turned out of the theater because Maguire, who meant to build another playhouse, had sold the Jenny Lind to the city for a town hall. So Junius engaged his father (at a large guarantee), the Chapmans, George Spear, Edwin, and some others to act in Sacramento under his management. They all steamed upriver, a ten-hour trip.

Sacramento was smaller than San Francisco, tougher and cruder and closer to the mines. Covered wagons choked the rutted streets and the miners streamed down from the mountains, not in their Sunday best as in Frisco but clay-caked, weather-stained, and tired out. San Francisco was infested with rats; Sacramento's plague was bedbugs.

A sudden depression had hit parts of California, one of those puzzling fits of caution and pessimism that clapped down on the gold country every year or so. The Booths opened confidently at Sacramento's American Theater, but after the first night their houses were thin. Finally all three took benefits. For his own Edwin played Jaffier to his father's Pierre in *Venice Preserved*. Before the performance Mr. Booth squatted on the doorstep of his primitive dressing room and watched the meandering, thoughtful approach of his younger son wearing a black velvet robe. "You look like Hamlet," he observed balmily. "Why didn't you try Hamlet tonight?"

"If I ever have another benefit I will," murmured Edwin out of his brown study.

Already Mr. Booth had had a bellyful of California. He had spent almost his entire take from San Francisco. He decided to go home, and he demanded pitilessly that Junius pay him the full guarantee for Sacramento in spite of the lack of profits. The family, though never criticizing Mr. Booth, always thought this insistence rather hard in him. In San Francisco his sons saw him off at Long Wharf exactly two months after his arrival. Booth sailed alone, without a guardian. Edwin had determined to stay behind. He was not yet nineteen, and the West had laid her powerful hand on him.

Moved by one of the premonitions that stir in men with a strong sense of destiny, Booth had some vague notion that his career had not long to run, and before sailing he lifted up his Richard's jeweled crown, from which the light flashed in a crisscross of filaments, and deposited it in the eager hands of Junius. "I shan't need this any more," he said.

Yet he was in a rollicking mood when he reached the wharf early, swinging his carpetbag, to superintend the stowing away of his luggage. The sailor in charge was too slow to suit him. "I'm no flunky," the man growled when Booth snapped at him to get a move on.

"What are you, sir?" Booth asked sharply.

"I'm a thief," sneered the man.

This happened to be a line from the play *Bertram*, in which Booth often acted. He picked up the cue.

"Your hand, comrade, I'm a pirate!" he cried, and the sulky seaman heaved himself erect and stretched out his hand with a broad grin.

II

California had an expression: "Seeing the elephant." It had been the title of a skit satirizing the gold rush that had run in San Francisco for months. "To see the elephant" meant to trek hopefully to the gold country and be (what most people were) viciously disappointed. The West took up the ironic idiom. All rugged travel, hunger, and heartbreaking bad luck were "seeing the elephant." Miners had elephants stamped on their letter paper and daubed them in red and black on their cabin walls.

The Booths had caught a glimpse of the elephant in Sacramento. Now Edwin got a good look from trunk to tail. At first, after his father left, he lingered on with Junius and Harriet in their house on Telegraph Hill, an exasperating guest. Having no work, he spent his time drinking in saloons where the bars were still warm from his father's instep. His nineteenth birthday came and went. Junius was mightily relieved when Willmarth Waller, an actor-manager organizing a company to play the mining towns, engaged Ted for the tour. "The name will help me anyway," said Waller.

Junius had learned a thing or two about how to survive in California: it was the survival of the cautious. His brother was a brash kid, and Junius advised him before starting out to "put a slug," which was a piece of gold worthy fifty dollars, "in the bottom of your trunk, forget you have it, and when things are at their worst bring out your slug."

Waller had hired George Spear, too, and Dave Anderson, another friend of Mr. Booth's. Anderson was a middle-aged widower with a humorous, kind face. He remembered well, he told Edwin, meeting him back East when Edwin was a child clinging to his father's hand. Before Mr. Booth left Frisco he had begged Anderson to keep an eye on Ted.

At Sacramento they all changed steamers and churned up the Feather River to Marysville. Then, piling into a coach, they jolted for miles across plains whose horizons were ringed at night by the red pillars of campfires. They inched in silence, muffling all harness noise, through bandit country where mustachioed highwaymen like Joaquin Murietta could be expected to take shape silently out of the brush. Now and then a grizzly lumbered across the trail. Through the night the coyotes howled. The sturdy horses braced their hoofs as they picked their way down pebbly forest paths. From the hilltops the swaying, singing coachload glimpsed an occasional white tent roof or a thread of smoke showing the whereabouts of some lonely fortune hunter.

Some of the mining towns had real playhouses with a sign over the door announcing THEATER or DRAMATIC HALL in five-foot letters, and inside kerosene footlights and drop curtains painted with pictures of elephants or of a miner recumbent, his pick by his side, dreaming of home. But often traveling actors played in a calico-draped saloon on a stage of boards held up by sawhorses, or in somebody's barn or warehouse where the all-male audience planted stools on the dirt floor and belligerently staked off places like claims.

Waller's troupe stopped first in Nevada City, a clump of shacks in a clearing among the tall pines, and Edwin acted his first Iago. They played next in Grass Valley, then in Rough and Ready, then in distant Downieville on the North Yuba at the deep bottom of a valley high in the mountains. The more remote the camp, the more electric the tension in the audience of tough-looking miners who sat with their guns handy in their laps. If you could capture them they showered you with gold pieces; if you disappointed them they tossed you in a blanket. Many of them knew the classical texts by heart and yowled with irritation when the smallest cut was made.

The actors were in Downieville when a tremendous blizzard struck. Waller herded them back along the trail as far as Grass Valley. Here the snow lay twelve feet deep in places, and food was so short and fantastically expensive that Edwin's precious slug, fetched out of his trunk to meet the emergency, bought the company no more than one dinner. They forced themselves out and on again to Nevada City, hoping to earn enough there to pay for the steamer trip home. But when they reached town on an icy December night they found the dramatic hall dark.

For many days neither food nor letters had got through to the camps. The stranded miners had no money for theaters. The stranded actors huddled around the stove in the dismal hotel and began to swap stories out of their accumulated experience of other catastrophes.

Edwin flung away and wandered off alone down the main street, which led out of the camp into a no man's land pitted like a moon landscape with gulches left by the gold diggers. The snow made the night look almost bright and the raw holes sculptured. He was on his way back when he saw a lantern bobbing, heard shouts and running footsteps.

"Holla!" rang George Spear's voice, sounding half-frozen, "Ted, is that you?"

"Yes, what's up?"

"There's a mail just in and a message for you."

"What news?"

"Not good news for you, my boy."

Edwin, like his father, occasionally had premonitions, true guesses at dark events. "Spear," he asked instantly, "is my father dead?"

Spear nodded slowly.

Mr. Booth, jaunty and unchaperoned, had arrived back across the Isthmus; not without mishap, for on the way his purse, which had in it most of his gold-coast earnings, was stolen. In New Orleans his old friend Noah Ludlow, manager of the St. Charles Theater, arranged a series of six performances that netted Booth over a thousand dollars. He ended the engagement with *The Iron Chest*, followed by his favorite comic afterpiece called *The Review*, or *The Wag of Windsor* in which he played John Lump, a Yorkshire boy ("I'ze zimple, zur, but I'ze willing to larn"), wearing a red wig, tiny hat, striped stockings, and a flowered chintz waistcoat.

Booth had caught a bad cold in New Orleans. He was beginning to feel ill when he left there on the steamer *J. S. Chenoweth* bound up the Mississippi for Cincinnati. The first day out he drank the cloudy river water, which most experienced travelers never touched, and by that evening he had a high fever. A passenger named Simpson noticed him pacing the saloon, his hands behind his back. "That's the tragedian, Mr. Booth," Simpson was told, and then he realized that he had just seen and applauded the actor on the stage of the St. Charles.

There was no doctor on board. The second day out Booth kept to his cabin, peering from his small window at the brown Mississippi bobbing with refuse and the deadly flat banks where the only signs of human life were the woodcutters' huts perched on stilts. After sunset the sky glowed weirdly from forest fires; black smoke peppered with scarlet sparks uncoiled from the ship's funnels backward over the water.

The germ Booth had picked up settled in his bowels. He lay in his bunk, weakened by vomiting and diarrhea, until the door opened and the passenger Simpson stuck his head inside to offer his help. Rousing from his fever to scan his admirer with a long, keen look, which the young man never forgot, Booth accepted. Simpson had the porter clean out the vilely neglected cabin and change the sick man's bed and body linen. In spite of all care Booth wasted away fast.

The *Chenoweth* crawled north, touching in the old familiar order at the southern ports he knew so well. On the third day out his jaws began to stiffen. The attentive Simpson dipped a rag in brandy and forced it between his teeth. But Booth made a stab to push the cloth away and muttered faintly: "No more in this world."

A day later, when he could hardly articulate, he seemed to be telling Simpson that he had suffered a great deal off in California and been exposed to many hardships. Simpson, who was young and inexperienced, felt at a loss. "Have you a message to send your wife?" he suggested.

At the word "wife" a look of longing passed over Booth's face. His eyes rolled feebly to stare into the other man's, but his slurred response was unintelligible.

"May I pray for you?" Simpson asked finally. Tears filled Booth's eyes and he bowed his head. When Simpson had finished and bent over to smooth the pillow, Booth tried gratefully to raise his arms and twine them around the good stranger's neck.

On the fifth day out, November 30, 1852, Booth died. It was one in the afternoon; they were just below Louisville and the dinner bell had rung for the other passengers. As he felt himself going, Booth's voice strengthened. He looked appealingly at the man sitting beside him and said in his deep, melancholy tones, with all his old forcefulness: "Pray, pray, pray."

Mrs. Booth, summoned by telegraph, claimed her husband's body in Cincinnati. The fearful trials of the life he had led her were dismissed and forgotten. "Yes," she said sadly, when they told her the story of his last days, "that was just what he thought right to do; to endure patiently, to suffer without a complaint, and to trouble no one."

So Booth came home. He lay in the dark green-and-gold-papered parlor in Baltimore. The mirrors were shrouded superstitiously with linen sheets, and a bust of Shakespeare was set at the head of the coffin. And as Booth lay there, his eyes half-open, there was still so much life in his face, so much humor and intelligence, that a spasm of hope seized his last audience and doctors were sent for. But this was not a trance. Far to the south in New Orleans the members of Ludlow's company, with whom he had played his farewell performance, wound bands of black crepe on their arms.

"What, Booth dead?" cried Rufus Choate when he heard the news. "Then there are no more actors!"

Snow fell in Baltimore on the day Booth's body was laid in a vault to wait for spring burial. And it was falling in Nevada City in slow, circling flakes as George Spear, holding his lantern low to light the path, guided Edwin back to the hotel. The picture of his father's lonely last journey even more than his death put the boy in a passion of tears and he sobbed out that he "should have gone with him." Like his mother, all he could remember now was the goodness and charm of the man who had died; the cruel faults had dropped away. At the miserable hotel his brother vagabonds gathered around to comfort him, but the boy could only repeat between sobs: "I should have gone with him," until kind Dave Anderson wrapped his arm around him and led him away.

The letter with the news of death had been sent to Waller by Junius, who begged that someone in the company would tell Edwin. A longing swept over Edwin to be with his brother. They two had been the last of the family to see their father alive. When next morning he heard of a plan put forward by a few reckless men to tramp through the breast-high snow to Marysville fifty miles away, he instantly said he would go with them. Out into the craglike drifts they plunged, walking single file, with each man treading in the footsteps of the man in front. They slept that night in an isolated shack, and Edwin picked up a banjo he found there and crooned the songs he used to sing for his father to the old mountain woman who had taken them in; the soft, friendly syllables called up a little Southland in the middle of the wind-lashed, frozen waste. By nightfall of the second day they pushed into Marysville. Edwin borrowed ten dollars to pay for the steamer down the Feather to Sacramento and from there to San Francisco.

At Junius' house he read two letters that had arrived from their mother. Mrs. Booth advised her sons not to come home. She meant to live at the farm with Rose and the younger children.

What she did not tell them was that no money at all had been found on their father's body—perhaps Simpson was not the first person to glide into Booth's stateroom. It was when Ludlow wrote to her in condolence that she learned of the large sum he had paid her husband in New Orleans. She had only a few dollars to go on with, but there was not a word of this in her letters.

Stay in the West, she encouraged her sons devotedly, for to a Marylander who had never been there, California was still the golden land.

III

Six months later San Francisco had a new personality. Friends called him Ted or Ned or Eddie, but he was known to the public as "young Booth," "Booth the younger," often simply as "Booth." People wheeled in their tracks for a sight of him tearing to rehearsal in midmorning on a high, white horse. He wore a black serape over his red shirt, a slouch hat, and Hessian boots, clamped a stubby pipe between his teeth, had a mass of black hair and a face like a cameo.

On that first harrowing trip through the camps this youngest Booth had been "never despondent," writes J. J. McCloskey, another of Waller's troupers, but had shown the spirit of "a true Bohemian." Now as the shock of his father's death wore off, Edwin Booth's natural gaiety, so long kept under, spurted up. He was quiet as ever, this would always be his way, but when his face unexpectedly gleamed—watch out, boys, to find a turkish towel boiling in your stewpot instead of stew, or your last clean shirt borrowed off your line. At rehearsals he was the life of the company. "His guying," says McCloskey, "was very neat and quick."

And with the overbearing pressure of his father's genius removed, Booth began to develop a stage presence of his own. Every evening guests on the hotel porch across from the theater could hear the applause that saluted the new favorite's entrance.

In San Francisco Booth had found prosperity stealing back, with Junius in work again as manager of San Francisco Hall, the new playhouse built by Tom Maguire. Junius had offered his brother a job. A man who had known young Booth in Boston saw him for the first time in the West sitting on the prompt table, swinging his feet, in the middle of the stage of San Francisco Hall. Booth was wearing a tattered hat, short monkey jacket, and burst-out shoes. He was broke, but gay as a grig and ready to try anything.

And this was what he did try. Comedies of manners like *The Critic* and *She Stoops to Conquer*, operettas, farces, and rowdy burlesques of local celebrities were all grist to the humming mill of Maguire's new theater. Some people grumbled that the place stank like a spittoon—the audiences used it as one. The walls halfway up were tawny with tobacco juice; you didn't dare sit down without looking close, and every few weeks the theater had to be shut for cleaning and airing. Others complained that its shows were thrown together. They certainly were, but they went with a swing. The little playhouse glowed like a lantern and rocked with the guffaws of hundreds of miners who groaned at the villain's entrance, joined hoarsely in the song choruses, and hurled buckskin purses stuffed with gold nuggets at their chosen actors, male or female.

The stars were the two Chapmans. Edwin often played the lover onstage opposite Caroline. Sometimes he cried when he thought of his father. In long rambles, which like his father he took alone, he explored the beach for miles, collecting gulls' eggs in his hat, and back in the greenroom he tipped them out as trophies into the women's laps.

Most of the actors lived near Junius and Harriet on Telegraph Hill with its view of the harbor. But out near the old Mission Dolores, which stood by the racetrack and the bull arena, far out of town on a winding road among sand dunes and chaparral where leafless plants grew in the shape of ghastly antlers and the wind blew in strong, there was a smaller, much less fashionable actors' colony known as Pipesville, and this was where the younger Booth lived.

Dave Anderson had struggled back from the mines with the rest of Waller's troupe as soon as rain washed away the snow, and he and Booth went to live together in Pipesville in a whitewashed shack they built themselves. In Pipesville everybody was a bachelor. They all shared the work, all except Booth, who refused to do one stroke. His eyes danced, he smiled his almost invisible smile. "It's a poor company that can't support one gentleman," he said charmingly.

Early each morning a bugle was blown, and the actors threw on serapes and raced their broncos into town to rehearsal. Booth and Anderson put themselves down in the city directory as "comedians and *rancheros*"—their joke, for their "ranch" was their two-room shack. They would jounce together into Frisco in a buckboard, pull in across from a butcher's, and Anderson would stand up, shaking the reins, and bawl out: "Kid?" meaning beef kidneys, their stand-by for dinner being so cheap.

With an actor named Barnes they used to gallop out to a roadhouse called The Lakes on the edge of a pond six miles from the city. One night Booth wheeled Anderson home in a handcart. Another night as they sat around drinking and spouting fierce lines from their plays like

Now could I drink hot blood

or

Here's the smell of blood still,

two detectives mistook them for members of the gang of the Mexican bandit Joaquin Corrilla, who was terrorizing the countryside, and trailed them furtively back to Pipesville.

Junius was a member of the vigilantes, and Edwin had joined the volunteer fire brigade; the engine his company was attached to was named "Old Dewdrop." For his debut at San Francisco Hall Junius had appropriately cast him in the part of Fred Jerome, hero of the melodrama *The American Fireman*. At the rise of the curtain on Act II, when Fred and his mother are eating supper in their humble apartment: "O Frederic," sighs Mrs. Jerome, "I have a strange foreboding, as if something dreadful was about to happen."

> FRED. Now, don't talk in such a melancholy way, when I feel so happy. . . . (*Distant fire bell heard.*) Hark! what's that? Fire! I'm off, mother.
> MRS. J. No, no—not without your supper!
> FRED. Supper—and do you think I'd stop for that? No! for while I remain to eat, some poor family may lose their all, which, were I present, I might aid in saving; the meal would choke me did I attempt to feast while others suffer. No, no, never. (*Exit hastily, center door.*)
> MRS. J. Brave boy! Heaven give you strength to save the unfortunate! (*Watches off center door, as scene closes. Music.*)

Then Booth did Dandy Cox, a strutting little darky in a blackface farce, then Colonel Mannering in *Guy Mannering*, then Furibond in *The Yellow Dwarf*. When the date was set for a benefit for the theater's scene designer, John Fairchild, it was Fairchild's privilege to choose the play, and he asked young Booth, over Junius' objections, to act Richard III. This was only the second time Booth had ever acted Richard, yet now there were moments when a startling authority in his tone or gesture showed the presence of a strong dramatic power, even occasionally the tentative working of an original mind. A Harvard graduate named Ferdinand Ewer, a scholar and editor, was standing in the wing that night watching Booth breathe flame onstage. Ewer saw (what Junius failed to see) the aura of a distinguished future surrounding the unconscious head of the absorbed nineteen-year-old.

Four days later it was Booth's own benefit. A journalist friend had proposed he play Hamlet and the actors standing around had bayed with laughter. "Too young," said Junius, also roaring. Then Booth approached his brother and murmured of the promise he had made their father. Good-natured June was not one to thwart a pledge around which death had hung a halo. Booth first appeared as Hamlet on April 25, 1853, with George Spear as Polonius, Caroline Chapman as Ophelia, and William Chapman as the First Gravedigger.

Advance work had been done in the press to "whoop her up," and all Booth's pals who were not performing sat out in front as a claque. Mr. Booth had had a true eye: when Edwin made his entrance he did look like Hamlet, the Hamlet of a fairy tale. The claque gave him an ovation that was almost too obvious, at which he made a cold little bow. But the moment his friends heard the quality of his voice in his first speech they knew he was "safe" and relaxed. On the word "father,"

> I'll call thee Hamlet, King, father,

and again on the line

> He was a man, take him for all in all,

Booth put across the clear image in his mind so that everyone there who had known Junius Brutus Booth instantly thought of him.

"You fellows overdid it," Booth objected afterward to his claque.

"Highly creditable," wrote Ferdinand Ewer in the *Daily Alta California*. "We can even predict a high degree of success for the promising young artist when he shall have overcome a few disagreeable faults in intonation and delivery, and reached a profound conception of the part."

Junius buttonholed his brother: "Yes, you've had a wonderful success, but you still have a lot to learn."

The very next night Booth touched earth again, being cast by Junius for Captain Absolute in *The Rivals*, and this same month Junius slammed him into Mr. Dombey in *Dombey and Son*.

It was now that San Francisco began to notice him. Mrs. Catherine Sinclair arrived, the woman whom Edwin Forrest had sued for divorce on the ground of adultery. The newspapers gloated over the case, but Mrs. Sinclair (she had taken her maiden name back) wore the dirty publicity like a smart dress; it somehow enhanced her charm and fastidiousness, made her heartbroken ex-husband look brutal. She appeared at San Francisco Hall and Booth played opposite her—Petruchio to her Katherine in Garrick's mutilated version of *The Taming of the Shrew*.

Katherine .... MRS. C. N. SINCLAIR, LATE MRS. FORREST
Petruchio .... ED. BOOTH

In May he acted his first Benedick in *Much Ado about Nothing* to the Beatrice of Caroline Chapman, at the end of June his first Romeo to her Juliet, and in September Shylock to Mrs. Sinclair's Portia. Ferdinand Ewer soberly advised him in print to study his parts better. It seemed to Junius that Ted's head was swelling, and he jerked him back to a regime of low comedy, which included the role of Givemsum in the burlesque called *Buy-it-Dear! 'Tis made of Cashmere*.

In one of the overnight turnabouts typical of California, Mrs. Sinclair became the manager and Junius and Edwin her employees. She had leased a new theater, the Metropolitan, a very grand house against which smelly little San Francisco Hall couldn't hope to compete, and she opened here on Christmas Eve, 1853, in *The School for Scandal*. She had engaged young Booth for juvenile leads. Soon he played opposite Laura Keene, the English comedienne whom Mrs. Sinclair had signed for guest appearances.

In England "Red Laura" had been a barmaid and then the wife of John Taylor, a tavern keeper who, having done something disreputable, had been deported. She had gone on the stage after Taylor's exile and soon afterward sailed with her two daughters (her "nieces" to the public) to New York, where she was well received until she broke her engagement at Wallack's Theater and decamped to Baltimore with a gambler named Lutz. Then she drifted west, a fragile, nervous, imperious woman with sloping shoulders, goldish-red hair and wide, angelic, come-hither eyes. She fluttered her gold lashes and wore frilly clothes, usually white. Her voice even offstage had a tender little sob in it, except when she raised it in peacock screams of rage.

She opened at the Metropolitan in *The Love Chase*, with Booth supporting her. An indefatigable and painstaking artist, which Booth was not, she considered her reception was less than her due and furiously blamed her "failure" on "Booth's bad acting."

Booth fluttered his black lashes in the ghost of a wink and quipped to McCloskey that he "felt it *Keenely*."

Something of the rhythm of "Oh! Susannah" churned in the blood of Californians. It was a restless rhythm that urged them forward:

Oh! Susannah, don't you cry for me!

Out in California, forward meant westward. By 1854 a number of actors had left to try their luck in Australia. The farthermost land beckoned to Booth, and when his engagement with Mrs. Sinclair ended, he, Anderson, Laura Keene, and a handful of bold spirits decided to push on over the water. They sailed from San Francisco the last day of July. Booth wrote to his family before leaving, bragging of the money he would make, but a letter from Junius advised them not to count on this.

It was October, the Australian spring, when the actors' ship was guided by the pilot boat through the needle's-eye gap of Sydney Heads into Sydney Harbor. They opened in Sydney in *The Lady of Lyons*, with Miss Keene as Pauline and Booth featured as Claude Melnotte.

After two weeks of so-so business they went on to Melbourne, where Booth turned twenty-one. To celebrate his manhood he had his picture taken, then gave Miss Keene the slip (she had struggled to control his high jinks), rushed out of the hotel and drank himself dizzy, rushed back and into the hotel yard, where he planted the Stars and Stripes and bellowed truculently that America was a bigger, better country than Britain.

And while they were in Melbourne he and Anderson went for a stroll outside the city and lay down luxuriously in the shade of a coconut palm. Suddenly some instinct made Booth roll over. A split second later an enormous coconut crashed on the spot where he had been lying. It was his caul that saved him, he whispered awestruck.

Business was terrible in Melbourne. The Americans' hopes drooped until at last they packed up their costumes in their champagne baskets and embarked for home. But when the ship touched at Honolulu, one of the first sights they saw ashore was a faded frame building with the magic word THEA-TER on it, so with their last fifty dollars they paid a month's rent and began preparations for a Hawaiian season. Halfway through rehearsals Booth and Laura Keene quarreled explosively and Miss Keene flounced out of the company to continue home alone.

This was Booth's breaking-in as a manager. They announced *Richard III*. The new king of the Islands, Kamehameha IV, yearned to see the show, but being in mourning for his father, the old king, he dared not appear publicly; so an armchair was rolled into the wing for him and there he sat, flanked by a smart French aide and a strapping Kanaka warrior. Booth had heard of a white man in town who could do Miss Keene's part of Lady Anne. The man turned out to have been noth-

ing but a grip, or stagehand, back in the States. He had a
Dutch accent, was under five feet, bowlegged and cross-eyed.
In female dress he looked worse, but they shoved him on and
Booth began Richard's speech:

Divine perfection of a woman.

Anderson and the other actors were hopping with laughter
just offstage. Booth was in a cold sweat. The dialogue seemed
endless, though it had been cut to the bone. The Lady Anne's
lip curled in rehearsed scorn; she had two front teeth missing.
Booth stuck grimly to the text:

Oh, teach not thy soft lip such cold contempt.

In spite of everything the audience of natives squatting on
the floor seemed well satisfied, and when it was time for the
coronation scene and Booth asked King Kamehameha if they
might borrow his armchair, which was the throne, His Majesty graciously got up and watched standing. At the end he
patted Booth's shoulder and told him in British English that
as a boy he had seen Booth's magnificent father play Richard III
in New York.

IV

The Booth family was like a frothing pot: try as you would
to hold the lid down, it boiled over somewhere. While Edwin
was in the antipodes, Junius had been home to Maryland, for
now it was Junius' wife Clementine who was threatening a
scandal by suing for divorce.

With Harriet, and this time also their little girl Marion,
born in San Francisco, Junius made the tedious trip east and
walked in unannounced on his mother at the farm. He managed the divorce discreetly and was back in California a month
before Edwin, who landed in San Francisco in April, 1855, with
about ten dollars in his pocket.

Through the account Junius brought west with him, Booth,
newly landed, caught a glimpse of home; of his widowed
mother coping valiantly and inadequately with the farm and

servants; of Asia, beautiful at eighteen and being courted by
Sleepy Clarke; of handsome, idling, unruly Johnny, who
thrashed his schoolmates and got drunk at sixteen. He was
worried about Johnny, Junius told Edwin; their mother spoiled
him.

With ten dollars to his name there was not a chance that
Booth could go home yet. He was lucky enough to find an-
other engagement at the Metropolitan, still managed by Mrs.
Sinclair.

During his travels his face had hardened a little, he had
gained in self-assurance. "He looked unusual and unique without trying to," explained Henry Sedley, who had known him
as a boy in the East and was with him now in California.

Booth still wore his slouch hat and Hessians, but instead of
the red shirt and serape he had toned down his dress to a plain
dark suit and an overcoat thrown around his shoulders cape-
style. He flavored his talk with Spanish—*muchas gracias, señor
. . . hasta luego*.

"He was exposed to much temptation," recalled Sedley. He
went to the races, smoked, and drank more than was good for
him, but in California in the 1850's "to keep fairly clear of
evil habits, which Edwin in the main did, was correspondingly
praiseworthy."

Once he was almost snared in a ruinous marriage by a
woman twice his age, and was rescued by a friend, probably
Anderson. He vowed a solemn vow never to marry an actress.

Catherine Sinclair had lost so much money that she had to
give up the Metropolitan. Booth found himself a billet in Sacramento. A friend saw him lolling on the hotel porch there,
script in hand, brushing up on *Hamlet*. Queen Gertrude for
this performance was played by Mrs. Judah, a West Coast
favorite, originally of the Boston Museum. She had been the
Duchess of York in *Richard III* on the night Booth made his
debut as Tressel.

Booth's style had strengthened. "If he will but apply himself!" This was the refrain of most reviews. "If he will but

apply himself *industriously, unceasingly* and *perseveringly* in his profession, he will ere long rank among the foremost of living actors."

But Booth was drinking hard. He would have paid with his life for one wild evening if his caul hadn't done its work again. The human instrument of his rescue was another actor, who pulled him dead drunk out of the Sacramento River and dosed him with brandy. "Who wo' me up?" Booth snarled.

A splendid new theater, the Forrest, opened in Sacramento, and Booth, Caroline Chapman, George Spear, and Mrs. Judah were all signed on. Booth's engagement lasted about a month; he was fired for drinking—the legend later given out by Asia in her books about the family was that the manager wished to "curtail expenses."

Then Mrs. Sinclair journeyed upriver to have another try at management. She rented the small, dingy Sacramento Theater on a back street and re-engaged Booth. The *Democratic State Journal* reviewed a performance of his Richard III in which he forgot his lines not once but repeatedly: "It was palpable that the part had not been studied with the deep concern which an actor of so much promise as Mr. Booth owes not only to an audience but also to himself."

They did a new melodrama, *The Marble Heart*, which told the story of Raphael Duchatlet, a sculptor in Paris hopelessly in love with Mademoiselle Marco whose heart is hard as any stone. Booth and Henry Sedley flipped for parts and Booth was stuck with Raphael. He loathed playing lovers. All through the rehearsals he drove the cast crazy with his tricks. On opening night McCloskey met him leaving his dressing room for his first big scene, after having walked through the earlier ones. Booth wore a short black velvet paletot and a red silk handkerchief around his throat.

"Want to see some good acting?" he asked.

"I haven't seen it yet," said McCloskey dryly.

"You'll see it now. Keep your eye on me." He gave his infinitesimal wink, then glided out on the stage, set as a sculptor's studio.

Music. RAPHAEL *is discovered seated, left, with his head resting on his hand before a statue, at which he has been working;* MADAME DUCHATLET *is seated in the great chair, right, looking anxiously at* RAPHAEL.

RAPHAEL. (*To himself, with passion.*) O, Marco, Marco! Like the fabled basilisk, death is in thine eyes. The wind is less inconstant than the rays of those beauteous lights of heaven's masterpiece—one instant they burn, the next they freeze, elate with hope and madden with despair. O, enchanting Siren! Where is thy heart?—where is thy heart?

MADAME DUCHATLET. (*Who has risen and quietly approached him, leaning on his shoulder.*) Raphael, Raphael, my dear son! have no secrets from your mother—tell me your grief. What is it Raphael?—my heart is cold with fear! (*Falls weeping into his arms.*)

RAPH. Dear mother, compose yourself; my tranquility shall soon return—for *your sake* I will chase from my heart the maddening chimeras that have estranged me from thee—till then, let me guard my secret.

Madame Duchatlet leaves. Raphael throws away his chisels and paces the stage in frantic excitement.

RAPH. I can work no more! (*With passion.*) O Marco! Marco! I cannot tear thee from my heart—thine image is graven there, never to be effaced! (*Taking a miniature from his breast and kissing it.*) Spite of my reason, I love thee—beautiful statue—marble heart—marble heart!

The tears poured down Booth's cheeks. Long before this the whole audience had begun to sob, men as well as women. There were trumpetings from the wings as the hard-boiled actors blew out their emotions into their silk handkerchiefs. "I suppose very few know," declared McCloskey, speaking for the newspapers years later—when the California he remembered was a place as remote and diminished as though he were looking at it through the wrong end of a spyglass—"I suppose very few know that Booth was a grand melodramatic, romantic actor of the Frédéric Lemaître style, and those who knew him in the early days are not so sure that it was not a mistake for him to follow the great tragedian roles rather than those of the romantic, picturesque school."

Next Booth was given the dual part of Fabian and Louis dei Franchi, the swashbuckling twins of *The Corsican Brothers*. Boozy George Spear—Old Spudge—was in the cast and so was McCloskey, and on opening night, which was New Year's Eve, McCloskey and Old Spudge stumbled onstage, hilariously drunk, and beat each other with a live chicken. Booth managed to keep sober this evening, but of another showing of the same play a few nights later the *Journal* observed that "Mr. Booth, who was cast to sustain the principal character, could hardly sustain himself, but he struggled through it, dragging everything down to the depths of disgust. Speaking mildly, he was intoxicated."

One of the managers in Sacramento was a certain loud-mouthed Ben Baker—"Uncle Ben" the actors called him—who eventually was fond of boasting that he "had picked Edwin Booth out of the quartz in California!"

Baker announced he was soon going east and offered, if Ted liked, to "fix up" some appearances for him. Anderson seconded the idea and advised Booth to engage Uncle Ben as his advance agent for his eastern debut.

Baker departed, talking steadily, and Booth, to earn some money in the meantime, joined a troupe of strollers and began another tour of the camps. Manager of this troupe was burly Ben Moulton, a coach driver by profession. The leading lady was his wife.

Early in July they started out with Booth prancing gaily ahead on a pinto pony he had bought for the trip and the others bumping after in a covered wagon that held ten actors, an orchestra of three horn players, scenery and costumes, and was plastered over with posters advertising THE IRON CHEST, OR THE MYSTERIOUS MURDER. On the back platform sat Booth's dress basket, which was to be used for the chest in the play. It was covered with canvas painted to look like iron and decorated with a skull and crossbones.

In Hangtown and Jackass Gulch near Shirttail Bend in the

northern mining region Booth was loudly invited to "git" by the unpredictable miners as he gulped through the woes of Sir Edward Mortimer. Traveling south, heralding their entry into each new town by a parade down the main street with all three horns blowing, Moulton's strollers forded the Moke-lumne River. Booth crossed on his pony and was almost sucked under by quicksand. A few days later in the town of Columbia a fight broke out in the audience while he was onstage. Shots were fired toward the footlights; no actors were hurt but two miners were killed, and in both these near fatalities it was his caul that had saved him, Booth claimed.

By an uncanny coincidence one settlement after another began to burn to the ground immediately after the troupe pulled out of it: Hangtown, Georgetown, then Diamond Springs. The cavalcade trundled into Nevada City. Before the calico curtain had a chance to rise this town also towered into flame; the best efforts of the local bucket brigade, augmented by the actors, were perfectly useless. Then Grass Valley blazed up. Some of the miners, suspecting a firebug, looked dangerously at Booth. They were beginning to call him the Fiery Star in ugly parody of the Fairy Stars, child entertainers like little Lotta Crabtree who toured the camps, singing and dancing.

Moulton's company had left a trail of bad debts as well, and in Downieville the sheriff caught up with it. Ben Moulton lit out. All the costumes, the three horns, and Booth's pinto pony were confiscated. Booth slung his flannel sleeping blanket over his shoulder, dug his hands in his pockets and slogged back to Marysville on Shank's pony.

"Booth's bad luck" was becoming proverbial. In Sacramento, dead broke again, he met an architect named M. F. Butler who was a patron of the theater. Butler spoke earnestly to the floundering young actor and the gist of what he said was: "My boy, you've 'seen the elephant' over and over. Now go back East. Take your father's place while his memory's still green."

Yes, agreed Booth, that was his own idea; but how to get

there? Leave that to him, said Butler. And he lined up a benefit for Booth at the Forrest Theater. Booth played the Cardinal in *Richelieu* by Bulwer Lytton, and after the show the stampeding audience gave him a present over and above the receipts, a pin of California gold shaped like a hand with a diamond between thumb and forefinger.

But when Booth had paid off his debts he hadn't a sou left. "Trust me!" said Butler and arranged a second benefit. Booth did Iago this time, and his present was a handsome copy of Shakespeare's plays.

Next morning he boarded the steamer for San Francisco. Every actor in Sacramento was waving from the river wharf and calling "God speed." The captain led him to the rail, as if for a curtain call. The theater band blared, and nothing was wanting to make all joyful but M. F. Butler with last night's receipts. Booth's eye was glazed, his mind busy with bleak calculations when, just as the gangplank was to be hauled up, a frantic voice shouted, "Stop! Stop! Hold the ship!" and Butler pounded down the landing place clutching the bag of gold, which he had simply forgotten to turn over to Booth.

At the Metropolitan in San Francisco Booth took a third benefit, acting King Lear for the first time. At his final call he whipped off his white wig and beard and astonished the audience with his boyish face, just as his father had once surprised his mother.

San Francisco had a last look at Booth's face two days later on September 5, 1856, as he stood at the rail of the steamer *Golden Age*, about to raise anchor off Long Wharf. It was not a particularly strong face. The strolling actor's life was in its expression. The chin was lifted; the curl of the lips just missed being cynical.

Booth was bound for Panama and from there east across the Isthmus, not on muleback this time, but by the new railroad; from there north to the farm in Maryland; from there, after a breathing space, out into the world again to bid for fame before eastern audiences.

As he leaned over the ship's rail, searching the crowd on the wharf for Junius and his friends, he felt that he was leaving home rather than returning to it. And when much later— trapped by fame achieved—he thought of California, he forgot the hardships, the jouncing disillusionments, and remembered only that it had been the golden land where for four swift years, with no hand to hold him back, he had been young, unjaded, spurred by the hope of fame, and perfectly happy.

CHAPTER 4

A New Star Rises

The royal tree hath left us royal fruit.
King Richard III, *Act III, scene* 7

"HE's FROM the diggin's!" cried the country boys as they lugged Booth's trunk into the farmhouse. The trunk was so heavy it must be full of gold, or of skulls "like actors carry around with 'em."

It was a forlorn household Booth came back to. He had always thought of his father as a rich man, so had everyone. Yet after Mr. Booth's debts were paid, all that was left was a few hundred dollars. Mrs. Booth had rented the Baltimore house and retired with the children to the farm, where she toiled to make it do well, but she had the amateur touch. Her farming was what her neighbors called "ornamental." The Booth crops failed, the Booth stock died of mysterious diseases.

Mr. Booth's discipline still lay heavy on his family. Asia and John couldn't bring themselves to kill their own animals and at last had set traps outside the grounds for some wild creature. All they had caught was one frantic opossum that looked up at them so pleadingly they almost shed tears and immediately let it go. Their cows ran dry except for one that gave only "pink milk," moving Johnny to declaim dramatically:

There is an old tale goes, that Herne the Hunter . . .
Doth all the winter time at still midnight
Walk round about an oak, with great ragg'd horns . . .
And makes milch-kine yield blood.

They were all living in a new brick farmhouse, called grandiosely Tudor Hall, which had been halfway built when Mr. Booth left. The original cabin, long outgrown, was given over to the Negroes.

Edwin's mother was much aged since he had seen her last. From a sulky schoolgirl Asia had grown into a handsome young woman, still reserved and passionate, capable of spasms of the wild Booth gaiety. It was John Wilkes who had changed most. At eighteen he was taller and bigger than Edwin, wonderfully good-looking in an exotic, theatrical way. His dark eyes glowed, fascinating as snake's eyes under crescent-shaped lids and silky lashes. His teeth flashed in an actor's smile. He was devouringly ambitious—"I must have fame! fame!"

At school he used to tell his friends, as they lay on the grass smoking clay pipes a yard long, that *his* was the name that would be remembered; and as he contemplated the impossible feats he might have performed if they hadn't been impossible (such as overthrowing the Colossus of Rhodes), his whole soul seemed to inflate itself with satisfaction. Violently stage-struck, he had made his debut in Baltimore as Richmond in *Richard III* in a benefit for Sleepy Clarke, who had gone on the stage too and was starring in *Toodles*, the comic afterpiece. It was premature, and John did badly. What Clarke was really after when he rushed Johnny into appearing, declared Mrs. Booth, was the family name.

Earlier, when he was at school, a gypsy in the near-by wood of Cockeysville had read John's palm. "Ah-h!" she muttered, "You've a bad hand, the lines all cris-cras! It's full enough of sorrow—full of trouble—trouble in plenty. You'll break hearts, they'll be nothing to you. You'll die young, and leave many to mourn you. You'll make a bad end, and have plenty to love you. You'll have a fast life—short, but a grand one. Young sir, I've never seen a worse hand, and I wish I hadn't seen it, but if I were a girl I'd follow you through the world for your handsome face."

Junius and Edwin, as the eldest sons, had sent money home whenever they could. Yet they had stayed away so long, it had come to be Johnny who ranked first in the house. Now their mother cautioned Edwin never to scold Johnny nor even to hint at any correction. She wanted no unpleasantness between her sons; she had told Junius the same when he was at home. And when Edwin, ready for the eastern debut on which his future hinged, looked over his father's costumes, which he had handled so often, and chose several to wear, his mother said to him firmly, "No,"—that she was saving those for John.

"Star or starve!"

Booth had boasted as much to Henry Sedley before he started east, and when a reporter in Sacramento asked him what his plans were he had answered with a vague and shining look: "Perhaps Europe!"

He meant, however, to conquer the New World first: the important cities on the eastern seaboard, New York, Boston, and Philadelphia. But when Uncle Ben Baker, arriving ahead, tried to make engagements for him, he was given the cold shoulder. Eastern managers didn't care to risk starring a youngster whom they remembered as performing very palely; the best theater Baker could elbow into was the Front Street in Booth's home city of Baltimore, where Booth opened on October 15 beginning with *Hamlet*, then going on to *Richelieu* and *Richard III*. He had a tendency to rant and strike attitudes, yet certain tones of his father's voice sounded in his own and told on the Baltimore audience with thrilling effect.

He headed south, with Uncle Ben as his seedy impresario. By mid-November they were in Richmond, playing at a theater stage-managed by Joe Jefferson. Booth, who had been sixteen when Jefferson first met him, had turned twenty-three on November 13. "There was a gentleness and sweetness of manner in him that made him far more winning than his father," was Jefferson's impression now.

After he had seen Booth act Richard that night, Jefferson drew his little leading lady to one side and told her: "Tomorrow, Mary, you'll rehearse Juliet to the Romeo of a new and rising tragedian."

Next morning the two young players in street clothes took their places for rehearsal. Mary Devlin was sixteen, hardly older than Juliet. She was slight, not beautiful, and yet as her part gained on her, her serious and eager face began to glow with a lovely intelligence better than beauty. Booth, who looked a perfect Romeo, was somehow never convincing in the character, didn't come to life until his fight with Tybalt. But he was young, he was handsome, and perhaps Mary Devlin saw through the trumped-up gallantry of his Romeo to the sensitive Hamlet behind it. Hamlet has his own charm for women. The interested company watched a spark kindle between the two.

After the performance, while Mary was sighing to Jefferson that Mr. Booth was the greatest actor she had ever known, that she was "inspired" and could "act forever" with him, Booth was writing home to his mother: "I have seen and acted with a young woman who has so impressed me that I could almost forget my vow never to marry an actress."

Mary Devlin had gone on the stage at fourteen because her father, in business in Troy, New York, had lost his money. It was a dubious career for a "nice girl" from a nontheatrical background, and the manager Henry Jarrett had entrusted her to the care of Jefferson and his wife, with whom she lived. When Jefferson saw a member of the notorious Booth family showing signs of interest in the inexperienced girl, he disapproved and ordered Mary to return the turquoise bracelet Booth had given her. Then Booth craftily bought another bracelet, the twin of Mary's and presented it to Mrs. Jefferson. This smoothed the path. At the end of the week Booth led his Juliet into the greenroom, where in a sham-heroic manner as though acting a scene in the play the pair fell on their knees before Jefferson and murmured: "Father, your blessing."

Jefferson caught his cue, held out his hands over their heads and answered in the voice of Friar Lawrence: "Bless you, my children."

But once bitten, twice shy: Booth had almost been trapped into marriage in California. His obsession against marrying a woman of the theater was slow to overcome, and he began to have scruples whether after all he ought to break his vow. When he and Mary said good-by nothing had been fixed between them.

II

On the road it was Uncle Ben who mended and cared for his star's wardrobe, sitting up long after midnight in their successive hotel rooms stitching and patching while Booth lay back smoking and threading the needles. From Mobile Booth wrote to Dave Anderson on the back of his hotel washing list and after finishing his letter added some remarks on the printed side.

Don't weep

WASHING LIST

It's all I own
Mr. *Booth's list of assetts*

. . . .

0 Night Shirts.
0 Bosoms.
1 Drawers.
2 Stockings.
Chemise.   *oh*
Caps.   *hum*
Dresses.   *he, he.*
Night Dresses.   *law!*
Corsets.   *Ha, ha, ha!*
Capes.   *I confess the cape.*
Pantalets.   *De lord*
Skirts.   *jamais*

Battle House, Mobile
1857

In Memphis Booth and Baker met Adah Menken, famous for her performance of *Mazeppa* in which, stripped nearly naked, she rode a white horse up a runway. The Menken conceived a "crush" on Booth, which he didn't return.

In Louisville a little Negro boy trotted backstage carrying a covered basket. Booth asked: "What's in that?"

The boy said: "Dunno, sah."

"Take the cloth off." The boy swept off the white cloth, then fled, screeching. In the basket was a skull wrapped in newspapers, the parts joined by springs and hooks. It had once belonged to a horse thief named Lovett whom Mr. Booth had befriended. Lovett had been hanged in Louisville and had willed Mr. Booth his skull to use in *Hamlet*. The doctor who prepared it now sent it over to Edwin, who stuck it up on a shelf in his dressing room, wearing Macbeth's red wig and a large jeweled and gilt crown.

In Chicago Booth played at McVicker's Theater. The lively, small stepdaughter of the theater owner, a little girl called Mary McVicker, took an imperious fancy to him, quite on the order of the mature Menken's.

As they worked back east it seemed that the billing Baker used to advertise his star got more and more flamboyant and preposterous. Booth violently disliked such titles as

THE WORLD'S GREATEST ACTOR
THE INHERITOR OF HIS FATHER'S GENIUS

and in Detroit he struck and sent word to Garry Hough, the theater manager, that he "insisted on being announced as simple Edwin Booth, nothing more."

Hough obeyed and proclaimed the

ENGAGEMENT FOR ONE WEEK ONLY
OF SIMPLE
EDWIN BOOTH

Someone had once called Boston "the Athens of America," and ever since then a patter of applause from the critical Bostonians was supposed to confer intense prestige, though, actually, the records of Boston box offices proved that what the old town really enjoyed, her lofty pretensions to the contrary, was not highfalutin classics but pantomime and spectacle, "blue flame and glitter."

Booth had set his heart on playing in Boston, and after repeated snubs from managers, Baker finally wedged him into the spring season of 1857. A diminutive notice in the Boston *Daily Evening Transcript* made known the starring engagement of Mr. Edwin Booth at the Boston Theater on Washington Street.

This Evening, April 20, 1857
Will be performed the play entitled
A NEW WAY TO PAY OLD DEBTS
Sir Giles Overreach . . . Mr. Edwin Booth

The night was cold and rainy. Bad weather didn't keep a crowd from flocking to the cozy little Boston Museum to see the popular Eliza Logan in the new melodrama of *The Duchess, or The Unnatural Father*. But young tragedians in the old plays were a dime a dozen. At the Boston Theater, a big barn of a place where all delicate effects had to be enlarged ("Might as well act on the Boston Common," troupers passed the word to one another), the audience was thin and made up mainly of white-haired playgoers who had known Booth's father. Cordial clapping greeted Booth on his entrance. This was his meed as his father's son. But after this gesture the Bostonians settled back in their seats and their polite attentiveness said plainly: "Now, young man, let's see what you can do for yourself."

Booth had chosen to open in this play because the first three acts, which were relatively tame, would allow him time to feel out his audience. Sir Giles Overreach, the principal figure, is a malevolent old scoundrel who has grown rich robbing widows and orphans. In the last scene Sir Giles does dramatically overreach himself; his wicked plans are thwarted; he collapses into raving madness.

This was the scene Booth was counting on. He paused in the wing to collect himself, then strode out on the stage as if it belonged to him, and just as his father had done in a country theater in Virginia almost forty years before, unleashed his powers on the startled audience. His eyes dilated and swept the stage—"like bassilisks," wrote one critic next morning.

"His father's eyes!" thought many people, and so they were in their remarkable way of emitting light, though like his mother's in their size and brown-blackness. But the next moment everyone forgot comparisons. A fearful sight fascinated them: they watched the mind and body of a man disintegrate. Sir Giles' face whitened and shrank; his lower jaw sagged like a dying man's; his upper lip writhed back baring his teeth in a lunatic grin. His hand flew to the hilt of his sword but his arm failed in its office. His guilty past rushed over him:

> Ha! I am feeble:
> Some undone widow sits upon mine arm.

At this point Junius Brutus Booth as Sir Giles used to bite a piece of carmine-soaked sponge hidden in his mouth, which made a red froth bubble on his lips. Edwin Booth disdained this particular trick. But as his body thrilled in a horrible spasm and pitched face forward to the floor, the whole length of it seeming to hit the stage at once, and there continuing to twitch and quiver, so strong a sense of evil poured out of it that half the people in the house turned away their eyes, feeling sick and shaken.

"Quite a triumph," ventured the cautious Boston *Transcript*. "Young Booth's success was decided. . . . It brought back the most vivid recollections of the fire, the vigor, the strong intellectuality which characterized the acting of his lamented father."

The next night Booth did *Richelieu*. Dr. Samuel Howe was in the audience with his wife, Julia Ward Howe, both ardent theatergoers. As soon as the new star began to speak, Mrs. Howe and her husband felt a peculiar chill go all through them. They looked at each other, nodded and whispered: "This is the real thing!"

For his benefit Booth gave Maturin's play *Bertram* and also disported himself in the afterpiece, a farce called *Little Tod-dlekins* about a young widower stuck with a great lump of a middle-aged stepdaughter—"Little Toddlekins"—who calls him "Papa." At the final curtain, when the boyish widower, Mr. Jones Robinson Brownsmith, is on the point of marrying a girl whose father is about to marry Little Toddlekins, Booth as Brownsmith, wearing a high hat and white trousers, tripped downstage to the footlights and appealed to the audience to unscramble the relationships.

BROWNSMITH. It's only some little boy fresh from school can do it. Is there any little boy here can help us? It's a nice little sum. My first wife's husband's eldest daughter's mother will now be my second wife's father's daughter-in-law's aunt; consequently, my present wife's youngest daughter's grand-mother will be her father-in-law's second wife's mother-in-law's husband. No—I can't do it. Is there any young gentle-man here, home for the holidays, who will undertake it?

"As a farce actor Mr. Booth did not impress us favorably," was one critic's clammy verdict. "The tragic prestige of an actor should not be trifled with."

Edwin Forrest sat out in front another night. "Why don't the young man learn his lines?" he grumbled.

In the house for a performance of *Brutus* was a plain-faced, stage-struck girl named Louisa May Alcott. Manager Barry of the Boston Theater had given her a pass to all performances. "Saw young Booth in *Brutus*," wrote Louisa in her journal, "and liked him better than his father."

During *The Iron Chest* the emotional actress Matilda Heron, in town for rehearsals of *Camille*, sat in a box and was so car-ried away that she peeled off her kid glove and ostentatiously threw it at Booth. Next morning a verse was in one of the papers:

> If Miss H. threw her "kid"
> For a popular bid,
> She blundered, we fear, where the stage-yawning
> Styx is,
> For 'twas plain to our eyes,

> If a good judge of size,
> That by shop-keepers' measure she did not
>   "throw sixes."
>
> But if tribute it were,
> Or professional spur,
> From an artiste in luck—young Booth don't
>   abandon it;
> For 'twill tempt you to aim
> At a still higher fame,
> And acknowledge the heart for the lack of
>   the hand in it.

It was passion, decided the critics, that was the governing quality of Booth's acting. His work was crude, but "crude," writes Henry Clapp, a seasoned Boston reviewer, "with the promise-crammed crudity of youthful genius."

He was most impressive in scenes of fierce action when, towering though his passion was, he always seemed to hold something in reserve. The critics preferred him as Brutus and Richard, agreed that King Lear was much too much for him at present, and disagreed over his Hamlet, pitched in a lower key and distinctly more thoughtful and more of a person than the fairy-tale prince he had created in California. The reviewer for the *Transcript* thought it feeble, barely up to average, even though Booth certainly looked the part. Still in fairness the *Transcript* printed the opinion of a correspondent "whose views differ somewhat from our own," and who could find only one word in the language to describe Booth's Hamlet, and that was "beautiful." "We have seen actors play the part with more energy, dash more at effects, . . . but the beauty of Booth's Hamlet was its abstraction and intensity."

Someone suggested to Julia Ward Howe that she write a play for Booth. She was interested, so he went to call on her. Although he was so much the actor in his appearance, Mrs. Howe was delighted with his natural gentlemanliness, his "modest, intelligent and, above all, genuine" manner. The fresh-faced Boston lady and the rather Hebraic-looking young man talked together quietly while in the adjoining conservatory the ferns rustled as the small Howe girls peeped around the door. One name slipped out of Booth again and again, that of "little Mary Devlin, who has been much admired," he repeated earnestly, "in several *heavy* parts."

The Boston Theater had made scarcely any money on Booth, yet his critical success with the reserved Bostonians had done him personally great good. Manager Barry, though, was worried half-sick by his star's dissipation, and William Warren from the Boston Museum, who was a cousin of Jefferson's, took Booth aside. Warren had played the Lord Mayor in *Richard III* on the epochal night when Booth played Tressel. "Now, Ted," he said sharply, "there is for you in a stage career either a fortune and the lead or—a bottle of brandy. You must cast aside Bohemianism. Be Hamlet everywhere."

Booth listened and did otherwise. "He used to pace Washington Street with a springy, elastic step," remembered one of his friends. "He wore striking suits, cultivated long, curly hair and smoked huge cigars. Chain-lightning couldn't hold him in those days!"

If Boston were the Athens of America, New York was Rome. All roads led there. After Booth's fine Boston notices Baker had no trouble getting him a New York contract with William Burton, manager of the Metropolitan Theater, where the French tragedienne Rachel had appeared in 1855. Booth had asked to open in New York as Sir Giles and to be billed modestly; there must be no flaunting his father's name—this above all. Burton, however, had other ideas. He had had a poor season. He needed a special attraction and he decided to handle Booth's best asset in the unblushing Roman manner. So he ordered posters to advertise that

EDWIN BOOTH
Son of the Great Tragedian

would open at the Metropolitan on May 4, 1857, in *Richard III*, his father's celebrated vehicle. He had Booth's best reviews published in booklet form and widely circulated. When it was too late for his star to back out, he sent a telegram to Ben Baker in Boston: "Mr. Booth announced for *Richard III* next Monday. Seats going like hot cakes."

After a farewell binge, Booth fell into the New York train. The Metropolitan was on lower Broadway in the heart of New York's theatrical district, and as he and Baker drove down the pleasant tree-lined street Booth saw himself emblazoned on the sides of buildings and in shopwindows.

SON OF THE GREAT TRAGEDIAN
HOPE OF THE LIVING DRAMA
RICHARD'S HIMSELF AGAIN

He groaned, clutched his forehead, ground his teeth, and shrieked to Baker: "I'm ruined!"

He went to rehearsal to meet a company as sore as he was. The veterans in it didn't relish giving their support to a comparative beginner about to swing into easy fame on his father's coattails. There was another beginner in the cast, Lawrence Barrett, who was down for Tressel. A hungry-looking youngster, all eyes and forehead, Barrett had achieved this, his first, season in New York only after making many weary rounds, and along with the rest of the company he was ready to hate Edwin Booth. But when Booth glided down the aisle and up onstage, all hostility melted. Instead of the pert aspirant the others expected, they saw a "slight, pale youth," so Barrett describes him, "with black, flowing hair and soft brown eyes. He took his place with no air of conquest or self-assertion, and gave his directions with a grace and courtesy which have never left him." Barrett was writing years later when he knew Booth well.

Thanks to Burton's advertising the house was full this night. Booth's performance of Richard, said the critics next morning (to Booth's chagrin, though he expected it) was marvelously like his father's. Through certain scenes young Booth walked tamely as his father had done when the mood failed him. Yet when Edwin Booth, like his father in this, too, took up a scene to make a sensation of it, "all his tameness instantly vanishes," cheered the New York *Tribune*. "He renders the passage with a vigorous truthfulness which startles his audience into wild enthusiasm."

When he came to the terrific speech

The North? What do they i' the North
When they should serve their sovereign IN THE WEST?

his face and body blazed with expression; his raging voice was like a lion's roar; he communicated an electrical force. All over the house men surged to their feet as if literally yanked up by the contagion of his summons and shouted in pure delight: "*Bravo! Bravo! Bravo! Bravo!*"

Tremendous untrained power and unfocused energy, an interior nervousness that showed in his acting: these were some of the flaws, possible seeds of greatness, that the critics pointed out. Booth hadn't yet learned control of his voice. His walk was rather awkward, like a very young man's. But it was the influence of his father that stood mainly in his way. From being so much with his father he had unconsciously acquired all Junius Brutus Booth's bad mannerisms; he had deliberately worked to imitate the good things. He was miserably aware the result was inferior.

In *Richard III*, for example, Mr. Booth used to say:

"Off with his head!"

at the same time striking one hand into the other; and his gesture amazingly conjured up the picture of the headman's block and the kneeling victim. But when Edwin Booth did the same, nothing happened. New York reviewers compared father and son monotonously until Booth, irritated and challenged, began to scrutinize his acting, and to pounce on and root out everything imitative.

There were two critics who looked at Booth freshly, being both young themselves. William Winter, a sporadic reviewer (later the dramatic oracle of the *Tribune* under Greeley), predicted that if Booth would only *reflect* more when studying his roles his name soon would "eclipse any which has adorned the

English stage within the memory of living man!" Winter's own memory was short; he was twenty-one.

Adam Badeau, another free lance, was a little older. Badeau had been loitering down Broadway one spring evening looking for copy when on an impulse he swung into the Metropolitan, cynically ready to be let down after William Burton's boasts ("Hope of the living drama!" "Richard's himself again!"). But instead he had been lifted up. His steel-rimmed spectacles grew cloudy with his excitement. When the show was over he took himself backstage, where his obviously sincere praise overjoyed and touched Booth.

Both Winter and Badeau came to know Edwin Booth well. Winter knew personally most of the actors of his day—Jefferson, Irving, all the great ones. He peered over their shoulders into their lives, talked and wrote familiarly about them, made himself the gusty chorus in the drama of their careers. As for Badeau, he soon began to spend whole days with Booth, and immediately taking in that the howling lack in Booth's equipment was his want of scholarship, he located books and pictures about the theater and thrust them on the raw young star. They visited libraries and art galleries together. Badeau reminded Booth how Kean had practiced his gestures before a full-length glass; how Garrick had deepened his sense of life by keeping his eyes open in the criminal courts, the madhouse.

But at night in Booth's dressing room the actor took over and the journalist leaned forward enthralled to watch the character for the evening come into existence. On hot nights Booth sat stripped to the waist, offering his face to the mirror. As the aging lines were penciled around the actor's mouth, the stylized crow's feet etched, the thin lips emphasized, as the rouge and false eyebrows went on and at last the wig, tunic, and tights, Badeau saw Hamlet or Iago or Pescara gradually emerge. Once he accidentally pulled apart Booth's scarlet robe as the actor sat smoking, ready for *Richelieu*, and Booth shrieked and quavered in falsetto: "How dare you, sir?" The next instant he was the Cardinal again.

He had plenty of humor, not particularly sweet, and while

he made up he chattered without stopping, exploding ghastly puns. But as they grew intimate Badeau saw him sometimes when all his gaiety had dropped away and he sat slumped before his dressing table staring straight ahead with the expression of a man who gazes into the lowest circle of the inferno. Through this depression there was no getting at him. "It was appalling to witness," writes Badeau, who used to find such melancholy hard to understand in a man with everything to live for, even though Booth tried harrowingly to describe it: the joylessness, restlessness, sense of drifting and premonition of some horror lurking in ambush—"the feeling that evil is hanging over me, that I can't come to good."

He longed for Badeau to share all his thoughts. He began to lean on Badeau. In their separations he scratched him quick little appeals: "Dear Ad, I am sick—took physic last night to make me sleep & laid awake all night; my cough is worse and my hoarseness d——dble! I am tired & in a bad humor!"

When he went carousing it was with other actors. He often got drunk with James Seymour, an actor about his own age. They would roll home in the small hours to Seymour's house far downtown, where tiny Willie Seymour lay sleeping in his crib. The father would snatch the baby up, cry, "Here, Ned, catch!" and toss Willie across to Booth who tossed him back.

Early in the summer Booth left for the road and was gone a long time, turning up again in New York at intervals. The trickle of his letters to Badeau sometimes stopped for weeks. "Likely as not you're on a spree," Badeau jogged him gently. "It's nearly five months since one of your performances of this sort and since I've known you, you've never missed one in that space of time. You might have waited until I could care for you."

III

When the old actresses in the stock companies Booth visited praised his performance, he would smile and arch his brows and say softly: "That was because I acted for you!"

On the whole, he liked old women better than the young

ones, dozens of whom sent him poems, flowers, Roman scarves, ostrich and peacock feathers, expensive rings and brooches to wear onstage, as well as perfumed notes on tinted paper with dainty monograms—"Though you do not know me, dear Mr. Booth, I have admired you so long and so warmly I can scarcely feel myself to be quite a stranger to you."

Booth hardly ever read these notes through. Sometimes he jotted lists on the back or scribbled his name as if idly practicing his sought-after, seldom-given autograph. In Boston, where he was staying with Orlando Tompkins, part-owner of the Boston Theater, an anonymous girl left a diamond ring for him at Tompkins' house at 12 Franklin Square, and Booth hung it on a string around the neck of the family cat, then dumped the cat on a cushion in the front window. "More than once," writes Adam Badeau, who absorbed whatever went on with a newspaperman's sense that all's grist, "Booth saved some foolish child from what might have been disgrace, and sent her home to her family. And he never injured a pure woman in his life."

In March, 1858, he acted again with "little Mary Devlin." They met in Baltimore, where Mary was playing at the Holliday Street Theater and living in a boardinghouse to which Booth saw her home every night. He had separated from Uncle Ben Baker and was doing excellently on his own. This summer, after Mary had played her first New York engagement at Niblo's Garden in Charlotte Cushman's company, Booth took a benefit at the Holliday Street Theater as Richard III, with his brother John Wilkes playing Richmond.

For every woman who ran after Edwin Booth there were two running after John's elegant figure in its stylish accouterments—a claret-colored coat with velvet lapels, a pale buff waistcoat and dove-gray trousers strapped down under the boots, a wide-brimmed tropical-straw hat. Restaurant waitresses swarmed to serve John. Hotel maids tore his bed apart for the ecstasy of making it up again. Like his father, John, who was twenty, had had several close shaves from getting in real trouble, though it was said of him, as Badeau said of Edwin, that he never seduced a girl he knew was pure. Clara Morris, a young actress, saw his method at work when Mrs. Ellsler, a manager's wife who was far from young, shook her finger at him for some forward remark, and John seized her hand, made a sweeping bow and kissed her fingers gallantly.

Yet appearing on the same stage with Edwin, John went mortifyingly unnoticed, though his brother did his best to give him the advantage and hide his mistakes, having noticed at rehearsal that John bucked corrections. In October in Richmond John played Horatio to Edwin's Hamlet, and when Edwin's final call came he pulled his brother down to the footlights and suggested to the audience: "I think he's done well, don't you?"

Privately he wrote to Junius: "I don't think John will startle the world . . . but he is improving fast and looks beautiful."

The end of October found Booth at the Boston Theater, where Mary Devlin was now playing. Again they acted opposite each other in *Romeo and Juliet*. The performance seemed remarkably real. "Few who saw it will ever forget it," exclaimed Julia Ward Howe. "The two true lovers were at their best, ideally young, beautiful, and identified with their parts."

Mary Devlin also played Margaret, daughter of Sir Giles Overreach, to Booth's rapacious Sir Giles. The entire family of theater-going Howes in a row at the matinee saw them act together in *The Iron Chest*. This creaky old melodrama was usually reserved for Saturday afternoons, and it struck the intellectual Howes as pretty silly stuff, which only Booth's personality saved from being ridiculous. As Sir Edward Mortimer, his first gloomy chords summoning from offstage, "Adam, Adam Winterton, come hither to me," were hauntingly thrilling and set the tone for the whole.

But the Howes were not moved by the pathetic climax in which Mary, playing Helen, Sir Edward's ladylove—charming in a white satin dress trimmed with point lace and silver, white silk stockings, white satin shoes, and a white velvet hat with ostrich plumes—threw herself into the black velvet arms of Booth, as the dying Sir Edward.

> HELEN. Where is he? Ill, and on the ground! Oh! Mortimer!
> Oh, Heaven! My Mortimer! Oh, raise him—gently!
> Speak to me, love. He cannot!
> SIR EDWARD. Helen—'twas I—that—killed—
> *(He struggles to speak, but, unable to utter, he falls and dies. Helen kneels over him as the curtain slowly descends.)*

Julia Ward Howe soon met and became very fond of "this exquisite little woman," as she called Mary, who was as much of a natural lady as Booth a gentleman. During this engagement Mrs. Howe saw Booth as Hamlet and her poem about him printed in the *Atlantic Monthly* was a tribute and a portrait.

> We sit before the row of evening lamps,
> Each in his chair,
> Forgetful of November dusks and damps,
> And wintry air.
>
> . . . . .
>
> And, beautiful as dreams of maidenhood
> That doubt defy,
> Young Hamlet, with his forehead grief-subdued,
> And visioning eye.

"My Hamlet," Mary called Booth. They were deeper in love than ever, and still Booth's recoil from marrying an actress kept them from becoming definitely engaged. He had left Boston when a Boston lawyer who had no such squeamishness proposed to Mary. She asked the advice of Charlotte Cushman. Miss Cushman, knowing the Booths, soberly advised her to accept the lawyer. Mary went so far as to write to Edwin that she had had an offer, and Booth's reaction was to drown his hurt in such rivers of alcohol that he landed in bed, ill as well as drunk, his acting at a standstill. Friends sent word to Mary, who caught the first train to join him. Between endearments the lovers agreed to be married as soon as they could, and that

Mary was to leave the stage—not a fit place for his wife, Booth ruled.

Even in the first haze of her happiness Mary had an inkling of what marriage to a Booth would be. To begin with, her future sister-in-law, the clannish Asia, was frighteningly hostile. Asia gave it out that Mary, being after the money Booth was making, had enticed him, drunk, into consenting to marry her. And when they were alone together, Booth told Mary about himself, somberly and painfully. "I remember," he wrote much later in a confession to a friend, "how she wept when I laid my blackened heart bare to her."

He had kept nothing back; he had confessed everything. "Before I was eighteen I was a drunkard, at twenty a libertine. I knew no better. I was born *good*, I do believe, for there are sparks of goodness constantly flashing out from among the cinders . . . I was neglected in my childhood and thrown (really, it now seems almost purposely) into all sorts of temptations and evil society. . . . I was allowed to roam at large, and at an early age and in a wild and almost barbarous country where boys become old men in vice."

When they were apart Mary strove to distill herself into her letters so that she might go beside her lover to guide and comfort. "Last night," she wrote, "I sat by the window thinking of you, and disturbed only by the mournful sighing of the wind. I wondered in 'this stillness of the world without, and of the soul within,' what our lives in the future would be."

Booth, shuddering and overwrought, had confided to her how a wind moaning could bring back the past to him, take him years back and start him dreaming. It was of this she was thinking. "It is not wonderful that *you* should have such emotions—sensitive natures are prone to them; then why, I ask myself, should my eyes have filled with tears, and trembled lest *you* should experience them again? Ah, dear Edwin 'twas a fear that they would lead you from my side and leave me once more alone. I am very wrong, doubtless, to have allowed so simple a fact to impress me, and am still more to blame to repeat it here; for have you not 'died into life,' as Keats says

—and I should wean you from all remembrance of the tomb; and so I promise to do."

What hundreds of young girls dreamed of, some idly, some passionately, was to be her destiny: to marry Edwin Booth. "You have ever seemed to me," she wrote, "like what Shelley says of himself—'a phantom among men'—'companionless as the last fading storm,' and yet my spirit ever seems lighter and more joyous when with you. This I can account for only by believing that a mission has been given to me to fulfil, and that I shall be rewarded by seeing you rise to be great and happy."

Her letters were full of his work. She had seen him in *Richelieu*. "The improvement you have made in the 'Cardinal' charmed me. You must not forget to tell me of your studies; they interest me alike with the movements of your heart— *my heart;* for 'tis mine. Did you not tell me so?"

She entered devotedly into his struggle to find his own style, one quieter than his father's. "The conversational, colloquial school you desire to adopt is the only true one, Edwin, for the present day."

Yet they both agreed an actor could go too far in it, as Matilda Heron had done.

"Could you see her!" expostulated little Mary, who had just done so. "She gives you too much of 'Mrs. John Smith,' and endeavors, or labors rather, to be so very commonplace that it is simply ridiculous."

This pedantic naturalness that does not idealize, that does not elevate, that, like the Heron performance in *Camille*, leaves out no detail of degrading reality—this is not art in its highest embodiment. Mary deplored the pulpy, salacious vehicles, many of them French imports, that were crowding pure tragedy out of the theaters. "Is it not outrageous to see an art so holy as the drama thus desecrated? . . . *You* can, if you will, change the perverted taste of the public by your truth and sublimity, and you must study for this. Dear Edwin, I will never allow you to droop for a single moment; for I know the power that dwells within your eye, and my ambition is to see you surrounded by greatness. . . .

"If my love is selfish, you will never be great: part of you belongs to the world. I *must* remember this."

IV

Already Adam Badeau, who in the late 1850's was contributing to the *New York Sunday Times*, under the pen name "Vagabond," charming, short essays on topical subjects (Longfellow's poems, the pre-Raphaelites, the death of Charlotte Brontë), had hailed Booth in several of them as the only representative in his generation of pure, poetic tragedy, the "gorgeous tragedy" that Milton wrote of, whose essential element is the spiritual, and whose peculiar accomplishment is to touch the soul through the senses. "Edwin Booth," exclaimed Badeau, "has made me know what tragedy is. He has displayed to my eyes an entirely new field; he has shown me the possibilities of tragedy."

In New York together, Booth and Badeau argued for hours over the interpretation of Booth's roles. At the last minute possible they would separate at the dressing-room door, one bound for the front of the house and the other for the wing. The lights dimmed, and with the portentous rise of the velvet curtain would occur a nightly miracle, which the journalist worked in vain to analyze. "How strange a thing it is, this genius!"

In their discussions it had been the writer's learning versus the actor's instinct. Now in performance how instinct triumphed! "You may be talking all day with a man or woman, perhaps studying with them the very part they are to play at night, quarrelling over their readings, criticising their conceptions, and then go and see them transformed, cry over the very line you thought they misapprehended, shudder at the gesture you declared would be ridiculous, and applaud as vigorously as anyone at the acting you contended against all day."

Was this the friend whose impatient arguments in support of his performance had been laughably untenable—this friend no longer, but a superbeing who burned with the divine fire? "This marvellous inspiration," cried Badeau, "that comes down on a man as suddenly and strangely and unaccountably to the actor as to the audience—that transfigures him before your face, like Rachel in *Polyeucte* or young Booth in *Richelieu*— this surpasses in strangeness any other gift vouchsafed to the race."

Booth, who wouldn't be a bachelor much longer, took Badeau with him to the Maryland farm for a night's lark and a look around the old place. In 1859 there was no one living at the farm any more except a handful of Negroes left to work the land. The family was scattered. Asia had been married in April of this year to John Sleeper Clarke. Her brother John was against the marriage, remembering how Clarke had coaxed him into making his stage debut before he was ready: it was the Booth name Clarke had wanted for his benefit. Johnny was cynically convinced it was the Booth name Clarke wanted from Asia, and he hissed to her before the wedding: "Always bear in mind you're a professional steppingstone."

John was acting in Richmond; the uncritical Southerners flattered and petted him. Joseph Booth, after a few gauche stage appearances—one of them with Edwin during which (the story goes) Edwin muttered to him between gritted teeth to "get off the stage for God's sake"—had decided to stay off and to study medicine. Mrs. Booth and Rosalie were living in a house in Philadelphia that Edwin had rented; he and Mary meant to make their home there after they were married.

It was early evening when Booth and Badeau galloped up to the farm. Giving their horses in charge of a decrepit Negro who grinned that he had "had Massa Edwin in charge more than once," they unlocked the door of the brick house and tramped through the half-bare, echoing rooms.

Some of Mr. Booth's costumes were still hanging there. His books were stacked on the shelves, and hundreds of his papers swamped drawers and cupboards, though not as many as there should have been. After his death Mrs. Booth, to destroy all references to his first marriage, had burned whole piles of his letters. Asia and Johnny howled in protest. They were planning a memoir of their father and saw their best material flying up in flames. But Mrs. Booth had gone ahead obstinately, almost sullenly, rereading, tearing, and burning—only stopping every few minutes to cry a little or rip off a corner of a page with some famous signature, which she handed as a sop to her children.

With a couple of lighted candles stuck in shoes beside them, the young men sat down on a closet floor to paw through what papers were left, first one, then the other, exclaiming with interest at an autograph on some mildewed playscript or a faded letter that still communicated the lively mood of its long-cold writer. They uncovered the tall counting-house ledgers in which Mr. Booth had pasted his playbills, grown yellow and their huge print turned brown. "It was strange," wrote Badeau in a *Times* article describing the nostalgic evening, "to look at these bills that were first handled fifty years ago and three thousand miles away; that told of the pleasures of people long since in their graves."

Clear in their minds' eye they saw the packed theater, the green baize curtain, the actors bowing like courtiers, and they heard the insistent clapping from hands fallen quiet forever. It was sobering to realize that those men and women, who at the moment of applauding and being applauded had felt so intensely of the present that they seemed to themselves to be immortal, had by now lain so long in their respective churchyards that the turf was sunken over them.

Badeau looked at Booth's face aglow with interest in the candlelight. It was not hard to see his father in him, and the journalist "thought of the long career of triumphs the father had gone through, and wondered whether fate had in store for the youth at my side a corresponding history."

Then they found a heap of playbills belonging to Edwin and compared the casts. "We thought of the time when some youngsters would be looking over these very lists, and we should have long since mouldered. The candles were getting low, you see."

They slept on two sofas with a mattress laid across. Booth couldn't stop talking. "I fell into a doze with his voice ringing in my ears," Badeau told his readers. "Some of his fair admirers would not have slept so long as he talked, and doubtless they envy me my snooze on his arm. But 'twas dark, and I couldn't see his eyes; besides, I had seen them all day."

The same voice woke Badeau late in the morning calling from the garden Sir Edward Mortimer's first words: "Adam, come hither to me!"

They washed at the pump, then had breakfast of some sandwiches. "Hamlet did the honors very gracefully," Badeau wrote. "You should have seen Lear washing a tea-cup, and Romeo making the bed. He had a way of doing even these that was worth looking at."

Booth made faces for his friend out of all his plays. Badeau begged for Richard's "What-do-they-i'-the-North" look, and Booth put it on for him. He hurled himself on tiptoe as Cardinal Richelieu launching "the curse of Rome." He pressed an illustrated Shakespeare on Badeau as a gift; examining it later Badeau noticed several of the plates were marked in Booth's writing: "Form this picture," and afterward he saw that Booth made the picture onstage.

Out of a wardrobe Booth rummaged antiquated wigs: one that Kean had worn in *King Lear;* one that his father had worn in *Othello*—this he tried on and unconsciously his face slipped into the lines of his father's. Some wild story about the old man clung to everything they touched, and Badeau took note how in telling these tales Booth's voice was reverent, though he missed none of the humor.

On their way to Baltimore in the afternoon they stopped at the cemetery where Booth, with some of the first money he had earned in the East, had raised a monument over his father's grave, a graceful obelisk twenty feet high of polished Italian marble rising from a pedestal of rough granite. Carved on one side was a sprightly epitaph:

Behold the spot where genius lies,
O drop a tear when talent dies!
Of tragedy the mighty chief,
His power to please surpassed belief.
Hic jacet matchless Booth.

On the second face of the obelisk was carved the actor's name with his birth and death dates, inanimate brackets enclosing the living man's turbulent history. There was also a medallion head carved in profile. Again Badeau was struck by the likeness to Edwin, standing at his elbow, handsome and serious. And again he asked himself: Into what triumphs and dangers would the genius as well as the beauty that had survived the father lead the son? What was the hold of the past on the future?

PART THREE

CHAPTER 5

The Fireside

She lov'd me for the dangers I had pass'd,
And I lov'd her that she did pity them.
              Othello, *Act I, scene 3*

 Booth HAD made another good friend, Richard
Cary, to whom he was writing excitedly from
New York at the end of June, 1860, that "this
day week 'young Edwin' is no more! A sober,
steady pater-familias will then—" when just at this point he
threw down his pen, jarred into a feeling of ill omen by the
strains of a popular but doleful song that had begun unwind-
ing from a hand organ outside. He knew the words. "Love
not," they ran,

> . . . love not! ye hopeless sons of clay;
> Hope's gayest wreaths are made of earthly flowers—
> Things that are made to fade and fall away,
> Ere they have blossomed for a few short hours.

On July 7 Booth and Mary Devlin were married at the
house on West Eleventh Street of the Reverend Samuel Osgood, an Episcopal clergyman. Badeau went to the wedding,
went with the bridegroom to give him support. Mary's sister

Mrs. Magonigle was there with her husband, and John Wilkes had traveled up for the event; after the ceremony he flung his arms around Edwin's neck and kissed him.

Booth invited his mother and brother Joe along on the honeymoon. They all shared a cottage on the Canadian side of Niagara Falls, and after a week Booth wrote to Badeau buoyantly urging him to join them, which Badeau did. Asia Clarke, who was living in Philadelphia, wished Edwin's bride would venture into the whirlpool of the Falls and be sucked under.

The newlyweds' friends were sent an announcement in the form of a visiting card.

Mr. and Mrs. Edwin Booth

Philadelphia

But when Booth brought his bride home, Asia let it be known that not only would she not call on her sister-in-law— she would not even meet her or go where she might meet her. So Booth and Mary left Philadelphia and rented an apartment in New York at the Fifth Avenue Hotel on the corner of Twenty-third Street.

In front of their drawing-room fireplace was a black bearskin. As the autumn days drew in, Booth, wearing a velvet smoking jacket, lay on the bearskin close to the snapping flames, his chin cupped in his hands, saying over his roles to Mary. Sometimes he frowned, without speaking, into the firelight, until his young wife took up her guitar and sang softly:

Come live with me, and be my love;
And we will all the pleasures prove
That hills and valleys, dales and fields,
Woods or steepy mountain yields.

The velvet curtains in the windows were drawn early, and they dined at a small, round table laid for two, while a greyhound Booth had bought for Mary crouched watchfully beside them. It was hard to leave the fireside for the theater. Booth was acting at the Metropolitan again, only its name had been changed to the Winter Garden; it was under new management. Mary sat in the stage box, demure and hidden from the audience by the box draperies until her husband entered, when she leaned forward absorbedly, her lips moving as she followed his speeches, in eerie, intimate communion with him. Once someone saw her shut her eyes and clench her fists: "Oh, I've said the wrong line and Edwin is saying it."

After the performance there would be a friend or two for midnight supper, since Booth was too keyed up to sleep. He saw Badeau almost as much as ever, and at the theater Mary and Badeau often sat gaily side by side. Dave Anderson rolled into town from San Francisco to assure Booth he had quitted the West in the nick of time. The legitimate theater was in a poor way out there. Minstrel and variety shows had taken over at the expense of the legitimate, and prominent actors (like Booth's brother Junius) were playing trivial roles. Junius was in debt; Edwin had already sent him $4,000, "which I may consider as lost, but it was my duty and I'm happy to perform it."

Except for intimates like Anderson and Badeau, the young couple held the world at arm's length. "We were all in all to each other," said Mary later of this first year of their marriage.

They were lunching downstairs one day in the hotel dining room, hating even such a semipublic appearance as this, but driven to it by a late rehearsal. Suddenly Mary's greyhound bounded in, trampled over the feet of a girl sitting at the same table with them, and exuberantly pawed the front of Mary's dress. Everyone in the place stared. Booth scowled, said something angry to his Negro valet who ran up with a leash, and Mary apologized winningly to the young lady. There was no need to apologize. Miss Lilian Woodman had been languishing for just such a chance.

Earlier in the autumn Lilian had seen Booth play Hamlet in Boston, had been hit hard, and not yet suspecting how very large was the sisterhood she had entered, had tremulously confided to her family that "that young actor would control her destiny." The Woodmans smiled. Not one of them had the least acquaintance with anyone in the theater.

Yet when they settled in New York for the winter, by a wonderful coincidence their apartment was in the Fifth Avenue Hotel down the hall from Booth's—and his bride's. Bravely enlarging her dream castle to include a princess as well as a prince, Lilian worshiped from afar until by a stroke of luck quite of a piece with her most purple imaginings, the royal couple were seated at her table. Hot with excitement, she stole glances at the faces opposite: Hamlet's and Juliet's, the one lowering, with darting eyes, the other beaming and tranquil.

Then in bounded the greyhound, after which Booth sat glummer than ever, furious at being made conspicuous, but Mary and Lilian began to talk; it was impossible to be shy with anyone so unaffected as Mary. A night or two later she called on Lilian, who never forgot the sight of her hesitating in the door: a slight girl with soft brown hair, in a soft, red dress with a chrysolite brooch—her husband's gift—shooting threads of green fire at her throat, and the magnificent dog like a guardian out of a fairy tale, stepping proudly and delicately beside her.

The round table was laid for four, and Lilian and her sister Mattie had dinner with the Booths. Hamlet's moroseness soon wore off. He came down from Elsinore and made them almost die laughing with his stories, as how on his travels he had seen three puppies suspended in a padded basket over a Pullman berth, and he threw himself into the character of each puppy as it howled and hung its head over the basket edge.

Dinner over, the sisters listened almost holding their breaths while he lay on the bearskin, rapidly reviewing his part to cues fed him by Mary. Then followed the nervous drive to the theater and the arrival while the house was still empty. Booth deposited the girls in the stage box and left them. Two hours later they were absorbed in the play when Hamlet himself, temporarily out of the scene, tiptoed up behind and startled them by whispering something in Mary's ear.

"Edwin, Edwin," Mary begged, "not so loud! They'll hear you speak."

Booth kissed her. "Why, they paid their money to hear me speak, and speak I will!"

New Yorkers did not receive actors into their houses as freely as Bostonians, though as the winter wore on a number of hostesses were not above inviting the attractive Edwin Booth ("with Mrs. Booth, too, of course"), who almost always declined. However, Badeau, impatiently anxious for Booth to know eminent people and hold the position Garrick had held in England, had arranged for his election to the formidable but cosmopolitan Century Club. The Club was giving a reception, and Mary and Booth dressed for it reluctantly—Mary in a crinoline of deep purple and Booth in his black evening coat and pencil-slim trousers.

Ready to go, he grimaced at the Woodman girls, called in to see them in their fine clothes. "Now every man, woman and child I meet will say the thing they always say: 'Mr. Booth, do you believe Hamlet was *really* insane?' "

Then, rolling his eyes like the distraught Prince, he offered Mary his arm and away they swept to the evening's ordeal, leaving their little friends bathed in the wake of their glory.

II

Playing at the Winter Garden this autumn, Booth came for the first time into direct conflict with Edwin Forrest. All through Booth's boyhood the leading tragedians in America had been his father and Forrest, competitors onstage and friends off. Before Mr. Booth left for California, he had proposed to Forrest that they appear together as Lucifer and Cain respectively in Byron's drama *Cain, A Mystery*. "I want to play the Devil," he explained.

"It seems to me," growled Forrest, "that you've done that pretty well all your life."

Among dozens of English imports Forrest stood out as the first world-famous, American-born star. He was massively and splendidly built, with a prodigious voice. His style had not the intellect of Mr. Booth's, but he made up in power what he lacked in subtlety. True, he used every known hoary stage device, like the trick sword that rattled in its scabbard when fear was indicated. True, at his worst he bellowed and brayed and had worked up a whole vocabulary of snorts and gurgles to express emotion when the words provided him were inadequate. Yet he could hold himself back as well as let go. In quieter scenes he was deeply affecting. At his best he played grand parts grandly. His King Lear was unforgettable and so were his noble, simple half-savages like Othello, Spartacus the gladiator, and Metamora the Indian chief—he had modeled this role on Push-ma-ta-ha, an Indian friend in whose wigwam he once lived familiarly.

Forrest was a dark man inside and out. After his wife Catherine Sinclair divorced him for "cruel and licentious conduct" —the countersuit for adultery, which he brought against her, having failed—he began to brood on himself as a man persecuted and a genius unappreciated. The loudest applause became not enough for him, the heaviest receipts left him dissatisfied. He signed his name with a manic flourish:

A bad notice of his acting would set him raving, and in the last few years there had been bad notices. A blackguard critic named William Stuart jeered (anonymously) in the New York *Tribune* that Forrest's Hamlet in the scene with the Players was like some huge gypsy watching to rob a henroost, that his vaunted Othello looked like a hangman. Any journalist, Forrest foamed, who disparaged his Othello was fit only for a lunatic asylum or to be kicked downstairs.

Stuart wrote with deliberate malice. He had been especially paid—some suspected by the *Tribune* itself—to write down Forrest. However, Walt Whitman, a completely unvenal critic, demanded in the *Brooklyn Eagle* if Forrest's blaring style were not a poor model for younger actors. These were only straws, yet they showed how the wind blew. When Forrest was young he had necessarily used a bold method to please a rough public. But during the thirty years of his supremacy that public, with more prosperity and leisure, had grown refined, while Forrest had simply grown older.

Just before Booth made his New York debut as a star in 1857, Forrest had been forced to retire temporarily because of rheumatism, a sign of age. Although he had been out of the theater three years, his prestige was still immense when in September, 1860, he returned to the stage, opening in *Hamlet* at Niblo's Garden in New York.

A part of the interest in his return was owing to the reputation Edwin Booth had made in his absence. Forrest's loyal, middle-aged friends panted to see him put down the upstart, while younger playgoers, who knew Forrest's glories only by hearsay, were eager to compare him with Booth. The seats for his opening were sold at auction, bringing huge prices, and at first his success was greater than ever. He had had the field to himself for several weeks, playing King Lear, Othello, Macbeth, Richard III and Richelieu, when in November Booth opened in *Hamlet* at the Winter Garden. Booth was just twenty-seven. In the next month he, too, was seen as Richard and Richelieu.

It was now that Booth made his first really deep impression on New York. Since he had played here last his acting had gained in depth and control. He still ranted occasionally, still was best in the lurid, mordant roles that gave his energy something to bite on, but his method was fining down. His individual style was forming, less noisy, more natural than his father's, and critics were beginning to recognize him as being more than a promising actor, to hail him as the leader in a new school, the embodiment of a new idea in tragic acting. "Since we saw him last," said the *Tribune*, "he has been at work, and his work has borne such noble fruit as can only be fully appreciated by those who knew him when he was the crude, unpolished, but still startling and original actor of three years ago, and who see him now, and note what gigantic strides he has taken."

Forrest's greater name and experience would have triumphed over youth alone. It was the "new idea" that was too much for him, this more nervous, natural, poetic, and spiritual style. Dimly he realized that in the short time he had been away from the stage the tendency of the public's taste had changed. There was no sharp swing away from him. Most older playgoers found in his favor, but the younger ones and the more progressive and fastidious critics were hot for Booth, who wrote cockily to Dick Cary: "I've had the best people, and the entire press yields me the palm."

One of the people (not the best) who came to see him was Mrs. Sam Cowell from England, the wife of a visiting singing comedian. Mrs. Cowell passed the time while her husband was hard at work entertaining by taking her daughter Sidney to serious plays, then writing up what she saw in her diary. She saw Booth in *Brutus*. "Sometimes a little tendency to rant distressed me, but the earnestness of his acting made amends for that fault. What eyes he has! . . . Nearly all the women are in raptures about him, and I heard many expressions such as 'Well, now, ain't he pretty?' 'Oh, there he is again, I don't care for anything when he is not there'—from the surrounding ladies. He annoyed Sidney and me by having one pertinacious lock of hair hanging over his forehead through the play, which we were always wanting him to push back, 'but he wouldn't.' "

The afterpiece this particular night was Garrick's *Katherine and Petruchio*. Mrs. Cowell thought Booth "very light and buoyant in Petruchio, only a little too boyish, jumping about the stage and playing all manner of school-boy antics." The part wasn't really Booth's dish, any more than Benedick in *Much Ado*, which he also tried now and then. His comedy had great elegance of a rather sinister brand and the jabbing irony that helped put across his Iago and Richard III. But he had never the relaxed, spontaneous gift of the born comic like his brother-in-law Clarke, who on his own low level could convulse an audience simply by looking at it and saying, "Whoops!"

Booth interrupted his New York season to do *Macbeth* in Philadelphia opposite Charlotte Cushman, who found his style effete. "She is down on me as an actor, says I don't know anything at all about Hamlet."

There was general disagreement about Miss Cushman's own Hamlet. The rare pleasure taken by this brawny, deep-voiced woman in playing men's parts was indulgently interpreted as the whim of a great actress, and she was very great, and in 1860 was at her peak. But as Hamlet or as Romeo, Cardinal Wolsey or Claude Melnotte, her peculiar, hollow tones, which seemed to belong to neither sex, hit on the ear perplexingly. Her large bosom, which couldn't be concealed, contrasted strangely with her masculine features; she looked neither man nor woman. Mary Devlin had once been her Juliet and during those performances, Miss Cushman confessed, she did indeed wish "that she had been a *man!*"

When she played Lady Macbeth, it was obviously the lady who wore the kilts in that castle. Booth's own private idea of the character was of a red-haired little enchantress, very feminine in her ambitions. Cushman's Lady Macbeth was a raven-haired Amazon who bullied her husband, stalked him into a corner and then, as somebody who saw her put it, regularly "pitched into him" with lifted arm and large, meaty fist. It was a wonderful performance in its way, pitiless, macabre, and fascinating. Yet every time that Booth onstage felt the clamp of her muscular fingers on his shoulder and heard the cellolike tones rise out of her chest in her famous line

He that's coming must be provided for,

he was terribly tempted to snap back: "Well, why don't you kill him? You're a great deal bigger than I am."

Not only their sizes (Cushman complained that so many "little men" played Macbeth), but also their two styles didn't pull well together. Cushman was forty-four, of the older method, and she shared Forrest's impatience with all but obvious meanings. She explained the discrepancy between Macbeth's words and deeds by supposing he was drunk through most of the play and his wife was drunk too. She considered Booth's performance underacted. His Macbeth was "a mere willow"—like his Hamlet, too soft and refined. "Exceedingly interesting," she boomed at him, "but, dear boy, don't be afraid of overdoing it. Remember Macbeth was the great-grandfather of all the Bowery ruffians."

Forrest took time off from New York to see one of these performances. When his rival came on, Forrest huffed with disgust. Booth strolled on excessively "naturally" from the side, gazing moodily at the ground. "What's the damned fool doing?" snorted Forrest. "He looks like a super hunting for a sixpence."

Forrest behaved himself through the next four acts until Cushman moaned sepulchrally that "all the perfumes of Arabia will not sweeten this little hand," and this was more than he could stomach.

"Little hand!" he scoffed. "*Little hand!* Why, it's as big as a codfish!"

The editor of "The Easy Chair" in *Harper's* for April called Booth's acting "the sensation of the city. New York rings with Booth's triumphs."

Over at Niblo's Garden, Forrest also played to good houses.

Yet as though conscious that the homage, which had once been his alone, must henceforth be divided, he grew greedier for applause than ever. When one night, in the middle of one of his tremendously delivered speeches, a well-meaning person in front hushed a rising murmur of appreciation, Forrest protested angrily afterward as he took his curtain call, saying that applause was the actor's reward; that it was his due; that anyone who would rob him of it would pick a pocket.

The theater had made Forrest. It had fed and clothed him; its literature had given him almost his only education. Now, with his home wrecked, his wife alienated, the theater had become his home, his wife, his everything. And as he felt the public, his children, just perceptibly beginning to turn away from him, he knew a bereavement and humiliation wholly incomprehensible to his young competitor, who left his fireside reluctantly to act for a living.

III

Booth wrote to Lawrence Barrett, who had bogged down in a stock company in Boston and appealed for help to get out: "Don't turn up your nose at the stock, Larry. . . . Starring about the country is sad work—a home is better."

Anticipating what would be Barrett's retort, he went on: "I *must* pursue the path Fate has marked out for me. . . . I'd rather there was no such thing as *starring*—I'd rather stay in one place & have a home, but of course I'd like to stand A.1. in my trade."

Already he stood perilously high for a man only twenty-seven, and Mary's greatest dread was that his career would "culminate too quickly." Booth himself feared his work was beginning to grow stale in commercial America, where "art degenerates below the standard even of a trade"—this was his withering verdict. He was convinced he needed to breathe the native air of art—whether in France, Italy, or England depended on the chance that offered, but wherever it flowed free, and that meant "away, away from here."

So he had written to Cary just before his marriage, and he

had expected then that Badeau would make the trip to Europe with him. "The only trouble will be, I shall have a wife to look after. . . . I can go on traveling through this country four, perhaps five, years longer, and make a great deal of money; but money is not what I want—nor position either, unless I can feel within the consciousness of deserving it. . . . I'm perfectly well aware that unless I aim at a larger circumference than the rim of the 'almighty dollar' (which one can't help in America), I'll go down 'eye-deep' in the quicksand of popular favor."

In the spring of 1861 he had a tentative offer to play in England. He still hoped that when he and Mary sailed Badeau could go too, but in April Fort Sumter was fired on, and men's worlds turned upside down overnight. On March 4 President Lincoln had been inaugurated. After Fort Sumter's fall he called out the militia to the number of 75,000 to defend the Union, and among the men to put on the blue uniform were Badeau and Cary.

New York was in wildest excitement. The streets were full of soldiers drilling; almost every morning the drum sounded early:—*rub-a-dub*. Almost every afternoon a new regiment swung along Broadway under the bright sun very warm for April, under a thousand flags big and little, past eight and ten story buildings that flickered from top to bottom with waving handkerchiefs, to "Hail Columbia!" and "The Star Spangled Banner," while the police cleared the way with their truncheons and the hurrahing crowds rolled backward and forward.

Booth was finishing his season at the Winter Garden in a house thronged with military men who hadn't yet left the city and with business men in from the provinces. Aroused, anxious, nagged by headaches from the glare and noise of the parades outside, his audiences were more ready than ever to enter worlds a step removed from reality and to identify themselves with heroes larger than life, sad beyond tears. "I remember well," writes Mrs. John Sherwood, prominent New Yorker whose opinions were often in the papers, "in the first year of our war, when we were profoundly miserable and frightened, what a relief it was to go and see Booth in *Hamlet*."

Edwin was for the North and so was Junius, but the War cut across the family. The English-born Mrs. Booth was first a mother; her loyalty was for her children and all she cared for was to keep them united. This was impossible. Although the two girls vacillated—with Asia finally coming to rest on the Union side—Joseph, though still a medical student in Charleston, served as a doctor with the Confederates in the attack on Fort Sumter; and John, who had been acting in Albany, New York, when the fort was fired on, railed at the North and praised the South so recklessly that the citizens ordered him to shut up or get out of town.

Joe was the only Booth even to sniff gunpowder. John had been in uniform just once, a borrowed uniform. In December, 1859, he had temporarily joined the Richmond Grays who stood guard under Colonel Robert E. Lee at the foot of the scaffold in Charles Town, Virginia, where John Brown was hanged. Johnny was a fire-eating antiabolitionist, but the would-be hero he knew in himself acknowledged the heroism in the doomed old leader. "He felt a throb of anguish," writes Asia, "as he beheld the old eyes straining their anxious sight for the multitude he vainly had thought would rise to rescue him."

Johnny told his sister: "Brown was a brave old man; his heart must have broken when he felt himself deserted."

On July 21 the Federals' Army of the Potomac was whipped at Bull Run. Washington streets seethed with the demoralized troops of half a dozen regiments pouring in from Virginia across the river. Yet while thousands of men had put on the uniform, blue or gray, a great many more thousands continued with what they were doing, as lawyers, cabinetmakers, clerks, horse traders, poets—and actors. Booth had given away his caul, his unique talisman, either to Cary or to Badeau—a mistake, he realized later, for on looking back it could be seen that his luck went with it. His vague European hopes had crystallized into an invitation to play at the Haymarket Theatre in London. Europe at last! "It is the grand turning-point of my career," he exulted to Cary (Captain Cary now), "though it pains me to leave my country at this time."

It suddenly occurred to him he had been scribbling "I, I, I," all through his letter with not a word for the friend soon to face battle. So, "God bless you, my boy!" he wrote. "Don't get tired of the hard fare; your patriotism is not in the stomach, I know, but stick to the flag, Dick, as I intend to do, though far away."

Lilian Woodman was worried about Mary, who was expecting a child, and she made Booth promise to cable from the other side "the very minute you have news."

Arrived in London, the first thing Booth and Mary heard was that a letter urging Booth not to come had crossed them on the way over. The Haymarket was a comedy theater, and the manager, J. B. Buckstone, now admitted late in the day that he was "rather afraid of tragedy." But since Booth was here, Buckstone persuaded him to open in *The Merchant of Venice*, against Booth's better judgment because Shylock was one of his least effective parts.

Something went wrong with Booth's chemistry as an actor on this long looked-for opening night in London, September 30, 1861. The manager's reluctance and the superciliousness of the English cast had dampened his flame instead of blowing on it. Americans in the audience felt puzzled and let down to see him walk through Shylock correctly and lifelessly. The reviews were cool.

Next he gave *A New Way to Pay Old Debts*, gave it to applause hardly loud enough to chase the echoes from the half-empty house, which was the wrong house, for one thing. As Buckstone explained, the Haymarket had neither the name nor the facilities for tragic productions. Added to this, Booth's time in England was badly chosen. Relations between England and America were strained; almost the entire British press was for the Confederates.

Booth tried *Richard III*, always a winner in the land across the water where art had fallen below the standard even of a

trade. Here in London, in art's native air, the production Buckstone threw together for his imported star was almost a burlesque. The supers' tin armor was so clumsy and heavy that
one actor who had knelt in homage couldn't get up again, while
another saluted and could barely bring his arm down.

For his last effort Booth announced *Richelieu*. The faintly
hostile Haymarket actors invited their friends backstage to
gloat over the biggest fiasco of all. But the tinselly melodrama,
which had not been seen in London for eleven years, had the
draw of a novelty, and when the curtain fell after the first act
they heard, not the polite spatter of token applause, but the
thunder of enjoyment. The famous old comedian Mr. Chip-
pendale, who had played Polonius to the Hamlets of Kemble
and Kean, was one of those spying from the wing and he
rushed over to Buckstone: "The finest piece of acting I ever
saw in my life, sir!" Buckstone, very deaf, stood with his hand
to his ear, torn between relief at his star's belated success and
chagrin that he hadn't opened with *Richelieu*.

Mary's confinement was near, and Booth left her in London
while he acted in Manchester and Liverpool. In Manchester his
Laertes, Cassio, Bassanio, and Buckingham were earnestly performed by a youth named John Henry Brodribb, who was
down on the bills as Henry Irving. He was a very ordinary-
looking young man, like a bank clerk or chemist's assistant,
but behind his rather sloping forehead raged an ambition of
the implacable sort that could prod a real clerk into becoming
bank manager—or embezzling bank funds. Irving's ambition
took another line: inhibited and self-conscious, he chafed at
his inability to do himself justice onstage and he devotedly
studied Booth, who was all that he was not and yet intended
to be.

Business in the provinces was mortifyingly below what
Booth was used to in America. He hurried back to London to
be beside Mary when their baby was born at Fulham on December 9, just at the time, after the Trent affair, when England
was within an ace of entering the American War on the Confederate side and British papers were storming against "that

spirit of senseless egotism which induces the Americans, with
their dwarf fleet, and shapeless mass of incoherent squads,
which they call an army, to fancy themselves the equal of
France by land, and of Great Britain by sea."

This was enough to make Americans in London who were
Union sympathizers twice the patriots they had been at home.
Galled and humiliated by his British reception, so far below
his hopes, homesick, and tormented by the thought that his
child would be born under a foreign flag, possibly an enemy
one, Booth made a canopy of the Stars and Stripes over Mary's
bed so that the baby, slipping into the world some hours later,
was literally born under it. "Thank God, all is well. A daughter," he cabled to Lilian.

He acted no more in England. "I think the fall will find me
in Boston again, a poorer but a wiser man than when I left
there," he wrote to Dick Cary.

Living in London on the savings he had accumulated in
commercial America, he went to the funeral of his mother's
mother, old Mrs. Holmes. Most of his time he spent with Mary,
who gained strength so slowly that it was March before he
was able to shepherd her, looking frail but radiant, and the
baby, named Edwina after him, to Paris, the Paris of the Second Empire. He didn't act here either, but took Mary sight-
seeing and to buy French gowns. For Edwina they engaged a
nurse, Marie Fournier, who came with them as they crossed
back to England and sailed for New York in August, 1862.

IV

When Booth reappeared at the Winter Garden he found
his London engagement had paid for itself by giving him a
certain added prestige in New York. Again Forrest played in
competition to him at Niblo's, and both stars had full houses;
there were audiences and to spare. While at Antietam dead
men lay rotting on the blasted fields (14,000 Federal casualties,
over 11,000 Confederate), the theaters were crammed to their
flag-draped roofs. The War had touched Booth too close for
comfort. He heard the news soon after landing that Captain

Richard Cary had been killed in action. For an instant Booth knew what war and battle meant.

"Dick was a hero born," he wrote to Cary's sister, Mrs. Felton, and three days later to his even dearer friend Badeau, stationed at Memphis on General Sherman's staff: "To talk about such old-time nonsense as my own affairs is now too trivial. . . . May the God of Battles guard you, Ad."

A letter from Cary, found among his things and forwarded by his widow, was delivered to Booth. Not long before writing it Cary had been in Baltimore, where he saw *Macbeth* starring John Wilkes, and he had believed Edwin might be interested in his opinion of his little brother's acting. John was much too melodramatic, Cary thought. Although some of his tones were remarkably like Edwin's, his face onstage was wooden, and the performance had reminded Cary of nothing so much as "a blood-and-thunder melo-drama full of sheet iron and burnt rosin and ghosts and other horrors," he had once seen in the old Federal Street Theater in Boston.

John had resolved to become a star when he read in the papers that Edwin had got five thousand dollars for a month's engagement in Boston. Billing himself as J. WILKES BOOTH, he exploded on the world as the evil Pescara in *The Apostate* in Montgomery, Alabama. This was in October, 1860. In February, 1861, he had marched north into what until then was Edwin's domain, acting Pescara again in Albany, and his performance in its fury and horror was so uncannily like his father's, which he had never seen, that a meeting of spiritualists in the city came out with a statement that the indomitable old man's perturbèd spirit must have been hovering about the son onstage. On February 18 President-elect Lincoln had passed through Albany on the route to Washington for his inauguration. John had watched as one of the crowd and glared. He hated the damn Yanks.

What he was after was to be "the Booth," to shoulder his way ahead of his brothers, to approach the level of his father's fame, and it was this ambition that kept him in the North even after war broke out and the South he loved was fighting gloriously. When Edwin sailed for England John saw his chance. He starred in St. Louis, in Chicago, then in Baltimore; and here in the city most intimately associated with all the Booths his posters proclaimed defiantly: I AM MYSELF ALONE!

In March, 1862, he made his starring debut in New York in the most famous of the family vehicles, *Richard III*. Both he and Junius were a little jealous of Edwin. It was irritating to Junius to be outstripped by a younger brother, discouraging to John always to stand in an older brother's shadow. "On account of the *likeness* the papers deigned to notice me," he had written dryly to Edwin from Richmond at the start of his career.

John had his share of their father in him: the very hairs of his head acted. The Harvard-educated Dick Cary might find him bombastic, yet there were critics who already rated him higher than his more polished brother—"the best of living Romeos," one of them considered him. The passion of his embrace lifted Juliet out of her shoes. Desdemona winced at the bang of his scimitar when as Othello he flung himself on her body. His Hamlet was mustachioed, hot-blooded, definitely insane. After *Richard III* he slept smothered in oysters to heal the bruises got during a stage battle fought in deadly earnest.

Mr. Ellsler, the Cleveland manager, who had known Junius Brutus Booth and who was partial to the old-fashioned technique, swore that John Wilkes "has more of the old man's power in one performance than Edwin can show in a year. He has the fire, the dash, the touch of *strangeness*."

At first sight Lilian and Mattie Woodman realized that things could never again be quite as they had been with Booth and Mary, who were subtly altered by their travels. A bloom was off them; a little veneer of affectation had taken its place. Whether owing to Mary's Paris clothes or to the baby squirming in the arms of its smart French *bonne* wasn't to be analyzed, but Booth and Mary seemed to belong more to this world.

They all met again at the Booths' apartment, and the young women had hardly had time to kiss and admire when there was the portent of a greater change. A card was handed in and Booth read it aloud: "Mr. and Mrs. Richard Henry Stoddard." Instead of frowning and shaking his head violently as he would have done a year earlier, he said: "Show them in," and then explained that he and Mary had never seen these Stoddards, but they had a friend in common.

Stoddard was a thin, bearded, pleasant-looking man. Mrs. Stoddard was an enigma to the young Woodmans. Angular and oldish (she was thirty-nine), with a face like a brown leaf, and wearing an arty brown dress woven with a white figure, she had *no* charm whatever in the girls' eyes. Yet they saw Booth, usually so reserved with women, hurry over to her with arms held out and gather up her hands. "Edwin!" she said intensely.

"Elizabeth!" he said. Delicately pulling undone her bonnet strings, he lifted off her bonnet himself and led her to a chair. And when both couples began gabbing intimately, as though they were old acquaintances, Lilian and Mattie slipped out of the room.

This meeting with the Stoddards opened a door to Booth and Mary. Their joint life altered almost from this moment. At home the baby was queen and reigned from the bearskin in front of the fire; one afternoon when Badeau called they all burst out laughing to see how exactly tiny Edwina's attitudes (creeping, rearing up on her knees and collapsing backward) were like her father's in *Richard III* in the fight with Richmond. But Booth no longer lay there himself and Mary's guitar hung silent, only vibrating when some heavy van rumbled by, while she in her most pronounced Paris gown and he in the formal blacks he loathed took their places in the circle of writers and artists the clever Stoddards had formed around themselves.

Richard Stoddard earned his living in the New York Custom House. Nathaniel Hawthorne, who had once worked—toiled, rather—in the customhouse in Boston, had got him the post. But Stoddard's heart, like Hawthorne's, lay in a world remote from his place of business. Both he and his wife were known as poets to readers of the *Atlantic Monthly* and *Harper's*. Elizabeth Stoddard had published a novel that, like herself, was too tart to be popular with the sweet-toothed general public, but had won critical praise.

Their modest drawing room in lodgings on Tenth Street was not as austere as the Century Club, where the names were greater. It was not as Bohemian as Pfaff's beer cellar under the sidewalk on Broadway, where baggy-eyed writers and cartoonists for the magazines sat eating German pancakes, and Walt Whitman, with his shirt collar open, tipped back his chair and his chin as he drained the steins at his special table. Nor was the Stoddards' group fashionable society. During their first evening at Tenth Street Booth and Mary were enchanted to meet Bayard Taylor, the author-traveler; Fitzhugh Ludlow, a writer who had smoked hashish and had a captivating wife; Launt Thompson, the sculptor, and a blond young poet, Thomas Bailey Aldrich.

Most actors chafe and burn to be the center of things, but not Booth. All the eloquence and aggressiveness that were somewhere inside him came out in his acting, but his role once put off, his public manner was defensively retiring. He was a lame curtain speaker. At banquets, including the ones later given in his honor, he seldom opened his mouth, except as a reporter once noted, "to put something into it." With scholars and those he called "educated men" he was shy and respectful to such a point that Dick Cary, after introducing Booth to his distinguished brothers-in-law, Cornelius Felton, professor of Greek at Harvard, and Louis Agassiz, the Swiss-born naturalist, had rallied him, laughing: "Why, my dear boy, these men are just like others!"

At fashionable parties Booth felt all legs. Louisa May Alcott, a sturdy wallflower herself, had a glimpse of him at a Boston reception. "Saw Booth at the Goulds," she wrote in her journal, "a handsome, shy man, glooming in a corner."

When they were married, his dear Mary had comforted him that she liked his backwardness, but then Mary liked everything in him. She had given freely of her candid, loving nature, and he had accepted unthinkingly and without thanks. She had her reward in that now, after two years of marriage, his face sometimes lit up with a ray reflected from hers; the terrible tensions that bound him had relaxed; even his jokes were less grim. The loyalty of her love had soothed and encouraged him until he could feel at ease in an unconventional circle like the Stoddards', to which he contributed more than he realized. He was the biggest lion the Stoddards had caught. Into their little drawing room he brought a breath of fresh, spicy air and a patch of color, the carnival colors of the theater against their intellectual black and white. "A splendid savage!" Fitzhugh Ludlow called him, and some of the others, "A natural." Even his clean-shaven cheeks, a mark of his trade, emphasized his exotic look among these gentlemen, every one of whom wore a mustache or side whiskers or a full beard.

There were teas and dinners and midnight suppers at the Stoddards', at Launt Thompson's in the Studio Building, where shrouded busts lurked on pedestals, and in the painter Albert Bierstadt's much grander studio stacked with landscape canvases. Then it was the Booths' turn to give a party. Lilian Woodman, the youngest guest there, was on tenterhooks to meet the bachelor poet and timidly plucked her host's sleeve. "Show me Aldrich, please."

"I mount! I fly!" said Booth, smiling.

He flew down the room to drag Tom Aldrich back, and with Aldrich's introduction to her the prince Lilian had dreamed about lost his Hamlet melancholy and became ebullient and a blond.

They sat down to supper at a long white-covered table lighted by candles in branched candlesticks. Glasses clinked as toasts were drunk. This was the first time Lilian had seen the Booths receive formally. In spite of her new preoccupation she noticed, not only what a genial host Booth made, with Mrs. Stoddard at his right hand, but also that he took no wine when the others did. Since his marriage he had drunk sparingly or not at all.

Mary's influence had restrained him, her influence and the

quiet life they led alone together. Yet now that they dined out almost constantly it was not so easy to say No and stick to it. Temptation was served with every gay meal, and before long Booth regularly accepted a glass, just one. Soon he tossed off glass after glass; the old days were back. And gradually a change came over Mary. She who had always been joyful was now only sometimes so.

CHAPTER 6

The Palace of Night

O my love! my wife!
. . . I still will stay with thee,
And never from this palace of dim night
Depart again.
        Romeo and Juliet, *Act V, scene 3*

 ON A November morning Booth and Mary with
the baby and her nurse left for Boston, where Booth
had an engagement. They were only to be gone
two weeks, yet it seemed to the Woodman girls
who stood waving after the carriage that there was something
ominous about this going, the sky was so heavily overcast,
and the husband and wife seemed unusually subdued.

Only a day or so before Booth's characteristically dramatic
knock had sounded on the Woodmans' door and he and Mary
had swept in. Her eyes glowing, Mary held out to Lilian a
beautifully painted miniature of her husband, set in a locket,
which he had just given her. She could hardly speak for pleasure, and laughing at her incoherence, pulled his head down
to hers and murmured Othello's words: "O my sweet, I prattle
out of fashion, and I dote in mine own comforts."

At the piano, she sent the first bars of Mendelssohn's "Wedding March" pealing through the room, then stopped playing, looked up at her husband and said in a tone so soberly emotional that it changed the whole atmosphere: "When death takes you, my best beloved, nothing will be more my solace than this last gift. I shall wear it eternally on my heart."

She had seemed to dwell on death lately and this time Lilian dared to ask: "Why do you always think and speak of Mr. Booth as being the one to go?"

"He needs me," Mary answered. "He needs me so." Her eyes were full of tears. She sprang up and threw her arms around him, and Lilian and Mattie, shyly looking on at a side of their friends' lives until now kept hidden from them, heard her prayer half-sobbed against his shoulder: "Almighty God, Merciful Father, spare him the cross! Take him first, I do beseech Thee."

A lady friend of the Stoddards, named appropriately Lucy Pry, mentioned to Mrs. Stoddard that she had "watched with sorrow Edwin's propensity to drink by the way in which he has drunk porter." Miss Pry had actually "counted five bottles a day that Edwin has drunk, which proves he has the appetite. I have once or twice expostulated with him but he would only laugh and make some funny reply. Mary did not seem to notice it at all."

Miss Pry was not the only one acutely aware of every glass Booth poured out, yet only those who knew Mary best suspected what she went through on those all too public evenings when she watched her husband drifting out of, and away from, his true self. "What is Edwin thinking about?" twittered Miss Pry. "Why does he give himself up in this way when he has everything to live for?"

"Mr. Booth is not well today," Mary only said quietly once or twice.

Once Lilian Woodman, intruding inadvertently, saw Booth pacing the floor of his apartment, holding his head in his hands. "Since daylight," he cried, "I haven't slept. No one can imagine the call of that desire. When it engulfs me I could sell my soul, my hope of salvation, for just one glass." And once—the only time she went so far—Mary spoke to Lilian of those mornings-after when, sick and heartbroken, her husband sobbed in her arms and fell before her in pathetic self-abasement to clasp her knees and promise . . . promise.

The Booths had not been their full time in Boston when a letter arrived for Lilian from Mary to say their plans had suddenly changed. Mary was not well, and the Boston doctor who examined her urgently recommended she spend the winter in some quiet place. Booth expected to act at the Winter Garden again in February, and Mary hoped to come to New York with him for this engagement of four weeks. But their home for the winter was to be in Dorchester, outside Boston, where they had rented a small house. She asked that the apartment at the hotel, which had been their first home together, be dismantled by their friends and their things shipped north.

Signs of disease in Mary's lungs had been detected, though she did not say so. The anxiety to be read between the lines of her sad, little letter was not primarily for herself. Booth did go back to New York in February, but Mary most reluctantly stayed behind. "Oh, take care of him, take care of him," she begged Lilian. Again for an instant the dark, hidden side of her marriage was revealed to the young girl.

In Boston hospitable Julia Ward Howe, who since the War's outbreak had distinguished herself forever by writing the "Battle Hymn of the Republic," gave a large reception for the Booths. She was still in love with them, called Booth "Great B." and Mary "Little B." "I do wish you to know Mr. Booth," she insisted to her good friend Senator Charles Sumner before the party.

"I don't know that I care to," said Sumner. "I have outlived my interest in individuals."

Mrs. Howe remarked in private that "fortunately, God Almighty had not, by last accounts, got so far."

"Like being dragged to hell, to go to meet a set of damned fools," Booth muttered when Mary roused him to dress for the Howes'. He had fallen asleep after his performance. Mary wore a dress of pale-colored silk, high in the neck and fastened with a brooch made from one large opal—an unlucky stone, people who had noticed it mused later.

"It was a real ovation to Edwin," she wrote with satisfaction to Elizabeth Stoddard. "All Beacon Street was invited and all Beacon Street was there."

"My child," Junius Brutus Booth had warned his son, "everybody knows Tom Fool." Radiating stiffness, Booth shook hands with "everybody," then fled with eight-year-old Maud Howe into a corner, where he sat on the floor and made dolls and rabbits out of his handkerchief.

Mary hid her shyness better, but "you know us both too well," she reminded Elizabeth, "for me to affect any delight at such a gathering—'twas tedious & perhaps heartless. I love Mrs. Howe though."

Many of the guests had shown curiosity combined with a reserve amounting to hardness, and Mary had noticed distinct condescension toward her and Edwin in the bearing of James T. Fields, editor of the *Atlantic Monthly* and junior partner in Ticknor and Fields, the Boston publishers. Yet almost the next day Fields called on Booth, who made an excuse not to see him. "And the cad," declared Mary, "returned with a request to see them at their home tonight: a regret is already written. How I hate such hypocrisy! They don't care for us."

Since the Booths had been in Boston, one or the other of them had sent the Stoddards a line almost every day. Ever since meeting these Stoddards they had been inseparable from them, were not put off by Elizabeth's terrible cleverness, which frightened most people, were if anything attracted by her independent manner. "Strange how completely you and Dick have entered into our life and thoughts," Mary marveled to Elizabeth when she first sat down to let her new friend know she wasn't well enough to come back to New York. "The first words we uttered after the cruel decision was—what you & Dick would feel!"

From living with Edwin she could better understand a temperament like Elizabeth's. "I have thought ever since I met you that your genius was struggling to get into the daylight. . . .

Edwin Booth after his return from California, 1857.

Father and son. Junius Brutus Booth and Edwin, 1849.

Edwin Booth at the time of his marriage to Mary Devlin, 1860.

You know I live with *genius:* am forced to bear the ills & restlessness of his untaught mind, his undefined purposes: & I know how dreadful it is to suffer as you & Edwin suffer."

At the Boston Theater Booth had had the best houses of any star in town. "Tell Dick that Edwin has made nearly $5,000 in the two weeks." Then Mary thought of the contrast with her literary friends' earnings. "Dear Elizabeth, who knows better than we do of your hard-pressed struggle. . . . We would share with you, but what is the use of such offering to your proud souls. The only thing we can do is to love you . . . & for your dear sakes lay by something to purchase joy for you & ourselves in books and pictures."

Yet whatever flowed into Booth's bank account seeped out again in a dozen directions, and he exploded to Dick Stoddard that he was "sick as hell & worried to death." His engagement over on December 20, he returned briefly to New York to untangle his affairs.

"Do look after Edwin," Mary appealed to Elizabeth. "He will be low-spirited enough without me, so pray do try and comfort him."

While he was temporarily away she moved with the year-old Edwina and the nurse Marie out to Dorchester, having chosen this town because a Dr. Erasmus Miller, celebrated locally for his treatment of consumptive cases, lived near by. "He has inspired me with a great deal of faith. All agree in saying that he is *wonderful!*"

Economy was one of her reasons for staying near Boston. Dr. Sims in New York would have cost her three times as much as Dr. Miller. But Dorchester was a lonely town, far out in the country. "An excellent place to study Sanscrit!" a lady had joked to her at Mrs. Howe's, and Mary had smiled ruefully.

"I know what I need, and my good sense bids me bear the isolation . . . providing I can keep Mrs. Howe & others like her at bay. She is the most importunate of her sex."

Mary had dined at Mrs. Howe's by herself and met Dr. Henry Beecher there, the brother of Harriet Beecher Stowe.

But she discouraged visitors, admitting to Elizabeth: "I saw my doctor yesterday! No, I will tell you nothing about it. All my courage is gone. I pass half my time in tears."

Then Booth came back and joined her in Dorchester for the interval before his engagement began at the Winter Garden, and for a short time all was bliss.

"He is so *happy* here," she told Elizabeth, her dearest confidante. "I look with dread and horror upon the four weeks' separation that must ensue. . . . How differently you & I are placed. Richard is so perfect a man, so free from human vices. . . . Well you know the demon that pursues a noble, ungoverned spirit like Edwin's. He is so gentle, so yielding, so *abstemious* now & I advise with him & he promises that the victory shall be his."

The *Transcript* had advertised Richard Stoddard's new narrative poem *The King's Bell*, and Booth and Mary read it together in bed, crying sentimentally over the hero Felix's death. Handsome Felix in his youth searches for happiness, tries wine, tries women; his desires

> Raging intensely like volcanic fires,
> Have burned away, and left a waste behind.

His own case exactly, Booth felt. And he wrote to Stoddard: "Dick! . . . I could tell you stories of my past, and I will some day, and they may cause you to think more leniently of the faults and wickedness of today. . . . Of course dear little wife knows all about my youth (ah, what a mockery! 'twas old age to me; my youth began with my marriage only). . . . My sorrows began at so green an age that the callow squab grew tough ere he had down to pluck."

Their little rented house was on Washington Street. Its windows at the back overlooked a snow-covered slope undulating down toward Dorchester Bay; you could see ice-skimmed water from the bedroom window. There was a great deal of sleighing, but Mary was not up to it. Hopefully each morning of this cold January, 1863, she stood in front of her mirror and pinched her cheeks to see if they had grown fuller. The rest of the day she lay on the sofa and her letters to Elizabeth in her pointed, rather elegant "lady's hand" were written on a book held in her lap. "I have laid all my plans for a home next winter in New York. . . . I do nothing all day but lay out bright visions for the future: it pleases me beyond all things to dream thus—but experience has taught me that it is all folly. We are masters of our destiny only to a very small extent."

She roused herself to drive into Boston with her husband to see John Wilkes act at the Boston Museum. They were recognized and applauded as they walked down the aisle to their seats. John had opened at the Museum on January 17, and if Edwin's Boston engagement had been brilliant, John's simply broke the record—"extraordinary," the *Transcript* called it. As a rival, John's hot breath was on Edwin's neck.

Edwin and Mary saw him play Pescara. "A bloody villain of the deepest red," exclaimed Booth with relish to Stoddard, "and my brother presented him rare enough for the most fastidious 'beef-eater.' . . . He is full of the true grit. I am delighted with him and feel the name of Booth to be more of a hydra than snakes and things ever was."

Booth loved Dorchester and the country life. He planned moonlight sleigh rides when Mary should be well enough. "He is so natural, so much himself when he is away from the stage," Mary explained to Elizabeth, "that I almost lament he is ever forced to assume the 'sock & buskin.'"

Could she go with him to New York in February? They almost quarreled over it. Booth was against her going. "I've given her my reasons and if she likes 'em—so; if she lumps 'em—so also."

This was to Dick. Elizabeth heard Mary's side, plaintively put forward. "Edwin got it into his head, I don't know how—that I wanted to go & stay during his entire stay there. This arrangement he very justly thought an extravagant & foolish one for we cannot afford to keep up two establishments. *I* had long ago decided not to go, or if I did, only for a few

days, but *he* did not so understand & after a good deal of talk
of the silly matter, I indignantly refused to go at all: giving as
my reasons, that he did not seem to appreciate my natural
desire to go on & see him for a few days—in doing which I
fancied I would be giving him great pleasure & content. The
'sorry child' then begged me to hold to my original plan &
assured me how happy he would be to have me there."

The question was settled for them when Mary, on top of
her other troubles, strained a tendon and Dr. Miller prescribed
absolute rest for her. Booth insisted to his friends later that
he had left her "in the bloom of health and hope, throwing
kisses to me as I parted from her."

Booth's perceptions these days were mostly turned inward;
he had few to spare, even for Mary, whose health was failing
steadily to any eye but his. To feel it fail and to be conscious
at the same time of her husband's need for her, of the inevitable danger in their separation, was a thing too bitter to
be dwelt on, and she did not dwell on it. But it was at this time
that alone in her bedroom she wrote to Lilian, who was all
aglow with her own love affair, for she had become engaged
to Tom Aldrich: "I send him to you. Oh, take care of him, take
care of him, for my sake."

II

The minute his friends saw Booth in New York they knew
something was wrong. He seemed lonely and restless and his
eyes were evasive. However, for the first few days all went
well. He opened in *Hamlet* with Lawrence Barrett as Laertes
and in spite of a bad cold played excellently and "to a house
overflowing," noted the *Times*, "with one of those peculiarly
fashionable and intelligent audiences for which he seems to
wear such a talisman of attraction."

Toward the end of the week his acting began to go to
pieces. Legend had it that when he was drinking, as he now
obviously was again, he suited his drunkenness to his role: got
melancholy-drunk for Hamlet, sentimentally drunk for

Othello, and savagely drunk for Richard III. His friends, with Mary in their minds, held a conference at the Stoddards', not daring to appeal to him outright; something in the way he looked at them made this impossible. "Notwithstanding the sweetness and simplicity of Mr. Booth's nature," said Lilian, "he carried always about him 'the divinity that doth hedge a king.'"

Suddenly Booth discovered that wherever he went he had company. Either Aldrich or Launt Thompson or Stoddard stuck with him, not to be shaken off. The unspoken truth flashed out only once when Booth and Aldrich, who was on duty that evening, were in Booth's dressing room and the Negro valet sidled in carrying a tall glass of something brown. Booth snatched for it, but Aldrich got there first. He and Booth exchanged expressionless looks, then Aldrich threw open the window and emptied the glass into the alley. He followed Booth into the wing and waited until his scene was over.

After they had left the theater and Booth began stepping out smartly in the opposite direction from where he was staying, Aldrich was right behind him. They walked all night. Two spectral figures of a man and a boy may have walked beside them—in Booth's churning thoughts, at least. At daybreak he gave up as his father had done, and he and Aldrich stumbled back to his rented room where they fell into the same bed and slept until noon. When they woke up not a word was said of the strange night, nor did either of them ever refer to it to the other in the years to come.

Early in Booth's second week John Wilkes, on his way from Boston to Philadelphia, swooped down on the Stoddards' apartment and found Edwin there. He came directly from Mary's side and brought the news that she was ill with a feverish cold. Depressed by being alone so much, she had ventured into Boston to invite a friend back to stay with her. Heavy snow had begun to fall; the horsecar had been delayed and in waiting for it on the exposed street corner she had been chilled through. At home at last she gasped to her maid: "Take me upstairs and put me to bed. I feel as if I should never be warm again."

For the next two days she was ill and aching, but when John left she sent a note by him to say Edwin must not be anxious, must on no account break his engagement, and John innocently seconded this by assuring his brother she seemed much better: her eyes were bright and her cheeks red.

That night or the next Booth got away from his chaperon and was so completely sodden when he made his entrance on-stage that his friends in the house were faint with pity and embarrassment, and Elizabeth Stoddard took it on herself to let Mary know. "Sick or well," she wrote, "you must come. Mr. Booth has lost all restraint and hold on himself. Last night there was the grave question of ringing down the curtain before the performance was half over. Lose no time. Come."

She had already notified Miss Lucy Pry in Boston of Booth's deterioration through the week. "I was not surprised," Miss Pry answered promptly. "I feared such would be the case when Edwin went without Mary . . . and I am sorry to say that I have heard of it from outside sources. . . . A friend of mine told me yesterday that a lady friend of hers who had just returned from N.Y. saw him so intoxicated that he could not walk and was being helped into a carriage."

In the last day or so Lucy Pry had seen Mary, who was very low indeed. Her cold had developed into pneumonia and, already depleted and ill, she had no strength left to fight. "She is completely prostrated. . . . You never would know it was Mollie, it seems to me that *our* Mollie has gone and that we have someone else in her place—she does not even look like herself." She seemed "perfectly indifferent" to everything about her and Miss Pry put it down to her utter weakness that she took no notice of any hints about Edwin.

In New York Booth, lying awake with a spinning head at two in the morning, felt a puff of air blow cold on his right cheek, once, twice. Thoroughly startled, he rolled over in bed and felt the same on his left cheek, like the well-defined pressure of cold lips, ghost kisses. Then distinctly he heard Mary's voice, smaller than in reality, but with the timbre of life, say against his ear: "Come to me, darling. I'm almost frozen."

Mrs. Miller, the doctor's wife, had moved into the Dorchester house to wait on Mary. "It's a shame you have to do all this for me," Mary said faintly more than once.

And Mrs. Miller answered, "It's a pleasure."

She held her patient up in bed while with a hand so feeble she could hardly control it Mary slowly shaped her reply to Elizabeth's letter: "I cannot come. I cannot stand. I think sometimes that only a great calamity can save my dear husband. I am going to try and write to him now, and God give me grace to write as a true wife should."

The evening of this day, Friday, February 20, Mary suddenly became so much worse that Dr. Miller called in another physician. Mary asked to be told the truth and was given it, that she had only a few hours to live. During the long two weeks of separation from her husband she had dwelt much in her dreams of the future when she would be strong again, and Edwin would be—wholly himself. Now, in the face of a need so immense and inexorable that the effort came easily, she put the future away and begged only that the doctors try to keep her alive until Edwin could be with her, "so that I may tell him."

Dr. Miller sent a telegram to New York.

"Seldom have we seen Shakespeare so murdered as at the Winter Garden during the past two weeks," clucked the New York *Herald*. "It would have been better to disappoint the public by closing the theater than to place Mr. Booth upon the stage when he was really unfit to act."

Booth was in his dressing room this night of February 20. An accumulation of three telegrams from Dorchester lay on his table, all unopened. Stoddard was with him but Stoddard's guardianship had a chink in it somewhere because Booth's face was gray below its paint; he moved like a man under water, and when his scenes were called for *Richard III*, he staggered out onto a rocking stage. The performance was just over when the

manager hurried into the room with a torn-open envelope
addressed to himself. He read it aloud: "This is the fourth
telegram. Why does not Mr. Booth answer? He must come at
once."

The last train north had left. At the Stoddards' apartment
Elizabeth brewed coffee over an alcohol lamp and gave Booth
cup after cup until he was enough restored to pace the room as
though it had bars around it, to halt and twist his hands, turning ghastly eyes on his hosts and monotonously appealing to
them to reassure him that things were not *so* bad . . . not the
worst? At seven in the morning he and Stoddard caught the
first Boston train. Booth sent a telegram from the station:
MARY, I'M COMING. Peering out of the train window he saw,
not the railway yard with its shuttling cars, but a clear vision
of his wife's face, unmistakable and yet unlike itself, with a
white cloth molded around the head and chin. And as the train
started and he turned repeatedly to the window, the quiet face
floated between him and the moving landscape.

Just before dawn the doctor's wife had called her husband,
who had been lying down. Mary laid her head on Dr. Miller's
shoulder. She was breathing quickly; her face was very pale,
her eyes were dark, and her long hair, falling loose, mingled
with his white hair. It grew slowly brighter. The French nurse
Marie slipped mutely into the room carrying Edwina, but
Mary motioned her away. As the water in the bay lit up with
the sunrise and the room filled with early-morning light, she
sank back and died, the doctor gently releasing her.

It was a few minutes after seven when Mary died and
Booth's train was gathering speed out of the New York station.
He made sure of this later, for it was then that he saw his wife's
face, disembodied and floating beside him. For the second time,
in a mysterious bridging of physical distance, Mary had communicated with him. Something like this the Negroes had fore-
told when Booth was born. And twice, his mother swore to
him, his father had appeared to her soon after death, to stand
beside her bed and vanish before she could speak. When the

train pulled into the Boston station and the helpful acquaintance who had brought his carriage to take Booth and Stoddard
out to Dorchester walked somberly up to them, Booth raised
his hand to ward off any talk and said only: "Don't tell me. I
know."

Not a word was spoken during the drive out. The small
house looked the same except that the blinds were drawn in
an upper window. Booth swung himself down from the carriage, was inside in three paces and up the stairs, hesitated outside the bedroom, then entered and shut the door, locking it.
He stayed there all night with Mary's body, no one disturbing
him. At dawn he emerged, and Stoddard, hovering by to offer any needed support, saw a strange thing: Booth held himself
erect and his expression was actually exalted. In the room behind him Mary lay; he had slipped a rose between her folded
hands and hung his miniature on her breast.

Services were held at Mount Auburn Cemetery in Cambridge, an endless, cold drive away along open roads. Stoddard
was in the chapel, and so were Mrs. Howe and William Warren
from the Boston Museum. Booth's mother was there. His
brother John and his brother-in-law Clarke had traveled up
together from Philadelphia, but Asia had not come; her resentment of Mary was like a splinter in her heart.

"As Edwin Booth followed the casket," writes Mrs. Howe,
"his eyes heavy with grief, I could not but remember how
often I had seen him act the part of Hamlet at the stage burial
of Ophelia. Beside or behind him walked a young man of remarkable beauty." This was John Wilkes. Mary's casket came
to rest—"hers was a most pathetic figure," Mrs. Howe recalled,
"as she lay, serene and lovely, surrounded with flowers."

Booth threw his long, theatrical cloak over his arm and
leaned against a pillar. The exaltation summoned up in him by
the first night's prayers had been wiped away; he looked
stunned. And as the clergyman Dr. Huntington began to
speak, a pain, like Booth's too sore and of the earth to be
comforted by prayer, welled up in all the mourners.

III

While Mary's body lay in a vault at Mount Auburn, the house in Dorchester was still warm with her presence. Booth roamed through it upstairs and down. His mother, who had stayed on with him, heard him calling: "Mollie, Mollie!" The silent house gave back silence. Outside a carriage drove past without stopping. Inside a door opened and he started: it was the servant.

He seized the pen Mary had held in her hand a week ago and wrote to Stoddard in New York: "What do they put people into the ground for? My father planted a penny once, expecting to find a guinea in the Spring. It wouldn't work. Would to God, Dick, that you and I could cultivate coffins."

To Adam Badeau he wrote: "If, while I was happy, I failed to keep you advised of my whereabouts and doings, you see I think of you in my misery. Can you believe it, Ad? I can't."

He sat listening to his half-drunken Irish cook spin out a story of two dreams she had had of him while he was away. Mary had suggested to her that those dreams meant a victory. "Yes, death's victory, was it not?"

He stood staring out at the white-capped bay, remembering the plans they had laid for this winter for rides through the snow to jingling sleigh bells. "Ah! the ride, sad and solemn; the bells, joyless and dull; but they came—the winter, the ride and the bells—to make a deeper impression than we thought they would."

Dr. Osgood, the clergyman who had married him and Mary, wrote to say he hoped Booth's art would console him. "The beauty of my art is gone," Booth answered. "It is hateful to me—it has become a trade."

And to Stoddard: "I wish to God, Dick, I was not an actor. Would to God I could write. It must be splendid! You don't think so? You'd swap with me, maybe, would you? Damn! Damn! Damn!"

"I am as calm outwardly," he assured Stoddard, "as though

a wedding had taken place instead of death—but, oh, the hell within me is intense! . . . My grief *eats* me!"

The chief cause of his agony was remorse. Had Mary not learned of his unworthy behavior while she lay suffering, she might have lived. From whom she had learned of it he knew not, but "had she had cheering news from me or of me," he cried hopelessly to his two dear friends—his and Mary's Dick and 'Lisbeth—"it would have given her strength to rally. My conduct hastened her death, when she heard that I—her all—was lost to all sense of decency and respect for her—her feeble spirit sank."

He climbed to the bedroom to look over her things and hide them from sight. "Her guitar is hanging on the wall. Her books lie all about me; her sewing, her dresses . . . all weep for her, all talk of her. . . . Every little toy of hers, every little scrap of paper the most worthless, are full of her because she has touched them. They recall her more vividly than the baby does. . . . My child should be a solace to me, but *she*, alas! was my child. . . . My child can never fill her place, for *she* was my child, my baby-wife. . . . Oh, Dick, only to think I've locked her up in a box and have the key of it; it doesn't seem as though she were in a coffin, does it?"

He had not yet heard from a number of his friends, among them Fitzhugh Ludlow, and, surprisingly, the Woodman sisters—"who pretended to be so full of Mollie. No matter, we all must go and be forgotten."

Then Ludlow did write—"a beautiful letter," and Lilian Woodman, in Boston for a visit, drove out to call. Several Boston friends with kind intentions invited Booth to dinner. "Are there not people in this world," he raved to Stoddard, "whose souls are formed of mud as well as their bodies?" Dismayed by his strange and terrible look, they offered sympathy. "I do not need their sympathy!" They spoke of Mary, and he began to cry, "to make a fool of myself." Nothing they could say was the right thing.

"What can they tell me? She is in heaven, and I must live

to meet her there. I know all this at least as well as they know it. . . . They tell me that time and use will soften the blow, that I shall grow to forget her. God forbid! My grief is sweet to me; for it is a part of her. . . . I look back now to my youthful days when I lost my father, a father most dearly, fondly loved! I look back without a tear, without a sigh, and it is difficult at this time even to recall his features. Great God! Will this ever be the case with Mary?"

The wind howled over the whitened fields. It was his fantasy, he used to tell Mary when they clung together at night during a storm, that the wind was the voice of some departed soul screaming in agony for the sins of poor mortals left behind. "I dread to think of what I used to say—there may be a voice in this wild music calling on me.

"Why don't Mary come to me? Can she so soon have forgotten all our past? I have called on her, prayed to her—have lain awake all night and strained my eyeballs in the darkness for her, but she gives me no sign. Am I so base? Does she hate me or does she fear to tell me she is unhappy? Oh, God! Could I but feel satisfied she is eternal! There is a damned unholy doubt keeps bubbling up in my boiling brain as to what we are. This dangling between the fiend and God is worse agony than to be damned outright. *So weep for my early education.*"

He sat up late, "more alone than Selkirk on his island," reading sad poetry while a storm raged outside. Something tapped on the glass of the window. He threw the window open and a small bird flew in past him. He was seized with a weird suspicion: half horror, half hope. But the waif ignored his coaxing and refused to nestle in his bosom. He ran after it, while it beat from wall to wall then dropped exhausted. "No, I don't think that Mary has yet, or ever will to me, make herself manifest. I don't think I am worthy of it. . . . I can't be good. I'm a fiend! I struggle upward as hard as I can but down I come plump into the sea of evil. I must drown—there's no use struggling."

Then he dreamed she stood before him and that as he knelt to implore her forgiveness, she turned her head away. This was justice. How many times in their life together had he not made her weep most bitterly when "cold, indifferent, like a statue I received her deep devotion. . . . Although my love was deep-rooted in my soul yet I could never *show* it. . . . If I were a poet I could tell you how I loved my bird, but as it is I can only say I loved and let you guess how deeply."

Dr. Miller persuaded him to go out sleighing, hoping to divert him. It was a useless effort. The Howes met him with the doctor on the Brighton road. "Such an image of sorrow I have never seen," writes Florence Howe. "His long black hair seemed a fitting frame for the dark, melancholy face, as he sat huddled together in the cutter, his head sunk upon his breast."

Wilson Barstow, who was Elizabeth Stoddard's brother, called on Booth and reported to his sister that he had found him "blue-chinned, unshaven," and smoking hard. Booth was smoking twelve to fifteen cigars a day ("I can't stop; half an hour, or an hour at most, is as long as I can go without it"), but there was one thing he was not doing, and that was drinking.

"Having forsworn the fiend," he explained in a note to Dr. Miller, to whom he was sending a leftover case of liquor, "I am anxious to rid my house of his presence—will you aid me by taking him into pound—thus bottled up and labelled 'Porter'?"

His drinking in New York had indirectly caused Mary's death, that coupled with the officiousness of the "damned good-natured friends"—their names unknown to him—who had been at pains to tell her about it. In a frenzy of self-reproach he laid bare to Elizabeth what he had long ago confessed to Mary: how he had been a drunkard before he was eighteen, a libertine at twenty. "All the accumulated vices I had acquired in the wilds of California and Australia seemed to have full sway over me. I added fuel to the fire until the angel quenched it and made me, if not a *man*, at least a little worthier than I was. There was one spark, however, left untouched. It was merely covered and it occasionally would ignite; still the angel kept it under. I dread lest it get full head-way again."

He was heroically resolved that it should not. "I'll struggle—I'll fight—I'll conquer, too, with God's help." From this time on he would be a man dedicated. "Mollie's goodness was while here thrown away upon me. But it was not wasted, for now I feel it, now it shows as it ever will, my guiding star through life. . . . I have dared to ask God why I have been thus tor-tured, and now I *feel* a voice which tells me it was to save me—to save her."

IV

Not until April was Mary buried. Booth drove over to Mount Auburn to choose a spot for her grave, "such a spot—I think—as she would have chosen for me; near Cary, and over-looking a valley, where the setting sun will kiss her good-night."

Then it was time to go, to leave Dorchester. The terror rose up in him once more that in the excitement of the world and his profession, soon to be renewed, he might stop thinking of her, might "live so long as to forget—not entirely, for that is impossible, but to be borne along by time into a misty recol-lection of something that has passed away; to turn the mouldy leaves of memory until suddenly remembering (with scarce a sigh, perhaps) a dream of happiness I had when I was young. Oh, Jesus! Spare me that!"

But he had reached a turning point, and he could hardly wait to get back to New York, where the noise of the city would deaden thought, even though he couldn't reason himself out of the conviction that he would somehow meet Mary there. For even yet he could not "make her dead," nor could he believe that she had wholly stopped being, in the sense of a flame blown out. In his night watches he had tried earnestly to put himself into direct communication with her, had waited breathlessly, listened intently. "But there is yet some impedi-ment between us," he told Elizabeth, "which prevents her from doing what I know she will do some day."

He had an appointment in New York with Laura Edmonds, the spiritualist and daughter of John Worth Edmonds, a former judge of the New York Court of Appeals. Lately the War had sent thousands of people drifting to the séance chambers in desolate, last-ditch attempts to deny the utter blotting out of sons or lovers killed in battle. Like them Booth pinned his hopes on the occult. "Oh, for the day with Edmonds! I shall tire her to death—but since I go to her in faith and for a holy purpose I feel sure she will assist me."

By May he was settled in New York with Edwina and his mother in a house on East Seventeenth Street rented from Putnam, the publisher. He had had his hair cut and he shaved regularly. The solitary vigils, the moon-bleached fields of Dorchester, the homely little rooms that spoke so agonizingly of Mary's presence fell back into the past. All about him the great city murmured. Yet "as I ever have lived," he wrote to Adam Badeau, "so live I now, within."

His work was soon to begin; his mind was pulled in a dozen directions. Still he sat on, and wrote on steadily. "Believe in one great truth, Ad.—God is. And as surely as you and I are flesh and bones and blood, so are we also spirits eternal."

The next day, May 19, was Mary's birthday, her twenty-third if she had lived. Booth chose this day for his first visit to Laura Edmonds. He walked out from the interview with his mind whirling, shaken and ecstatic. "I feel a load lifted from my heart," he exulted to Dick and Elizabeth. "Oh, how beautiful, how good is my angel wife! Oh! how I love her! My soul yearns—but not painfully—for her. I feel she is nearer—dearer to me than she could ever be on earth; she told me beautiful things yesterday—many things I longed to hear. Every Wednesday we are to meet—every Wednesday my soul will become freer and happier. Yesterday seems like a world of itself—apart from all time & all mine. Oh, how I long for Wednesday!"

The Wednesday came and others after it, but with each one Booth's ecstasy subsided a degree and his mind was more torn. He complained to Badeau that "the result of my four or five visits is not satisfactory; of course nothing I can get on earth can be. . . . I sometimes believe beyond a doubt of her existence and her constant love; but then again I feel the deadness of an outcast soul."

He had read in the *Herald* that Badeau had been wounded, and the news suggested an awesome possibility. "My dear Ad., we may never meet again; you may even now be quitting earth for the bright home I have longed for. . . . Ad., if you do go, *come back* to *me*, and assure me of the reality of what perplexes us all so often."

Most people who cared for him were displeased and worried by the new line he was taking. Elizabeth Stoddard had some time ago urged him austerely to "cultivate the intellectual," and he had answered piteously that this was "impossible for him."

He refused to give up hope. "I won't believe for the millionth part of a minute that Mary's deep love for me is buried in her grave; and living and loving still, why should she not seek me even yet?"

But his remarkable plea to Badeau was made in confidence. "Keep it to your heart," he wrote. And of the séances: "I may as well tell you, some marvelous things have been said and done. . . . My father and Mary have both been with me there, and have written and spoken with me through Miss E— in a curious manner . . . *almost* convincing . . . but we cannot help our doubts, you know. . . . I want something beyond a doubt. . . . So if you remain on earth I'll acquaint you with my proceedings; if you go to her and can come back, do so; I will, to you."

Slowly Booth gathered up the threads he had dropped. There were still some places he could not bear to go; the Fifth Avenue Hotel was one. Even now his mind couldn't let alone the same, worst, sore spot, which seemed never to heal. "Had the hateful knowledge of my conduct been kept from Mary, I should feel more quiet and patient, but the consciousness of my baseness and the agony it caused her is a curse that will ever weigh upon me—God forgive us all!"

This was to Stoddard. Not long after this the blow fell. Lilian Woodman believed what happened was that Booth discovered the letter from Elizabeth telling of his being drunk, which Mary had tried to answer the day before she died. Whether he discovered it or not, he learned who had been the informant, and whenever someone had wronged Booth or had hurt one he loved, no excuses could excuse, no reasons could explain the injury. After the first shock he would blaze with the awful anger of pure disillusionment. Perhaps he expected too much from his friends, but when any of them proved themselves to be less worthy than he had thought them, they simply ceased to exist for him. He was through with both the Stoddards.

The cruel letter Booth had learned of, written by a friend he trusted, had not been a friend's letter. Yet now mysteriously, as if to restore his faith in his kind, a letter reached him from a stranger who was indeed a friend. Booth had opened again at the Winter Garden on September 21. "I no longer feel an interest in acting," he had told Dick Stoddard before their breakup. "There was but one whose opinion I valued in the least."

Then the mysterious letter was delivered to him. "My dear Mr. Booth," it began, "it is because I *do know* that you mourn your wife truly, I appeal to her memory now as the surest spell to win your attention to what I have to say, and now that her voice is silenced, and her loving spirit has passed away, to speak to you as she might have done about yourself."

The letter, which was unsigned, had been written by a man, evidently a New Yorker, who with his wife had admiringly followed Booth's career up to Mary's death. Booth was a public figure, and his audiences hung with romantic interest on every detail of his private life. Hundreds of people had been glad with him at Edwina's birth, had regretted his drinking, felt sorrow at his loss, and unknown to him, had discussed among themselves what he ought to do next. The anonymous writer had noticed that since Booth's return to the stage his voice, affected by too much smoking, could hardly be heard even in this small house; that his breathing was oppressed and he looked gray and ill.

The letter continued, like a quiet voice. "You are reckless, and heedless of life and health, you say. . . . This is not as it should be! *You* have a motive for every act of self denial, a prompter for every high and noble aspiration, which should make you rise superior to all selfish considerations. Another life is bound up in yours—a sacred trust has devolved upon you alone. . . .

"Can you not rouse yourself to a sense of your responsibility, and determine to fight life's battle with renewed courage for the sake of the helpless girl entrusted to you? . . . determine to preserve for her the support and protection which a father's arm alone can afford, and to devote yourself to the culture, and elevating for another life, the immortal soul you hold within your influence for good or evil? *This* is worth living for. . . . And now for the advice."

The stranger urged Booth to smoke less and to give up drinking strong coffee. "Seek *good* medical advice and have done with quacks. . . . Come out of your memories and combat your despondency. Believe me, you have many and warm friends."

At the foot of the page was written: "Be good enough to burn this letter *as soon* as you read it."

But Booth laid the letter carefully away after noting on it: "It is too precious to burn."

He had said of little Edwina that she "climbs my knee, and prattles all day long to me; but still she is not the baby I have loved and cherished so devotedly."

Florence Howe writes that "it was pitiful to see him with his little motherless child." Once immediately after Mary's death he had seized his daughter in his arms and raked her face with hungry eyes, yet when a likeness to her mother seemed to peep out at him he had burst into such a flood of tears that when his eyes cleared the resemblance was gone.

Now months had passed. He was growing used to his loss; he accepted it. And inevitably, as what he dreaded began to take place—as the vivid image of the person he had most loved imperceptibly effaced itself—his power of loving and hopes for the future fixed on a new object. Edwina needed him, and this, as the wise stranger had shown, *this* was "worth living for."

He bought his own house this fall, on East Nineteenth Street, where his mother and Rosalie could live with him and look after Edwina, who was not quite two. "All my hopes and aspirations now are clustering like a halo about her head," her father cried. "She is the light of my darkened life."

More and more he saw in her a likeness to Mary. "Full of her sweet mother's soul, she brings Mary back to earth; her eyes, voice, manner, her ringing laugh bear me backward in pleasurable pain to the days when I first knew her mother."

PART FOUR

CHAPTER 7

A Suit of Sables

I have that within which passeth show.
Hamlet, *Act I, scene 2*

DURING the past summer Booth had seen Asia in Philadelphia. They were friends again. With the girl she hated six months dead, Asia's feud with her brother had worn itself out. Years later in a little book she published about Edwin she went so far as to speak of Mary Devlin as "a good woman"—a modest enough tribute compared to the praises others had heaped on Mary, yet from a woman of Asia's curious nature, possessive, belligerent, and ingrown, it meant a great deal.

John Wilkes occasionally stayed with Booth in New York, flashing in from Boston or New Orleans. As an actor, he had a pass across the battle lines and traveled freely between North and South, being recognized everywhere by his picturesque overcoat with its astrakhan collar, deep sleeves, and flowing cape; his broad hat worn low and on the bias; and his jet-black mustache. In the spring he had been arrested in St. Louis for saying he "wished the whole damn government would go to hell." He was set free after swearing allegiance to the Union and paying a fine.

John had been in New York this summer when the wounded Adam Badeau, after weeks spent in hospital, was brought to Edwin's for his convalescence. Edwin and John carried him upstairs, dressed his wound and nursed him in shifts. Badeau thought John was "very captivating, though not so distinguished as his greater brother."

And, "imagine me," said John afterward, laughing grimly to Asia, "helping that wounded Yankee with my rebel sinews. If it weren't for mother I wouldn't enter Edwin's house. . . . If the North conquer us, it will be by numbers only, not by native grit, not pluck, and not by devotion."

Asia exclaimed: "*If the North conquer us?* We are *of* the North."

"Not I, not I!" cried John. "So help me holy God! my soul, life and possessions are for the South!"

When, after his own daughter's death, the great Macready returned to playing the part of the grief-stricken father Virginius, he recognized in his acting a tragic authority it had never had before.

Booth had demanded of Badeau in the fullness of sorrow: "Do you think now it is possible for me to recite some passages in a play without a something in my heart and throat?"

At first his new insight nearly made him break down onstage as the poignant application of some of Shakespeare's lines to his own case came home to him. Then as his grief became more manageable, his technique absorbed it, and by degrees the work that had seemed empty to him after Mary's death began to engross him completely. Strange how each night the play became a fresh creation, a tale never told before!

He was not drinking. When people jocosely condoled with him about this he would say: "I dare not, I dare not, I dare not!"

He smoked hard instead, and drank black coffee. Now that he was no longer wasting himself he could give his profession the best that was in him. He would make his acting a monument to Mary. He began to appreciate the moral value of his art. "Whatever I may do of serious import," he wrote to

Cary's young widow, "I regard it as a performance of a sacred duty I owe to all that is pure and honest in my nature—a duty to the very religion of my heart."

His main opposition in New York this autumn of 1863 was Edwin Forrest, laboring again at Niblo's. When Forrest played Spartacus or Metamora he could still pack the house, with people sitting on campstools in the aisles, but when he tried Shakespeare, especially *Hamlet*, his audiences declined. New York had a new Hamlet now, and Forrest had not one but two Booths against him, as was shown earlier in the year when he and John Wilkes were both acting in Philadelphia and John deliberately scheduled *Macbeth* for the same night as Forrest and drew a bigger house.

His season in New York over, Edwin Booth took to the road, and in Washington Secretary of State Seward gave a dinner for him, and President Lincoln saw him act Shylock at Ford's Theater on Tenth Street. "A good performance," said the sad-faced President in his oddly soft voice, "but I'd a thousand times rather read it at home if it were not for Booth's playing."

Lincoln often escaped to the theater, having arranged with Washington managers that he should enter unobtrusively by a side door. He had been warned he was foolhardy to go without guards, such rashness was uncalled for. "The fact is, I am a great coward," Lincoln had replied. "I have moral courage enough, I think, but I am such a coward physically that if I were to shoulder a gun and go into action, I am dead sure that I should turn and run at the first fire—I know I should."

He was not the only one. "If it were not for the fear of doing my country more harm than good," Booth admitted to Badeau, "I'd be a soldier too; a coward always has an 'if' to slink behind, you know. Those cursed bullets are awkward things, and very uncivil at times; and as for a bayonet charge, I don't hesitate to avow my readiness to 'scoot' if there is a chance. Bull Run would be nothing to the run I'd make of it."

By March, 1864, Booth was acting in New York again, and he offered a new melodrama, a real tear-jerker called *The*

Fool's Revenge, based on the same story as the opera *Rigoletto*. Booth played Bertuccio, the hunchbacked court jester who, not knowing what he does, helps kidnap his own daughter and hand her over to a libertine. Then he learns his mistake.

> BERTUCCIO. (*With a wild cry.*) My child! My child! wronged! murdered!
> DELL' AQUILA. Ha! by whom?
> BERTUCCIO. (*Wildly.*) By me! by me! Her father—her own father!

It was a huge hit.

II

A year had slipped by since Mary died. There was a change in Booth, and he could see it. The great lesson he had learned from Mary's death was that of submission. "Nothing but the blow which fell could have awakened me. I learned to feel it was in kindness, not anger, that God spoke thus to me."

For the first time since the days when he took care of his father, he thought of others, not of himself. When Cary had been killed, Booth was shocked and saddened, yet it was a thing apart from him. When Badeau was wounded, Booth thought of his own need first. Now early in the summer of 1864 Mrs. Cornelius Felton, who was Cary's older sister and had been like a second mother to Booth and Mary, died in Cambridge, and this time Booth's sympathy flowed not only from his knowledge of sorrow; he had got beyond sorrow to an understanding of what true consolation is.

"Oh, that I could give you," he wrote to her family, "the full companionship of God's love as I have felt it since Mary's death, the peace that has filled my soul, and the strength that has flowed steadily into it since that terrible day. Oh, be assured, dear, dear ones, that they *are* together. They never forget us, never cease to love and care for us. Oh, I feel such an intense love for God when sorrow touches me that I could almost wish my heart would always ache—I feel so near to him. . . . How distinctly I can see Richard and Mrs. Felton—

much more so than I see Mary. Isn't it strange? I see her, though, in Edwina."

Edwina was almost three. Just as Booth's earliest memory was of his father's small, hard hands swinging him terrifyingly down from horseback through the woodland, dipped in darkness, so one of Edwina's first memories was of being cradled in her father's arms and laid back softly in her crib from the nursery floor, where Booth had found her when he arrived home after the theater.

The elder Booth's voice rang through his son's childhood. "Your foot is on your native heath!" shouted Junius, and no forest goblin dared dispute him. But when Edwina remembered her young father's voice, as she did later, it was as a musical caress. Often she sat on his lap while with one arm clasped around her in a gesture divinely protective he recited poetry— a verse by Tennyson:

> What does little birdie say
> In her nest at peep of day?

And his tone was so sad and the words as he said them so full of pathos that the child pressed her face into his shoulder and burst into tears.

Edwina was her father's "birdie," his "little bird," as her mother once had been. She realized dimly that he was not like other parents. To begin with, there was only one of him, whereas other children had a mother as well. And so did she, he reminded her earnestly, looking at her with eyes that seemed to enter her. She had a mother who was waiting for them both in heaven. But to Edwina, seeing was believing; she *knew* her father. Young though she was, she sensed his sadness, and it was her father's solitude, not her own, that seemed to her forlorn and unnatural. He could be with her only in the short, darkening hour before his early dinner. Then he frolicked with her, very gently.

"Far-r-ther, don't go," she trilled at him as he left for the theater.

"Birdie, it's to bring you bread and butter."

"I don't want any bread and butter."

He returned at midnight, to watch his darling from the lighted door or to stand by her crib.

"Go to sleep, baby."

"Far-r-ther is my baby," she told him.

Junius Booth had traveled East again, holding by the hand his little girl Marion, his and Harriet Mace's daughter. Poor pretty Hattie had died in California, and Junius had left her under a tombstone which bore a marble figure, her name, age, the date of her death, and the words, DON'T CRY.

Edwin had helped Junius with money before. This time he gave him a good business position connected with the Winter Garden. Booth and his brother-in-law Clarke had taken the bold step of leasing the Winter Garden to play there under their own management for several seasons to come. As a third partner they had signed on a plausible person who called himself William Stuart, though his real name, which he had reasons for dropping, was O'Flaherty. He was the writer who for pay had systematically written down Forrest in the *Tribune* and made him a laughingstock. Stuart was not a wise choice for a partner, the truth was not in him. But Booth and Clarke hadn't yet scratched below the surface of his Irish charm and they installed him as house manager at a large salary.

Booth's home was the perch for all three of his brothers whenever they were in New York, but he had had absolutely to forbid any talk about the War when John was staying with him. John had championed the South and coarsely cursed "old Abe" until Edwin finally blurted: "Why don't you fight if you feel so strongly?"

"I promised Mother to keep out of the quarrel," retorted John, "and I'm sorry I promised."

He was more frank with Asia in Philadelphia when she taunted him that "every Marylander worthy the name is fighting the South's battles."

After a scorching silence he answered painfully: "I have

only an arm to give. My brains are worth twenty men, my money worth a hundred, my beloved, precious money—Oh, never beloved till now!"

He might have added that his flattering eyes were worth a regiment, that his voice, intimate and coaxing, ought to be valued at a division. Observing, as he put it, "how women rule the Nation," he had begun to ingratiate himself with ladies in the highest circles, especially the government circle in Washington. His attentiveness was one of his charms. Having started his fair friends talking, he lowered his disturbing gaze and smiled as he listened, like the sultan at Scheherazade's voice.

John was forever and feverishly on the move these days, though, strangely enough, not acting much. Often he turned up at Asia's house plastered with red mud and occasionally so late that he let himself in with his own key and tumbled asleep on the couch downstairs in his clothes and riding boots. He still detested Clarke—"I'd never darken his door but for you, Asia."

Early in the War when he and Clarke had been on a train together and Clarke had sneered at Jefferson Davis, John hurled himself on his brother-in-law, almost throttling him, and yelled: "Never again if you value your life speak to me so of a man and a cause I hold sacred!"

Yet he was freer in this house than in Edwin's because Clarke was usually on the road, and Asia kept her questions to herself. She had them, however. Night after night when John was with her she would hear a soft tap at the front door, then the unmistakable creak as he opened the door and then guarded voices, one or two of which she thought she recognized, but when she called down there would be no answer.

Edwin followed the war news that inflamed his brother with only a part of his mind. The bloody battles—Chickamauga, Chattanooga, The Wilderness—in which soldiers of both sides, each man to himself vividly central, gave their lives for a yard of ground, might have been fought out on the plateaus of the moon for all they affected a busy actor. Parke Godwin of the *Evening Post* stopped in to see Booth one day at noon and found him stretched on a sofa breathing like a runner and covered with sweat. "Not ill, I hope?" Godwin asked.

"No," said Booth, "it's this abominable speech. I've been practicing it all morning. I've shouted it and screeched it and roared it and mumbled it and whispered it, but it won't come right."

That night Godwin heard the speech onstage, heard it frantically applauded.

Booth was his own producer, too, now, since he and Clarke had taken the Winter Garden, and he meant to do nothing but the great plays, to do them as they should be done—perfectly. He spent most of the hot summer of 1864 in the wardrobe room and scene shop of the theater poring over designs for new sets and costumes to be shown off during his first season in this house as part proprietor. In September he acted for two weeks in Philadelphia, rushing to New York and back over the week end. The pace was fearful, too much for any man, "bodily, mental and spiritual 'hammer and tongs,' " he complained to Mrs. Cary in a letter.

He was not quite thirty-one, and for the first time in his life his body went back on him. In New York again, worn out by his elaborate preparations for a season that hadn't yet opened, he was first crippled by neuralgia, having to sit up straight with his leg in a sling, and then laid low by a series of such blasting nervous headaches that the slightest noise seemed to split his head open.

A Federal army under General Grant was pressing the siege of Petersburg. "Oh, God! give me leave to see the end!" John sighed to Asia one night. He looked haggard and distraught.

Asia begged him: "Don't go South again, my poor brother. Don't go."

"Why, where *should* I go, then?" he demanded and glaring at her with half mad, half somber eyes, began to sing a parody of a popular song in which each verse ended on a rhyme to a year.

"In 1865 when Lincoln shall be king!"

John sang.

Asia shook her head violently.

"Oh, not that. That will *never* happen."

John leaped to his feet. "No, by God's mercy! Never *that!*" he cried. Then he whispered savagely, his tormented face close to hers: "This man's appearance, his pedigree, his coarse low jokes and anecdotes, his vulgar similes and his frivolity are a disgrace to the seat he holds. . . . He is walking in the footprints of old John Brown, but no more fit to stand with that rugged old hero—Great God! No! John Brown was a man inspired, the greatest character of this century. *He* is Bonaparte in one great move, that is, by overturning this blind Republic and making himself a king. This man's re-election which will follow his success, I tell you—will be a reign!"

On November 25 Edwin gave *Julius Caesar* at the Winter Garden for one gala night only. The profits were to swell the fund for a statue of Shakespeare in Central Park, New York's new pleasure ground, which had been a wilderness three years before. Junius and John were in the cast with him. This was the first time they had all played together, and Stuart, in charge of publicity, made the most of it by advertising

THE THREE SONS OF THE GREAT BOOTH

JUNIUS BRUTUS,

EDWIN AND

JOHN WILKES

Filii Patri Digno Digniores

There was already a saying in the theater that Edwin Booth ruled the East, Junius Brutus, Jr., the West, and John Wilkes the South. Since Stuart had taken over publicity at the Winter Garden he had devoted himself to promoting Edwin in a flock of posters, leaflets, and even statuettes (suitable for drawing-room tables) distributed through the whole city, so that the name Booth alone, in New York at any rate, had come to mean Edwin, and "Booth-like" was an accepted synonym for dark, handsome, and melancholy. However, now that Junius had established himself in New York, the papers occasionally called him *the* Booth, "so I must brush up or lose my laurels," said Edwin.

"Ah," said Junius, eyeing his brother's success, "Ted has got the public, and they're running wild over him. Yet let him act for a thousand years and he never will be able to approach father."

It was John who felt really diminished by Edwin. John was no longer a schoolboy and yet his dream was still to overthrow the Colossus—"I must have fame, fame." The unspoken rivalry between him and Edwin was exploited by managers. When he played in Washington the management billed him not only as the "Son of the Great Junius" but as the "Brother and Artistic Rival of Edwin Booth." The Southern press naturally favored John. A notice of his Richard III in New Orleans boasted that "in *physique* Mr. Booth is greatly the superior of his brother Edwin, being a much handsomer and larger man, and in no other particular . . . is he at all inferior to that much-admired actor."

Because *Julius Caesar* was given as a benefit, all prices were raised and the best seats sold for five dollars. It was worth the money to see the three Booths outdo themselves, each at the top of his form: Edwin as Brutus, Junius as Cassius, which had been their father's part, and John as Mark Antony. "Edwin was nervous," Asia noticed. "I think he trembled a little for his own laurels."

Asia was standing downstairs while her mother and Rosalie sat in a box at the side. As the band struck up and the brothers made their entrance in Caesar's train the ovation rocked the house. When the act was over they stood in line before the curtain, bareheaded, wearing white togas and sandals, and bowed to the audience and to one another. Junius, sturdily built for the lean Cassius, looked the most like his father, though he was taller and heavier. The jutting jaw, bold carriage of the head, and air of domination all were the same, but the electric

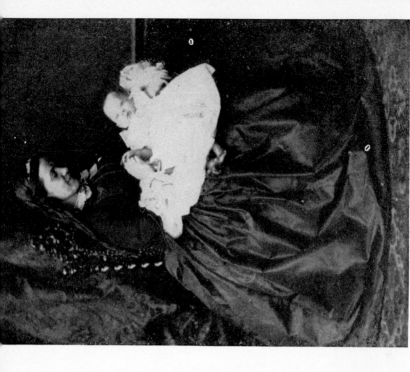

Edwin Booth with Edwina, about 1864. (*Museum of the City of New York*)

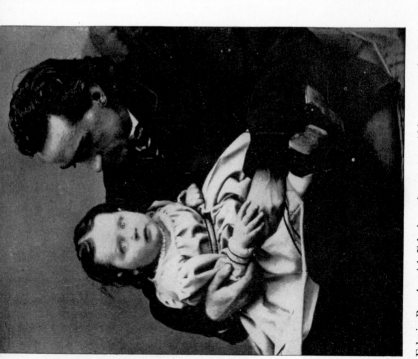

Mary Devlin Booth with Edwina in London, 1862. (*Museum of the City of New York*)

Playbill for the performance of the three Booth brothers in *Julius Caesar*, November 25, 1864. (*Harvard Theatre Collection*)

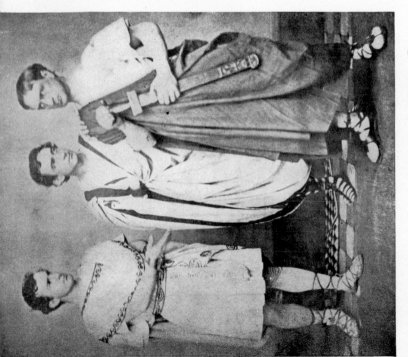

John Wilkes Booth as Mark Antony, Edwin Booth as Brutus, and Junius Brutus Booth, Jr. as Cassius in Julius Caesar, November 25, 1864. (*Harvard Theatre Collection*)

fire that had seemed to zigzag like forked lightning from the eyes of the elder Booth was missing from the eyes of Junius.

Edwin looked fragile between his brothers. His thoughtful eyes roamed over the house. He seemed to illustrate Brutus' words about himself:

> I am not gamesome: I do lack some part
> Of that quick spirit that is in Antony.

John had shaved off his mustache for the performance. His eyes sparkled like black diamonds. Most of the applause was for him and he knew it. He threw back his head, set beautifully on his neck, and his moist lips parted, his teeth glinted, as he laughed his acknowledgments. Asia, listening eagerly to the people around her while they compared the brothers, heard somebody exclaim: *"Our Wilkes* looks like a young god!" She turned to see a man whom she recognized for a Southerner staring like one hypnotized. As the demonstration rolled on unchecked, old Mrs. Booth sat beaming down at her sons— who made a special bow to her—and at their father in them. This was worth everything.

The audience was engrossed in the picture of Brutus pacing his shadowy orchard just before the Roman dawn broke when a screech and a roar in the street outside jolted everyone back to New York. Several fire engines clattered to a halt in front of the theater, and three or four firemen burst into the lobby. There was a mutter of panic through the house. Brutus stepped quickly to the footlights, commanded silence with a look, and in the low voice of most of Booth's curtain speeches announced there was nothing to be alarmed at. The noise died down and the play went on. But next morning the papers explained that the fire endangering the Winter Garden (the actual blaze had been next door in the Lafarge House) was one of a dozen or so, deliberately set in public buildings all over the city in a co-ordinated plot of the Rebels to demoralize New York.

At breakfast on Nineteenth Street one of the forbidden political arguments broke out. Junius blustered that in California the men who set those fires would have been strung up. Edwin said firmly that a few days earlier, voting for the first time in his life, he had voted for Lincoln's re-election; and at this John began to rave that his brother knew not what he had done, that he would live to see Lincoln the king of America.

III

The night after *Julius Caesar* Booth opened in *Hamlet*, which was the first of the perfect productions he had been lovingly working on all summer. Stuart predicted it was so good it would run six months. Booth, more conservative, gave it about four weeks, but the four weeks stretched into six, then eight, ten, twelve. Evidently this *Hamlet* was going to set a record. For Shakespeare a run of three weeks was very fair and to pass the twelve-week mark was extraordinary.

Stuart was walking on the clouds, but Booth, who had to carry the show and Stuart and the Winter Garden and everything else on his own back, was almost dropping under the strain of "this terrible success." Never in his life had he played a part so long. One night onstage he reached a dead stick, was prompted and forgot again, was prompted and forgot still again and at last signaled the stage manager to lower the curtain. After this he urged Stuart desperately to agree to a change of bill. Stuart shook his head until it wobbled and smacked his palm with his fist. "Dear bhoy, keep it up, keep it up. If it runs a year, keep it up, *keep it up!*"

The monumental scenery of the new *Hamlet* and the rich stuffs and colors—green, gold, crimson, violet—of the costumes, contributing to the beauty of the spectacle, helped to make it go. But what, after all, gave it its siren-lure was Booth's peculiar fitness for the main part. From his first entrance upstage left every eye was riveted on that forward-drifting, small, lithe, elegant, saffron-faced figure in shabby black with the dark hair hanging to the shoulders. Booth looked more Italian than Danish, but anyone reminded of this in the moment of watching him would have brushed the suggestion away as of no account while waiting impatiently for him to begin the first of the famous soliloquies that to both star and audience were like operatic arias, each a test of quality in the performer.

Left alone, Booth roved from side to side.

O God! O God!
How weary, stale, flat, and unprofitable
Seem to me all the uses of this world.

On the midnight battlements, more native to him than the castle chamber, Hamlet stood apart from his friends and questioned the air with rolling glances. He seemed a figure created by the night: shadowy, fantastic, moonstruck. A few years before, Booth had sometimes worked himself up so in this scene that he was incoherent, but since then he had learned restraint. His acting had a quiet ease now, an intensity of emotion without rant; yet breaking every so often into what seemed a spontaneous explosion of tragic power, as when he commanded Horatio and Marcellus to swear by his sword—they standing resolutely on either side of him while he held the crossed hilt high, his head thrown back, his face dazzling and impassioned under the calcium flare:

Never to speak of this that you have seen,
Swear by my sword.

. . . . .

Never to speak of this that you have heard,
Swear by my sword.

Booth gave the great speech on suicide sitting near the footlights, his chin in his hand, his solitariness intensified by the sweep of the empty stage. The touches of emotion were so slight, yet to a sensitive listener suggested such depth of feeling, that the least touch more would have been unbearably crude. He began almost in a whisper:

To be, or not to be.

The audience sat rapt, its thousand faces as immovable in the half-light as a painted backdrop; its thousand minds alert, while the six words on which the actor had lavished as many weeks of labor seemed to be spoken not to but within each separate consciousness, as though each man and woman in that worldly place heard his own thoughts speak.

Booth was usually a bad stage lover; however, Hamlet's scene with Ophelia is renunciation rather than straight love-making and into the line

> I did love thee once

he poured so much poetry and tenderness that half his audience heaved an envious sigh.

"You felt," mused Mrs. John Sherwood, "that Ophelia was a poor creature; that if she had been grander, nobler, and more of a woman, the play need never have been written."

After his biting dismissal of Rosencrantz and Guildenstern,

> . . . though you can *fret* me, you cannot *play* upon me,

Booth flung away the recorder with so much fierce energy it sailed up into the flies. Then Polonius entered, and another member of the feminine half, Lucia Calhoun, considered his greeting to the obsequious old man,

> God bless you, sir!

was one of his finest single lines—"such utter weariness, such scorn of this miserable, dishonest, luxurious court; such despair of a noble nature set upon by ignoble natures; such impatience of this last crafty, unscrupulous, lying courtier, that the grace of speech is more bitter than a curse."

It was the awful quiet of his reproach to the Queen—

> Mother, you have my father much offended

—that indicted and terrified. He was never brutal or loud; when he addressed the Ghost of his father his voice quivered with love, and when the Ghost ordered,

> Speak to her, Hamlet,

he put his arm around the shuddering woman.

In the macabre place of burial Hamlet stood contemplating

the jester's skull. Said the actor Otis Skinner: "Booth's 'Alas, poor Yorick,' was the most melodious thing of the age. He breathed the word 'Yorick,' but did not speak it. The audience knew what he was saying, and the effect of his reading was tremendous."

In a voice that had already something of the detachment of the dying, Booth gave the lines that were his favorite in Shakespeare.

> If it be now, 'tis not to come; if it be not to
> come, it will be now; if it be not now, yet it will
> come: the readiness is all.

He was fire and elegance as he fenced with Laertes. He was a dashing, expert fencer and West Pointers in front sat on the edge of their seats and nodded approvingly. The match ended; the character of the scene changed. Hamlet, wounded to death and turning convulsively in Horatio's arms, breathed his last words in tones that the actor, who *as* an actor was now wholly forgotten by his audience, deliberately invested with sublime pathos.

> O! I die, Horatio;
> The potent poison quite o'er-crows my spirit.
> . . . The rest is silence.

And the silence in front continued after the curtain had glided down. There was not even applause until the orchestra struck up the "Dead March" from *Saul* and snapped the charm.

Booth never lost the name he made this season.

"The fashion and the passion, especially among women," was how the New York critic who signed himself "Nym Crinkle" described Booth's Hamlet.

The *Times* pronounced it "a part in which he has no living equal."

"What Garrick was in Richard III or Edmund Kean in Shylock, we are sure Edwin Booth is in Hamlet," suggested the editor of "The Easy Chair" of *Harper's* for April, 1865.

"Booth is altogether princely. . . . His playing throughout has an exquisite tone, like an old picture. . . . The cumulative sadness of the play was never so palpable as in his acting."

"Edwin Booth's Hamlet," writes William Winter, "was the simple, absolute realization of Shakespeare's haunted prince, and raised no question and left no room for inquiry whether the Danes in the Middle Ages wore velvet robes or had long flaxen hair. It was dark, mysterious, afflicted, melancholy."

Possibly the keenest comment came from John Wilkes who thought much the same as Winter. John could be generous in spite of rivalry and when at rehearsal one day some actors were discussing well-known Hamlets with him, including his own, "No, no, no!" insisted John, "there's but one Hamlet to my mind; that's my brother Edwin. You see, between ourselves, he *is* Hamlet—melancholy and all."

IV

Booth was engaged to be married again, and he explained that it was for Edwina's sake. The young woman was a Miss Blanch Hanel of Philadelphia; they planned to be married in the summer. Yet his allegiance and preoccupation remained unchanged, very strangely so for a man recently engaged. He kept Mary's books and belongings intimately about him and he wrote to Mrs. Cary: "I feel that all my actions have been and are influenced by her whose love is to me the strength and the wisdom of my spirit."

And again: "Do you think the freed spirit loses *all* interest in earthly things?"

He meant Mary and his friend Richard. Did they not rejoice together in heaven to see his improvement in his noble art? "I think they do." He felt mystically, literally, guided from above. "I cannot help but believe"—this was to Emma Cary, Richard's sister—"that there is a sufficient importance in my art to interest Mary and Richard still; that to a higher influence than the world believes I am moved by I owe the success I have achieved."

Acting every night, he was busy all day mounting a magnificent *Richelieu* to be on a level with his production of *Hamlet*, whose record run lasted just a hundred nights. All New York was proud, and a committee, which included Governor Hoffman, planned to present Booth with a fancy gold medal on the hundredth night, March 22, 1865. But when the date came the medal wasn't finished. Tiffany the jeweler was still working on it, and the presentation had to be postponed.

Another of Booth's brothers paid him a wry tribute. Junius admitted that while their father "could make the cold shivers crawl down my back, he couldn't possibly have played Hamlet as Edwin has done for one hundred consecutive performances and done it well."

It was sometime in February or March this year, so says Adam Badeau, that Booth, on his way to Philadelphia late one night, was waiting on the railway platform in Jersey City on the fringe of a crowd of passengers all buying sleeping-car space from the conductor, when he saw a tall young man, pressed by the crowd up against the car body, lose his footing as the train began to move and fall into the gap between the wheels and platform. Booth dropped his valise, stuck his ticket between his teeth, and striding forward, caught the helpless man by the coat collar and hauled him back up.

The young stranger, who recognized the actor from his photograph, panted gratefully: "That was a narrow escape, Mr. Booth." It was Robert Lincoln, son of the President.

Booth left New York for Boston near the end of March. He had expected to take Edwina, but when the time came his mother warned him against exposing the child to the bleak winds off the Boston fens, and Booth was twice warned after losing Mary from a fatal chill in Boston. So Edwina went to stay with her Aunt Asia, though he knew in advance how much he was bound to miss her. While he was there he would visit Mount Auburn, though not Dorchester. "It would kill me almost to visit Dorchester, and yet I can go to Mary's grave."

He was happier now than he had been. He had the comfort of his bride-to-be ("sent in answer to dear Mary's prayers,

I faithfully believe. She will do what Mary struggled, suffered, and died in doing"), and more important even than this, he had found himself at last in his profession. Convinced that his work exerted an influence for good "even beyond the range of *my* little world (the theater) I begin," he wrote to Emma Cary, "to feel really happy in my once uneasy sphere of action."

It was a profound and hard-won change. "I believe my growth in spirit is shown more in the appreciation of that which God sent me here to do, than in aught else that I have experienced in my life."

In the larger world the terrible War showed signs of ending. Besieged Petersburg could not hold out much longer. The Confederate Army was being beaten to its knees, still dealing heroic, though feeble, strokes like one of Booth's hard-pressed stage warriors. In Northern cities there was hope in the air. People sang in the streets and shook hands with strangers, promising one another: "It will be over by spring!"

Booth, too. "Oh, how I long for the spring!" he cried to the widowed Mrs. Cary, for whom the War was already over. "Yes, our news is indeed glorious. I am happy in it, and glory in it, although Southern-born."

CHAPTER 8

Johnny

Between the acting of a dreadful thing
And the first motion, all the interim is
Like a phantasma, or a hideous dream.
Julius Caesar, *Act II, scene 1*

 GENERAL GRANT's blue-coated soldiers surged into Richmond on April 3, 1865, almost in the same hour that the gray-coated Confederates galloped out of the city. On Palm Sunday six days later, in a frame house on the edge of Appomattox, General Lee, wearing the finest of his swords and a fresh uniform, faced the bluffly courteous Grant, who had not dressed up for the occasion, and signed the agreement surrendering his army.

It was as though one shout of joy rose from the North. A gigantic spree began to the clashing of bells, the boom-boom of cannon, the wail of whistles from factory roofs. Hundreds of thousands of buildings flapped with red, white, and blue bunting. Offices were slammed shut and homes left empty as people poured outside to join in parades to the cockerel-tooting of "Yankee Doodle," while drum majors flourished their batons, boys turned cartwheels, and men and women, drunk on free beer, reeled and whirled in the red light of bonfires.

Yet underrunning all was the note of religious thankfulness. The words were heard everywhere: "God be thanked"; "Thank God." Twenty thousand businessmen in New York bared their heads and sang "Praise God from Whom all Blessings Flow," and Trinity Church, thronged to capacity, quivered with the soaring chant by the choir of the *Te Deum*.

Booth was in his last week at the Boston Theater, staying with Orlando Tompkins in Franklin Square. On Friday night, April 14, he played Sir Edward Mortimer with William Warren as Adam Winterton. Early Saturday morning his Negro dresser rushed into his bedroom without waiting to be rung for and pushing a newspaper at him sobbed: "Oh, Massa Edwin, the President has been shot! And, oh, Massa Edwin, I'm afraid Massa John has done it!"

Long afterward, speaking as though the very shaping of the words hurt him, Booth confided to Joe Jefferson that when he was told this news "it was just as if I was struck on the forehead with a hammer."

Yet he accepted the fact instantly, even though it was not yet certain that John Wilkes was the guilty man. As Booth's eyes raced over the account of the lurid scene in Ford's Theater, of how the assassin leaped from the stage box and, flourishing a dagger, shrieked, "*Sic semper tyrannis!*" he knew beyond doubt that it was his brother—knew it, not from the sketchy description of the man's looks, but from the arrogance, the melodramatic devices of the leap, the flourish and hurled defiance, the fanaticism behind the act. The Booth blood had spoken. John Wilkes Booth—son of a father who wept to see the sparrow fall, yet in his frenzy could stab to kill—had shot the President. Edwin stood confounded. His brain refused what his instinct recognized.

"But . . . *Johnny!*" he whispered.

II

Some months earlier in Philadelphia the loving Asia had asked John in a low, anxious voice: "A man came here the other day for *Doctor* Booth. What does that mean? I thought it was someone who had known Joseph as a medical student."

John said lightly: "I'm he, if to be a doctor means a dealer in quinine."

The Southern hospitals were desperate for quinine; there was money and glory in smuggling it. Asia sat aghast. "*You* send it! How?"

"In horse collars and so forth."

"You run the blockade?"

"Yes."

"I knew now," writes Asia, "that my hero was a spy, a blockade-runner, a rebel! I set the terrible words before my eyes, and knew that each one meant death. . . . I found myself trying to think with less detestation of those two despicable characters in history, Major André and Benedict Arnold."

Blockade-running was the least of it. What she did not know was that her brother, living in a room in Washington at the National Hotel, had been for nearly a year plotting the "capture" as he liked to call it (the word sounded more heroic than "kidnaping") of President Lincoln, who was to be spirited away to Richmond and then exchanged for Confederate prisoners, badly needed by the South. The route must be traced in advance, all kinds of arrangements made; and this was the reason for John's comings and goings in an atmosphere of thick hush-hush.

The others involved were Michael O'Laughlin and Sam Arnold, second-rate young men who had been at school with him; David Herold, a moronic boy of around twenty who loved to shoot partridges and follow brass bands; George A. Atzerodt, German-born, once a carriage maker, thickset and with a face like a monkey's; and Lewis Paine, a tough-looking deserter from the Confederates.

The conspirators' meeting place was a boardinghouse on H Street run by Mrs. Mary Surratt, a widow and "the real Secesh." Her son John was in on the plot. Only a motive that dared not show itself to the light could have bound Wilkes

Booth to men so drearily unworthy of him. Asia once asked casually about O'Laughlin, whom she remembered as his school friend.

John gave a quick start. "What possessed you to ask about *him?* Forget his name." On another, later visit he handed his sister with a portentous air a sealed package to be opened "if anything should happen to me."

Junius saw John in Washington in February. He had always thought of his younger brother, whom he much admired, as a born leader, but now he changed his mind as he watched Johnny face in the direction of beleaguered Richmond and with streaming cheeks cry hysterically: "Virginia, Virginia!"

Their mother had sensed for some time that all was not well with her favorite. She wrote to him uneasily; she was miserably lonely in Edwin's house with the others away so much. "I don't think I am much cared for. . . . I never yet doubted your love and devotion to me—in fact I always gave you praise for being the fondest of all my boys, but since you leave me to grief I must doubt it. I am no Roman mother. I love my dear ones before country or anything else. Heaven guard you, is my constant prayer."

John was secretly engaged to Bessie Hale, the daughter of Senator John Parker Hale from New Hampshire, a Lincoln supporter. "Not exactly a secret," Mrs. Booth hinted, "as Edwin was told by someone you were paying great attention to a young lady in Washington. . . . Her father, I see, has his appointment, would he give his consent? You can but ask . . . you know in my partial eyes you are a fit match for any woman. . . .

"Now I am going to dinner by myself why are you not here to chat—and keep me company—no you are looking and saying soft things to one that don't love you half as well as your old mother does."

She was probably right. John was not a one-girl man. His good-time favorite was Ella Starr, whose sister Nellie ran a high-class whore house on Ohio Avenue, and about this time he kept a tryst with Eva, the daughter of another senator, who scribbled on an old envelope:

> For of all sad words from tongue or pen
> The saddest are these—it might have been.
>   March 5th, 1865
>   In John's room

Two plans for the kidnaping had misfired. Between these fiascos John, wearing a slouch hat, gauntlets, spurs, and a satanic scowl, was present at Lincoln's second inauguration on March 4. Through Bessie Hale's influence he had a ticket for the platform, where he stood quite near the President.

It was later in March that he called on his friend Charley Warwick, an actor who rented a back room in a house across from Ford's Theater. Having tugged off his boots and slung his spurs across the gas fixture, John filled his pipe, then stretched out on Warwick's bed and smoked himself to sleep. "Who would think," writes Warwick, "to look on that handsome face, so calm and peaceful in repose, that beneath it slumbered a volcano? Who could raise the curtain of the near future and peer upon the picture of the dying President on that very bed?"

Delay and failure had made John savage. He paced Mrs. Surratt's parlor, lashing his boot with his whip. On the day Richmond fell he signed a hotel register in Newport, Rhode Island: "J. W. Booth & Lady." The girl with him was very likely Ella; they were given room No. 3. John was on his way to Boston, where he had a last altercation with Edwin over the War. "Good-by, Ned," was his parting. "You and I could never agree about that."

Back in Washington, on April 11, a soft, misty evening, he lingered with Dave Herold among the thousands on the White House lawn listening to Lincoln speaking from a balcony in favor of giving the ballot to the Negro. "Nigger citizenship!" hissed John to Herold when the speech was over and the brass band was pumping out "Dixie." "Now, by God, I'll put him through!"

The ending of the War had made kidnaping the President obsolete. It was the last stroke: To be thus crushingly thwarted in his sacred determination to rescue the South from tyranny, and in doing so to make his name flame forever in men's minds, had set at work strange, unhappy and inherited impulses in John Wilkes Booth.

During the ten days after Richmond's fall Jack Deery, who kept a bar near Grover's Theater, noticed that his friend and good customer Booth who, "while a steady drinker, I had always found to respect the amenities and 'drink square,' as we used to say . . . —he could absorb an astonishing quantity and still retain the bearing of a gentleman— . . . now sometimes drank at my bar as much as a quart of brandy in less than two hours. . . . It was more than a spree, I could see that. . . . He seemed to be crazed by some stress of inward feeling, but only one who was very intimate with him could have told it."

"If Wilkes Booth was mad," said Asia later, "his mind lost its balance between the fall of Richmond and the terrific end."

III

April 14 was Good Friday. Like most actors John got up late, and it was about noon when he stopped at Ford's Theater to collect his mail. As he swung along Tenth Street, accenting his steps with the tap of his cane, Harry Ford, brother of the theater owner, standing at the door with some friends, turned and said emphatically: "Here comes the handsomest man in Washington!"

In the lobby John heard for the first time that the President and Mrs. Lincoln and General and Mrs. Grant were to see the show this night. About four hours later Charley Warwick met him on Pennsylvania Avenue. Booth was riding a yellow mare, "sitting his horse like a Centaur," Warwick noted. "He was faultlessly dressed, elegant riding boots with a slender steel spur were on his feet."

Booth reined in his horse and leaned over to shake hands. A circle of acquaintances seemed to spring out of the ground around him and he dominated them all from the height of his horse, talking and laughing and lifting his chin in a fascinating, theatrical awareness of his power to please until a carriage rolled by down the avenue toward the railway station. Inside sat a familiar burly figure biting on a cigar. "Hallo," cried Booth, "there goes Grant."

As if the sight reminded him of something, he said good-by, wheeled his horse around, and trotted off in the direction of Ford's Theater. General Grant had decided to send regrets for the evening and he and his wife were leaving town, but Booth did not know this.

The play at Ford's was Tom Taylor's comedy *Our American Cousin*, starring Laura Keene. Miss Keene's chief comedian Harry Hawk was to act Asa Trenchard, a role created by Jefferson. Also in the cast was old George Spear, who had broken the news of their father's death to Edwin in California when Johnny was only fourteen.

At seven o'clock John left his hotel, asking the clerk as he swaggered by the desk if he meant to go to Ford's. "There'll be some fine acting there tonight!"

Then he passed out into the spring evening. A mist from the Potomac hung over the city. Organ-snatches of the *Miserere* floated occasionally from Catholic churches, draped inside with mourning for Christ's passion and death. In the saloon next to Ford's Booth shouted for brandy. The talk turned on actors and one of the drinkers twitted him with: "You'll never be the actor your father was!"

A peculiar expression stole into Booth's face as he answered: "When I leave the stage I'll be the most famous man in America."

President Lincoln's empty carriage was waiting outside the theater. The doorkeeper Buckingham—"Buck" to his friends —stood with his back to the entrance and his arm across it to keep people out when someone behind him gently pried up two fingers of his hand and shook them. He wheeled around and there was Wilkes Booth. "You'll not want a ticket from *me?*" Booth suggested winningly.

Buck melted into smiles and introduced Booth to some men from out of town lounging about the lobby as "our distinguished young actor."

After an interval, during which he fortified himself with another brandy at the bar, Booth strolled ostentatiously into the theater, humming a tune, and up to the balcony where he leaned against the far wall, glancing back and forth from the bright shell of the stage to the shadowy audience. When he moved next his bearing had completely altered. He made not a sound nor a spare motion as he glided down the sloping side aisle past row on row of absorbed spectators.

The soldier supposed to be guarding the President's box had sneaked around the corner to a seat in the balcony, and when Booth noiselessly eased open the door of the anteroom that led into the box, not a soul challenged him. He put his eye to a gimlet hole in the box door; it was suspected afterward that he had bored this hole himself during the afternoon. There sat Abraham Lincoln in his special rocking chair. The inside of the box was like a little drawing room. It had a carpet, and the walls were papered in deep red with a design of flowers; there were armchairs and a sofa. Mrs. Lincoln, her plump shoulders bare in a billowy evening dress, sat beside her husband, and beyond them were their guests, a Major Rathbone and his fiancée. All watched the performance.

Down on the stage the "English society lady" Mrs. Mountchessington swept into the wing after depositing a snub on the American Asa Trenchard, left standing by himself.

MRS. MOUNTCHESSINGTON. I am sure, Mr. Trenchard, you are not used to the manner of good society, and that alone will excuse the impertinence of which you have been guilty.
> (*Exit. Trenchard, left alone, soliloquizes.*)
TRENCHARD. Don't know the manners of good society, eh? Well, I guess I know enough to turn you inside out, old gal—you sockdologizing old man-trap.

This was the moment in the play, when one actor stood on-stage alone, that Booth had counted on. He stole into the box, silent as a current of air, aimed a tiny pocket derringer at Lincoln's attentively bowed head, gave a half-shout, half-roar, then fired. His cry was, *Sic semper tyrannis*, the noble Brutus' cry to Caesar and the motto of Virginia, which many people swore afterward they had heard him yell as he crossed the stage. Lincoln slid sideways in his rocking chair; his head fell gently against the red wallpaper.

Major Rathbone sprang up to grapple with Booth who shook him off. Booth forged to the front of the box, put his hand on the rail and vaulted over. One of the spurs Warwick had admired caught with a tearing sound in the hated Union flag draped over the box front, and he landed with a crash on the apron, his left leg folded under him; a bone had been snapped just above the ankle. "If I hadn't been very courageous," he boasted later, "I'd have given up right there. I thought for an instant I was going to faint."

Wrenching himself to his feet, he crossed the stage in a motion "like the hopping of a bullfrog," under the very nose of Harry Hawk as Asa Trenchard. In the wing he brushed between Laura Keene and a young actor named Ferguson, standing ready for their entrances, brushed them so close that his brandied breath warmed their faces; struck aside Miss Keene's tentatively raised hand; plunged down a passage, dragging his hurt leg and slashing with his dagger at two men in his way, and burst through a back door out into the alley where his yellow mare waited. Except for hoofbeats on the cobblestones heard by some of the actors backstage, the theater was comparatively quiet, with only a rising hum of astonishment until a scream from Mrs. Lincoln froze everyone's blood. "He has shot the President!"

The audience rose, as audiences so often had risen like one man at a Booth's exit. Men swarmed over the footlights, a surprising number brandishing revolvers. "What happened?" "Who was it?"

A few people let drop the name Wilkes Booth; they believed they had recognized him. In nearly the same moment the name was being spoken far more confidently by Booth himself.

"Who are you?" the sergeant at the Navy Yard bridge challenged the rider on the steaming, bright-skinned mare who galloped down on him in the moonlight.

"My name is Booth," was the ringing answer. The sergeant let him pass. Far behind him in the glare and hubbub of Ford's Theater, where people fell over one another, swooned, were trampled on amid screams and hoarse exclamations, six soldiers carried the President slowly out of the box, slowly through the anteroom, up the balcony aisle, down the stairs, across the lobby, and into Tenth Street by the same route that Booth had followed thirty minutes earlier. They carried Lincoln across the street into the house and the room that Charley Warwick had occupied and laid him down on the bed that Booth had lain on.

IV

Later that night the actor John McCullough tore open the door of Edwin Forrest's bedroom in the Metropolitan Hotel in New York and gasped out to Forrest that Lincoln had just been assassinated and that Wilkes Booth was said to have done it.

"But I don't believe it," McCullough added.

"Well, I do," snarled Forrest. "All those God damned Booths are crazy!"

In Boston several members of Edwin Booth's audience, creeping home in the horsecar from the Boston Theater, paid almost no attention to one of the passengers who tried to convince them he had heard the news of Lincoln's assassination over the electric telegraph.

When Lincoln died early next morning, the heavy bells began to toll far and wide across the country. Edwin Booth heard them tolling in Boston. Lincoln was dead; the crime had become murder. Booth sent off a telegram to his mother, begging her to keep up her courage: it was not yet established that their John was the murderer. Then he sat alone, his head in his hands. Tompkins' house where he was staying was draped in black immediately, as were most other houses.

In the middle of the morning a message was laid before Booth from Henry Jarrett, the current manager of the Boston Theater; the theater's façade was also being hung with crepe. "The President of the United States," wrote Jarrett, "has fallen by the hand of an assassin. . . . Suspicion points to one nearly related to you as the perpetrator of this horrid deed. . . . With this knowledge, I have concluded to close the Boston Theater."

Booth roused himself to answer: "While mourning, in common with all other loyal hearts, the death of the President, I am oppressed by a private woe not to be expressed in words."

The bells tolled in Philadelphia. John Sleeper Clarke was shaving when he heard a shriek from Asia, who had had the morning paper brought up. While he was trying to calm his wife, a United States marshal pounded on the front door, threw a guard around the house and forbade anyone to leave or enter.

The bells were tolling in Cincinnati where Junius Booth was filling an engagement. He wandered into the hotel lobby after breakfast and the clerk warned him not to set foot outside, as a mob, hungry for a lynching, had ripped down his playbills all over town. Junius looked simply bewildered. When the news was broken to him "he was the most horrified man I ever saw," the eager clerk told a ring of reporters. "For the moment he was overcome by the shock. I suggested to him that it would be better for him to go to his room, and he did so. He had scarcely gone upstairs before the room he left was filled with people. The mob was fully five hundred in number. They would have hanged Booth in a minute if they could have laid hands upon him. We finally smuggled him away."

In New York Lilian Woodman drove down Fifth Avenue through the tolling bells between rows of flags flown at half-mast to the house on Nineteenth Street, which already looked sinister. People on the sidewalk pointed at it fearfully. In the front room Mrs. Booth sat with Rosalie. The mother was past grief; her world had turned over. A few hours earlier, if someone had told her John had blown his brains out, she would have counted it the heaviest cross God could have laid on her. Now it was all she had left for which to pray. She moaned: "O God, if this be true, let him shoot himself. Let him not live to be hanged."

Just then the postman blew his whistle and handed in a letter from John, written the day before, when he was a peaceful citizen. "I only drop you these few lines to let you know I am well. . . . With best love to you all I am your affectionate son ever."

Aldrich wrote to Edwin: "Is there anything I can do for you here or elsewhere? God knows my heart is tender for you this day."

Faithful William Warren hurried over from the Boston Museum to sustain his fellow player in this hour of shame for their profession. Warren had comforted Booth at Mary's funeral. He found it harder to give comfort now.

In St. Louis Junius' eldest daughter, Blanche, a talented actress and a passionate Secessionist, was in her bedroom, with some fetching new costumes laid out on the bed, contemplating a bright future in the mirror in the person of her Boothesque self, when her Negro maid ran in with the story of "Nunkee John."

In Richmond John T. Ford, owner of the theater where the crime was committed, heard a report that Edwin Booth was the murderer. "Impossible!" Ford exclaimed. "He's not in Washington." Then with the same shock of recognition that had come to Edwin, Ford reflected that the foolhardy Wilkes Booth was there.

On Easter Sunday, April 16, Edwin wrote to Adam Badeau: "You know, Ad, how I have labored since my dear Mary was called from me to establish a name that my child and all my friends might be proud of. You know how I have always toiled for the comfort and welfare of my family. . . . You know how loyal I have been from the first of this damned rebellion. . . .

"Alas, how frightful is the spectacle! What shall become of

me? Poor mother! I go to New York today expecting to find her either dead or dying. . . . I was two days ago one of the happiest men alive. . . . Now what am I? Oh, how little did I dream, my boy, when on Friday night I was as Sir Edward Mortimer exclaiming, 'Where is my honor now? Mountains of shame are piled upon me!' that I was not acting but uttering the fearful truth."

After Booth had been questioned and his trunks searched by deputy marshals he was free to leave Boston. Tompkins went with him, and a few courageous friends met them at the New York station early on Monday morning, April 17. There was nothing to be said. Booth's face was perfectly stony as he stepped off the train.

Men's sense of fitness was offended because Abraham Lincoln had met his end in a playhouse. On Easter Sunday and for weeks to come the theater and its people were anathematized from Northern pulpits.

"Would that Mr. Lincoln had fallen elsewhere than at the very gates of Hell," groaned one clergyman.

And another: "We remember with sorrow the place of his death. . . . It was a poor place to die in."

And still another: "The theater is one of the last places to which a good man should go . . . the illumined and decorated gateway through which thousands are constantly passing into the embrace of gaiety and folly, intemperance and lewdness, infamy and ruin."

It was a sad time for actors. They were reminded once again that they were vagabonds. The martyred Lincoln's blood was on their heads. Those who had known Wilkes Booth bore a special stigma, yet they did not wholly cast him off. "He was so young, so bright, so gay," mourned Clara Morris. "Many a painted cheek," she went on, "showed runnels made by bitter tears, and one old actress, with quivering lips, exclaimed: 'One woe doth tread upon another's heel, so fast they follow!' but with no thought of quoting, and God knows the words expressed the situation perfectly."

The hue and cry sounded: "Arrest *all* actors!" Ugly-tempered crowds milled about stage entrances. When a Washington storekeeper bravely defended the people of Ford's Theater, who were his best customers, the mob threw a rope around his neck; he was barely saved from being lynched. Because Wilkes Booth was so much at home in Ford's, the Secret Service was convinced someone in the company had been his accomplice. John T. Ford, Laura Keene, and Harry Hawk were arrested, though Miss Keene and Hawk were soon let go through the intervention of Lutz, her gambler lover. The actors at Ford's had to report to the police daily.

But it was the helpless Booths who were caught like insects in the circle of a spotlight. Hundreds of letters, truculently and foully abusive, and mostly unsigned, were received by every member of the wretched family: "We hate the name of Booth leave quick or remember. . . . Bullets are marked for you. . . . Revolvers are loaded with which to shoot you down. . . . Your house will be burnt. . . . Your life will be the penalty if you tarry heare 48 hours longer."

Sensation hunters overran the Maryland farm and wondered aloud if the Judas tree on the lawn mightn't be taken as a symbol of the former household. A Belair Negro, hostile to the Booths, gabbled malevolently of their secret "doin's." A neighbor swore that Johnny had been a cruel boy who tortured the forest animals. An abandoned trench, which John and Asia had dug one summer looking for arrowheads, was rediscovered as "an underground store for secreted arms." The Clarkes' rambling old house in Philadelphia (reporters described it as "mysteriously built") was ransacked twice by police. Every scrap of paper belonging to John was confiscated including a small photograph of him that he had hung over the beds of Asia's children, saying charmingly: "Remember me, babies, in your prayers."

Just as the North went on a spree of joy when the War was won, so now she went the other way: on an orgy of sorrow, a spree of grief. Once again cannon boomed. The bells that had pealed now tolled everlastingly, and the drums were muffled. Most men wore black bands and even the skies were leaden those first few days.

On April 21 the solemn funeral cavalcade with Lincoln's body set out from Washington. In the procession escorting the hearse along Pennsylvania Avenue a torn flag was carried, the flag that had caught Wilkes Booth's spur and might yet, through the injury inflicted on him, catch the fleeing criminal.

On April 24 the body of the man Wilkes Booth had murdered arrived in New York, after being borne ceremoniously across on the ferry from Jersey City. Edwin Booth was in New York then, where every building was festooned with black crepe. He was in New York when Lincoln's body, drawn by sixteen white horses in funeral trappings and followed by floats, wreaths, and floral monuments, moved toward City Hall between fields of faces to the nerve-racking beat of the funeral drums. He was in New York while the body lay on a catafalque on somber display at City Hall, and thousands on thousands of people filed past to look down on it.

Alongside the columns bordered in black that described at lugubrious length the funeral train's progress, the condition of the body, and the royal reception in city after city, the papers ran stories about all the Booths. It was suggested that John was an eater of opium, but his taste for women provided the best copy. Typical was one reporter's tale of a well-born young girl in Philadelphia who had pursued John and been squarely warned by him that he felt no love for her, "though a sufficient desire." "Go home," John was quoted as saying, "and beware of actors." But the girl persisted and was debauched.

Another story, which was true, told how the actress Henrietta Irving, during a drunken evening in John's hotel room in Albany, had stabbed him in the face, almost spoiling his profile. Within the last few days John's sporting-house sweetheart Ella Starr had unsuccessfully tried to kill herself. She swallowed chloroform, then lay down to die with his picture under her pillow.

The authorities discovered that Junius' daughter Marion was born while he was still married to the mother of his first child Blanche. The public was reminded of Edwin's former drinking. It was served up the morsel of the elder Junius Booth's adultery. The murderer of Lincoln was born out of wedlock. The whole fantastic tribe was illegitimate; their strain of Jewish blood made them kin to Fagin and Shylock. In their rout and agony the Booths might have echoed the defiance of Edmund in *King Lear* when he cried:

Now, gods, stand up for bastards!

The Clarkes remembered the package John had given Asia. They took it out of Clarke's safe and opened it, finding inside a letter written the previous November by John to his mother in which he entirely cleared his family of any complicity in Lincoln's kidnaping—his plan at that time—and also a much longer letter addressed "To Whom It May Concern." In this last he had tried to explain his motives for the kidnap plot; it was a shrill, self-pluming, illogical apologia. Clarke turned over both letters to the United States Marshal. Because the inflammatory "To Whom It May Concern" had been in his possession, he was arrested, sent under guard to Washington and thrown into Old Capitol Prison, where John T. Ford was, and the conspirators who had been rounded up: Mrs. Surratt, Paine, Atzerodt, O'Laughlin, and Arnold. John Surratt had fled to Canada, and Dave Herold had escaped into the night with Booth.

Asia expected a child in August, a child that John had hoped would be named for him. Her doctor certified she was unfit to travel, otherwise she too would have been haled to Washington. A polite detective was assigned to follow her as she paced heavily from room to room and to read her letters, which she placed in his hand without look or word; many of them were from Edwin. "Think no more of John as your brother," Edwin had written, "he is dead to us now as he soon must be to all the world, but imagine the boy you loved to be in that better part of his spirit in another world."

And again: "I have had a heartbroken letter from the poor little girl to whom he had promised so much happiness." This was Bessie Hale.

The young detective implored Asia to let his wife ("who actually cried to think how ill-treated and sick Mrs. Clarke was") take over his duty. Asia cut him short, "Obey your orders, but tell your wife I thank her very kindly"—adding later, "I should rather have been watched by ten men who could keep quiet than by one chattering female."

Another to feel the hand of the law fall on his shoulder was Junius, who shortly before the murder had written to John urging him in a brotherly way to give up the "oil business." Federal agents were suspicious of what "oil business" meant (it meant what it said; John had been speculating in oil stock) and Junius was clapped into jail. "I wish John had been killed before the assassination for the sake of the family," were his bleak words, almost his only words, as he drooped beside his guard in the train to Washington where on arrival he filled another cell in Old Capitol. Perhaps their name's dishonor meant more to the Booths than the blood on their brother's hands.

Owing to the pressure brought to bear on the authorities by his influential friends, Edwin was not arrested, though his movements were watched. Tom Aldrich stayed with him in the house on Nineteenth Street. Little Edwina, blissfully unaware of her Nunkee's change into a bogeyman, a threat to frighten other children, was still in Philadelphia with her Aunt Asia.

It was dangerous for a Booth to be seen abroad, but sometimes after dark Edwin and Aldrich slipped out for air, keeping close together in the shadow of the brownstones. With the rest of the family Booth waited stoically for news of John's capture. To his southern niece Blanche De Bar Booth, to whom John had been almost like a brother, Edwin wrote during this trial of waiting: "I would have you, Blanche, if you can believe me true and worthy of some share of your affection, to open your heart to me when care oppresses you, to confide in me as your dear friend and loving uncle."

He never spoke of John, whose portrait hung in his bedroom and had not been removed. When he and Aldrich lay down at night the light of the street lamps shone in through the shutters fastened against the hostile city, and in the faint gleam the portrait seemed to come alive and to watch them intently as they closed their eyes, though not to sleep. Each knew that the other was thinking with pity of the fugitive.

V

"He may take the wings of the morning and fly to the uttermost parts of the sea! He may make his bed in hell; but he will not escape," thundered an outraged divine to his congregation in Boston. The manhunt was on.

The War Department circulated bills informing all citizens that

THE MURDERER

Of our late beloved President, Abraham Lincoln

IS STILL AT LARGE

$50,000 REWARD

Will be paid by this Department for his apprehension.

BOOTH is Five Feet 7 or 8 inches high, slender build, high forehead, black hair, black eyes, and wore a heavy black moustache, which there is some reason to believe has been shaved off.

Hundreds of people had seen the murderer. Turbaned seers in dingy back rooms saw him in their crystal balls; astrologers read the stars to locate him. Police stations filled up with him;

he had already been arrested in Canada, New England, out west as far as Chicago. The real Wilkes Booth was much nearer Washington than any of these places. By April 22 he had got no further than the Maryland shore of the Potomac at Nanjemoy Stores, where he crouched in the marshes waiting for his chance to cross into Virginia.

Day was just breaking, and Dave Herold had slunk off to the nearest house to beg for food. Booth's clothes were wet and slimed; his mustache was gone; his stubbly cheeks had fallen in; his skin was gray; his eyes glared out from pits of shadow. His broken leg had been roughly set, but gangrene had begun and was spreading through his body. Keeping his head cautiously lowered and slanting his page to catch the pale daylight, he wrote in pencil in his diary: "After being hunted like a dog through swamps, woods, and last night being chased by gunboats till I was forced to return wet, cold, and starving, with every man's hand against me, I am here in despair. And why? For doing what Brutus was honored for—what made Tell a hero."

He had read every newspaper he could lay his hand on, and what had he learned? That he had brought misery on his family, that every Booth that breathed was under suspicion of treason, and that a nation sickened with sorrow and rage compared Lincoln to Christ and himself to Judas. Unhappy the city that had nursed him—"pity, oh, pity unhappy Baltimore."

Speaking through the mouths of their public men the North raked him with curses, the South repudiated him. "At the moment he struck down Mr. Lincoln he also struck himself from existence. There can be no more a J. Wilkes Booth in any country. If caught he will be hanged. If he escapes he must dwell in a solitude. He has the brand of Cain upon his brow."

"I am sure," Booth wrote in his diary, "there is no pardon in the Heaven for me, since man condemns me so. . . . God, try and forgive me, and bless my mother."

He had perfectly expected to be hailed as a hero. All during his flight he had boasted of his deed, acknowledging and even flaunting his identity as a sort of reward to whoever gave him and Herold a helping hand. "Do you know who I am? Yes! I am John Wilkes Booth, the slayer of Abraham Lincoln!"

It was as well for him now, lying disconsolate, that he had no vision of the place he had won for himself in history. Already there was mourning for Lincoln's death among the British masses, the French masses, and students of Paris; in Scandinavian harbors flags hung at half-mast. And as the name of Lincoln was to become famous to the far ends of the earth so, coupled with it, was Booth's deed to became infamous, though his name might be forgotten. Years later Count Leo Tolstoy, traveling in a remote, savage region of the Caucasus, put a photograph of Lincoln in the hand of a Circassian tribesman who looked down at it so mournfully that Tolstoy questioned him. "I am sad," the man answered, "because I feel sorry that he had to die by the hand of a villain."

But this was a future Booth could not know. In the swamps of Maryland he lay in hiding, writing painfully on his cramped page; and now a great gust of reviving arrogance whirled up in him, fanning his pride, so near its embers; floating like a red haze in front of his eyes; blinding and inflating him. "I do not repent the blow I struck. . . . I think I have done well. Though I am abandoned, with the curse of Cain upon me, when, if the world knew my heart, that one blow would have made me great, though I did desire no greatness. Tonight I try to escape these bloodhounds once more. Who, who can read his fate? God's will be done. I have too great a soul to die like a criminal. O, may He, may He spare me that, and let me die bravely."

Four days later, when lower Maryland and all Virginia were bristling with soldiers, a troop of cavalry commanded by Colonel Everton Conger and Lieutenant Luther Baker surrounded a tobacco barn belonging to a farmhouse in a forsaken stretch of country near Port Royal, Virginia. It was about two in the morning of April 26. Inside the barn lurked Booth and Herold, awakened suddenly by footsteps outside.

"You must surrender in there," roared Baker. "We give you five minutes."

On the white-painted, pillared gallery of the little southern farmhouse the women of the farmer's family huddled in their nightdresses, listening to the male voices bandying challenges back and forth. The Negro farmhands swayed goggle-eyed below. They could all hear the trapped Booth as he called: "There's a man in here who wants to surrender."

The barn door opened just a slit to let out Herold who blundered into the starlight, reaching for the sky, prancing and jittering in a cakewalk of terror. "I always liked Mr. Lincoln's jokes," he simpered.

"If you don't shut up we'll cut off your damned head," growled one of the soldiers as they tied him still chattering to a tree.

Booth, alone now and as fantastically outnumbered as any hero of the melodramas he starred in, tried to go on parleying. "Captain," he called ringingly, "give me a chance. Draw off your men and I'll fight them singly. Give a lame man a show."

When no answer came he went on almost gaily: "Well, my brave boys, you can prepare a stretcher for me. One more stain on the old banner!"

Colonel Conger tossed a burning brand inside the barn. A heap of straw caught fire and the interior was lit up brilliantly. Through the horizontal crevices between the slats the lone, black figure of Booth became instantly as visible to his audience as if he stood on the stage of a theater. "Behind the blaze," recalled Conger, "I saw him standing upright, leaning on a crutch. He looked like his brother Edwin, whom he so much resembled that I believed for a moment the whole pursuit to have been a mistake. . . . His eyes were lustrous like fever, and swelled and rolled in terrible beauty. In vain he peered; the blaze that made him visible concealed his enemy. A second he turned glaring at the fire as if to leap upon it and extinguish it, but it made such headway that this was a futile impulse and he dismissed it. As calmly as upon a battlefield a veteran stands amidst the hail of ball and shell and plunging iron, Booth, shifting his carbine to his left hand and drawing his revolver, turned at a man's stride and, in a kind of limping-halting jump, pushed for the door and the last resolve of death, which we name despair, sat on his high, bloodless forehead."

There was a loud crack over the hiss of flames. The watchers saw Booth gather himself up, seem to tower above his true height, then fall headlong. One of the men outside, Sergeant Boston Corbett, immediately claimed to have shot him. But Booth had threatened repeatedly to kill himself if he were cornered, and many of the friends who knew him best were always sure this was what he had done.

Lieutenant Baker leaped inside and dragged out Booth's body. Booth lay unconscious on the dewy grass under a locust tree while the officers stooped over him. It was the dark, cool hour before dawn. Booth might have been a soldier, honorably wounded, in the arms of his comrades. Water was poured into his mouth. He blew it out feebly, opened his eyes and moved his lips to shape the words: "Tell . . . mother. . . ." Then he fainted again. When he came to, he finished his sentence: "Tell . . . mother . . . I . . . died . . . for . . . my . . . country."

Baker, who was washing Booth's face with ice water, pointed out his wound, which was in the back of the neck. The bullet had passed through the spinal column.

The heat from the burning barn was getting so fierce that Booth was carried by the shoulders and feet up to the farmhouse porch. The soldiers were proceeding inside when their burden, overcome by a longing for the open air, begged weakly: "No, no, let me die here."

"The damned Rebel is still living!" drawled one of the officers.

A straw mattress was laid across the doorsill and Booth was eased down onto it so that he rested half in and half out of the house. His arms, legs, and body from the waist down were paralyzed. His eyes screamed with agony. He gasped: "Water, water," then hoarsely begged to be turned over on his side, then on his back, then on his face.

"You can't lie on your face!" objected Colonel Conger.

"Kill me, kill me," pleaded Booth.

In the east the sky was turning red; the meadows began to be flooded with pink light. A young woman, belonging to the family on whose porch Booth lay in suffering, had stolen down from the gallery and drew near him as though pulled by strings, knelt, dipped her handkerchief in water and moistened his lips. She slipped a pillow under his head and stroked his forehead. The morning air, steadily lightening, made the others shiver, but Booth did not feel it. His body was like a sheet of flame. In a gurgling voice he cried again: "Kill me, kill me."

"We don't want you to die. We want you to get well," retorted Lieutenant Baker. Both officers, without waiting the few minutes necessary for all to be over for Booth, were pawing through his clothes. The meager discoveries were passed around: a knife, a pipe, a nail file, a compass, a diamond pin and, found fastened to the helpless man's undershirt, his little red leather-bound diary with a pocket in the back containing the photographs of Bessie Hale and four pretty actresses.

While the officers, talking across Booth, discussed arrangements to carry his dead body back to Washington, the dying man indicated he wished his paralyzed arms to be lifted so that he could see them. He stared at his hands, and his lips moved for the last time, producing a thread of sound, as he whispered: "Useless, useless."

A moment or two later he died. The attentive Southern woman asked in a low voice if she might have a lock of his hair, which was cut off and given to her.

VI

Mrs. Booth in New York had had a telegram from Philadelphia urging her to come at once, as Asia was ill. Launt Thompson drove with her to the ferry for Jersey City. In the street he heard a newsboy yell: DEATH OF JOHN WILKES BOOTH! CAPTURE OF HIS COMPANION! He slammed down the carriage windows, made an excuse to draw the curtains and talked loudly to cover the shouting but, like the refrain of a song, the same strident cry met them at every crossing.

When they reached the ferry, Thompson shepherded Mrs. Booth into a quiet corner on deck. No one recognized her behind her widow's veil. At the Jersey City station, where Edwin had rescued Robert Lincoln, Thompson settled her in the train, then left her to buy a newspaper. Hurrying back to say good-by, he put the paper in her hand, and shielding her with his body from the passengers in the aisle, he said: "You will need now all your courage. The paper in your hand will tell you what, unhappily, we must all wish to hear. John Wilkes is dead."

The one topic in the crowded car was the murderer's death, which most people agreed had been too good for him. He had cheated the gallows. Behind the broad pages of her newspaper Mrs. Booth read the story of her child's last hours. Over the coarse voices, his living voice spoke to her intimately, though all the world might read his message: "Tell mother I died for my country." She gave no cry, made no sudden movement. Those sitting near her noticed nothing strange. Her grief was like an inward bleeding.

Asia Clarke was in bed when old Mr. Hemphill, employed at Philadelphia's Walnut Street Theater, asked to be let in to see her. In the middle of the room he steadied himself by a hand on the table and refused to meet the young woman's eyes. His face worked; he had known Johnny. The very way he stood told his news, and Asia demanded tonelessly: "Is it over?"

"Yes, madam."

"Taken?"

"Yes."

"Dead?"

"Yes, madam."

She sobbed with thankfulness. As she fell back, her face to the wall, she heard the old retainer, who was sobbing himself, leave the room, and after an interval, the street door close.

Edwin Booth had a number of letters from self-styled "widows" of his brother who wrote from various cities demanding that the family acknowledge their claims. One of these women got hold of poor Rosalie and swindled her of what money she had.

John Clarke and Junius were let out of prison. Clarke, furious that Edwin had gone scot free, was boiling with rage at his bad luck at having married into the family. The Booths were all "Iagos, male and female"; he loathed their "secretiveness." He demanded a divorce from Asia, "which would be *his* only salvation now."

In the end he stayed with his wife, but Johnny's warning, once enigmatic, flashed back to Asia: "Bear in mind that you're only a professional steppingstone."

Not only her husband, but also some lifelong friends, showed Asia a side of human nature she would not have believed in, had it not been proved to her. "There is no solidity in Love," she wrote bitterly, "no truth in Friendship, no steadiness in Marital Faith."

The nurse she had engaged for her confinement refused to attend her. The family doctor, though he had seen the Clarkes through many illnesses, could barely be induced to come to the house. Among those who did come was a blond young actor named Claud Burroughs who prattled glibly that he had been sent secretly to Mrs. Clarke by her brother Edwin to obtain "the paper she had placed in her bosom."

Asia later asked Edwin if this were true. "I *never* sent Burroughs or any other actor, or any human being to your house on any mission or with any message whatsoever," he told her.

Then she had one letter, alone of its kind, and therefore more precious—"sufficient," she cried, "to set the faithlessness of the world aside, and almost revive belief in human goodness." It was from a young actress, one of those whose photograph had been found in John's diary. Effie Germon, a family connection of the Jeffersons, had played the title role in *Aladdin, or The Wonderful Lamp*, in Washington at Grover's Theater, the rival of Ford's, on the night of the assassination.

"Dear Madam," her letter ran, "Although a perfect stranger to you, I take the liberty of offering my sympathy and aid to you in your great sorrow and sickness. If my mother or myself can be of the slightest use to you in any way in this world we should be only too happy. I should have offered before, but illness prevented. May God help and bless you, is the constant prayer of EFFIE GERMON."

Edwin's friends also showed their true colors. Elizabeth Stoddard ("a good hater," one of her circle called her) wrote to her brother in words that had a shrill crow of satisfaction: "I never was more overwhelmed by any outside matter than by this. . . . Your news of Edwin's marriage is about as astounding as the rest. Is it Laura Edmonds or Mattie Woodman? Do find out. Two or three nights ago I had a dream of him. He will undoubtedly go to the devil sooner or later. *All* the elements that make up life are in his composition, except one—that of courage. John B. has brute courage. Do you believe at all in human fidelity? Think of Edwin's marrying again. I pity the woman, unless she has a dramatic genius superior to his and then she can overpower him. I shall be most curious to learn who the person is . . . but won't this business break it up?"

Booth had assured the good Cambridge spinster Emma Cary, one of those whose friendship had not been found wanting, that in Philadelphia "there is one great heart firm and faster bound to me than ever," and he meant his fiancée, Blanch Hanel. But Mrs. Stoddard's cool surmise was right. Blanch Hanel's father put his foot down against marriage to a Booth, and the engagement was broken off.

Announcement of John's death brought Booth an overdue letter of condolence from Richard Stoddard, which began without other salutation: "Edwin—When I heard of the dreadful calamity which has fallen upon us my sorrow was twofold—for the nation and for you. My impulse was to write you at once and say so, but I did not for several reasons.

"First, I could say nothing which could for a moment miti-
gate your grief or which you would not be likely to hear from
others.

"Second, it seemed best to me that you should be left to
yourself alone with your woe and God.

"Third, I knew that if you ever understood me—and I think
you did once—you would understand my silence as well as my
speech.

"Fourth, I have always made it a rule of my life when I have
lost a friend or a friend has lost me to take no step, and to
permit none to be taken with my sanction, toward renewing
the old relationship. There is no cement in this world . . .
strong enough to mend a broken friendship. . . .

"Now I write you—and why? . . . Because John is dead,
not by the rope which he could not have escaped (and by
which I would not have had him die, for your sake and your
mother's and the fame of your great dead father), but fighting
for his life. Because it is all over with him, I write you re-
joicing, though with tears, for your sake and his own. For my
own part I remember him well and kindly. I saw no ill in him
when I met him at your house and shall think of him, or try
to as he seemed to me then, not as we are told he was later, and
as we know he was at last. That God may sustain you and bless
you and pardon him is the prayer of your once friend, never
enemy. Farewell, RICHARD."

A letter from Badeau was just as much in character. At the
first news of John's crime Badeau, who didn't share Stoddard's
confidence that it would be best to leave their friend alone with
his woe and God, had written instantly: "Try, dear Ned, and
bear up. . . . Try and be a man. . . . Dear Ned, my heart
bleeds for you."

Professor Louis Agassiz, one of those scholars and gentlemen whom Booth looked up to as being of a different clay
from poor players, slapped the table when his name was
solicited in support of Booth. "Indeed he shall have it! I love
that boy!"

There was Julia Ward Howe. With all her zeal for the

North and Lincoln, she addressed a poem to John Wilkes Booth, which she called *Pardon*. There was Launt Thompson, who, at the very height of hostile feeling, appeared in public with the mother of the murderer, and Tom Aldrich, who moved into Edwin's house to be as near as possible to him in his trouble.

On May 10—the day John would have been twenty-seven— the trial of the conspirators opened in Washington. Aldrich and Lilian Woodman watched one session. They were leaving the courtroom on the second story of the old Arsenal when they met a man running lightly up the spiral stairs. It was Edwin, summoned by the defense, which was preparing a plea of insanity and trying to prove that Wilkes Booth had had such power over the minds of others as would easily sway his associates. Yet after interrogating Edwin narrowly about his brother they dared not risk calling on him.

While he was in Washington Booth went to see Junius, at that time still in his prison cell. The lackadaisical Joseph Booth, landing in New York from San Francisco, was arrested, grilled up and down about John's affairs, of which he knew nothing, and finally set free.

On July 7 Lewis Paine, George Atzerodt, David Herold, and Mrs. Mary Surratt were hanged in the courtyard of the Arsenal in the presence of a lip-licking crowd. Fierce afternoon sunlight pounded the prison yard, making mercilessly clear every detail, how Herold grinned idiotically at the spectators, how the woman's skirts were tied around her legs. The bodies were lifted down, tumbled into coffins and shoveled into waiting graves in a corner of the yard, a stone's throw off from where John Wilkes lay buried. "It is a great blessing," Edwin wrote to Emma Cary, "that I have had so much occupation all this while, else I should have gone mad, I fear." And to another friend: "When will all this trouble leave me?"

William Bispham took turns with Aldrich in staying close to Booth whose dazed, wretched face and ceaseless brooding over his lost plans ("beautiful plans I had for the future—all blasted now") made them afraid that if he didn't go mad, he would begin to drink again. One of his comforts was to remind himself how he had saved Robert Lincoln from possible death. He described this to Bispham over and over, and at last to distract him Bispham coaxed him to set down what he remembered of his boyhood in the form of letters to Edwina. The scheme worked. Bispham, reading almost over the writer's shoulder, found the memoir delightful, and, remarkably in the circumstances, full of humor. And as Booth relived his rich past a little of the savor of life came back to him—but not the whole, ever.

He had been struck down twice with too short a time between the blows. He was like some poor insect trodden under by a giant foot, which after a pause creeps forward, is trodden again, and with heroic vitality still feebly stirs its filaments of legs and crawls on mechanically, but with no faith or joy left in its insect existence. Years later Booth told William Winter: "All my life I have thought of dreadful things that might happen to me. I believed there was no horror that I had not imagined, but I never dreamed of such a dreadful thing as *that*."

Asia put the case for her family. "Those who have passed through such an ordeal," she wrote, "if there are any such, may be quick to forgive, slow to resent; they never relearn to trust in human nature, they never resume their old place in the world, and they forget only in death."

She and Edwin felt the shame the most after their mother. Junius had written quite cheerily to Edwin from prison that "we must use philosophy—'Tis a mere matter of time. . . . I feel sure Time will bring all things right—that is, as right as we have any right to expect."

Junius and Joseph, not having within them the passionate earnestness that had made their name great, suffered less, accordingly. But when Edwin and Asia turned back to the world, the faces they showed were branded with suffering.

PART FIVE

CHAPTER 9

Another Juliet

This is not Romeo, he's some other where.
Romeo and Juliet, *Act I, scene 1*

"Is THE Assassination of Caesar to be Performed?" the New York *Herald* raved when Edwin Booth's return to the stage was announced for January 3, 1866. "Will Booth appear as the assassin of Caesar? That would be, perhaps, the most suitable character."

Booth appeared as Hamlet. At first after his brother's crime he had sworn he would never act again. In the stupor of his anguish he longed to go far off, to sit alone, to shroud his face in a classic pose of mourning, to ruminate on his shame. Nothing but the most routine necessity drove him back to the stage. The whole family was enormously in debt, for no one had been working, and ironically the only trade these people knew, who shunned the eyes of men and whose only wish was to hide their heads, must be carried on in the full sweep of the limelight.

Other newspapers spoke up in defense of Booth, the *Tribune* cordially predicting that "the Winter Garden will be thronged tonight as it has rarely been," and, sure enough, a dense crowd milled excitedly in and out of the lobby; even the

Lafarge House next door was jammed with ticket seekers. Ladies in evening dress wandered unescorted through the crush as they would never have dreamed of doing on an ordinary night. Twice as many police as usual were on hand. Poor John Wilkes, seeking fame for himself, had willy-nilly built up his greatest rival's fame. Men who never went to the theater and had never before heard of Edwin Booth had heard of him now and were yelling for admittance.

This was not an audience; it was a mob. What would it do to Booth? The curtain rose and an instant went by before the crowd picked him out, sitting in the middle of the brilliant Danish court—he had chosen to be discovered rather than make an entrance. And then the sight of that slight, black, seated figure did something to them all. As one man they leaped to their feet and cheered and cheered; not a single person was left sitting down. From gallery to pit the house was white with waving handkerchiefs. "Three groans for the New York *Herald!*" somebody shouted, and three hollow "Boo-oos" went shuddering through the house.

Booth trembled in his carved chair; his head drooped onto his breast. After several minutes of this pandemonium, he slowly stood up and bowed very deep. His eyes were swimming with tears. And as the ovation by the audience said many things, so Booth's deliberately low obeisance meant much more than the thanks of the player who must please to live. It was the acknowledgment of a man long on trial, to whom acquittal by his peers has restored his honor.

Next Booth put on *Richelieu* in the ornate new production that had been almost ready a year earlier. Rose Eytinge played Julie, the Cardinal's ward. During Booth's tragic time away from the stage, his physical health had improved. He had even gained a few pounds, but was outraged when people complimented him—"I don't feel as I look!" A few weeks back at work soon pulled the weight off. A few weeks more, and the chronic shooting headache knocked at his brain like an old acquaintance returning. His sleep was troubled; if someone woke him suddenly he would start up and grope for something to throw.

"What a change!" was all one actor could say who had played with him in 1857 and remembered him brimming "with life and vivacity," and who met him again now. "What a change!"

Most reluctantly, looking most gloomy and sad, Booth began to go out socially again. Always there was the danger that some sly accident would tear off the skin that hid the Booth shame. And one night one did. At James Lorimer Graham's the men had trooped into the library after dinner and Booth, drifting a little apart, was austerely inspecting the bric-a-brac after the way of lonely guests.

"As his fate would," recollected William Dean Howells, who was there, "he went up to the cast of a huge hand that lay on one of the shelves."

"Whose hand is this, Lorry?" he asked, picking it up and turning it over. Graham didn't answer, and Booth asked again: "Whose hand is this?"

"It's Lincoln's hand," said Graham desperately.

Howells, who like the rest had winced with pity, writes that "the man for whom it meant such unspeakable things put the cast softly down without a word."

"These things are agony to me," Booth muttered to a fellow guest at another formal party where he stood backed against the wall with eyes begging for rescue and arms folded across his chest. The women's gush especially tortured him. They were all intruders, these would-be admirers.

"Dearest Edwin," began a letter, directed to the Winter Garden box office, from an eighteen-year-old girl who signed herself "Edith,"—"I have taken this opportunity to let you know of my intense devotion to you, and now notwithstanding strong opposition declare my love. . . .

"Of course I would insist on your leaving the stage, having enough to support us both in luxury—I never could endure to see you take the lover's part with any one but myself. It is agony to me now to see Miss Eytinge in *Richelieu*. . . ."

Booth's home was his refuge. He spent at least an hour every day sitting with his mother, and the reminiscences they matched together consoled the stricken old woman, whose family life was her whole source of interest. He and the four-year-old Edwina went to have their pictures taken. Booth sat in a studio armchair with Edwina first on his lap, nestling her head in his bosom, then standing beside him as close as possible; her hand was curled in his, her small, white-stockinged legs were pressed against his knees. He had almost a horror of allowing her backstage. Only now and then before a matinee she might sit in his dressing room and watch him paint his face. There was one name she had heard him called by so many times in the theater and at home that once at the table when somebody offered her "a piece of omelet" she chirped: "Why, that's Papa!"

A year had gone by since Booth's return to his profession, almost two years since the tragedy that had made him leave it. On January 22, 1867, after the curtain had fallen at the Winter Garden, it was immediately pulled up again, the scene was dismantled and modern furniture lugged in so the stage could be reset as a drawing room. Then Booth, looking foreign and delicate among the clubmen all gathered to pay homage to the one divine spark their sturdier clay lacked, was at last presented with the much talked-of gold medal to commemorate his hundred nights of *Hamlet*.

For now more than ever, New Yorkers agreed, an actor-manager who gave serious plays the distinguished productions Edwin Booth did, deserved to be honored. All too many managers, smiling alertly, shrugged off any responsibility for elevating the public taste. Tony Pastor had opened his so-called Opera House on Broadway; his variety program catered to an all-male audience that kept its hats on. And made bold by the success of Adah Menken, who in *Mazeppa* had worn a Greek chiton with nothing underneath but invisible fleshings, the management of Niblo's had allowed to open an extravaganza called *The Black Crook*, in which the young chorus women pranced on in black tights.

The innovation tore the town apart. Parents and clergymen all but shook their fists, and the mass of the public rushed to Niblo's to see the double row of shapely underpinnings flash along the stage like suave black scissors.

Later this January Booth gave *The Merchant of Venice*, which failed to hold the stage long chiefly because of his inadequacy as Shylock. His performance had wonderful moments. At the Jew's first appearance halfway up a flight of stairs, bargaining with Bassanio, the laconic

> Three thousand ducats; well?

was like the attack of an instrument in a virtuoso's hands. The line,

> This Jacob from our holy Abram was,

conjured up the generations reaching back and back in pride of race.

But his grasp of the character was not sure; he couldn't get the clue to Shylock. "Somehow I can feel no sort of inspiration or spirituality in the atmosphere of that play," he complained to Dr. Horace Furness, a typical academician with his nose to the page, who studied Shakespeare analytically in contrast to the actor's method, which relied on intuitive flashes and explosions of sympathy. Yet when Booth studied Shylock no flashes broke, nothing exploded. "I can't mount the animal—for such I consider Shylock to be. . . . He seems so earthy that the little gleams of light that I have perceived while acting other parts are absent."

Booth was directing, imaginatively and painstakingly, the productions he starred in. After *The Merchant* closed, he gave *Othello*, and for a change he acted the Moor instead of his usual devilishly fascinating Iago with the "leopard tread." His portrait of Othello was of an entirely noble, dedicated character, and while most men in the audience thought it rather tame, the other half of the house was smitten almost to a woman. In a soft green silk robe that showed the movement of muscles,

Booth looked Oriental, exotic, sumptuous. His face framed in a white headdress was bronzed, not blackened, by desert suns—Arabian, not African. "A proud, beautiful face!" cried Mrs. John Sherwood. "Desdemona was not worthy of it."

Like Amphion's lyre, which charmed the stones to move, Booth's voice in the lines,

> If it were now to die,
> 'Twere now to be most happy,

could not be heard without tears. Otis Skinner, who saw the performance some years later, was one of the few *men* to be deeply touched by it. In the alternating spurts of hot pride and moodiness, romantic idealization of the thing loved and bursts of weakness, this Othello had a human, and at the same time poetic and lovely, quality, "very much," said Skinner, "like Booth himself."

On March 22 Booth did Payne's *Brutus*. The grand scene of Rome burning was so realistic that the glow from the stage lit up the auditorium. At the end one spark was not quenched. It lived on through the night, a live worm of fire lengthening and fattening while the Winter Garden gloomed dark above it and the only permanent occupant, William Stuart, slept in his apartment at the top. At nine next morning Stuart was shocked awake by the tong-tong of fire engines. He stumbled to the balcony and saw the theater carpenters far below scattering across the stage while flames darted through the openings in the orchestra pit by which the musicians entered. Smoke was rolling up the stairways, so, snatching on his trousers, he dashed down and out of the doomed building onto the sidewalk, where thousands of New Yorkers gaped.

Old Mr. Booth would have loved the spectacle: the uplifted, "ohing" faces; the curveting horses that pulled the scarlet engines; the waltzing jets of water sprayed by hand pumps and almost totally useless against the Goliath of a fire, which roared to the roof, leaving in its wake the charred skeleton of the famous little playhouse where Jenny Lind had sung, and Rachel had acted; where Edwin Booth had made his debut as a star before the metropolis, and the three Booth brothers had matched their talents for the first and last time.

Mr. Booth would have been in the thick of things, plying the pumps shoulder to shoulder with the caroling Irish firemen. But Edwin stood on the sidelines looking on. Theater fires were common, and so was the sight of an owner or manager helplessly watching his investment burn. Inside the expiring Winter Garden was Booth's whole professional wardrobe, including stage weapons and jewels, all his new splendors for *Richelieu* and *Othello*, as well as other costumes more precious still, for they were historic and hallowed by having belonged to his father.

II

"Not even a wig or a pair of tights left," Booth said calmly, smiling faintly.

He had been through so many worse things that a mere loss of property (roughly forty thousand dollars' worth) left him almost indifferent. And he had begun to realize the power that was in him. What was this loss to one who had the golden touch? "If I live & don't lose my *grip* in 5 years I'll be rich!"

He would build his own theater! build it like a palace, dedicate it like a temple. He had tried to make his acting a monument to Mary; so would his new theater be. As at the Winter Garden, he would give the great plays with distinguished casts in lavish, peerless settings. He felt the power pouring out of him; he had the golden touch.

Just before the fire Clarke had sold his interest in the Winter Garden to Booth because he was leaving for England to make a fresh start in life. They had both been anxious for months to get rid of Stuart, who was a trouble-breeder. Stuart's policy was good-humoredly and slyly to turn people against one another, including his best friends, with the idea that he was thereby accumulating a reserve of advantage for himself. Booth was finally onto him, having caught him out in some of his double-dealing, like his advising Booth to give all reporters the cold shoulder because "they'd murder their grandmothers for a line of type," then sidling up to them himself to hint smoothly that Booth was really "a dull man, who made fun of the press."

Booth had dreaded a break; he hated to hurt feelings, but now the fire had set him free. "All Booth's mistakes and most of his troubles," moaned William Winter, a head-wagging supervisor of his friends' affairs, "resulted from the amiable weakness with which he sometimes permitted himself to become entangled with paltry, scheming, unworthy people."

For his new theater Booth needed a new partner. He decided on Richard A. Robertson, a businessman from Boston, "kindly enough," Winter granted, "but of ordinary taste and meagre abilities, and in no way fitted to be associated with a theater otherwise than, possibly, as a janitor."

Robertson had, though, one comfortable gift: he could make saying a thing seem as good as doing it, could make the mere mentioning of large sums seem like cash in the pocket. Booth found this highly encouraging. In proposing the terms of partnership he insisted only that the theater was to be in his own name and that he should have the option to buy out Robertson at any time. For five years a percentage of the profits would go to Robertson. Then Booth would pay Robertson any surplus needed to make up Robertson's investment in the project and also award him a hundred-thousand-dollar bonus. Meanwhile, they figured that the combined costs of the land and construction would come to half a million. Booth appointed Harry Magonigle, who was Mary's brother-in-law, to represent him and Robertson, and he put his brother Joseph in as treasurer. Joe's medical studies had fizzled out.

Magonigle shopped around for a good location. The entertainment district was creeping uptown, and he chose a site for the theater on the southeast corner of Twenty-third Street and Sixth Avenue. It cost one hundred and sixty-five thousand dollars, which was more than Booth had counted on, and hardly had the earth been turned over when the shovels banged against a layer of rock; the blasting was hideously expensive. Well, in for a penny—! Besides, Robertson had promised to contribute seventy-five thousand himself immediately, later the same amount again. To be sure, he hadn't done it yet, but the solid sound of the money was in his voice.

Booth paid down fifty thousand in cash, then departed on a strenuous tour to earn the balance, leaving behind some notes of hand signed in blank—the amounts to be filled in by his partner. Every dollar he could spare he sent back to Joe, who passed it on to Robertson. It was wearing work to build a theater this way, not by the simple toil of the hands but by a nightly creative effort and giving out of vital nervous energy.

In Chicago he played at McVicker's opposite Mary Mc-Vicker, whose stepfather owned the house. He had seen her here before in 1857, when he had smiled down at the self-willed little girl who had taken a fancy to him; he had been courting another Mary. At eighteen Mary McVicker was a tiny tag of a woman with a little, sallow, heart-shaped face and dark hair worn elaborately frizzled. She had beautiful if rather distraught-looking brown eyes, and these she fixed on Booth. Grown up at last, she was on equal terms with him. She seethed with plans and ambitions. By her Irish wit and sharp sense of fun she pulled Booth out of himself, got him to laughing again as sweeter, timider young ladies hadn't been able to do. Onstage she played a rather crude, vivacious, "western" Ophelia to his Hamlet and Juliet to his Romeo. When he left Chicago she went along as his leading lady. And when in Baltimore he was pinked in the arm during some swordplay in *The Apostate* and the doctor ordered him to rest a few nights, Mary McVicker was somehow right there to nurse him most capably in his cheerless hotel room.

As soon as he could afford it Booth had reimbursed the Virginia farmer whose tobacco barn had been burned down during John Wilkes' capture. A fairly large sum was still deposited in John's name in a bank in Montreal; John had visited Canada six months before his crime. The bank had advertised for the heirs to claim the money, but Edwin sternly forbade any member of the family to touch it. At the entreaty of his mother, half-childish in her grief ("She seems to have still a lingering hope in her heart that all this will prove to be a dream"), he had written to Secretary of War Stanton, begging for custody of what was left of his brother's body, on which an exhaustive autopsy had been performed before it was dumped under the dirt floor of the Arsenal. But Stanton had ignored his letter.

Booth tried again in September, 1867, writing from Barnum's Hotel in Baltimore. This time his appeal was to General Grant, who had succeeded Stanton as Secretary of War and had once offered to do Booth any service after his rescue of Robert Lincoln. "Sir," Booth addressed Grant, "I now appeal to you—on behalf of my heartbroken mother—that she may receive the remains of her son. You, Sir, can understand what a consolation it would be to an aged parent to have the privilege of visiting the grave of her child."

Grant made no reply.

There was no shaking off the dominion of that forlorn, defiant spirit whose shell remained in strangers' hands. Since his brother's crime Booth had steadily refused to play in Washington. Baltimore was as near as he would go, and special trains ran between the two cities so that Washington theater-lovers could see him act. It was the odium of John Wilkes' name that had driven Clarke to move to London, where Asia soon joined him. The child that Asia was expecting at the time of the assassination had turned out to be twins. In the fearful months when Edwin, at Bispham's sane encouragement, was setting down what he remembered of his boyhood (he later destroyed the manuscript in a spasm of disgust), Asia had gone on doggedly with the memoir of their father that she and John had planned. The writing opened all her wounds, but to finish the work they had begun together was all she could do for John.

Her worshiping little memoir of Junius Brutus Booth was printed, and soon after it appeared she had a letter from a stranger, probably a woman, who signed herself "M.K." "Dear Madam: I have just finished reading, for the third time, your Book. Long years have passed since I saw that form. But every lineament, Word, & every Gesture of that Haunting recollection has been with me still. I remember him well. . . .

"Last Winter I went to the Winter Garden wearied of Life (for I have drained the cup of Life's sorrows to the dregs) during the Engagement of your respected Brother. When I looked upon that Fragile Form (which I know well needed rest) when I saw him the Embodiment of Energy & perseverance, I returned to my home determined to overcome any Obstacle, which Fickle fortune threw in my way. It would be gratifying to see my Innocent children's eyes light up at the name of Edwin Booth. Oh that Heaven in its Mercy may Bless him with its peace Love & Happiness. He must know that there is one home whose Children are taught to emulate his Gentleness & Goodness & Virtue. Yours Devotedly. . . ."

In her published memoir Asia simply painted over the blots on the Booth escutcheon. She conceded that by her father's early misalliance "there was one son who, if alive, is still a resident of London, and of whom we possess no further knowledge." Yet her half-brother had lived for years in Baltimore. She didn't mention her father's divorce. Over his furtive courtship of her mother she threw a gossamer of romance and announced that her father had married her mother in London on January 18, 1821, "at the residence of the Hon. Mrs. Chambers." There really was a Mrs. Chambers. A wistful tradition in the Booth family may have inspired Asia's claim; possibly her parents did go through some sort of ceremony.

To hear Asia tell it, no family life was ever more idyllic than the Booths' in their Maryland hideaway. In her pages every relative put his best foot forward. Her grandfather Richard Booth—so often dead drunk that he couldn't be relied on to supervise the farm work—was a picturesque old gentleman, "tall, slender, arrayed in knee-breeches, shoe-buckles, and with snow-white hair wrapt in a queue." Her good-for-nothing uncle Jimmy Mitchell was "an eccentric Scotch Biblomaniac," who sedately spent his time "reading the Bible and writing commentaries on it." Even old Joe, the servant, "swarthy giant of the woods, boasted his lineal descent from a Madagascan prince "

And Mr. Booth, the head of this household, was strictly a gentleman-farmer who never, his daughter emphasized, sold his vegetables at the Baltimore market as some of his contemporaries were sure they had seen him do. In Baltimore he was always scrupulous not to smoke on the street and to take the curb side "when passing or walking with a female." Asia never spoke of her father's drinking. She alluded to his madness as "slight aberrations" and "seasons of abstraction."

There was one stain on the shield she could not wipe away. "We, of all families," she mourned, "secure in domestic love and retirement, are stricken desolate. The name we would have enwreathed with laurels is dishonored by a son—'his well-beloved—his bright boy Absalom!'"

Had Booth bitten off more than he could chew in the theater he was building? He labored and labored. Othello's rage, the distress of Hamlet were turned on and off until he couldn't sleep at night for fatigue, but sat up in his hotel bed counting the strokes of the city clocks in Toledo or New Orleans, or lay twisting in a train berth while half the states in the hard-won Union flashed by under him; and always the cry from Robertson in New York was for more money, more and faster. Already Booth's theater, still a long way from being finished, had devoured the half million dollars expected to cover the whole cost, and Robertson had borrowed on the credit of Booth's name. Booth's debts had increased so fast they had a narcotic effect, "would frighten any one," he allowed, "whose bump of 'don't-care-a-tiveness' was less than mine."

He was too inept at business, too dazed with work, too tired, and most of the time too far away, to keep a check on Robertson. More than this, he was too busy with the future to care much about the present. All at once his interest in another Mary and the delicious renewed vision of a wife and fireside had not only shoved the complicated theater enterprise into second place but "everything connected with it," as it seemed to him later, suddenly "became hateful to me, and I lived a sort of troubled dream-life, thoroughly disgusted with my 'hobby,' and altogether indifferent as to the result. I let things go."

The cities fled past, the months fled past. Booth was thirty-five in November, 1868. He had been acting nineteen years, during which his style had grown steadily less flamboyant and more natural. The actor had become less to him and his art more. "The fitful power," applauded Lucia Calhoun in the *Century*, "that dazzled and delighted in great bursts has become a diffused strength, which sustains the whole."

Like all New York she expected wonderful things of his new theater, had found only one fault in his Winter Garden productions, so striking in their scenery and costumes. The supporting company had been "impossible to defend. . . . Surely," she volunteered, "it is not too much to demand of Mr. Booth to insist that the gentleman who plays Richmond shall speak the English language; or that Antonio shall not altogether dispense with a pocket handkerchief; or that the nobles and gentlemen in general should look at their parts once or twice before playing; or that Ophelia should be told that she is not a singing chambermaid. If, in the new theatre, he will but give us Shakespeare with an intelligent actor in every part; if the courtiers who stand with folded arms will but *be* courtiers and not boobies, the world will owe him a debt it will gladly pay in honor, in praises, in fortune."

Booth thought so too. He aimed at bringing together the best casts available. He had already tried to sign the Bohemian tragedienne Madame Janauschek for the heavies, and when she decided she hadn't time to learn the parts in English he engaged Mrs. D. P. Bowers, who was also first-rate. His leading lady, however, was to be Mary McVicker and here, right at the beginning, his heart overruled his head. Nothing daunted Miss McVicker. She did all the great heroines from Portia to Ophelia, and William Winter's comment was that "had she chosen to play Irish girls in farces, she would have succeeded."

And before Booth realized it, the lower ranks of his new company had taken on considerable dead wood. The very first actors he had made places for were Dave Anderson and

Willmarth Waller from California, both past their primes but the fondest of old comrades. They swarmed into his life again pumping his arm and thumping his back in their joy and relief—dear old Ted! Then there was Mark Smith, who had acted with his father in Mr. Booth's last performance in New Orleans; Booth made him stage manager. There was "Polly" Drummond, who was practically doddering and also penniless, so Booth let him in for such odds and ends as the Physician in *Macbeth*, the Priest in *Hamlet*, and An Old Man, Uncle to Capulet at the masque in *Romeo and Juliet*, a three-line bit that managers usually left out.

For the opening performance he had invited Forrest to play Othello to his Iago. Forrest could have any price he asked, any terms at all. He refused, would have no terms, nothing to do with Booth. He would have been wiser to accept; affairs had not gone well with Forrest. In proportion as Booth's star soared, his own had drooped. In 1865 he had been partly paralyzed, but his doctor recommended that he go on acting: the machine, if stalled, would rust and drop to pieces. Forrest did go on, but fewer and fewer people came to see him act, and those who did come were older and older. It seemed that the young people had never heard of him. Soon even the faithful began to dwindle. Forrest was bewildered. He had clung to the fable that there is a sentimental bond between the public and a star, causing the public to look tenderly on age and infirmity in one who has served it so long.

He resorted to the provinces, began to accept engagements in second-class cities, then to play in remote villages that smaller stars scorned to visit. It was the same story everywhere. The old actor glowered with humiliation at the reports from the box office. He dreaded his openings, dreaded his first entrance when the puny applause showed the thinness of the house. He searched the local papers for a word of praise and pasted into his scrapbook, beside the notices of his acting by leading critics belonging to his great days, the silly effusion of some cub reporter on a small-town journal.

Attacks of rheumatism wore down his remaining strength.

In the peak scene of *Damon and Pythias* one of his exploits had always been to leap from Pythias' arms up to a scaffold three feet high. Lately it had been necessary to cut the height to two feet, then to one, at last to six inches. There came an evening when as Forrest tried out his leap just before curtain time everyone onstage saw that he couldn't make it if the height were more than three inches.

"Will this do?" asked the stage carpenter, after dislodging a couple of boards.

Forrest turned away his head and whispered sadly: "Yes."

III

Three stone towers rose over Twenty-third Street and up from the central one shot a flagpole flying a flag with the glorious legend BOOTH'S THEATER. Into the raising of these towers had gone some thousands of hours of Booth's vitality. For the past two years he had acted at least nine months of each year, six nights a week, three hours a night.

Now that his theater was nearly finished, the dull part over and the time come finally to cast and rehearse, his fanatic enthusiasm revived with a rush. This didn't escape Robertson, who was becoming discontented with his lack of real ownership. Three weeks before the theater was due to open he wrote Booth a letter demanding plaintively: "Why should I not be a fair owner in this building? Why, Ned, should I not have something which I can feel a pride in as much as yourself? . . . My fine idea is that we should own equally together, but if this cannot be allowed then make it 3/7. . . ."

Booth made it three-sevenths, admitting that Robertson "struck at the proper moment, just as my fire was hottest, blowing me to a white heat. To get that theater open I would have said 'yes,' had he asked for all of it."

The theater did open on February 3, 1869, and so did the heavens. First rain, then damp snow splashed on the long crocodile of smart carriages that crawled along Twenty-third Street and pulled up, each carriage in turn, at the main entrance. Outside everything glistened: carriage roofs, umbrella tops, tall silk hats. Inside all was orderly and breath-taking. From both the central and side entrances richly dressed patrons swarmed into a vast semicircular lobby, walled and paved with Italian marble. The section of the audience that had seats in the balcony flowed up the marble staircase past Thomas Gould's bust of Junius Brutus Booth in a niche halfway up. Mr. Booth in life had acted in Drury Lane and Covent Garden but never in a theater to compare with this one. This was New World magnificence! His marble image looked out on it a little ironically.

William Winter ambled through the blue-ribbon crowd, taking mental notes for his column in the *Tribune* next day. He saw "many a face that study had paled and thought exalted. Grave judges were there," Winter noted, "and workers in the field of literature, and patient, toiling votaries of science, and artists from their land of dreams. The eyes of beauty, too, shone there."

The reporter from the *World* snooped about, picking flaws. Next day in his column he deplored the defiling of the lobby by "imitated wood and imitated marble, and other little lies. . . . All the exterior decoration is as dead as Julius Caesar," carped the *World*.

The auditorium was as big as a meadow and shaped like a horseshoe. From the ceiling a monster gasolier hung, its jets lighted by electric sparks. A fan worked by steam pressure agitated the atmosphere in a stately way. There were seats for almost two thousand people, most of whom couldn't as yet be induced to sit down, they were so busy admiring the painted Apollo, god of poetry and music, on the vaulted ceiling; the freshly gilded cupids and initial *B* in gold over the doors of the boxes; the busts of Garrick, Talma, Kean, Cooke, and Betterton along the walls and the noble statue of Shakespeare enshrined over the proscenium arch.

After Forrest had failed him, Booth had chosen to open with *Romeo and Juliet* as the best vehicle to launch Mary McVicker in New York. When the house lights had been dimmed, he slipped out in front of the curtain in a suit of perfectly new evening clothes ("evidently prepared for the occasion," the *Herald* whispered to its readers), murmured a stiff little speech of welcome and bowed himself off. The orchestra began to play soft strains; the fringed curtain stole upward and arranged itself artfully in a series of festoons framing the stage, and the audience sank back into its plush chairs to wait for its money's worth.

It got what it came for. With a loud alarm and clanging of bells a full hundred young men of the rival houses of Montague and Capulet shot out from the wings and up and down the unusually wide and deep apron, their steel blades weaving and chattering—a professional *maître des armes* had been rehearsing them for weeks in the gymnasium upstairs. In the masque at the Capulets, which was gorgeously staged, a corps of trained dancers performed. The balcony scene had *two* balconies. Romeo bounded over the garden wall wearing a yellow satin tunic, a rolling collar of green silk, flowing sleeves, and a pointed hat of silk and solferino velvet with a plume of cock's feathers. When he took his hat off, his blond hair gleamed in the stage moonlight, which also shone on Juliet's form in white satin, leaning on the rail of the lower balcony, her skirt looped with pearls. More pearls were twined around her neck and a tiara of diamonds rested on her streaming, waist-long black hair.

Many years ago Booth had played Romeo to another Mary at the Boston Theater in the inspired performance of which Mrs. Howe had written that "few who saw it will ever forget it," and which had been one of the exceptional times when the part of Romeo didn't freeze something in him.

"Whether he was not actually a good lover," speculated Badeau, "or whether he felt a certain delicacy about lovemaking in public, the fact remains that he was always more effective in parts that represent harsh or violent emotions."

Scoffed the *Herald* the day after the grand opening: "Mr. Booth knows as well as we do that he can't play Romeo. He seems almost to writhe under the load of sweet fancies . . . when the face should be lit up with a glow of passion it is almost funny to see his struggles. . . . Feeling the impossibility of expressing with his immobile face the eager impatience of the young lover, Mr. Booth sought the aid of his heels, danced and clogged about the stage. The passage of old Capulet's wall was a bit of harlequin business which brought out the great gymnastic ability of Mr. Booth."

Then came the lady's turn. "Miss Mary McVicker, for whom Mr. Booth thus gallantly sacrificed himself, we are pained to say is in no way worthy of the sacrifice. She is not a delicate geranium, rising from a Sèvres vase, but a strong, practical Western woman, with but little artistic training but a good deal of raw vigor and rude force; and while she can never realize the graceful, buoyant, lovely Juliet of Shakespeare's creation, we have no doubt would manage Romeo's business after marriage with considerable effect."

The actor most applauded was not either of the principals but Edwin Adams, a popular leading man, for his Mercutio. The real hit of the night, though, was the theater itself. When the drop curtain fell at the end of Act I, it got its own round of applause for the Italian landscape painted on it. The critic for the *World* fussed that Romeo's and Juliet's costumes didn't "go well" together—the colors clashed. And Romeo's blond wig was not becoming; Nature knew what she was doing when she made Booth a brunet. But the *World* praised the scenery and compared it favorably with the handsome mountings given imported French farces. "Now the diamond of poetry is set more exquisitely than was even the quartz of prurience," gloried the *World*.

William Winter ended his rapturous review with a pearl of a quotation. While managers like Booth are active, "we can cease," he exulted, "to grieve for 'the good old days.' '*Angels are bright still, though the brightest fell!*' "

IV

Not two weeks after the opening Booth, whose life these days seemed to the public to be one lived wholly in the light, a series of happy triumphs, wrote to President Andrew Johnson beseeching and imploring for custody of the body of his brother. He begged also that an ancient trunk once belonging to John, now held at the National Hotel under seal of the War Department, be returned to his family. "It may contain relics of the poor misguided boy," Booth wrote, "which would be dear to his sorrowing mother, and of no use to anyone."

This was his third attempt, and it succeeded. In gloomy secrecy John Wilkes' remains were exhumed and shipped to Baltimore. Edwin could not bring himself to go, but his intrepid mother, with Joseph and Rosalie and a few others who had known John, identified the body there in a back room at Weaver the undertaker's on February 17. The black hair appeared to have grown riotously; the white teeth grinned in the lipless face.

"Yes, that is the body of John Wilkes Booth," said Joseph, speaking with rare firmness. He avoided the word "brother."

Mrs. Booth sat in a corner with Rose by her side. A lock of hair was snipped from the head and given to her, and she moaned as she blindly and mechanically drew apart the still beautiful strands between her fingers.

President Johnson had ordered that no monument should flaunt the place where Lincoln's assassin lay. The suffering Booths agreed, but they were determined to bury John honorably. While his body waited in the undertaker's vault, the bodies of his father and grandfather Richard along with the monument Edwin had raised to Mr. Booth were moved to a new burial lot in Greenmount Cemetery in Baltimore. The remains of the children that had lain for over thirty years in the willow-shaded burying ground at the farm under a shattered tombstone (shattered with an ax, the legend ran, by Mr. Booth in his frenzy over little Mary Ann's death) were brought to Greenmount so that all the Booths might rest together—all except Henry Byron, dead in his thirteenth year in England.

On June 26 Mrs. Booth, Edwin, Junius, Rosalie, and Joseph drove openly to Greenmount. A number of old friends were on hand, all who could be persuaded. John Wilkes' body in a fine casket was carried to the grave on the shoulders of several actors in whom the loyal blood of the profession ran strong. Deposited next to it was a smaller box holding the dust, for not much more was left, of the three children who had been dead before this brother was born. An Episcopal clergyman from New York had been called in to read the burial service. He had not thought of asking whom he was to bury, and did not find out until he arrived at the cemetery. It was an unlucky oversight. Because he had read the service over Lincoln's murderer, his congregation threw him out.

But the thing was done. The train of events that John Wilkes Booth had set in motion would go on unfolding until time was no more. But this was the end of the man. His still loving mother wailed with despair as her son's body sank into the grave, away from her forever. Her living children, who had only lost a brother, tried in vain to comfort her.

Even when Mary McVicker was still no more than engaged to Booth, she was forever in his dressing room. Dr. R. Ogden Doremus had found her hovering there when he called on Booth to discuss a reading by him of Byron's *Manfred* before the Philharmonic Society.

"Please don't ask Edwin to read *Manfred*," interposed Mary. "He's already so overtaxed he can't get the sleep he needs."

Booth smiled at her and went on making his arrangements.

"But suppose Mary doesn't like your pipe?" someone suggested to him before the wedding.

"I can't give up my pipe," he said softly.

He and Mary were married on June 7, 1869, at the McVickers' summer home in fashionable Long Branch, New Jersey. "My little wife," he told a friend at the end of the summer, "is a quaint, cosy, loveable little body, and we get on famously. She and Edwina are all in all."

Booth had loved deeply once. He was through with passion.

CHAPTER 10

The Worldly Hope

*O! now, for ever
Farewell the tranquil mind; farewell content!*
Othello, *Act III, scene 3*

 A RIVAL Hamlet was in New York. Charles Fechter, the French actor, was making his American debut at Niblo's Garden in January, 1870. Fechter's Hamlet, which, shattering tradition, was a beefy blond with reddish-gold hair and a sing-song intonation, had been quite the rage abroad. It was an artichoke among Hamlets; to enjoy it was a sign of cultivated taste. Actually Fechter hardly understood the role, insisting that Hamlet never put things off but went ahead with so much energy the Ghost had to slow him down.

"Do you not recall," chanted Fechter to an interviewer, "the Ghost's words to the Prince in the Queen's closet: 'I come to *wet* thy almost blunted purpose'?"

Fechter had confused *whet* with *wet*, and never bothered to look up *blunted*.

The blond prince did well in New York, but Booth's dark one at his own theater did even better. One thrilled critic urged his readers to "go and hear a madman on Blackwell's Island

225

soliloquize, and make a point of watching his eyes as he communes with himself. Booth has caught the very trick."

Booth took Edwina to the Olympic to see the burlesque of himself in the part by the comedian George L. Fox, who slogged up and down Elsinore ramparts in a heavy fur cap and collar, mittens and arctic overshoes, told Ophelia to "get her to a brewery," and when the Ghost ordered him to "swear!" let out a string of oaths in a richly vibrating voice.

Edwina, eight years old, was at school outside New York and happy to have a mother to come home to. Her letters ended with "love and kisses to dear Mama," to "*chère petite Mama.*" In February there was an exchange of valentines. "Dear Mama," Edwina wrote, "I was much pleased with the valentine you gave me. the pink is pretty and so are you. from your loving daughter."

By Booth's wish Mary had left the stage before their marriage. They were living in a studio apartment above the theater, and when his late actor's day began, Booth had only to walk downstairs to be at work. "His life was his theater and there he virtually lived," writes Augustus Pitou, who was in the company.

Raptly supervising the coming into being of one of his great productions, Booth hovered and prowled—into the wardrobe room, prop room, armory. He bent over work tables, poked in cupboards, scanned shelves, laid his hand on this, held that up to the light. He talked costumes with his designer; loitered on the paint frame, smoking with the painters, or simply stood with his head high and hands behind him, expansively contemplating the world he had made.

Underneath his broad stage was a brick-paved chasm into which an entire scene could be lowered by hydraulic machinery. In his huge scene shop were numbered pieces of the modern box sets, the last word in scenery. He had given over five floors to airy dressing rooms, and there was a pretty greenroom hung with theatrical engravings and framed playbills.

On July 4, 1870, while the New York heat beat against the shaded windows of the apartment over the theater, Mary

Booth bore a son. Her pregnancy had lasted a month beyond the normal term. The infant at birth weighed ten pounds, which was much too large for the mother's delicate frame. After an agonizing labor the doctor took the baby with instruments, and in the operation its head was crushed. Little Edgar Booth lived only a few hours. When Mary was recovering from the effect of the anodyne, her terrible sorrow and weakness were "something not to be described," said Booth.

While that other Mary had given Edwin a daughter named after him, who grew in his love, the son that she herself had borne had passed out of life on the day he entered it, with only his mother to mourn his passing. The child was buried beside Mary Devlin Booth in Mount Auburn Cemetery. Those walking by and reading carelessly the inscription on the stone over his grave would be sure to take him for the first wife's son. His mother's small face tightened with misery. Unsuspected by her husband and stepdaughter, a bitter rage began to build in her.

Booth's Theater this fall starred Jefferson in *Rip Van Winkle*, who jammed in the crowds, while Booth, away on tour, did likewise. He was fighting to reduce the mortgage on his theater. Box-office profits for the first year had been over a hundred thousand dollars, but this was a drop in the bucket to what he owed. From New York Robertson wrote as usual screaming for more money. Booth sent him back checks to the amounts of three thousand, five thousand, seven thousand, to be sucked away like dew in the sun. "William!" he scribbled desperately to Bispham, "when that pile of granite is paid for, I'll retire."

Jefferson in *Rip* ran from the middle of August to early January—five fat months, and yet in spite of them the profits for the second year were only eighty-five thousand. Robertson began to wail that Booth's devotion to "high art" was losing them money, and to pull for "livelier shows and bigger names." Booth was willing to try what strong names would do, but it would be expensive he warned his partner because "all these half-baked *stars*, such as Barrett, Adams, and even Wallack and Davenport (all excellent in the stock) require their $300 per week . . . their names to be at the head of the bill, and in the largest letters, to say nothing of declining to play seconds to each other. . . . I will try Barrett and Adams and see what can be done. . . . If we can make these damned idiots pull together, I don't care what we pay them."

To meet the call for more popular plays he revived *Richelieu*, a perennial draw because of its exciting story and melodramatic passages in which Booth still let go with everything he had; his audiences would have felt cheated otherwise. Most purple and most famous was the Curse of Rome speech. People swore that as he delivered it Booth grew seven feet tall. They were right. He did, by an artful illusion endlessly rehearsed. A young actress, Kitty Molony, who later appeared with him, has given away his secret: it lay in the timing.

Under a splash of light the scarlet-robed Cardinal shelters his ward Julie in her gleaming bridal dress from a shadowy horde of black-velvet enemies. "Mark where she stands!" he thunders,

> "around her form I draw
> The awful circle of our solemn Church!"

As he began to speak Booth plucked back with his left hand the ermine-bordered sleeve that fell over his right, with which he traced an imaginary circle around the girl.

> Set but a foot within that holy ground,
> And on thy head—yea, though it wore a crown—
> I launch the *curse of Rome!*

On "Rome" he whipped his right hand high over his head with two fingers raised and in the same instant lifted himself on tiptoe, his feet hidden by the train of his robe. And as Booth rose, all the others abased themselves: Julie, Father Joseph, and the courtiers sank to their knees and bowed to the floor before the lurid figure of the Church triumphant.

Laurence Hutton, who was an avid playgoer, remembered hanging about in the wing one evening with Booth during *Richelieu*. Away across the stage they could see Julie waiting at the opposite entrance. Booth, puffing on a meerschaum, pointed out to Hutton the greasy white paint with which she had plastered her neck and shoulders. "If she gets any of that stuff on my new red cloak I'll pinch her black and blue."

He heard the cue. "Don't let my pipe go out!" Hutton found himself holding the awkward thing while Booth flowed majestically onstage. Julie fluttered into his arms; sure enough, she smeared him and he made a face over her shoulder at Hutton. Then the Curse of Rome began. The actor's voice soared. Suddenly the watcher in the wing became conscious that he had taken off his hat and his legs were shaking.

"I forgot all the tomfoolery we had been indulging in," Hutton marveled. "I forgot Booth's pipe and my promise regarding it; I forgot that I had been a habitual theatergoer all my life; I forgot that I was a Protestant heretic, and that it was nothing but stage-play. I forgot everything except that I was standing in the presence of the great, visible head of the Catholic religion in France, and that I was ready to drop on my knees with the rest of them."

The more Booth succeeded, the more some people hated him. The jilted Stuart had begun a whispering campaign. At least half the spiteful stories about Booth that crawled into print had been started by Stuart. There were jokes, too. Booth stood about five feet, seven inches, and a wit suggested he ought to hire Tom Thumb, the midget, for Macduff the next time he played Macbeth. His early drinking gave the enemy another handle. Five days after his new *Richelieu* opened, an article was published by a man named John Moray describing Booth in the same play in Cincinnati in 1860. Moray recollected that he had met the stage manager in the street that long-ago morning and had asked him solicitously if the young actor were "likely to draw."

"If he'll leave —— and whiskey alone," the manager grumbled, "he'll do well enough. He's not a great actor, but his father's name would pull him through."

"Why," said Moray, "isn't he studious?"

"Gas!" snorted the manager. "Not one of old Booth's boys but hates a book as much as he loves a bottle."

That night in the theater after a long restless delay the curtain was at last signaled up, "and there on the stage," recalled Moray with relish, "sat the son of Junius, the brother of Wilkes, who by alternately standing on the tombstone of each has managed to make a pretty good thing of it.

"They had opened the flats on the second scene when Booth was discovered actively engaged in throwing up his situation and—I am ashamed to add—his dinner along with it. He tried hard to recover himself, commenced saying that he had 'found Franze rend dassunder and lu-lu-lu-lumnuss wings,' and staggered about the stage. The curtain fell; the manager came out to say: 'Ladies and gentlemen, we advertised Mr. Booth and we have shown him to you. We are sorry his beastly habits have led to your disappointment. Your money will be returned at the door.' "

II

Now that he had his own theater there was always a conflict in Booth between what he wanted to do and what was expedient. When some poor devil, pathetically spruce, cringed or swaggered into his office and bravely asked for a part, it took a heart harder than his to turn the old-timer off without a promise of some kind of help. Lurking at the back of his mind was the vagabond's inkling that some day, by the whirligig of Fate, the tables might turn.

Outside, too, he had regular petitioners. To a struggling artist, Jervis McEntee, who had appealed for a loan, he replied promptly: "I send a check here for $1000 of those damnable can't-get-along-without-'ems, and in a week hence will let you have another. Will a week be time enough?"

McEntee was neurotic and overconscientious. "My dear boy," Booth wrote again soothingly, "you let this little affair trouble you too much. I do not require any interest—that's all *bosh*. Don't think of the thing a moment."

But the troubles of a manager! Booth supervised everything, standing onstage before the curtain rose while the grips staggered past him and confusion raged around, but oh, the incompetence! And to be the star too who must carry the show. Often he blazed with anger and cursed a full minute long at the dundering fools who had spoiled his scene—"a *prod* at their *bums*" was what they needed. Once he grabbed a book and hurled it at a super who stood gawking in the wing in plain view of the audience. Every time he all but begged pardon five minutes later.

During intermissions he saw visitors in a little parlor off his dressing room, sitting in state in a gilt armchair drawing on his meerschaum or a cigar. His diminutive wife, modishly dressed, curled, and bejeweled, received with him. Like Mary Devlin, she was concentrating absolutely on her husband's career. When Dr. Osgood, who had married Booth and his first Mary, wrote to ask for tickets to a performance, Booth, after answering that he would be pleased to be of service, volunteered—in words that would have been outrageous to him a few years before—"and be pleased to introduce my wife, who is the counterpart of that dear angel you blessed on our wedding day."

He invited Dr. Osgood to visit backstage. "Several clergymen have trod the unhallowed ground—so you needn't hesitate to take a peep."

He had had a letter from another "Reverend," a stranger to him, who inquired cautiously if there were a back door to Booth's through which he could slip in after the lights were down because his parishioners mightn't like his being there.

Booth's whole background had bred in him a longing for what was decent and respected. All that was best in him, all that was purest, most aspiring to good, had gone into his theater and was behind the reply he gave the fearful clergyman.

"There is no door in my theater," Booth wrote back, "through which God cannot see."

The troubles of a manager! Booth had gone out of his way
to give Edwin Adams and Lawrence Barrett, who had each in
turn been his leading support, a chance to star. Each time he
did he lost money, on Ned Adams in *Narcisse*, and this spring,
1871, on Barrett in three productions: *The Winter's Tale*,
with Barrett as Leontes, and two modern plays. And Barrett
was becoming a problem. He had been something of a problem for the past ten years. As far back as 1860, when he was
acting in stock at the Boston Museum, he had tried to touch
Booth for money and influence. "You say in your letter,"
Booth had then answered the plea for a loan, " 'a friend who
can assist me if he will.' Larry, my boy, if those words came
from your heart they should have stood thus, 'who *will* assist
me *if he can.*' "

Barrett's mother had taken in washing. His father was an
Irish immigrant whose name, rumor had it, was not Barrett but
Brannigan. Their son had fought so desperately to improve
himself that he could take nothing lightly, always had a chip
on his shoulder. His face with its craggy Celtic cheekbones
and bulging forehead looked like a monk's, but the hunger in
his unhappy eyes was not for God. Fate was unjust, for Booth,
who had been born to fame, could have been happy if the world
had never heard of him, and here was Barrett whose unique
desire was to be recognized by the world as a great, a *great*
actor.

For the season of 1870 to 1871 Booth had offered Barrett a
place in his company as leading man at a weekly salary of a
hundred and fifty dollars. And when Barrett hesitated to accept a position that was less than the very top, Booth reminded
him gently: "How many old and disappointed actors do we
know who now curse their 'pride' which prevented them from
'stooping' just a little?"

With an ill grace Barrett consented to come, but demanded
a salary of two hundred and fifty, which was more than Booth
could easily afford. Alas for ambition unsupported by what
Booth called "that lucky knack of drawing dollars." Intense
and really interesting actor though he was, Barrett couldn't

draw. When at the end of the spring Booth generously starred him in *The Winter's Tale* and *The Man of Airlie*, the public stayed away in such droves that the theater lost almost twenty thousand dollars.

Booth was already immersed in next winter's plans. *Julius Caesar* on a grand scale was to open in December with himself as Brutus, Barrett as Cassius, and Adams as Mark Antony. He had agreed to pay Barrett four hundred a week though this was a drain on him, especially since the recent flop proved that Barrett's name brought almost no cash to the house. Still, as he had said to Robertson: "If we can make these damned idiots pull together, I don't care what we pay them."

Now, diplomatically, he hinted to Barrett: "The only trouble will be your (and, I presume, Adams' also) wish to be *first* on the bill."

The name EDWIN BOOTH would of course head the bill. But directly below would it read

LAWRENCE BARRETT *as Cassius*   EDWIN ADAMS *as Mark Antony*

or the other way around? It was a hideously nice question. "*He* may not care about it," Booth coaxed Barrett. "But if he *sticks* shy you must remember not only that these little trifles are of no earthly account outside the greenroom, but that your salary will doubtless be much larger than his. . . . That last point must be kept secret."

His autumn season opened with the kitten-faced Lotta Crabtree in *Little Nell*, a choice of star and play that was a distinct sop to Robertson. Minstrelsy was Lotta's gift. In all her parts she played the banjo, danced a clog or breakdown. She was not quite at home in a theater like Booth's. People were not used to going there to see her, and her spotty business lost the management some two hundred dollars a week for six weeks.

Robertson began to nag again that his partner's standards were too "highbrow." He was ready, he said, to buy out Booth's interest. When *he* was sole owner of the theater he would make it into a variety house—"I appreciate your artistic feeling, my boy. I can't expect you to stoop to that; but it won't make any difference to me, as a business man."

Booth instantly offered to buy out Robertson. An accountant was called in to calculate the amount of Robertson's interest. But the precise amount was impossible to fix because the theater treasurer, the muddle-headed Joseph Booth, had somehow mixed up the costs of construction of the theater with the production figures for *Romeo and Juliet* and for *Othello*, the second play produced. The wild-eyed expert finally approximated Robertson's interest, which originally had been a free gift from Booth to his partner. Now Booth found himself buying it back for two hundred and forty thousand dollars. He scraped the sum together. Something else brought to light in the accounting was that Robertson, for all his cozy talk of money, seemed never to have put a single solid dollar into the theater.

More than ever, now that he was master on his own stage, Booth's desk boiled with letters, all of them asking for something. Everyone had some favor that only Booth could grant. An admirer named Miss S. Levin Dilkes wished an inscribed photograph, offered to pay if it could be taken especially for her—"I would be willing that it should cost $10."

"Sir!" commenced a letter from a would-be playwright, submitting a manuscript called *The Gipsy's Revenge*, "I am Unknown 'tis true. Does that prove that I have no wit no intelligence no imagination? I am poor. Have I for that to die from misery and despair? No! I will not give up before having exhausted the last ray of hope."

"Dear Sir," began a milder request from the mother of young Garrie Davidson, the theater errand boy; "my son Gennaro Garrison Davidson his working at your Theater i wish you would keepe a watchful eye on him that he don't forme any Bad ashoates he as allways been a very good boy to Me but New York his so ful of temtations."

An important message came in from Clarke in London, who sent word the Lyceum Theater there was temporarily free and proposed that he and Booth lease it jointly. Here was Booth's chance to control a first-rate house in London in which he could act regularly. He was tempted. But the Lyceum had the name of being an unlucky house. And—Booth hated decisions. He let this one drift, and while he hesitated a more enterprising, less superstitious manager, H. L. Bateman, and his wife, who had been Sidney Cowell, Mrs. Sam Cowell's daughter, snapped up the lease. It was a fatal hesitation. Henry Irving, the English actor, who since 1861, when he supported Booth in Manchester, had bided his time, making every day count toward his advancement, persuaded Bateman to produce *The Bells* in which Irving acted Mathias and scored his first overwhelming metropolitan hit. A star had been born whose angular shadow was to fall across Booth's path.

Late in September the great Charlotte Cushman emerged from ten years' retirement to appear at Booth's as Lady Macbeth, Queen Katharine in Shakespeare's *Henry VIII* and Meg Merrilies. This last role was her sure money-maker. Actors playing with her these days whispered that as she gave her final death shriek in the part, she pounded her breast, which was known to be on fire with cancer, so as to make her famous cry one of real agony.

Cushman brought in money, but the profits were wiped out by the next star, John E. Owens, a dear fellow and a topnotch comedian of the old school, but no longer quite able to hold his own with the fashionable opera season running full tilt against him. "My expenses are fearful," Booth confessed to Barrett in a letter. "I have only made thus far $49 dollars this season—losing *all* & more on Owens than I made on Cushman."

He was writing to reopen the delicate subject of names and print for *Julius Caesar*. Although he alluded to it in all modesty, there was no denying what the real capital of Booth's Theater was. "I think it is definitely proved that the 'draught' to this house lies in *my* name, and it follows that greater prominence should be given to the article that sells best. . . . If by doing what no other 'star' has done or will do, I accustom the rabble's eye to a constant view of my name made much less prominent than formerly by a combination of others—perhaps not so attractive (theatrically speaking) I shall soon destroy the power of my own."

Barrett must lump the idea that from now on if he played at Booth's he would play second fiddle. Booth could no longer afford the luxury of starring those whom no one came to see. "It was surely demonstrated last season that—much as you were liked by the intellectual few—your name had no attraction for the multitude. . . . My real desire has always been to do away altogether with 'star' type—but, alas! it cannot be— *humbug* & large letters have got such a firm hold upon the age we live in that I begin to fear all my dreams of high-art, refinement & delicacy in our profession are Utopian;—*dreams* & nothing more. I must, I find, live *with* the time since I am doomed to live in it, and must necessarily do as others do— look out for No. 1. I hate to say all this—I hate myself for feeling it, but it is a *rotten* truth."

Julius Caesar opened on Christmas night, 1871. Booth began as Brutus, a part he hadn't done since the benefit with his two brothers. It was one of the roles he was born to do. "A masterpiece!" exclaimed Laura Keene, writing in the April *Fine Arts* of the mature performance of this actor with whom she used to quarrel in days so far off now and themselves such tiny figures in them. She called attention to his Brutus' "tender love for Portia, his sorrow at her death, and the grief-laden meaning he gives to the short phrase:

Speak no more of her . . .

so indifferent in word, so affecting in delivery."

When the toga'd Barrett stalked into the Forum he was Cassius to the core, Cassius whether he would or no, for the same nature was in him. He too was the lean and hungry one: gloomy, combative, suspicious, intellectual, grudging in tendency, yet capable of generous deeds and with a streak of nobility.

In February Junius Booth took Barrett's place. Junius had turned fifty; his figure had thickened like his father's until

Caesar's description of Cassius as "lean and hungry" was a worse fit than ever on him. He had copied a piece of business from his father in the part, which was to strut with heavy ostentation right across the murdered Caesar's head. Edwin wrote to Barrett, who had quitted the company, that "June's Cassius was the gayest old burlesque you ever saw—by Jove! it was funny!"

Early in March Booth moved into Cassius and William Creswick, a reliable if shadowy player, took over Brutus. Negotiations with Adams to be Antony had fallen through. For the first weeks Antony was done by Frank Bangs, of whose performance William Winter murmured that it was "efficient." "Bangs," added Winter, "considered it to be sublime."

On March 11 Booth played Antony. Creswick shifted into Cassius, and Bangs tried Brutus. Booth's acting of the three principal parts prolonged the run; his fans wanted to see him in all three. "In all of them," decided Winter, "he excelled his competitors as to the element of sympathy. That was an attribute peculiar to Booth."

"In Mark Antony," said Laura Keene, "Mr. Booth rose out of himself." What stirred her most was the wonderful oration over Caesar's body, "its art, its elocution, tact and subtle management of the crowd, with the quicker and quicker delivery, till it swelled to a torrent of words; finally, the leap from the tribune (a trick, but a clever trick), and his thunderous denunciation of the traitors. . . . The house was swept away."

Booth had set his production in the Rome of Augustus Caesar because it was grander than the city of Julius. The scene of the Forum was all blue sky, white marble and a sense of space. In the Senate Chamber a curving backdrop spectacularly reproduced Gérôme's painting of Caesar's murder, showing tier on tier of stone benches rising on three sides above a dais. "Scene-painter's drama!" was what the failing Edwin Forrest called the production to Barrett soon after the opening. Forrest had no patience with fancy scenery. He remembered his youth, when an actor created the illusion called for with little more to help him than his voice and body. There were giants in those days when, as Forrest liked to put it, it was absolutely necessary to be an *actor!*

Lately Forrest had proved himself superior to any accessories. He had played King Lear in New York, the last engagement of his life there, with poor support and dingy settings, yet never had he acted the part more movingly. As he slowly advanced onstage, inclining his head to the faint applause from the half-filled benches, he made such a figure of ruined majesty that the handful of spectators could hardly keep their tears back. The critics no longer scoffed at him. "He is the King Lear of the American stage," declared one. "He gave to his children, the public, all that he had, and now they have deserted him. They have crowned a new king, before whom they bow, and 'the old man eloquent' is cheered by few voices."

At last Forrest saw clearly that he was discrowned. After one neglected performance a reporter cried to him: "Mr. Forrest, I never in my life saw you play Lear so well as you did tonight!"

The old actor rose. He drew himself up. "*Play* Lear?" he retorted. "What do you mean, sir? I do not *play* Lear. I *play* Hamlet, Richard, Shylock, Virginius, if you please, but by God, sir, I *am Lear!*"

III

Central Park Lake froze over this winter. Booth wrote to Edwina, shut away at school: "I've been learning to skate, but I make a poor 'foot' at it. When I was a little boy I had no opportunity to learn the different games and sports of childhood, for I was traveling most of the time. . . . *You* must learn."

There was not much time for skating now. Although *Julius Caesar* seemed from the front to run on greased wheels, in the regions backstage the actors jockeyed and intrigued, each one beating his ego like a tom-tom. Booth labored to keep the peace, to be all things to all people. He confided to Barrett that "Mark Antony has ruined Bangs. *He* wants to *star*. . . . I expect trouble with him. . . . Davenport is insulted because I told him he wouldn't draw as a *star* . . . he's very *indig* with me." This was E. L. Davenport.

Booth took the production to Philadelphia after suspending Bangs for a tiff with another player. But the man he put into Bangs' part, "though he does the *bus.* as well as Bangs could have done it got rats from my press-friends."

Another actor who reached Philadelphia on Monday morning to take over Cassius found his name advertised in small type, wrote Booth an insulting letter, and huffed out of the city on the train he had arrived in. A tyro was moved into his place; there was a two-night old novice for Antony. Booth was the Brutus. "Great G! what a performance! It d——d the play. . . . Ah! well, the result was I had to let up on Bangs."

He mused: "It's a very delicate thing to handle—this self-esteem."

He was planning for next fall, and he had bad news to break to Barrett. "Now, my boy, I am going to hit you square in the eye. . . . It is absolutely necessary that I should secure the strongest *paying* attraction & by filling my season with the sure cards endeavor to redeem a little of my losses. . . . Until the *grand revival* of 'Caesar' I have not made a penny over my rent this season—& with its fearful expenses it has not more than kept my head above the surface. . . . It is not as tho' my debts were paid & I stood free to serve a friend & damn the expense! I *cannot* do it. . . . I must tell you at once the plain & bitter truth—I cannot give you time next season."

Barrett took this fairly well. The real rift between him and Booth came the next winter when word flew south along the grapevine to New Orleans, where Barrett was acting, that Booth was about to put on a historical play called *Marlborough*. Barrett panted for the title role of the military Duke. When Booth fixed his choice elsewhere, Barrett accused Booth of breaking an engagement with him.

His tone was irritable with his chronic grievance, and Booth thrust back sharply: "Your accusation is utterly false and you well know it. . . . My dislike to say unpleasant things causes me, I know, to convey sometimes a wrong impression, and this weakness of mine doubtless led you to suppose yourself engaged by me, but now—since you have so grossly charged me with an act I have not committed . . . I will no longer be considerate or 'mealy-mouthed' but talk blunt business facts to you. I cannot afford to *star* those who have proved to be unprofitable to me."

Besides this, "You are physically so unsuited to the character of Marlborough," wrote Booth, "that I regarded your proposition to perform it as simply absurd."

It was this final adjective that cut most cruelly. When Barrett answered, which he did at once, on New Year's Day, 1873, his professional pride was oozing blood.

"My dear Sir," he began, "it may not be unprofessional in *your* eyes to say to an artist that his desire to perform any character is 'simply absurd' but it is a word I choose to use and if the atmosphere in which you breathe were not made too dense by the flattery of your dependents and hired agents, you might perhaps be able to hear the same things said of yourself. . . . No man ever yet attained greatness permanently by making everybody else pigmies and you will be no exception. . . . I have stood by *your* side and have suffered, I think, not much by the comparison.

"I am anxious that you should understand how deeply and unnecessarily you have estranged the friendship of one who at least is not to be despised. I shall not accept the humble role you allocate to me. If *you* really stand at the head of my Profession then *you* only are my compeer . . . and when Time gives his judgment, I may not after all be so very far behind your illustrious self, whom I care now as little to see or hear from as I was once anxious and delighted. Your silence will please me better than any reply to this."

A sight of Booth's face as he read would have pleased Barrett best of all. Booth scrawled furiously across the page: "Preserve this as a souvenir of the blackest ingratitude."

It was like the famous quarrel they had acted so often when the harassed Brutus cries,

"Away, slight man!"

And the stung Cassius answers,

"O ye gods! ye gods! Must I endure all this?"

No time for skating, no time to make up for lost time. But
there are some things that drag on forever. It was one night in
February or early March, 1873, that Booth instructed Garrie
Davidson, who did the odd jobs, to wake him up in his apartment at three in the morning.

Many years later Garrie Davidson, an old man now who
still did odd jobs in theaters, told everything that had happened on that eerie, dark early-morning to Otis Skinner, who
gave the story to the world.

Snow was falling thick outside when Booth and Garrie
stole down together into the furnace room under the stage.
Obeying orders, Garrie lighted a gas jet, then stoked the fire.
Over in one corner waited a large trunk tied around with ropes.
Still at Booth's direction, Garrie cut the ropes with an ax and
knocked the lid off, letting out a powerful smell of camphor.
They saw some wigs and swords lying on top and packed
underneath a heap of tarnished costumes.

It was like a dream to Garrie Davidson: the hour, the place,
the mysterious business to be done. Down in the heart of the
sleeping theater he stood at attention in front of the furnace
fire that scorched his face every time he stuffed into it one of
the costumes silently handed him by Booth. In silence ("It was
awful to watch him," said Garrie) Booth shook out each piece
and studied it, occasionally exposing the initials *J.W.B.* inked
on some of the linings. There was a Hamlet hauberk sewn
with jet beads, a satin waistcoat worn for Claude Melnotte,
Mark Antony's toga, and a robe for Othello made of Indian
shawls, gossamer-fine. At last he pulled out of the depths a
purple velvet tunic and an armhole cloak trimmed with ermine, wrinkled and shabby. He sat down on the edge of the
trunk and to the embarrassed boy's horror began to cry.

"My father's," Booth said. "Garrie, this was my father's

Richard III dress. He wore it in Boston on the first night I went on the stage as Tressel."

Garrie asked in a subdued voice: "Don't you think you ought to save that, Mr. Booth?"

But Booth was on his feet again. "No," he said, "put it in with the others," and he snatched the long-handled poker and stirred the disintegrating mass himself.

Finally everything in the trunk was gone, even two daggers thrown into the fire to melt, a few paste jewels, and a pair of women's satin slippers that had lain at the bottom. It was almost dawn. Booth motioned to Garrie to chop up the trunk. The splintered boards and the ropes were tossed onto the flames. Booth looked searchingly around, then told the boy to shut the furnace door.

"That's all. We'll go now."

IV

That things were not well with Booth's Theater was known in greenrooms all over New York. Bispham had heard the gossip in business circles outside the profession. Box-office receipts even of a hit like *Julius Caesar* could barely keep abreast of the cost of producing plays as sumptuously as Booth insisted on producing them. Harry Magonigle, one of the few at his elbow whose advice was worth anything, was always imploring him to cut down expenses, especially where the identical effect could be got for less money, but Booth only smiled with the shining, obstinate look of one who sees a vision.

The theater's financial basis had been shaky from the first. The original building costs had been let grow much too large. While the theater was going up, Robertson, apparently not chipping in with a dime himself, had raised the money needed (beyond what Booth faithfully sent him) through short loans on the credit of Booth's name. Instead of one long-term mortgage, which would have been easier to carry, Booth and Robertson had taken out several short ones at killingly high rates. There was no system, or plan adopted, only a scramble from month to month to make ends meet. Booth was all alone in deep waters now. He worriedly consulted Junius, who offered to lease and manage the theater for five years, thus freeing Ted to act in the provinces where the real gold lay.

Booth started out, leaving Junius in charge. But the brothers had no luck. Just when there was stark need that business should be good, the panic of 1873 clapped down on the general economy. Financial houses—empires, even—began to crumble and theater audiences naturally fell off. Junius borrowed money. He flaunted star after star to keep Booth's Theater from turning its lights out. Unfortunately, his main opposition was Tommaso Salvini, the Italian tragedian, doing a brutal, exciting Othello at the Academy of Music. This was Salvini's American debut. He was someone new, and those who had any money left to spend on the theater were spending it on him.

Salvini was a man towering and leonine, almost fat, who showed his white teeth in smiles of the south and breathed out physical charm like a hot wind. His Othello made New York gasp. "Revolting!" Clara Morris found it. "When Othello entered," she writes, "and fiercely swept into his swarthy arms the pale loveliness of Desdemona, 'twas like a tiger's spring upon a lamb. . . . His gloating eyes burned with the mere lust of the 'sooty Moor' for that white creature."

In the scene of Desdemona's murder Salvini would hurl himself on Signora Piamonti, his leading lady (no American actress would play opposite him), swing her over his head, stride across to the wide, low, cushioned bed, suggestive of the seraglio, then crash her down on it and himself on top of her, she writhing, he grunting and snarling.

William Winter was nauseated. "Plebeian! Carnal!" he called the exhibition, and solemnly reminded his readers in the *Tribune* that "Edwin Booth's learnedly accurate, steadily poetic and brilliantly pictorial setting of this play remains the best, and by far the best, that this public has ever seen."

But this public was perverse. After reading Winter it flocked to see Salvini.

Next, without warning, all Booth's creditors swooped down on him at once with hard, frightened faces. The panic had hurt them too. They must have their money from him. They threatened to foreclose the mortgages. It was utterly beyond Booth's power to pay them. In desperation he hired a lawyer named T. J. Barnett to examine his finances and advise him what to do.

He had plently of trained and reliable friends—Bispham was one of them—who would have been eager to help. He turned to Barnett instead. He had met the man a comparatively short time ago through a gushing letter Barnett had sent him praising his acting. Booth now put all his affairs in Barnett's hands. Barnett was a talker, like Robertson. Faced with the mess his client had made of things, he was philosophical. "All experience must be bought," he prated. "It is the rudder of life and is often its best treasure. Youth don't listen, won't heed. When the blood burns and hope is high and ambition strong, the gallant mind, restless as the wind and aspiring as the eagle, sweeps to its point, reckless as impulse itself."

Booth had hoped Barnett could sell the theater. After eight weeks of busy ineffectiveness Barnett proposed what amounted to giving it away. On November 12 the property into which Booth's dreams and best strength had gone was conveyed "for no consideration" to a man named Clark Bell, who was to protect and carry it until it could be sold. On January 26, 1874, Booth, nudged again by Barnett, filed a petition of voluntary bankruptcy in the United States District Court. The newspapers estimated his liabilities at about two hundred thousand dollars. His assets, which were also published, were valued at something under ten thousand. They included his wife's jewelry, all his furniture, books, paintings, chandeliers, professional costumes and one pair of dumbbells.

Booth had been forty on his last birthday, forty and a bankrupt. His friends wrote to him after the fiasco was known, as they had done in other bad times. "Your letter," he answered Jervis McEntee, "so full of what is beyond all price—the genuine sympathy of sound and solid friendship—gives me great consolation."

And to Bispham: "My dear boy. . . . This is by no means the heaviest blow my life has felt."

Critics who disliked Booth brayed with triumph to see him brought down. The *New York Times* told him what in its opinion had been wrong with his theater: "Such a company as only the most assiduous searching from Podunk at the east to Peoria at the west could ever have collected. Among such 'sticks' any star would shine!"

"Booth's Theater," smirked the Philadelphia *Press*, "has been the tomb of his fortunes and his renown. Mr. Booth did, it is true, shine in it to advantage, but it was as a brass tack does on an old-fashioned hair trunk. His company was one of the worst ever gathered together in this country. . . . Mr. Booth failed, of course."

There was no "of course." Booth called himself resigned, yet the ignominious failure wormed in him. This was a very different thing from the accidental burning of the Winter Garden, because bitterest of all was his dim recognition that his theater need never have failed if its business had been handled better, that even when the crash came it could still have been saved for him if he had engaged an able lawyer instead of the woolly-witted Barnett. He could have climbed to success on a ladder of *ifs*. Something he had learned, the hard way: "If ever I control another theater I shall subdue the painter & costumer & spend the money, thrown away on them, for good plays & actors."

McVicker, a canny theater manager, believed Booth's Theater could have been "bonded for all the indebtedness . . . such was its true value . . . Had Booth's financial affairs," McVicker pursued, "been conducted with anything like the ability he displayed in artistic matters, only success would have been the result; unfortunately, he was of a confiding nature."

"He was a dreamer," writes Winter. "The temperament that made him fine in Hamlet unfitted him for practical affairs. . . . In every part of his life I saw the operation of Hamlet's propensity to view all things as transitory and immaterial, and to let everything drift."

It was this strain that had tempted Booth's father to seek refuge from the sham of the stage in a lonely lighthouse where he could meditate on what was real. To father and son, in their brooding on a world elsewhere, the world they lived in grew shadowy. The spur of fame that drove other men on was dulled and blunted. Everything passes.

"My father ever seemed," said Booth—and he spoke for himself as well, "to muse with Omar Khayyam, thus:

> The worldly hope men set their hearts upon
> Turns ashes—or it prospers; and anon,
> Like snow upon the desert's dusty face,
> Lighting a little hour or two—is gone."

PART SIX

CHAPTER 11

Peace and Quiet

Say, is my kingdom lost? why, 'twas my care;
And what loss is it to be rid of care?
                    King Richard II, *Act III, scene 2*

 BOOTH spent the summer of 1874 with Mary and Edwina in a little retired house called Cedar Cliff at Cos Cob, Connecticut. He had his long actor's hair cropped close to his head in the short "warrior cut" that was always his first luxury on vacation. His chronic nervous indigestion eased away. He lay sunk in a hammock outdoors in the shade and smoked. One afternoon a tall Yale student trudged over through the heat to put a momentous question to the great actor. Ought he to go on the stage? "Young man, I wouldn't," said Booth. "It's a dog's life."

The boy looked unconvinced; he had the fever badly. His name was William Gillette.

Away in the steaming city the lawyers wrangled over Booth's ruined enterprise. It was like the funeral of an old friend held in another country, too far away to hurt much. But Booth came across the first fawning letter he had ever had from T. J. Barnett and his pencil bit into the paper as he scrawled along the envelope: "First letter I remember to have received from this damned scoundrel—would to God it had been the last."

The summer could have been pleasant even for a bankrupt except that Mary was behaving very oddly. Her nerves were all on edge, and she took out most of her irritability on Edwina, who in winter was usually away at school. Ever since her marriage Mary had gone conscientiously to school entertainments and during holidays had heard her little stepdaughter say her prayers, tucked her in bed at night, and read Dickens to her. But as Edwina grew closer to being a woman she was becoming as passionately devoted to her father as he to her, rapturously sniffed the smell of tobacco clinging to the letters he sent her at school—it brought him nearer to her—and at home ran to do him ardent little services, to wake him from his nap every afternoon and brew the tea that was all he took before leaving for the theater. She and her father had a special bond in their united quiet devotion to an idealized, angel figure (a memory to Booth, a legend to Edwina) until Mary McVicker Booth, shaken by a fury she could not control, shrilly forbade Mary Devlin's name to be spoken in her hearing.

Besides his own debts Booth had Robertson's to pay. When he bought Robertson out he had assumed all outstanding liabilities. Back on the road this fall on a long tour aimed at large profits, he plugged away doggedly—"a galley slave chained to the oar . . . something always prevents my getting free."

At the turn of the year Booth's Theater was surrendered on foreclosure to the Oakes Ames estate. McVicker, with his daughter's happiness in mind, stepped in to the rescue and bought up his son-in-law's debts, making himself Booth's only creditor and extending him lenient terms. In March, 1875, Booth was discharged from bankruptcy, though it would be a hard pull still to pay McVicker.

They spent the summer at Cos Cob again. There was neither peace nor quiet to be found under the same roof with Mary. She was really ill mentally, and the doctors traced the sly growth of her illness back five years to the birth and death in one day of her lost son, the infant Edgar. The shock of the loss had jarred into actual hysteria what must have been a tendency. Mary began to suspect slights where none existed. She nursed a sullen obsession that everyone was against her, showed a craving for sympathy that was almost imbecile, and flew into demonic rages at a word. Booth humored her and carefully warned Edwina never to cross her. Outsiders' mouths dropped open at scenes like the one every night at ten when Mary pointed to the clock with a small, jabbing forefinger and snapped: "Edwina!"

Edwina would immediately say good night and whisk upstairs. Half an hour later—"Edwin!"

Booth would lay down his book, rise obediently, say an affectionate good night and fade out of the room.

"Mrs. Booth," writes Margaret Townsend, who saw this happen, in her *Theatrical Sketches*, "was one of the most extraordinarily small and precise of women, and it was difficult for the observer to discover wherein lay her attraction for the great actor, likewise her claim to such absolute control as she practised over her family."

Booth's vacation this summer blew up in August with a bad carriage accident when one of his horses bolted. Born with a caul and used to a charmed life, Booth was astonished and rather aggrieved to find he had broken his arm and two ribs. The surgeon called in set his arm crooked, so that later another surgeon had to break the arm and set it again and *he* set it crooked. For the rest of Booth's life it was shorter than the other. He couldn't raise it in a straight line. Something else spoiled was his hurtling fall to the ground at Richard III's death. After his accident he had to give it up—a pity, because it was one of the most startlingly deadlike falls ever seen in the theater.

II

A newspaper sniped that "Booth is now 40 years old. He will never draw as he once did." Booth was almost forty-two, and the paper missed again in its prophecy. When he showed himself on the stage of Augustin Daly's Fifth Avenue Theater in October, 1875, carrying his broken arm in a black silk sling, a packed house shouted its welcome. He hadn't acted in New York for two years. At Booth's Theater, where he had been seen last, George L. Fox was popping up from trapdoors and jumping through policemen's legs in *The Adventures of Humpty-Dumpty in Every Clime*.

With Booth at Daly's in the cast of *Hamlet* were two green players, Maurice Barrymore as Laertes and John Drew as Rosencrantz. Maurice Barrymore, almost an amateur since he was the first in his family to enter the profession, soon after this married Georgiana, John Drew's sister, and had three children, Lionel, Ethel, and John. Young Drew's mother was Louisa Lane Drew, who remembered Junius Brutus Booth and was now manageress of the Arch Street Theater in Philadelphia. Because of the boy's eminent connections Winter noticed him in his review: "The gentleman who played Rosencrantz evidently had an engagement with a friend after the performance, so hurried was his speech and so evident his desire to get through with his part."

At Daly's Booth played Shakespeare's Richard II for the first time and superbly; the doomed, charming Richard has a good deal of Hamlet in him. He played King Lear. When he had first brashly acted Lear in California he was twenty-three. He was twenty-seven when he admitted the part was too much for him and dropped it out of his repertory. But he still studied it, and when he tried it again after ten years his performance had attained a stature that made some people consider Lear the most wonderful of all his roles, though the gallery always liked his Hamlet better. Booth's Lear was a connoisseur's dish, like Bernhardt's Phèdre or Jefferson's Bob Acres. The public monotonously yelled to see Jefferson as Rip Van Winkle, Bernhardt as Camille, and Booth as Hamlet.

Booth showed Lear incipiently mad at the rise of the curtain, dimly and agonizingly aware of his deterioration. His most moving passages were toward the end, the pitiful, bemused recognition by the brain-sick old king of his one faithful daughter,

> Do not laugh at me;
> For, as I am a man, I think this lady
> To be my child Cordelia,

and the threnody over her dead body,

> Thou'lt come no more,
> Never, never, never, never, never!

"I remember him," writes Winter, "—indeed, who that saw him could ever forget?—his attenuated figure, his haggard face, his beseechful eyes, his bewildered glance, his timid, hesitant, forlorn manner as he gazed on Cordelia, the doubting, questioning look . . . the piteous, feeble movement of the hands, one upon the other, and the pathos of the heart-breaking voice."

Money was so short that Booth and Mary exchanged only the simplest gifts this Christmas, though, shutting his eyes to the cost, Booth took Edwina to the French opera. Better days were coming. In January, 1876, he left New York to make a grand tour of the South under John T. Ford's management. Ford had agreed to pay him thirty thousand dollars for fifty performances. Mary went along, though thoroughly unfit to travel, refusing to let her husband out of her sight. From Richmond Booth wrote to Edwina: " 'Twas in this city, darling, just twenty years ago, that I first met your angel mother. . . . Your grandfather Booth was much beloved here."

The deeper they penetrated into the reconstructed South the fiercer was the curiosity centered on Booth as John Wilkes' brother. In Mobile he had a request for free tickets from Sergeant Boston Corbett. "I am sure," Corbett reminded him in his note, "you will not refuse . . . when I tell you that I am the United States soldier that shot and killed your brother." Booth winced, and sent the tickets.

State legislatures shifted their hours of meeting so members could see him act. Crowds collected at railway stations to gape at the aloof, handsome man with the glossy, black hair overflowing the space between the brim of his silk hat and the fur collar of his coat. In Chattanooga a brass band, stridently hospitable, met his train. In Nashville women plunged after him in the street in a mania to touch him, gabbling: "That's him!" "That's Booth!"

News of his approach threw the stock companies he starred with into a perfect dither. Thirty-two supers (the lesser stars got ten) were hired for his stage armies in *Richard III* and *Macbeth*. The actresses, who graded their costumes by the magnitude of the visitor, brought out their choicest dresses, and on opening night the awed, local Laertes, Richmond, or Macduff could hardly hold his weapon for his sweating palm in the fight at the finale.

With Mary every molehill was a mountain. She couldn't sleep on a moving train, so they had to wait out the nights on a siding. Physically indefatigable, she walked thirteen miles across rough country at Mammoth Cave and next day side-saddled fourteen more, wearing out the men. But she was ridden with nervous fears, and at Virginia City when they had a chance to go down in a coal mine she hysterically refused and forbade her husband to go.

"Mr. Taylor!" she ordered one actor, "the resemblance between you and Edwin is so *remarked* when you are onstage together as Hamlet and Horatio that I wish you would wear a blond wig." Mr. Taylor did as he was bid.

The Southern tour had ended. They were on their way west. Booth had had an offer from John McCullough, proprietor and manager of the new California Theater in San Francisco. It was twenty years since he had seen the West Coast. He had left San Francisco in 1856 with five hundred dollars. Twenty years later he hadn't much more than that, his fine profits from Ford having been passed on to McVicker. Yet California was still the magic land of new beginnings and on hand to greet him and Mary was a jaunty old couple who had just made a fresh start, Dave Anderson and his bride; she was the actress Marie Everard, a West Coast favorite in the golden days. Other faces familiar to Booth of yore were there to be picked out, among them Mrs. Judah's, fabulously ancient.

San Francisco itself was wonderfully transformed. The sea wind still raked it from end to end and the precipitous streets still rushed downhill to the white-capped harbor bristling with masts and pennants, but the city's sparkling, flimsy, fairy-tale look of having been scattered on the hills from the hand of a swooping djinn was gone. San Francisco had grown roots and a history and stone houses and settled citizens, become parents and grandparents, who could trace back their residence for a quarter of a century.

The California Theater exuded wealth, especially when filled at night with an opulent-looking audience dressed to the nines. Booth was used to noisy ovations, but the one he got here topped all: the mental picture most of the old-timers had of their little *ranchero* tearing down Market Street, waving to his friends, superimposed itself on the shape of the mature actor bowing his acknowledgment of their wild greetings with a faintly tired, regal smile.

And to Booth it seemed that if ever he had had a home it was in California, where he had been most vagabond. He and Anderson sat back and reminisced voluptuously. Booth felt young and stimulated and hopeful. He went on a stealthy pilgrimage by himself to find the "ranch" where they had lived their glorious bachelor life, but what had been an open space in the sand hills had become a back street swallowed by the metropolis. Their shack was gone, and on its site stood a tenement house. The change was ruthlessly complete.

Booth's San Francisco engagement ran eight weeks and smashed all records for the dramatic stage in the United States. A good-looking lad, David Belasco, whose home was in Frisco, got work as a super and managed to "walk on" with Booth at least once in every play he did. Hundreds were turned away each night, and the receipts swelled to over ninety-six thousand dollars, fifty thousand of which went to Booth and from him to McVicker to shave down his debt.

He was back in the East in November and fully middle-aged again. The waters of work closed over his head. "My correspondence and conversation must needs be vapid," he wrote distractedly from Boston in May to Ferdinand Ewer, one of his earliest serious critics and his friend ever since. "The foot-light limit is a sealed Greek book to me. I rarely know who's President." There was a brighter side: from November to May he had earned upward of seventy-two thousand dollars, which changed hands rapidly. And now at last his debt to his father-in-law was paid in full. He could keep the next dollar.

III

One afternoon Dr. Osgood on West Eleventh Street was surprised to have a call from Booth, who looked worn and depressed and begged in a low voice to be allowed to see once more "the room where I secured my greatest happiness." This was the book-lined study where Dr. Osgood had tied the knot between the rising young star and Mary Devlin.

Booth's second Mary, in a bad state, rested through the summer of 1877 at a sanatorium, but she was out by fall, in time to insist on going with her husband on the road. From Chicago Booth scratched Anderson a line about family doings: "June is building a hotel at Manchester—sits still—smokes and bewails his hard lot. Aggy *jobs* and looks as though her hair dye had affected her health. Joe 'loafs and invites his soul' at Long Branch and wishes he was a sea-gull."

Joe Booth had married and was dabbling in New Jersey real estate. He was becoming rather a curmudgeon. His brother hoped that marriage would "moderate and civilize him." Aggy was Junius' new wife, formerly the actress Agnes Perry, who was very good-looking and three years younger than June's daughter Blanche. June had married her in 1867 and had had four sons by her. Now he was leaving the stage and starting out in the hotel business in Manchester-by-the-Sea, Massachusetts. He had a Booth's grand dreams, and his unfinished hotel was to be a hulking, showy creation with terraced gardens, a dance hall and a staff of fifty. Consequently, the handsome, painted Agnes "jobbed" or acted in short stints to help raise the money.

Edwin wrote again to Ewer that his health was fair and his houses were crowded. "This is about all I know beyond the limit of my fancy world, where I dream my life away."

Some people who had seen him act in his fiery younger years felt he was beginning to refine his art too much, was losing his hold on life. Adam Badeau thought back regretfully to the "awful bursts of passion" that had thrilled him in Booth's early work. Jefferson warned his old friend not to overdo the polishing.

"Don't elaborate, don't refine it any further," begged James E. Russell, critic on the New York *Sun*.

Booth wrote back: "I appreciate all you say, my dear boy, but how in hell can I help being refined? (The above is a specimen of it)—I can't paint with big brushes—the fine touches come in spite of me. . . . I'm too damned genteel and exquisite."

Cried Walt Whitman: "Edwin had everything but guts: if he had had a little more that was absolutely gross in his composition he would have been altogether first class instead of just a little short of it." Whitman was all for the big voice and the broad-ax gesticulation. He had adored Junius Brutus Booth and gone overboard for the acting of Forrest and Salvini, who, when they let themselves go, Whitman gloried, could "make me forget everything else and follow them!"

In comparison with their huge oratory the younger Booth's was a "still, small voice," heard to the last corner of the house yet seeming in the soliloquies to speak from inside the listener. Edwin Booth's mature style had a quiet grandeur. He had inherited the grandeur; the quietness, which was his own, was his link with the future. E. H. Sothern, twenty years old and a star in the making, now first saw Booth's Hamlet. "His genius," marveled Sothern, "shone like a good deed in a naughty world. His light was so steady and pure and his acting so free from exaggeration that he baffled imitation."

In the eighteen months since he had paid off McVicker, Booth had struck a winning streak and was heaping up money.

Now was the time. With determination, with a certain self-consciousness, rather with the air of someone whose right hand knows not what his left hand does, he began to lay discreet plans and pull wires for acting in England again. His ancient near-failure there still smarted.

And since Booth had acted there Henry Irving had become England's top star. When H. L. Bateman, the manager of the Lyceum in London, died, his widow and Irving had carried on the theater together, with Bateman's daughter Isabel as leading lady. In 1878 Irving had taken over the management from Mrs. Bateman. Ellen Terry, who slipped into Isabel's place, considered that "he had to be a little cruel, not for the last time in a career devoted unremittingly and unrelentingly to his art and his ambition."

From across the Atlantic Booth had watched Irving's rise a shade wistfully but with a generous admiration uppermost. As actor-manager of the Lyceum Irving was doing what Booth had failed to do: making "a go" of producing and starring in worth-while plays. A rumor was afloat that Irving with Miss Terry planned to tour the United States, and Booth had an inspiration, one that had first come to him several years earlier when his business manager had written to Irving to propose a simultaneous exchange of countries and theaters: Booth to play at the Lyceum and Irving at Booth's. Irving never answered, and Booth had persuaded himself that the letter never reached him. This time Booth wrote in his own hand in March, 1879. "I have now no theater to offer you in exchange for such a courtesy, but whatever service I may be able to render you among my countrymen I will cheerfully perform."

He still recommended that Irving when in New York should play at Booth's Theater, which "still retains," he emphasized, "nor can it ever entirely lose its Shakespearian prestige." And he mentioned a letter just in from his sister "in which she expresses her great interest in your Hamlet." This was retouching the truth a little, because Asia had thought Irving's Hamlet frightful, called the English actor "a pallid ghost" and urged

Edwin to hasten over to show the Londoners what good acting really was.

Asia longed to see her brother. To friends who visited her abroad she poured out her desperate homesickness. Her married life was a disaster. She hated her husband and he had hated her ever since John Wilkes' crime. "It is marvellous how he hates me, the mother of his babies—but I am a *Booth* that is sufficient. I call myself in secret the ladder that he mounted by."

She had never come back with Clarke on his business trips home. A second parting from so much she loved would be too hard to bear. She remained in England, would die there—an exile. "I shall bless God," she told Edwin, "when my hour comes to relieve me from the thralldom."

Often she thought of her youth, of the farm in the vast forestland. Soon after Johnny died, Joe had gone down to sell some of the furniture and rescue the heirlooms, but for many years afterward a few old theatrical costumes still hung in a wardrobe in one of the rooms, among them a dark, rich suit with gold buttons. As time went on one of the tenants tore them into strips and braided them into rugs.

In 1878 old Mrs. Booth had sold the farm. It had passed out of the family's hands, yet the imprint the Booths left behind could not fade completely. Some fifty years later—long after every child of Junius Brutus Booth's had gone back to dust—an old lady in the neighborhood still recalled them: their taking ways; their wooing voices; their dark, sparkling faces. "How beautiful was Asia! How handsome John Wilkes Booth!"

On April 23, 1879 (Shakespeare's birthday), Booth was acting Richard II at McVicker's Theater in Chicago and was in the middle of the last soliloquy, spoken by Richard in prison at Pomfret. The sad young king says softly:

> "I have been studying how I may compare
> This prison where I live unto the world:
> And for because the world is populous,

And here is not a creature but myself,
I cannot do it."

A calcium light blazed on Booth. Always in this scene he sat in the same attitude, a slender, rejected, yet still royal figure; the fair brown hair he wore for the part drooping to his shoulders, his head bowed at an angle that varied only infinitesimally from one performance to the next. But this time, for no clear reason that he could ever fix on, he changed his usual business by impulsively standing up, and in that instant a pistol shot cracked. Jerking his head back, he saw the flash as a second shot went off. One self watched his other self make the three strides down to the footlights to point up into the balcony at the moving shape, which was poising to shoot again. "Arrest that man!" he called.

At the police station the would-be assassin allowed that he was a clerk in a dry-goods store in St. Louis. He spun several fascinating stories: that in shooting at Booth he was defending his sister's honor (the reporters pounced on this and did what they could with it); second, that he was Booth's illegitimate son and like his father a tragic genius, only Booth had thwarted him.

His third statement was even more titillating: "My name is Mark Gray. My reason for attempting to shoot Booth is that he mocked me. I saw him a few nights since in *Richelieu*, and Booth said in one of the scenes: 'Mark where she stands!' He had a peculiar emphasis on the word 'Mark.' He said it sneeringly, and I know he meant me. Besides, Booth is not as great an actor as Barrett."

Mark Gray, obviously mad as a hatter, was locked up in the asylum at Elgin, Illinois. Among dozens of letters inspired by the shooting, Booth had one from Jefferson submitting that it would be "an interesting theme in the future history of the stage that the only man who thought Barrett was better than Booth turned out to be a lunatic."

From England, Asia wrote that her husband was ragingly disgruntled because an attempt had been made on Booth's life

Booth's Theater on Twenty-third Street between Fifth and Sixth Avenues, New York City.

terior of Booth's Theater showing
t of the first scene of *Romeo and
iet* with which the Theater
ened February 3, 1869. From a
tercolor drawing by Charles W.
tham. *(Museum of the City of
w York)*

(Above) The Palace and Play scene for *Hamlet*, Act III, as produced in Booth
Theater in 1869. The play within the play was performed both behind and in fro
of the low arch back center. This is one of the first uses of the box set on any Ne
York stage.

(Below) The last scene of *Richelieu* as presented by Edwin Booth at his theater
1870.

Both of these illustrations are from watercolor drawings made by Charles V
Witham, who was Booth's scenic artist. *(Museum of the City of New York)*

that not only didn't scratch him but would make the public feel sorrier for him than ever. When the news reached London, Clarke had burst open Asia's door about two in the morning with a blow "that sent it back against him," with his hat on his head, and in a loud, excited voice exclaimed over and over: "Bear in mind one thing! Edwin is safe and hearty. He has been shot at on the stage and is not hurt."

"He dwells upon that," Asia told her brother, "not *touched*, not *hurt* as if it was a great pity to have escaped." Then Clarke had launched a tirade on the Booths, "who get all the notoriety without *suffering!!* Look at me! *I* was *dragged* to jail by the neck, literally *dragged* to prison, and Edwin goes scot-free—gets all the fame, sympathy. Who thinks of what *I* endured?"

The shooting had ripped open the barely healed wounds of all the family. Booth's mother couldn't rid herself of the picture of this son too lying dead. Mary dreamed of revolvers and woke up shrieking. When the first shot went off she had been standing on sentry duty in the wing, keeping her ever-vigilant eye on her husband, and Booth had had to excuse himself to the audience and hurry back to soothe her before finishing the play. Next morning he had a delayed fit of nerves himself as he realized how all that had saved him had been his unpremeditated rising from his chair. "My caul saved me! Second sight—premonition—warning! I don't account for what I did, but there's no other explanation."

He could never talk about it without getting a little wild-eyed. Yet like Hamlet, who joked excitedly after the Ghost had gone, Booth went into fits of nervous laughter over the shooting, which he called "the Fool's Revenge." He had one of the bullets pried out of the scenery, mounted on a gold cartridge cap inscribed *From Mark Gray to Edwin Booth*, and wore it on his watch chain.

Gray bragged that he had been scheming to kill Booth for three years. From jail he sent a letter of the twisted, illiterate type that all the Booths were used to receiving, warning Edwin that he must pay nine hundred dollars or "be hurt til he dy," later another letter from the asylum admitting he had made a mistake, "got the wrong pig by the ear. Well, as the learned 'heads' say we all are not infallible, hence its human to err. And to forgive is devine. . . . I wish you a happy New Year and manny of them."

Fate had her hand in, and now ordained another threat. A peculiar, raised black spot, large as a silver dollar and furry to the touch, appeared on Booth's tongue, which began to feel swollen too big for his mouth, was always burning-dry, and had to be kept constantly moistened. Booth, who feared the spot was cancerous, sought out one doctor after another, tragically opening each interview with: "Doctor! I'm the man with a black tongue!"

At home he paced the floor and every five minutes sprang at the mirror, put out his tongue as far as it would go and glared in panic. At last Dr. Ghislani Durant, a New York cancer specialist, diagnosed the trouble as a rare type of fungus. The doctor scraped off the parasite and treated the tongue with phenic acid. The condition cleared up. Marvelously relieved, Booth went off with Mary to Saratoga to recuperate. A few weeks passed, then Dr. Durant had a despairing telegram: "BLACK, BLACK, BLACK, BOOTH!"

Microscopic specks of the fungus had been left on the tongue and had multiplied until the spot was as alarming as ever. Dr. Durant took the train to Saratoga and began all over. Every day he delicately and painstakingly scraped the diseased tongue and treated it with acid. At the end of six months Booth was really healed. He had paid Dr. Durant's fee, but, as the token of a gratitude beyond fees or words or any recompense, he also sent the doctor an exquisite silver loving cup from Tiffany's around the rim of which was engraved from *Macbeth*:

> The mere despair of surgery he cures.

IV

It was December and Henry Irving had not yet deigned to answer Booth's letter written in March. This made twice he had ignored a letter. "He has 'the big head' a heap," was Booth's opinon.

If Irving was slippery, Booth was stubborn. He decided to go to England anyway. "People accept Irving *faute de mieux*," insisted his friend E. C. Stedman, who was visiting in London, and Asia didn't leave off emphasizing that her brother was bound to succeed there if only because Irving's acting was so bad.

Through a London agent Booth reached an understanding with Walter Gooch, manager of the Princess Theater. Booth remembered the Princess as a very fashionable house, and so it had been twenty years before when he first played in London. But since then it had degenerated steadily, and though located in the West End, it catered now to an East End public that jammed the cheap seats to see shockers like *Drink* and *Guinea Gold*. Gooch, however, had tremendous plans for the house. He meant to do it over—all new, all beautiful—and swore to Booth that by the next autumn a transformed Princess would fling her doors wide and her future policy would be to show "good plays."

Booth was delighted at the chance to open what would be like a new theater. It seemed a happy omen. "Irving has the A.1. position," he explained in a letter to Dave Anderson. "But maybe I may get an English pat on the back (or a kick, mayhap) while there."

He was acting in New York and on the road. Although almost every city he stopped at held some piece of family history, he had no home love left for any place now. Once he had felt such a love for California, but no longer. Only when he passed through the stage door and saw the lighted stage waiting to receive him behind the lowered curtain did he feel he was at home.

In Boston (where June's gay daughter Marion acted Katherine to her uncle Edwin's Petruchio) a letter reached Booth out of the blue from Lawrence Barrett. It was a plea to forget their seven-year-long feud that Barrett's furious words had started. They called on each other, Booth remarking afterward to Anderson that Barrett, obviously on the make, had "blarneyed" him to his heart's content—"all of which I meekly swallowed for the nonce. *Mum!*"

Later this spring he played at his own theater, or the theater that had once been his—played there most unwillingly, for he found the place "peopled with countless ghosts." In the company was a jolly, eager boy named Otis Skinner, who did Laertes. Every night, during the tedious wait between Laertes' good-by to Ophelia and his next appearance three acts later when he bounds on to avenge Polonius' death, young Skinner would stamp up and down his dressing room flaying his emotions, and when his cue finally came would hurl himself into the scene. After several nights of this Booth sent for him during an intermission. Booth was smoking as usual and playing solitaire.

"Young man," he said thoughtfully, "I've been watching you and you're killing yourself. You've got some high-tone notion you're supposed to *be* Laertes. Relax! Read a book, write letters, play pinochle. Loaf about in the wings. Don't try to work yourself up, it can't be done. Just wait for your cue, then, when you hear it, *go on the stage and act!*"

Booth and Mary were in a furnished apartment at the Hotel Brunswick overlooking Madison Square and each sunny day Booth spent minutes at the window—"the view is lovely—with the budding trees and young grass springing."

He had a gloomy letter, suggesting solitary heart-eating behind drawn shades, from the still struggling artist Jervis McEntee, to whom he had lent money and whom he now did his utmost to cheer. "Come out of the shadows!" Booth summoned him in words that were almost an echo of the unknown stranger's words, which had done so much for Booth so many years ago.

"Come out of your memories and combat your despondency," that nameless friend had written then.

And now: "Don't stay in your den and rust in corroding recollections," Booth warned the brooding artist, "it's damned selfishness to do so. . . . I did the same once and realize the stupidity—the ingratitude of my conduct. We owe something to God and to those we mourn for. They expect us to make them some better return for their dear love than mere moans."

He had his own troubles. The summer before, when they were at Saratoga, Mary's nervous illness had been violently stimulated by what Booth considered was the deliberate malice of one of her intimate friends, "a devilish work," and Mrs. —— was a "fiend," an "envious, malicious devil."

The result of this woman's repeated suggestions to one whose mind was already disturbed was to begin to turn Mary against her husband. Mary's mother, who had never liked Booth, helped the mischief on. Booth confided to Laurence Hutton, who had been living near them in Saratoga when the fuss started, that "the damage that Mary and her vile-tongued mother and Mrs. —— have done me—socially, I mean—is more than you suppose. I've been busy the past few months listening to and refuting horrible stories about myself."

It was not yet a year since he had written to Asia that after ten years of marriage he found not a fault in his wife—one of the loveliest things he had ever written to her, his sister answered as she forlornly contrasted his marriage with her own. It would, she feared, take Clarke a long time to enumerate "all *my* deficiencies."

Then came Saratoga, and Mary's condition took a jump for the worse. At the theater this spring her behavior was the talk of the greenroom. On her bad days she would let no one, including his dresser, speak to or come near her husband. "She would attend to all the robing and make-up," Otis Skinner writes, "and in parts like Richelieu and King Richard would gather up the trailing robes and, walking close behind, follow him to his entrance, never releasing him until his cue was spoken from the stage."

Sometimes the actors gave impromptu parties onstage after the play, but Booth was not allowed to attend them. Mary expected him, however, to be at her side when she served tea in the anteroom to her special friends. She would beckon the nearest member of the cast. "Where is Mr. Booth?" They always knew, though they never admitted, that Mr. Booth would be down in the cellar drinking beer with the grips.

These were his only escapades. At home he held the wailing girl in his arms. Not only was her mind worse, the doctors looked serious over a hacking cough she had.

For hours in the tense afternoons before the performance or late at night when his work was over, Booth rocked her on his lap like a child, laid his cheek against hers, stroked her hair, coaxed her back to reason. The room was not large enough to hold her restlessness. The years flew back and it was his father whose mad feet pounded through a hotel bedroom; he could smell the dust, hear the *plink-a-plink* of a boy's banjo. As Mary grew wilder, he grew more tender. She could not help herself, not even when, her mania coming on her, she screamed that she hated him, was persecuted, martyred. "The peculiar phase of hysteria has increased and has manifested itself in worse form than ever," he told Hutton.

Early in June the once well-known actor John Brougham died. He had been a favorite in his day, yet at his funeral there was a poor turnout. The arrangements made by his friends were cheap and skimpy, even the black crepe ran short. Booth, who was a pallbearer, found it a "shamefully sad affair," in spite of which, perhaps because of which, he risked a small joke at the sparsely attended graveside. Brougham had been a very large man. His coffin had been partly lowered when it had to be hauled up into view again so the grave could be widened. "It is the *last recall!*" Booth murmured to Winter standing beside him.

So much for an actor forgotten. A few days after Brougham's funeral a champagne breakfast was given for Booth at fashionable Delmonico's as a send-off before he sailed for England. Invitations were at a premium. An orchestra strummed away. Hothouse flowers were massed overpoweringly around a bust of the guest of honor. Among the favored ones invited were Barrett; Jefferson; Dr. Durant, asked at Booth's request;

and Winter ("Weeping Willy," Booth called him), who was slopping over with tearful farewell sentiments.

Barrett had hinted ahead of time that his seat at table must be above the salt. " 'Tis my part to be quiescent in this business," Booth parried.

The fun started at noon and lasted until night, leaving its mark even on the reserved guest of honor who, though he had dreaded the occasion beforehand, exulted to Barrett afterward: "Wasn't it *jolly* as well as grand? Everyone was *limber*, in fact I found myself 'quite so' and have small knowledge of how or when I reached home. First time I've been so for ages— sick yet!"

Weeping Willy Winter had his shrewd side. His eyes were quite dry when he advised Booth to open in London with *Richelieu*, which could be counted on to please, rather than with *Hamlet*, which would seem like wanton defiance of Irving, whose Hamlet had become the towering performance of the London stage and had run for two hundred nights, twice as long as Booth's.

On June 30, 1880, Booth walked up the gangplank of the ship *Gallia* with his blooming daughter on his arm. Edwina was eighteen, the age her father had been when he first saw California. On Booth's other arm hung his tiny, pining, fading wife.

After changing her mind a dozen times, Mary had decided to go. She was temporarily buoyed up by a vision of triumph over the unbearable Irving, and it was she ("impulsive, belligerent . . . meant well but had no tact," fumed Winter) who in the course of the trip over talked her husband into opening in *Hamlet.*

CHAPTER 12

A Pat on the Back

So foul and fair a day I have not seen.
Macbeth, *Act I, scene 3*

 With high hopes they landed at Queenstown. They stopped in London just long enough for Booth to shake hands with Walter Gooch, who was still scurrying in and out of his theater with insectlike industry as he renovated. Then they crossed over for a pleasure tour of the continent, lasting several weeks.

In Paris Booth took Edwina to the Porte Saint Martin to see the same play he and her young mother had seen there in 1862 and to his astonishment the same actress as heroine. That pantheress of a star Madame Sarah Bernhardt was out of the city, soon to leave for America to make her New York debut at, of all places, Booth's Theater, but they saw Coquelin *ainé* at the Comédie Française. Luster, intellect, finesse—Coquelin's art had them, and yet to Booth the French style was too academic; it wanted soul.

With high hopes they crossed back to London. If California in Booth's memory had a golden haze around it, London was an etching, a black and white with outlines smudged by fog. After twenty years the picture was still true. The autumn weather was chill and dull as he settled his little family into an awesomely expensive suite at the smart St. James Hotel in Piccadilly, then went off to begin rehearsals at the Princess.

And now for the first time his heart misgave him. The theater as Gooch had done it over was handsome in a stiff way, but Booth, struck with sudden foreboding, began (too late) to wonder if the long association of this house with trashy thrillers could be lived down overnight. The scenery was ordinary. As for the company, there were only two acceptable actors in it, and it was a discouraging omen that one was killed in a train wreck before the opening, while the other was finally kept from appearing by a complication about his contract. And everywhere Booth went it seemed the chief thing talked of was Henry Irving's latest equipment and crack casts at the Lyceum.

Booth opened ("I went in head first!") in *Hamlet* on November 6. London's American colony was present to a man, all Americans having for weeks boastfully harped on the string of how superior Booth was to Irving. The English playgoers waited to be shown. A few had seen Booth act in his own country and had been pleased in their composed fashion. Lord Houghton, for example, on his return to England was asked his opinion of Booth and gave it, that "Booth was a really fine actor—quite so."

But the suspicion, gathering and darkening as the dread night drew near, that with his usual instinct for business he had for the second time steered his London engagement into the worst possible theater was fatally depressing to Booth. So were the well-meant warnings of friends that he was not to mind if the London critics were—reserved. When he walked on at last into Gooch's shoddy settings he was fatally resigned, fatally calm, stern and cold, and his mood touched his performance with a fatal kiss. Said the *Standard*, reviewing the opening: "A disappointment."

The *Observer:* "Artificial . . . uninspired."

The *Daily News:* "An actor's Hamlet . . . cold and classical."

The *Times* conceded that Mr. Booth gave "a thoroughly intelligible and consistent reading of a favorite part," that only occasionally was he "laboured and tricky."

It was a mixed reception, by no means all bad; the disheartening element was its faintness. Booth's genius hadn't caught the public. On his second night, still more on his third, his initial coldness wore off as his work gripped him, but by then it was too late. His first impression on the critics had been made beyond unmaking. It was possible, too, that he had waited a few years too long to come back to London, the city that was the pace-setter of things theatrical in the English-speaking world. The *Saturday Review* regretted some of his "odd and old-fashioned tricks" like "taking the stage": to command all eyes, Booth would strike a pose up center, the attention-riveting figure of an obvious tableau.

"The days of the old classical school are dead and buried," scoffed the *Telegraph's* critic, Clement Scott, and he made fun of the American Hamlet's "poor and unattractive dress, his tangled black hair hanging in feminine disorder down the back—this was Edwin Booth, who looked as if he had stepped out of some old theatrical print in the days of elocution."

Scott had felt something, though, of a spell impossible to analyze—"impossible," he admitted, "to keep the attention off that remarkable face, that strange power of expression, those eyes that rolled and changed."

Booth on his side had coldness to complain of and wrote to Hutton three days after the opening: "They tell me my success is *great!!!* and all that. But the Press damns me with faint praise—the audiences are cold and dead, truly British."

He had had from them none of the warm response to individual points that Americans always lavished on him, especially in *Hamlet*, a play that was his touchstone of the quality of audiences. Famous lines such as

The play's the thing,

whose launching in America called forth storms of enthusiasm, in London fell almost flat and brought down the confidence

of the actor with them. At home the American papers were
spreading the word of Booth's disappointing reception and
vowing vengeance if Irving came to their shores. Americans
in London growled of "insular spleen." They annoyed and
embarrassed Booth. "I think the *gush* of my countrymen here
has injured me somewhat. There's no restraining the eagle
when he feels like screeching and he 'scroched' too much for
me."

This last was to Barrett, written some weeks later, by which
time Booth was putting the best face he could on things. He
assured Bispham that "the purity of my English is invariably
praised," and to Stedman he insisted bravely that "the feeling
for me is warming every day." So it was, a little, his houses
having dwindled to a handful of true admirers whose enthusiasm every night gave him the heart to hang on. But the
box-office sheet, cool criterion that takes no account of a sensitive artist's need to encourage himself, showed mortifyingly
small profits.

Booth took off *Hamlet* and tried *Richelieu*, which Winter
had advised him to open with, and as by a charm, the receipts
climbed, though only temporarily. But the daily press was not
to be won. The *Times* was at pains to point out that Booth
and Bulwer Lytton, the author of *Richelieu*, were the same
sort of artist: both were thinly endowed, though well trained
and resourceful.

"I hardly think," Booth ventured, "the critics have shown me
a kindly spirit, but they are very provincial and 'little' in their
views of art matters. . . . In New York or elsewhere in
America Mr. Irving, Monsieur Fechter might appear while I
was in full swing & yet receive kindly and impartial treatment—
yet here, in this great world of London—a poor stranger is
cold-shouldered as a trespasser."

Almost overnight he was in the position of suing for favor,
who in his own land was the star of stars. "If I get no other
benefit here," he wrote, "I shall learn to appreciate the good
will that has always stood by me in the American theaters."

Yet almost every night a man or woman from one of his scanty audiences took the trouble to seek Booth out backstage to make certain he knew of their deeply felt admiration. A sprinkle of titles came to see him, which flattered him, coming as he did from democratic America; besides, titles were supposed to help business. Royalty, however, had held back so far. "The Queen," Booth complained of the aging, stoutening, still grieving widow Victoria, "is too 'stuck up' to patronize me—so's Wales."

He was asked out a great deal and accepted invitations for Sunday evenings for himself, Edwina, and Mary, was dined and wined—only he was drinking no wine these days. His hosts and fellow guests stared blankly at his empty glass. He was too busy and fearful of ruining everything by his poor head for drinking to accept the stag invitations. "Perhaps this gives the 'boys' a wrong notion of me—but in the end, I think, my sedate and very proper behavior will tell."

At one of the great houses the Booths met Robert Browning, very loud-talking and self-congratulatory and wearing what seemed to be a blue-checked flannel shirt. The actor, demure in his correct swallowtail and his determination to do the right thing, was repelled—"that's all affectation!" And, "Oh, how provincial it is!" he cried to Anderson of upper-class London, which was so completely one large family. "I often fancy myself in Belair while listening to the really unsophisticated though highly cultured Briton."

One of the humblest and dearest of the old friends at home whose comfortable face he longed to see was Anderson, and now he reminded Davy that since his London opening he had had congratulations from hundreds of persons, "but not a line from thee. Now, this is not meant reproachfully, for I know there is not a heart that throbs on earth that doth more rejoice at my success than thine, my Davy, but, nevertheless, would I be happier to have had a line of greeting to that effect." Many English actors, of a more manly and generous breed than the critics, had cordially wished him well. John

Ryder, who played the Capuchin Joseph in *Richelieu*, "with tears declares that I have toppled his idol (Macready) to the ground, and is as anxious of my success as a father may be—as *you* are."

The Booths ate their Christmas roast beef at the Clarkes' house, where John Clarke occupied rooms churlishly separate from his wife and children. Booth was on fairly friendly terms with him and took some of Asia's accusations with a grain of salt. "John's a good fellow, if you can get under his shell."

This was the first Christmas he and Asia had spent together since they were children. Booth longed to have their dear old mother with them—"What a miserable existence is the actor's, especially if he is domestically inclined!"

Asia was rewriting her book about their father and he persuaded her to leave out the euphemism "boyish *mésalliance*" when speaking of Mr. Booth's first marriage. She planned to add a section about Edwin's youth. He obligingly dredged up what he could to pass on to her of his wanderings with his father, then of his bachelor adventures. It was more exquisitely disturbing to live over the happy times. "You may well imagine my feelings at this late day," he told Anderson, "taking our midnight rides to 'Pipesville,' and sailing the seas toward t'other side o' the globe."

Soon after writing this he heard from Anderson. A pressed flower grown in California tumbled out of the old actor's letter.

II

Two nights after Christmas Booth opened in *The Fool's Revenge*, his most indifferently received bill yet, though during its short run his first English royalty in the persons of the Prince and Princess of Wales materialized in the royal box. The chunky, bearded, beribboned Prince loved the good things of life, the latest of which he had discovered was blonde Lillie Langtry, the "Jersey Lily." Summoning Booth into his presence in the manner of one who crooks a finger, he said to the pleased and expectant player: "I'm glad to see you, Mr. Booth. I sent for you because I wish to get your opinion about Mrs. Langtry's chances of success as an actress in America."

After the New Year, Booth's contract with Gooch was due to lapse. Gooch pressed hard to renew it. His reputation as a "cheap-John" manager was so well known to all except Booth that he had had trouble finding any star to reopen his theater until the American signed with him. But because profits trailed far behind what had been expected, he stipulated that a larger cut be made before the star got his fifty per cent.

Booth gave in. He was no match for "Gougy Goochy . . . who is, perhaps," he wailed to Barrett, "the most contemptible little ingrate I've ever dealt with. With my usual foresight and business tact I signed a contract which placed me completely in the little Jew's power. . . . The little pig has tricked me into reducing terms, and—desiring to prolong an engagement, which might have been originally made for any length of time I chose—I've had to yield to his extortion."

To add to his frustration, Booth had heard the critics actually joked ahead of time about the way they planned to go for him ("Let 'em go!") when he gave *Othello* as his next production, acting the two principal parts alternately. Three inches of wet snow fell during the run of this play, giving some excuse for the sagging box office. His engagement, neither success nor complete failure, muddled along dismally until one gray day in January his door opened and, lo! it was Henry Irving come to call—Booth having now been in London three months.

The contrast between the Irving of 1861 and of 1881 was one of the wonders of the profession. His apprenticeship as an actor (the period that Booth in California had spent in skylarking and not learning his lines and succeeding in spurts through a genius that couldn't be kept under) Irving had spent in diligent self-improvement, toiling, observing, strengthening his weak spots, never missing a chance to advance his career. Booth had remembered Irving vaguely as a rather colorless young man not long out of the West Country with frank, commonplace features. Now the saying went that there were three men in London whom people turned to stare after: Gladstone, Cardinal Manning, and Irving.

Irving had transformed a pair of long, skinny legs into props of distinction, had made a guttural, halting voice into an abused but talked-about hallmark. He wore his blue-black hair in a lumpish thatch over his collar. His profile was pale, pronounced, distinguished, but the candid expression of his youth was a sacrifice to this ruthless metamorphosis: the new Irving looked secretive, almost furtive. Everywhere except on the stage itself, even in his dressing room and as far as the wings, he wore pince-nez on a black cord over darkly glowing, small, somewhat close-set, nearsighted eyes. His manner to strangers was exceedingly courteous, gentle and indirect. "He is a very *gentle* man," said his leading lady Ellen Terry, "though not in the least a *tender* man."

Avoiding any mention of the letters Booth had written to him, which, to do him justice, he had probably forgotten, he smilingly reminded Booth how he, Irving, owed his final success to Booth's hesitation in taking up the option on the Lyceum. "He is apparently a good fellow," Booth speculated to Hutton, "but his first impression on me (owing to embarrassment, doubtless) was not at all pleasant."

A London throat specialist, Dr. Morell Mackenzie, was treating Mary Booth's persistent cough. It was soon after Irving's visit that Dr. Mackenzie called in Sir William Jenner, the Queen's physician, for consultation, and the two doctors broke the news to Booth that his wife's cough was caused by tuberculosis of the throat and lungs in an advanced stage. Besides this, her mind was failing fast. "She doubtless has uterine mania," Booth wrote to Hutton.

She was not herself; her spiteful words were not her own. "My great pity for her," Booth wrote, "has overcome all feeling of resentment, & my hatred for those who really caused her to act as she did is increased tenfold. . . . Seeing my wife suffering here before me makes me mad."

In February he tried *King Lear* and this time at last he struck it. "Nothing finer of the kind has been known upon the English stage!" applauded E. L. Blanchard in *The Era*.

Charles Reade, playwright and author of *The Cloister and the Hearth*, came to see Booth. In Sacramento in 1856 one of Booth's acting chores had been to dress up as a priest in Reade's melodrama *Two Loves and a Life*. Now Reade was bowled over by Booth's Lear and, as he always did when deeply moved by acting, seemed to take it as real. "Poor old man, they have broken his mind, but see how he holds his dignity," Reade whispered to his friend Edward House as Booth stepped forward bowing only slightly for a curtain call.

House was an American and he was also a friend of Booth's. He sent a line to the actor to tell him how much both he and Reade had admired the performance. "I'm sorry that Friday was the night Mr. Reade saw me," Booth answered, "for I was unusually disturbed then."

That night in his dressing room halfway through the play Mary, who ought to have been at home in bed, had flown into hysterical convulsions, with contortions of the face, tossings and lashings of the head and limbs. Dr. Mackenzie was sent for and warned Booth it was touch and go whether she could live an hour. Booth forced himself away from her side to finish the performance and take his calls with the dignity that Reade admired. Afterward he rushed her home through side streets where the horses could go at a gallop. Both her doctors absolutely refused to treat her any longer unless she were kept away from the theater.

They gave her only a few weeks, in any case. "The poor little girl whose ill-balanced brain has caused me so many years of discomfort is passing away from us," Booth wrote to Hutton on March 12 at two in the morning. "They tell me she is dying & that I may expect her death at any time. All that is gone before, so far as she is concerned, is nothing now. . . . It is very pitiful to see her (half crazy all the while) fading before our eyes, while Edwina—(deprived of sleep & half dead with sorrow for the only mother she has known) & I—worn with my nightly labors & watchful all the while, sit turn by turn to cheer her. . . . You can imagine the condition of my poor wits just now. Acting a madman every night & nursing a half insane, dying wife all day, and night too—for that matter, I am scarce sane myself."

Tennyson came to see *King Lear*. Tennyson never went to the theater unless a free box were given him, so Booth provided one. Next day, a Sunday, Booth dined with the poet. Booth had brought along poor Mary's autograph album.

"I hope you don't expect me to compose anything for it," gloomed Tennyson.

"Oh, certainly not," said Booth.

"I never give my autograph," Tennyson rumbled on. "I had a request for it today all the way from India, and I refused." At last he condescended to poise his pen over the little book and actually inquired what quotation Booth would like. Booth murmured that a couple of lines from *The Bridge* or *The Brook* would do nicely, that his wife was very fond of both, before he remembered miserably that *The Bridge* was by Longfellow.

Although his King Lear was a critical success, he had made hardly more than hotel-money out of it. His houses were papered, and word that the great Booth was playing to deadheads must be all over the theater world. He could tell by the way Gooch's company looked at him. His pocket-book was almost bleeding. What with the enormous expenses of Mary's illness he would soon have to draw on his capital at home. But the loss of prestige, the undeserved loss, depressed him most. If just once before he left England he could show himself with a first-class company! He swallowed his pride and asked Irving if he might give some matinees at the Lyceum. He had seen something more of Irving now and was beginning to find him "a very pleasant fellow and kindly inclined." Irving most agreeably and unexpectedly proposed that instead he and Booth should costar in one of the Lyceum's superproductions—of *Othello*, taking turns in the main roles. It was the change of luck, the stroke of luck, Booth had been waiting for.

But when the papers announced that he and Irving would soon act together, Booth's business at the Princess was knocked flat. People were waiting to see the two stars at once. Booth's last effort under the dingy banner of Gooch, which was a double bill of *The Merchant* and *Katherine and Petruchio*, was played to houses that could be counted.

Charles Reade continued faithful, and was often seen in a box at the Princess sitting alone ("to shut out England," he said) as he concentrated on the all-sufficient world down on-stage where Booth, nearly sick with anxiety over his wife, fought tides of nausea, drove himself and drew on his reserves. His powerful acting won emotional praise from Reade, who snorted: "The London press is an ass!"

Edward House, furious at the indifference shown Booth, retaliated by printing in one of the London papers a statement of the average annual income (over $100,000) earned by Booth in the United States. House then compared this with the much smaller incomes earned by the best British stars in England in the same period. "Not the most delicate method for celebrating our countryman," he acknowledged, "but it was soothing."

Some of Booth's friends were puzzled why a man whose wife was dying should distress himself so over poor houses. They were not actors. On March 26 Booth closed his season at the Princess. "At last my *great* London engagement is ended," he exploded to Stedman. "Thank God a thousand times, again and again repeated. I never had such an uphill drag of it."

Rehearsals with Irving hadn't yet started so he used the interval to hunt for cheaper rooms. He could no longer afford the elegant St. James. He found a rather dreary house with smoking chimneys on Weymouth Street for less than half what the hotel had cost and moved into it with Mary and Edwina, who was to do the housekeeping.

After making the invalid, lost to reality, comfortable with her nurses, he went to pay a call on his public—kind Mr. Reade—in Knightsbridge. He listened absorbedly while the old writer reminisced of the acting of Junius Brutus Booth in

1836 during Mr. Booth's last trip to England. "He was not so grave as you, young sir. He was full of life, full of fire. . . . Blank verse came from his lips like music. You have the art too—his example, no doubt. I think too I caught an echo of your father's voice in Shylock. I have a good memory for voices. You have the same accent—the very same. With my eyes shut, I think you might lead me back to my place in the pit fifty years ago."

Reade, who had never been to America, was a hot Yankophile: "Is it credible, I ask you, that the leading actor of England should visit America, and be received there as you are here?"

Booth carefully reminded the angry old man of Henry Irving's hospitable offer.

"Irving may have many motives," Reade retorted, "and they may all be good ones."

III

Back in the dreary autumn when Booth first opened at the Princess one of the many published cartoons of him and Irving had shown the potential rivals, with hands in pockets, sourly looking each other up and down. The legend underneath ran:

Cox (An English Hamlet)—Who are You?
Box (An American Hamlet)—If it comes to that, Who are You?

Now that Irving had noticed Booth by calling on him, Clement Scott of the *Telegraph* hastened to put on a large party in Queen Square in honor of the two stars, who were much and half-maliciously eyed as they stood chatting together in almost the same attitudes as in the cartoon, though with looks politely attentive and giving frequent nods of agreement. Booth took the time to see Irving in *The Bells*, his most famous vehicle, in which he played a murderer whose guilty conscience hounds him to his death. Irving's extraordinarily graphic performance went in strong for agile pantomime, like a story-telling dance, and cunningly descriptive use of properties—had rather "a lot," Booth suggested in a letter to Winter, waiting in America with his mouth ajar for news, "of red silk pocket handkerchief in it."

Booth met Ellen Terry for the first time at a special benefit at Drury Lane in which Irving happened to be taking part. Booth was behind the scenes sitting quietly in Irving's dressing room, his back to the door. "Here's Miss Terry," exclaimed Irving, and the visitor glanced around quickly to see a tall, lean young woman with reddish hair, tiptilted nose, piquant, cleft chin, and radiantly playful expression.

Ellen Terry, it developed, never did think much of Booth as an actor and was even a little contemptuous of him as lacking the drive and tough, fighting spirit by which Irving, with none of Booth's natural advantages, had thrust his way to the front. But she never forgot that first impression of Booth. What she saw was a rather small, swarthy-pale man whose features had begun to thicken and whose black hair was salted with gray. Then he looked up at her. She almost caught her breath. "I have never in any face, in any country, seen such wonderful eyes," she recalls. "There was a mystery about his appearance and manner—a sort of pride, which seemed to say: 'Don't try to know me, for I am not what I have been.'"

Rehearsals for *Othello*, twinkling with two stars, began at the Lyceum. A letter was delivered to Booth in his dressing room from Irving's estranged wife, and the mother of his two sons. Irving hadn't spoken to her for ten years. There was a story that Florence Irving sometimes read a newspaper as she sat in a box during her husband's performances. Now she wrote to the guest at the Lyceum instead of to her husband. "Dear Mr. Booth, can you spare me a box? I should like to have my sons see what good acting is."

Miss Terry was to be Desdemona. Irving was doing Iago first. Booth was immensely and favorably struck by this actor-manager's genius for directing. Irving was a master at handling crowds, and made each actor on the Lyceum stage excitingly aware of his relation to the others, of his contribution to the whole effect. While rehearsals were going on, the "Gov'nor" lounged out in front, so low in his chair that only his broad-brimmed hat and shock of hair could be seen from behind, and issued his instructions in a monotone, requiring everyone up there from Ellen Terry to the boy who played the Messenger to repeat a line or piece of business over and over until it was *right*.

"It's no better," sighed Miss Terry once after they had spent half an hour over a short dialogue.

"Yes, it's a little better," said Irving, "so it's worth doing."

When they rehearsed a scene in which the guest appeared Irving would considerately inquire how he wanted the action. Booth would smile deprecatingly and wave his hand and murmur: "I leave it to you, Mr. Irving."

Only occasionally he offered a suggestion: "This is how I usually do it—" and his lackadaisicalness really shocked both Irving and the conscientious company. Brought up in a school that was resignedly tolerant of poor support, Booth had never entirely freed himself from the independent habit of the old-time star who thought of his performance as an affair of the emotions between himself and his audience.

"At rehearsal," recalls Ellen Terry, "he was very gentle and apathetic."

After the first one she had said sweetly: "Do you know, Mr. Booth, that I just hated you when you first came to London?"

Booth's response was polite rather than interested. "Why so?"

"Because," cried Miss Terry naïvely, throwing out both arms in Irving's direction, "I thought you had come to dethrone my god."

The same thrust was driven home harder in another cartoon. This one was labeled "The Lyceum Lion," and showed a lion with a human face and several little human-faced dogs snapping futilely at its feet. The lion's features were Irving's, complete with eyeglasses on a black ribbon, and one of the dogs was Booth.

To gleeful Ellen Terry in her early prime the middle-aged

Booth seemed "broken and devoid of ambition." "He had not the spirit," she concluded, "which can combat such treatment as he received at the Princess, where the pieces in which he appeared were 'thrown' on to the stage with every mark of assumption that he was not going to be a success."

A reporter in an interview proposed to Booth what a happy arrangement it would be if Booth could take over the Lyceum while Irving toured America. This had been Booth's dream for years; now he shook his head. "I went through all that at Booth's Theater."

Especially after seeing Irving in action he realized the impossibility. "There was a time when I had the energy and experienced all the evident delight in these things which Mr. Irving feels. I do so no longer. I am an actor, not a manager."

Irving's deepest motives in inviting Booth to act with him at the Lyceum were variously interpreted by friends of both sides. Whatever they were, Irving was the one who risked most, and his timely invitation was a lifesaver to Booth. Yet Ellen Terry intuitively laid her finger on it as being a main cause of their guest's sad listlessness. Grateful though he was, "I cannot be sure," she writes, "Booth's pride was not more hurt by this magnificent hospitality than it ever could have been by disaster. . . . I could imagine Henry Irving in America in the same situation—accepting the hospitality of Booth. Would not he too have been melancholy, quiet, unassertive, *almost* as uninteresting and uninterested as Booth was?"

To be "interesting" counted a great deal with Miss Terry. "Irving's hold upon *me* is that he is INTERESTING no matter how he behaves. I think he must be put down among the 'Greats,' . . . Constantine, Nero, Caesar, Charlemagne, Peter, Napoleon, all 'Great,' all selfish, all, but all INTERESTING."

Mary Booth, whose hoarse, lunatic yells could be heard up and down Weymouth Street, was not expected to live the week out. Her rapid decline was followed in the newspapers. "Mrs. Booth," said a bulletin, quoting one of her doctors, "is like a soldier in battle. She may be shot at any moment."

"Last night we thought would be her last," Booth wrote to

Bispham on April 7. Yet she hung on, and on April 20 he notified Hutton with the composure of one who has been through
everything that, though she still lay "helpless—very weak and
emaciated—utterly demented," she might linger for weeks.

His nightmare—he couldn't help himself—was that she
would die at the beginning or halfway through his engagement
with Irving, which promised to be momentous, and cut it
short. Every good seat was already sold, even though prices
had been hiked up to the opera scale: a guinea in the stalls,
half a guinea for the dress circle. All over London the posters
advertised BOOTH AS OTHELLO! IRVING AS IAGO! There had
been nothing to equal it since 1817 when Kean and Junius
Brutus Booth faced each other like gamecocks on the stage of
Drury Lane.

IV

The Lyceum, which was Irving's kingdom, was a quite
differently conceived house from Booth's Theater, being
pretty and intimate instead of gorgeous and vast. When he
took it over, Irving had had it repainted in sage green and
turquoise blue. He had had it hung with blue silk draperies
and given it a sky-blue and gold ceiling, stalls upholstered in
midnight-blue velvet, lace curtains in the boxes, and dainty
shields shaped like scallop shells for the footlights.

On the night of May 2, 1881, several hundred people who
usually sat in the stalls had been driven by the raised prices
and demand for tickets into the upper circles. Edwina with
her Aunt Asia and one of Asia's daughters occupied a box. The
American Minister and the Consul General were there.

The audience, though not unusually fashionable, was a very
alive one, full of intellectuals and artists, including the twenty-
five-year-old Oscar Wilde, and it warmly greeted Irving when
as Iago he walked on with Roderigo. Irving was brilliantly
arrayed (he overdressed the part, said the Boothites) in a
crimson and gold jerkin, a green cloak, and a hat like a gondo-
lier's, and he was hung from crown to kneecap with jingling
silver charms with which his slender, active fingers toyed.

The really deafening ovation was saved for the next scene when Iago and Othello, with the characteristic gaits, jerking and gliding, of their respective interpreters entered together—Booth looking eastern and graceful in a flowing, gold-embroidered gown looped up on the left hip by a jeweled fastening, and a Moorish burnoose striped in gold and purple, pearl hoops in his ears. The picked, sensitive audience, appreciative of everything about Booth, from his gloomy home life to his ordeal at the Princess, was making up for past neglect.

When the applause subsided Irving's jangling yet compelling voice began:

"Nine or ten times
I had thought to have yerk'd him here under the ribs."

As Irving said it, it was "thut to have yairked him," given with a wrenching back of the lips.

Booth's answer dropped each word with each syllable rounded:

"'Tis better as it is."

Backstage the Lyceum actors avidly kept score: so many calls for the Gov'nor; so many for Booth; so many for the two together. Out in front the eagle and the lion couldn't agree about which star got the more frenzied welcome. To the American Edward House it seemed that Booth's reception "carried everything before it, like the rush of a river."

But the counter-impression of Percy Fitzgerald, a Britisher, was that "audiences have unfortunately but little delicacy. In their plain way they show their appreciation of whom they think 'the better man' . . . and I remember how this audience insisted that the encouraging applause which it gave to the new actor should be shared by his host."

Here at last were Booth and Irving on the same stage. Irving's tendency as an actor (as a director, too) was to pile on the details. His bustling realism left nothing to the audience, "would have been most eloquent to an audience of the deaf and dumb," as somebody aptly hit it off. In his popular production of *Hamlet*, for example, Irving's own first appearance was always much worked up, with music, a parade of the courtiers, then an imperceptible but effective dimming of the lights and the entrance of the Prince all alone. By contrast, Booth's Prince in recent years was discovered at the rise of the curtain seated quietly with the rest of the court, and to those susceptible to this method his somber repose was as impressive as Irving's elaborately stage-managed display.

But now in *Othello* on the Lyceum's busy stage Booth's acting, as the lone example of a more formal style, seemed static and alien. His poses were out of a museum; the music of his voice was like some stately dance tune played by lutes and viols. "I shall never make you black," he had promised Ellen Terry early in the rehearsals. "When I take your hand I shall have a corner of my drapery in my hand. That will protect you."

He meant it would keep his sooty Othello make-up from rubbing off on her, impossible to prevent when Irving, a fierce layer-on-of-hands in his realism, played Othello. "I'm bound to say," she admitted, "that I thought of Mr. Booth's protection with some yearning the next week when I played Desdemona to Henry's Othello. Before he had done with me I was nearly as black as he."

She granted too that Booth's elevated performance helped her Desdemona (a fey and charming heroine—personality was Miss Terry's strong point) because "it is difficult to preserve the simple, heroic blindness of Desdemona to the fact that Othello mistrusts her if Othello is raving and stamping. Booth was gentle in the scenes with Desdemona until *the* scene where Othello overwhelms her with the foul word."

At week's end the stars exchanged roles. The general opinion of press and public after sampling the exchange was that both Iagos belonged in the very first rank, both Othellos in the second. Neither Booth nor Irving really had the temperament or physique for Othello. They were not simple or primitive enough; Booth was too short and Irving too lanky. Irving

lacked even more than Booth the massive, rough-hewn qualities the part needed, and even his admirers admitted the most
serious defect in his acting was his want of genuine tragic
force. He was too light an actor for high tragedy. He could
be pathetic, since pathos can be simulated, but his displays of
passion never rang quite true.

"In his whole composition," read a dispatch sent from London to the New York *Herald*, "there is not a gleam of that fire
which illuminates the best of Edwin Booth's impersonations.
. . . On the other hand," pursued this correspondent with
penetrating fairness, "*take from Booth his one most precious
gift* and allow him with his own nature and instincts, all the
qualifications that distinguish Irving, and he would never have
secured more than the most ordinary place in his profession."

But both Irving and Booth could do villains, especially the
complicated ones. Booth's Iago, very diabolic, very Venetian,
and so personally captivating that a girl who saw it asked how
Desdemona could have been left alone with him without a
chaperone, had been recognized in America for years as one
of his masterpieces. Ellen Terry, however, was cool to its attraction. She thought the diabolism archaic and obvious and
the whole performance "deadly commonplace after Henry's,"
which was overhung with ingenious new readings and clever
bits of business, just as Irving's person was with jingling orna-
ments.

A critic for *Macmillan's Magazine* agreed with her only in-
sofar that "it is truly said of Mr. Irving that he is never commonplace, but this freedom from commonplace may sometimes be purchased at the expense of common sense. . . . Irving is never content to do as others have done, to find the same
meaning in words that others have found, to read human nature as others have read it."

As Iago, Irving picked his teeth with his dagger all through
one speech, then wiped the blade on his sleeve (the front of
the house loved this), and as he stood listening while Cassio
talked with Desdemona in the scene at Cyprus, he casually
plucked and ate a bunch of grapes, then spewed out the seeds

one by one. "Though the action is easy and natural enough," agreed Mowbray Morris in *Macmillan's*, comparing the two Iagos, "yet how much less really natural to the character than Mr. Booth's still, respectful attitude, leaning against the sundial, alert to execute any command, seemingly careless what goes on so long as he is ready when wanted, yet ever watching his prey with sly, sleepless vigilance."

"A magnificent reader," was Irving's opinion of Booth; a comment that both praised and damned, though true as far as it went.

But a few years after Booth's performances with Irving, Julia Marlowe, a young girl at the time, was to see his Iago. And she writes: "As I had never seen Booth, I did not know him when he appeared on the scene. Suddenly I discovered a figure at the back of the stage intently watching the Moor. You could see plainly that he contemplated some demoniac act. His eye and manner at once caught the attention of the house long before he had said a word. The look on his face was crafty and devil-like. This one incident proved to me that there was very much more in acting than the polished delivery of lines." Miss Marlowe's subject was "The Eloquence of Silence."

To the public the Booth-Irving engagement was a contest, with patriotism involved and the talented rivals, pitted against each other, as good as brandishing the flags of their nations. The stars themselves did their best to play this aspect down, but it was what kept audiences flocking and talking, enabling Booth to write to Anderson of a "ponderous success," and to Bispham on May 16 that "business is still great." Although, "I've not done myself justice yet," he added, "being so depressed by my domestic troubles."

V

In her lucid intervals Mary knew she was dying. "O Asia," she whispered to her sister-in-law, "my life is going from me."

Her disordered mind dwelt savagely on her stepdaughter. Pulling Asia's face down to hers she whispered on, with what little voice she had left, for her disease was destroying it, that her husband was loving and sweet when she had him alone, that it was Edwina who caused trouble, that Edwina "often shook and pinched her when she was asleep, woke her roughly and made awful faces at her to frighten her—and *dared* her to tell her father. I mention this," wrote Asia in a note to her brother, "to show you how she may talk to a stranger—who would believe her."

The McVickers had been sent for and were in London, making a painful situation worse by siding with their deranged daughter in every family difference. Asia warned Booth to collect his wife's jewelry and lock it up, because if any were missing there was no telling whom Mary and her parents might accuse. Mary had complained to Asia querulously that she had begged and begged Edwina to put her jewels away for her and that Edwina *would* not. In spite of everything Asia's heart turned over with pity for the dying girl, so joyless and loveless. "Poor young thing," Asia wrote, "her brain is too great a burden for her fragile body."

Now in his letters home Booth expressed little sorrow. "Poor Mary," he called his wife occasionally. What was there more to say? He was growingly aware in himself of an immense—not fatalism—but a sense of God's will that was overwhelmingly, somberly resigned. When Maggie Jefferson, Joe Jefferson's daughter, who had married an Englishman and was living in London, held out her album to him one day with a request to write his name and something suitable, he chose the lines, profoundly comfortless, from *Richard II:*

> Nor I nor any man that but man is
> With nothing shall be pleas'd, till he be eas'd
> With being nothing.

Booth was negotiating with German managers for a visit to Germany, but before acting there he meant to tour the English provinces and was making arrangements with the English manager Wynn Miller; several actors had already been signed. Then he abruptly changed his plans, postponed everything until fall, though it was an expensive business to withdraw from his commitments. He and the McVickers had decided to take Mary home if she lived long enough. When her mind was clear, she was restless and unhappy if Booth were not beside her, so the doctors advised him to go with his wreck of a wife, not to send her away with her parents.

The season with Irving ended on June 10, and on June 18 the whole party sailed from Liverpool. It was thought perfectly impossible that Mary could survive the trip by more than a few days. Before leaving London Booth had written to Bispham in New York to reserve two state-rooms for Edwina and himself on the *Gallia*, August 17, for the return journey.

CHAPTER 13

A Kiss from the Heart

Now are our brows bound with victorious wreaths.
King Richard III, *Act I, scene 1*

 AT THE Windsor Hotel in New York a swarm of reporters stung Booth with questions, the same reporters that had buzzed around Madame Sarah Bernhardt on her own landing in New York eight months earlier. La Bernhardt had been equal to them. Narrowing her glittering eyes under her frizzy bangs and extracting some "red stuff" from her purse with which she touched up her lips, she had smartly parried questions like: "How much do you weigh, dressed and undressed?" "Is it true that you have four children and no husband?"

Booth was equal to them too. When, with their exquisite instinct for prodding a tender spot, they demanded what he really thought of Irving, he countered imperturbably that Irving was a delightful man, "always obliging, and always kind in every possible way. . . . A very superior actor."

He had not been home three days when President Garfield was shot in the back by an assassin. It was the end of summer before Garfield died, and while he lingered and the doctors kept the nation on tenterhooks with their bulletins on his fluctuating condition, the papers raked up and paraded the details of the shooting from behind of President Lincoln by another "mad killer."

"That horrible business will never be buried!" cried Booth. It was this sort of thing that kept Asia a permanent exile. Now a man named Nahum Capen wrote to Booth at the Windsor to demand new facts about the unmentionable brother, and Booth beaten into acquiescence, answered him.

"Dear Sir, I can give you very little information regarding my brother John. I seldom saw him since his early boyhood in Baltimore. He was a rattle-pated fellow, filled with Quixotic notions. . . . We used to laugh at his patriotic froth whenever secession was discussed. That he was insane on that one point, no one who knew him well can doubt. . . . He was of a gentle, loving disposition, very boyish and full of fun,—his mother's darling,—and his deed and death crushed her spirit. He possessed rare dramatic talent, and would have made a brilliant mark in the theatrical world. . . . All his theatrical friends speak of him as a poor, crazy boy, and such his family think of him."

Booth was full of care about his mother, who at seventy-nine was failing fast. Rosalie, who nursed her, was fifty-eight; the world had always been too much for Rose. The two women, the aged and the aging, were living with Joseph, and Booth sent a message with his love through Laurence Hutton to Hutton's mother: "I wish she could spare a moment to see my poor old parent." How more than happy he would have been to look after them himself if his life had been arranged differently.

But by all that was wonderful, Mary seemed better. The much-feared ocean trip had superficially improved her. She looked well, ate with appetite, enjoyed being driven into the country. The American doctors predicted she might live until November, which meant Booth must postpone going back to England. "It may be she will live years from what I've heard lately of similar cases," he wrote to his English manager,

Wynn Miller. "Doctors know nothing of such indomitable women."

Still she was doomed, and he could only wish for her death, "or for my own." It was all to no purpose that he had come home with her. Since they left London she had turned against him too. "Her antipathy to Edwina still exists," he told Hutton heavily, "& she barely tolerates my presence." And a few weeks later: "Mrs. Booth drove me from her room a month ago last Saturday & I've not seen her since."

The McVickers had carried Mary off to a house they had rented on West Fifty-third Street. Booth and Edwina stayed behind at the hotel—"the parents have shut us out completely."

Mrs. McVicker was greedily credulous of Mary's tales of Booth's cruelty, making no allowance for the girl's sick mind. But James McVicker had been a good friend to his son-in-law once. Now that the marriage was cracking Booth suspected, rightly or wrongly, a more sordid motive in both parents than mere distrust of him. "Their object is to get valuable property I gave my wife and which they fear I will get back at her death and so they steel her against me. . . . From many little hints I've had I think the old folks have induced Mary to will my Chicago property (in Mary's name) to them."

It was an ugly mess. Booth was impatient to be back in harness, which was most unlike him, but work was the one thing left. "Idleness would only intensify the sadness that is hovering over my domestic life."

On October 3 he opened an engagement at Booth's Theater. This at least went well. His season with Irving had flicked New York's interest in him. But the press got hold of his feud with his in-laws, and several papers jumped to take the McVickers' side and inform their readers, as something quite new, that Booth had been a drunkard and a bankrupt, that he had married Miss McVicker for her money and was such a brutally abusive husband that his dying wife flew into convulsions whenever he came near her.

Booth had his dresser, Henry Flohr, mail Hutton a copy of

Edwin Booth in three of his most famous roles: Iago, Hamlet, and Richelieu. (*The Players Collection*)

Edwin Booth, 1889.

Edwin Booth in his last years.

the *Dramatic News* "with Mc*Wicked's* abuse of me," and he wrote to Edwina, who was visiting her Uncle Joe, that he had heard lately how he had squandered all Mary's money, ten thousand dollars, and owed her father seventy-five thousand. He attributed this fable to the mother. "Isn't it funny? The old lady beats Edison in the way of inventing."

He paid Mary's bills as they were presented, and returned them to McVicker, who duly sent hem back marked "Paid." When he left New York for the road Edwina went with him. Poor Mary's spurt of health was only on the surface. Booth was in Philadelphia on November 13, his forty-eighth birthday, when he had a telegram: "Mrs. Booth died at five o'clock."

The still girlish body, in white satin with fine white crepe *lisse* around the neck and sleeves, lay in the flower-crammed space between the front and back drawing rooms of the Mc-Vickers' rented house. The parents, relatives, and their friends were in one room, the Booths with their own following in the other. Booth sat near the head of the open rosewood casket, holding Edwina, who had not seen her stepmother since they left the steamer, tightly by the hand. And he shed tears. It was not so long ago that he had writen to Asia: "After ten years of marriage I find not a fault in my wife."

Over Booth's bowed head the Reverend Robert Collyer, who was a McVickerite, intoned a eulogy of Mary that, without saying outright anything against her husband, implied volumes. Eyebrows were raised all over both drawing rooms, but Booth sat shielding his eyes with his free hand and gave no sign of having noticed. Hutton and Winter kept him company on the train to Chicago, where Mary was buried on a dark, gusty day of steady rain. "Now, what next discomfort?" he wrote to Will Bispham, another loyal friend, " 'What more sorrow claims acquaintance at my hand which I know not?' . . . Well, I have tried to be strong in all my sufferings, but I fear that I have been most feeble."

Adam Badeau, back in his own country after years lived abroad, had spent the night with Booth in New York between the funeral and the burial trip. Often while he was in Europe and watched some royal personage hold a levee or ride in procession, Badeau had been reminded of his friend Booth acting the king or prince onstage. "No Guelph or Bourbon," said Badeau, "went through his part with greater dignity or grace than the young American who had never been at court; the magic of genius arrayed him in a majesty which all the reality of their grandeur could not inspire."

This was "that majesty, that look above the world," Booth's father in his youth had hungered for and found wanting in the first real king he set eyes on.

Now Badeau was struck by the dignity and self-control of the man he had known long ago as a headstrong, dissipated, often nervously irascible boy. Booth's expression had gained greatly in strength, but there was nothing young about him any longer; the last freshness of youth had gone. His features were worn and hardened, a little coarsened, with the actor's stamp of years of use. His hair had receded, his face was heavier, his jaw squarer. Barring his father's marks of dissipation, Booth's own face had become much like his father's in middle age.

II

The papers went on blackening Booth in his domestic life, printing items that originated with the McVickers and were added to by any malicious journalist who had it in for the actor. McVicker himself occasionally sent his son-in-law vicious clippings from the papers through the mail, "sent while tight," Booth guessed, "else he tried to disguise his writing. The donk!"

Edwina, not used to slanderous attacks, having been a child at the time of her uncle's crime, was beside herself with hurt and rage and implored her father to contradict the stories. Booth only shook his head and even smiled. But to Hutton he admitted that "all I ever feel anxious about in this beastly business is on Edwina's account. If I should die before all this slander is cleared from my reputation it will be a life-long sorrow for her. . . . If I were vindictive I could tell my story and expose the McVickers to my heart's content, but I keep old Satan behind me as well as I can & will be patient."

' "Compassion for poor Mary alone has kept me silent," he explained to Barrett, "but consideration for Edwina may force me to expose, not only the McVickers' villainy, but poor Mary's *insane* wickedness." He had first written "poor Mary's wickedness," then went back and inserted "insane" with a line under it.

His friends were under no such constraint. Booth and Edwina were in Boston when an unsigned article by a journalist named Junius Henri Browne, who evidently knew more of Booth than Booth knew of him, appeared in the Boston *Herald* refuting the slanders. After describing in a balanced way what the reserved, quiet-loving Booth had had to put up with from his well-meaning but officious little wife long before her disorder showed itself, Browne's article went on: "Booth never spoke of the incongruity between them; he was always patient, tender, chivalrous, and in nearly all cases allowed her to have her way, as strong, self-disciplined husbands, not afraid of being thought hen-pecked, always do. Mrs. Booth was subject to periodic derangements. . . . During their continuance she was entirely irresponsible. . . . A good deal of the time she was a lunatic, and a lunatic who could hardly be controlled."

After her return from Europe, said Browne, Mary "began to disclose a marked aversion" to Booth. "She refused to receive the visits of her husband and, as his presence in her chamber threw her into convulsions of rage, he at last, after trying in every way to placate her, kept carefully out of her sight. But he still took every care of her."

To account for the parents' venom: "There may have been some disagreement concerning financial questions, because in the event of Mrs. Booth's death, the whole, or part, of what Booth had given her—and he had been very liberal—would have gone according to the particular law of the State, to her mother, Mrs. McVicker. This lady has . . . hated Booth long and bitterly and has, by her energetic manifestation of it, earned from him some degree of reciprocity."

While the McVickers were branding him a mercenary out for what he could get from their helpless daughter, Booth was busy making certain arrangements by letter with Bispham. From the Hotel Vendome in Boston he wrote to ask Bispham in New York to look out for a flat of four or five "cozy rooms." To Booth a home was always a place that was small and cozy. His idea of home was romantic as a calendar picture: a thatched cottage deep in the countryside or a dot of an apartment in the heart of the city—a nest for two. He was doomed to hotel life himself at present. He wanted the flat for a special friend of his, "a poor player, who struts, etc., but one I love with all the tenderness a son might bear for a father—one of the oldest and the dearest of duffers the good God ever made."

This was Anderson, whom Booth had persuaded to come back East and who was on tour with him. "He approacheth now the time," said Booth, "when the oil burneth low and the wick waxeth brief. He wants to settle in New York—his dear old wife and he—and I want them to settle near me. . . . Can you give me an idea of rent, cost of furniture, servant's wages, and other little details requisite for the comfort of a dear old couple of antique babies?"

Not until a second letter ("more about my 'flat' friends") did Bispham discover it was Booth who meant to pay for everything. "This *entre nous*. I thought I'd relieve them of all cares for the future. No one but you, they, and I are to know the *facts*, and even you must be ignorant as far as they know."

Booth was playing at Boston's Park Theater. He had his own troupe traveling with him this time, and on Christmas Eve, 1881, he invited everyone to a late holiday supper in his rooms at the Vendome. At twelve o'clock Edwina kissed him and departed. The others sat on, listening to him reminisce.

He exclaimed happily: "Yes, my brother John and I—" The words withered on his lips. He brushed his hand across his eyes but the stricken company could see the tears as he corrected himself. "Yes, my *unfortunate* brother John—"

From Albany on April 14 he wrote to Hutton: "In this hotel, 22 years ago, I passed my first marriage night. What a world of memories is conjured up." He had time for his memories, having suddenly great trouble in sleeping, and after the play would sit writing long letters to his scattered friends, then read through the hours left until dawn.

The days, to make up, were almost gay. He and Edwina traveled in a private hotel-car with piano and bookcase, the rest of the troupe in a special Pullman. Booth often asked the others in to lunch and afterward, while they bounded along over the rough roadbed, Edwina would rattle the piano, Louisa Eldridge, a veteran trouper called "Aunty" by everybody, would give them a song, and the two old Andersons (Mrs. Anderson had been allowed to come for the trip, though she wasn't acting) would nod their heads in time. Booth simply watched, his eyes dwelling on his daughter. Whenever Edwina stopped playing she hurried over to him. They sat close beside each other and always with some comforting contact of arm through arm or hand in hand.

They must make the most of their time together. Edwina was engaged to young Downing Vaux, son of Calvert Vaux, the architect and landscape gardener who had designed the plans for Central Park. She was not to be married immediately, and expected to sail with her father for Europe in May. But back in New York about two weeks before their sailing date she came down with pleuropneumonia. She almost died. Booth, alternating between wild anxiety and a dreadful, genuine calm—for he had long anticipated the death of his beloved and only child as the logical last blow fate might have in reserve—kept trying to fortify himself by saying over Brutus' stoic lines:

> With meditating that she must die once,
> I have the patience to endure it now.

They gave extraordinarily little comfort.

Edwina improved, and on June 14 they were able to sail after all. Just before the sailing Booth renewed a friendship long at a standstill and harking back to a remote, young, tumultuous self—his friendship with Richard and Elizabeth Stoddard.

During their estrangement of almost twenty years he had once, as was inevitable, met Elizabeth Stoddard head on at a party, had gazed into "her cold eye, and bowed to her coldly." Now Mrs. Stoddard was the first to write. He answered her letter on June 1, 1882. "Dear 'Lisbeth, no forgiveness, no mercy is required: we are friends and I hope will ever be so. I'm sure we shall, for I am older, sedater, though mayhap not wiser, and I suspect that you and Richard be so also. . . . Dear, dear Mollie! She lives again, thank God! in her good daughter, whom I am sure you will love."

III

Booth was bursting with spirits on shipboard. Julia Vaux, Edwina's future sister-in-law, was traveling with them, and he tramped the deck with a girl on either arm. He wrote to Anderson: "Davy ahoy! I'm afloat! you old bloat!"

He opened in London on June 26 at the Adelphi Theater playing Richelieu. Barrett, Winter, and Aldrich were in London too, and Hutton soon joined them. Hutton's mother had died in the spring, and the desolate bachelor did not forget how in the first hours after her death Booth had stolen in to put his arms around him and whispered: "I know, my boy, I know."

Arriving in London after Booth, Hutton found him cheerful but poorly. Booth smoked too much, took no exercise if he could help it, ate stodgy foods, and had begun to have dizzy spells. His doctor told him he must get outdoors more, so Hutton made it his business to walk to and from the theater with him every night.

Late one lovely evening when the moon whitened the whole city, Barrett, Winter, and Aldrich met them on the way home, and the five Americans wandered into the cloisters of Westminster Abbey. A helmeted policeman nodded and let them pass. The place was deserted. The bell in the clock tower chimed the quarters as they drifted from one tomb to another. Booth, who was forty-eight, began to speak musingly of the men, once so eager, once so celebrated, whose dust lay under the stones: Dr. Johnson; Sheridan, the sparkling playwright; Garrick, greatest of English actors. The living men, each of whom had some small reputation to hug to himself, were plunged into deep seriousness and paced back to their lodgings almost without a word.

They made another and a very different night of it when this world was all too much with them. Booth mentioned it afterward in anguish to Hutton: "I fear I made a fool of myself. It's a pity that my poor brain cannot withstand the least stimulus; a child's can safely carry that which floors me. I suffer so intensely, too, long after the *fun* is over. As I look back to that evening my mind is filled with all sorts of disgusting things. It seems that ever since the Delmonico breakfast my head has been weaker than before. Tell me the worst I said and did. I know I made an ass of myself and among the very people whose respect I value. I can't laugh at such slips as jokes—they are agonies to me. I find that simple water is my only safe tipple—I stuck to it for years & must let it float me to the end, I suppose. It's rather difficult to be jolly on cold water—and to get up the spirit for tragic acting without stimulant now & then. No more o' that."

Business at the Adelphi was "English!" he joked to Anderson. The entire profits for his six weeks there amounted to five hundred dollars. But the critics were kinder than the year before, and the sparse houses were friendly. "Don't fret if you don't get work," he soothed Anderson, who was unemployed and hated his leisure. "When funds run short, let me know."

In August he took the girls on a quick trip to the continent. They saw *Die Jungfrau* by moonlight, and at Bingen in Germany they sampled the beer (at least Booth did); it was dark, creamy, maddeningly satisfying. In England again, he set off on his provincial tour, which had been deferred dangerously long, because in the interval Irving had gone over much of the same ground with his spectacular Lyceum productions.

Booth's English manager had simply smiled when Booth described the "good stock scenery" he wanted to have built to take with him. "Shakespeare, my dear sir, won't draw a handful of people in the provinces unless it's presented as Mr. Irving gives it at the Lyceum. Mr. Irving has been through those same places with the Lyceum scenery, and the people will never go to see Shakespeare again unless it's equally well put on. They'll say your show isn't as handsome as Mr. Irving's."

Starting in Sheffield in September, Booth finished in Birmingham three months later after covering most of England as well as Dublin and the main Scottish cities. The tour was fun, even though it barely paid expenses, even though in Liverpool he was so nervously exhausted that he finally saw a doctor, who prescribed absolute rest, the logical remedy—impossible to follow.

Edwina's fiancé, Downing Vaux, joined them in London in December, but their Christmas was only half merry, for the young man was far from well.

As an actor, Booth was through with London, doubted if he would ever act there again. "I could never be made *fashionable!*"

So off with England, on to Germany where, his instinct told him, had told him for years, he would prosper. He dared not trust instinct. He was to open in Berlin at the Victoria Theater the middle of January, "open and shut, too, perhaps," he warned Anderson and himself. "It may be a startling fizzle."

IV

Certainly it began badly. The manager of the Victoria had a comic hit called *Frau Venus* running and refused to close it. He insisted Booth would have to wait. Booth was in despair when his German agent hastened in to tell him that the Residenz Theater was available owing to the sudden illness of the woman star who was to open there. Booth signed at once with the manager of the Residenz, which was a smaller house than the Victoria, promising less cash, but more intimate and elegant.

He was to act in English, the others in German. Most of the company had never done Shakespeare. Now they were handed copies of *Hamlet, Prinz von Dänemark* and ordered to study their parts. At dress rehearsal Booth noticed that the First Actor in the band of Players visiting Elsinore was got up as a very old party with a white beard to his waist. Through an interpreter he asked the man why on earth he had made himself so decrepit. "In America the First Actor is always played as much younger."

"Oh," said the German, waving his translation, "Shakespeare himself is my authority, for does he not have Hamlet address the First Actor as 'old friend'?"

Booth explained that in English this isn't taken literally, but the German's finger froze to the text. He beamed and nodded. Hamlet says "old," the Shakespeare meant "old," *nicht?*

The German star Ludwig was appearing as Hamlet at the Royal Theater. The American had already been advertised (*Erste Gastdarstellung des Herrn Edwin Booth*), and Ludwig, a fine actor in a monumental way, was determined to outdo him. Ludwig's Hamlet was on the order of Forrest's. He marched up and down the stage flexing his muscles and trumpeting,

"Sein oder Nichtsein,"

and the delighted Berliners, who were used to this method, predicted that "Booze could never equal him." Their disbelief showed in the attitude of the Residenz stage director, who ran the rehearsals like a Prussian drill master and treated Booth with cold, hostile politeness.

It was Christmas-card weather, snowy and crisp. On opening night, January 11, 1883, the little Residenz was packed. During the introductory scene between Horatio and the soldiers a couple of the actors, not at ease in costume plays, tripped over their swords and the audience guffawed. As the curtain rose a second time, every opera glass in the house swerved simultaneously to focus on Booth, sitting still as a statue with his dark head bowed, the most somber of all stage Hamlets. He lifted his head and swept the audience with far-seeing eyes as the King turned on him:

> *Doch nun, mein Vetter Hamlet und mein Sohn.*

And he gave the famous first aside:

> A little more than kin, and less than kind.

These were the first words to be spoken in English and in a style utterly different from that of the other actors. To the Americans in the theater it seemed like a message straight from their own country. More remarkably, the one short foreign phrase brought instant tears into the Germans' eyes. Booth's peculiarly moving quality, which had so often missed its mark in England, struck home in Germany. Accustomed though they were to a loud, declamatory manner, the emotional Germans instinctively responded to the grandeur and intensity that underlay Booth's quietness.

The production blundered on. Ophelia was so silly in her mad scene that the audience lay back and laughed. Booth strode through his part, "dignified, gentle, handsome and in-spired," wrote an American there.

He had mentally to recite in English what the rest were saying in German. When they stopped he took the pause for his cue and began his own speech. He slipped just once, when in the graveyard scene he started a fraction ahead of time, then quickly recovered himself; hardly anyone noticed the mistake. The strain on him was made worse by the dead silence in front. No heartening applause interrupted the scenes; there was only a subdued "bravo" now and then. But as the final drop fell, the other actors stood rooted and strangely attentive, and the Prussian stage director, who had been so cold to Booth, ran out from the wing, bent his knees, seized Booth's hand to bring it to his lips and said simply: "*Herr Meister!*"

It never took much to make Booth's eyes moist. The intently watching actors were already weeping. The front of the house was white with handkerchiefs. Now the long delayed demonstration broke out with "bravo" on "bravo" topping the handclaps. Booth was recalled twenty-four times, and after the audience, still jabbering with excitement, had drained out of the theater, there were more tributes backstage. The flushed actors pressed close around him. One after another they kissed him on both cheeks, heedless of his look of distress, his flung-back head and plaintive cries of, "Mind the paint!"

And they shouted: "*Danke! Danke!*"

"They thanked me over and over," wrote Booth, who was too stirred up to sleep, later this same night to William Winter, "for what I know not."

The reviews next morning were lyrical with praise. Caricatures blossomed in the shop windows showing Ludwig bidding a forlorn *auf wiedersehen* to the Tragic Muse. Wrote Oscar Welten in the *Tägliche Berliner Rundschau:* "Booth is the best Hamlet I have ever seen. . . . You can understand him perfectly even though you may not know a single word of what he utters."

The *Staatsbürger Zeitung:* "How can the eminently practical American, we ask—he that is said to have ropes for nerves —be in sympathy with the most subtle character that a poet ever created? The spiritual, sublimated Hamlet soul, with all its nervous, dreamlike and melancholy attributes—how can this be conceived by such a man? For an answer, look at Edwin Booth."

The *Berliner Fremdenblatt:* "Booth's Hamlet is a masterpiece of the actor's genius . . . towering above all his rivals. . . . The curtain fell upon the most wonderful impersonation of Hamlet that Berlin has ever seen. . . . This Hamlet was not played, but *lived*."

Booth was used to applause in all forms. It seemed as though he had had his first taste through his father, having been with his father so long. But the solemn adoration and reverence heaped on him now by the German actors was a new experience, "and stimulates me strangely," he told Anderson. "I feel more like acting than I have felt for years."

This was in spite of new cause for sorrow. Downing Vaux, who had come on to Berlin with them, from being nervously disturbed when he left New York had sunk into an alarming apathy. His memory was affected. All his faculties were deadened, and he showed no more interest in the wistful Edwina than in his sister Julia. Three times in Berlin Booth called in Dr. Leyden, the great German specialist in diseases of the nerves and brain. It was finally thought best to send the young man back to America with his sister. To see Edwina so forlorn took the edge off Booth's success, "or rather my enjoyment of it. . . . She is lonely & depressed of course—having no companion but old fogy me."

He played King Lear, Iago, and Othello—all received with delight. The Crown Prince and Princess came to see him. A court reception was in the offing at which he was to be presented to Emperor Wilhelm and a command performance was talked of. Then Prince Karl, the Emperor's brother, died, cutting short these bright prospects and leaving Booth to fume to his friends that "one of those little German princes had to die, the stupid jackass, and the Court went into mourning."

His artistic conquest remained dazzling, peerless. When he left Berlin the Residenz actors presented him with a silver laurel wreath inscribed "To Edwin Booth, the unrivaled Tragedian." In Hamburg, where he played next, the press went wild, and the audience formed a passageway from the lobby to his carriage, forcing him to run the gauntlet while they clutched at and tried to kiss him—an ordeal for a man who loathed being pawed.

The stage director of the Hamburg Theater, seventy-seven years old—he had been a pupil of Ludwig Devrient's, Germany's greatest tragedian—threw his arms around the American, who seemed like a boy to him, and called him *"Meister."*

The almost equally antique stage manager, who remembered Talma, titan of the French stage during the Revolution and Empire, exulted that Booth was Talma's peer—*"Meister, Meister!"*

The little girl pages in the Hamburg Theater waylaid Booth

after *King Lear* and murmured bashfully: "Mr. Booth, you make us cry. We do want so much to kiss you."

And so it went: in Bremen, in Hanover, and Leipzig. It must be confessed that while the houses were excellent, they were not always cram-full. "As it is in England," Booth wrote to Bispham, "no money is to be made here. That, however, I did not expect."

He had earned something more. Americans abroad grew used to the raptures of their German friends: "*Ihr Landsmann! Der Edwin Booze!*" The tokens poured in. In Hamburg it was a silver spray of laurel. In Bremen a second laurel wreath was offered him on a velvet cushion by a young actress while the theater director read out a fulsome speech and the actors, weeping and kissing, made a circle around the venerable, white-bearded Booth, dressed in King Lear's robes, who looked frightened to death and stammered his thanks. In Hanover it was a silver goblet; in Leipzig still another laurel wreath, as well as a death mask of the mighty Devrient.

In one of the cities after a matinee, women from the audience swarmed up on the stage and overwhelmed him as he stood, this time young and in his Hamlet sables. They formed a line and filed past. Each thrust out her hand to be shaken, then her face, shiny with expectancy, to be kissed. When he told the story afterward to Kitty Molony, Booth's own face unconsciously froze into the trapped expression it must have worn then. Finally an uneasy-looking lady rustled into position. She poked out her fingertips. Booth accepted them, swayed forward mechanically getting ready for the salute, but she flinched. "I am an American!"

"Oh, I beg your pardon, and thank you so very much."

In March he was in Dresden on his way to Vienna. He did not act in Dresden, but sent a letter from there to Richard and Elizabeth Stoddard. He was writing of Mary, his first Mary whom they had known, thinking of her in relation to this wondrous success of his. He could look back on her calmly now, almost without a sigh, as of a dream of happiness he had had when young. "I know that dear Mollie foresaw my present—what shall I call it?—condition, but she often feared that I would 'culminate' too soon. It may be the vanity of age—but I fancy that I am still going on & that my work is better & fuller now than ever."

Vienna was his last stand. And there at first the critics hung back a little. They didn't altogether admire his Hamlet, didn't consider his idyllic Othello powerful enough. But his King Lear was a triumph beyond any that had gone before. During Lear's mad scenes and his recognition of Cordelia all restraint in the audience was shattered, and even the listening actors sobbed in the wings and hugged one another and whispered raptly: *"Ach, wie shön! Und sein Organ!"*

On his last night in Vienna Booth was given the fourth and finest of his laurel wreaths. Its leaves were gold and silver and on each one was etched the name of a member of the company. The Viennese begged him to stay on. The German managers implored him to come once more. Russia, Italy, France, and Spain sent invitations, but he refused them—"I am thoroughly tired and yearn for rest."

He had had his dream of acting in Germany. Mingled with his exhaustion and the reaction of depression after the exciting strain was his inkling that this season of late-come, perfect triumph had, like those golden years in Calfornia, a peculiar, self-sufficient happiness not to be pursued or known again.

PART SEVEN

CHAPTER 14

Gray Hair

Hath sorrow struck
So many blows upon this face of mine
And made no deeper wounds?
King Richard II, *Act IV, scene 1*

 IT WAS in the middle 1880's that a certain Harvard graduate, fresh out of the academic mill, had his only glimpse of Edwin Booth offstage. Charles Townsend Copeland saw Booth onstage whenever he could. He was trudging up Park Street in Boston one winter morning when with a thrill he recognized the actor threading his way down. It was brilliantly sunny. The steep street was white with rutted snow, and on Boston Common to Copeland's left the undinted drifts glistened. There must have been other people in sight, but Copeland could never remember them. The picture that bedded itself in his mind was of a solitary black figure moving slowly toward him down the glittering slope through this world of whiteness.

And though young Copeland stared and stared, almost taking off his hat on an impulse of reverence, the great man seemed not to notice him, "seemed," Copeland writes, "to be looking in, not out, with the curious introverted gaze of his own Hamlet. . . . As he came toward me, stepping lightly though not quickly, his head a little bent and his hands in his pockets, he looked like Hamlet in a great-coat. I thought then that I had never seen so sad a face, and I have never yet beheld a sadder one."

Booth had had his winter home in Boston since the autumn of 1883. Back from Germany at the end of May that year his one first thought had been to make a place somewhere for himself and Edwina. He had bought land on the rocky Rhode Island shore two or three miles outside Newport, had built a cottage, and they had spent the summer there. He called the place "Boothden." Only a few miles away was Oak Glen, the Samuel Howes' farm. It was years since Julia Ward Howe had seen so much of her pet actor and his little girl, who at twenty-one was very like her mother, slender and light of step, with eyes full of soul, and a gentle, winsome manner. Whenever Booth let fall Edwina's name his voice was reserved, but the expression of his face adored her. The Howes' large family and Booth's small one of father and daughter had a picnic together under the trees by a brook at Oak Glen.

Booth and Edwina had been still over in Europe when word was sent Booth that Downing Vaux was much worse. On their return, Edwina's engagement was dissolved. Booth had been at a loss at first how to break the terrible news to her. Later he thought thankfully of the danger she had escaped, but at the time "God help us!" he cried. "What a curse is on the Booths, and for what? We must go back beyond any records that I have found for the cause of all the horrors that are heaped on us!"

They stayed at Boothden well into the fall. In the shortening evenings he sat with his daughter by the Franklin stove that radiated comfort into the room, and he tried to help her weave new plans for happiness—"the interest she has felt in this lovely little house I've given her has diverted her mind . . . though of course she has her moments of depression. I do all I can to keep her up."

On September 17 Junius Booth died of Bright's disease in Manchester. Edwin and Joe went on for the funeral, but their mother was too frail to go, and Rose stayed to nurse her. Of Junius' children, four were living: Blanche, his daughter by his first wife, Clementine; Marion, his daughter by Harriet; and his sons Junius III and Sydney by Agnes. Not one of them showed the Booth genius, though Blanche and Sydney were fairly successful in the theater. Junius III had the taint of strangeness from his grandfather Booth. Later, in middle life, he was to kill his wife and himself in their lodgings in Brightlingsea, England, where he ran a movie house.

Of Marion, called "Marie," her uncle Edwin wrote to Anderson at the time of June's death that "she's a jolly dunce & should be incarcerated in some mild asylum for dunderheads. Poor girl! I suppose her 'dear, sweet, old, darling, beloved, sugarplum uncle' will have to care for her & be bored to madness for his reward." At his own death Booth left Marie ten thousand dollars. She could use the money, having been deserted by her actor-husband and forced to appeal to the overseer of the poor in the New Jersey town where she was stranded.

Booth's old friend from California, Ferdinand Ewer, died soon after Junius, leaving his wife and children in real need. Booth wrote to Mrs. Ewer immediately to offer her with the utmost delicacy "some little aid. . . . I beg that you will not deny me the privilege of doing for you what he would have done for mine in similar circumstances."

In September or October he bought a winter house in Boston for himself and Edwina to settle in "for aye." It was at 29 Chestnut Street on select Beacon Hill, a gray stone mansion built sideways to the street with a smart iron fence hugging its grass plot and panes of purple glass in the drawing-room windows. Up from Newport, he took Edwina the long drive out to Dorchester to see a much smaller wooden house overlooking the bay, where she had lived once, though she had no memory of it.

Booth's Theater had given up the struggle. It had closed its doors forever on April 30, 1883, with the same play that so spectacularly opened them. Juliet this time was the Polish actress Helena Modjeska; Romeo was Maurice Barrymore.

Workmen pulled apart and tore down the building and a block of shops replaced it. Booth's Theater was no more.

But the theater in general flourished. New names were in the headlines: LILLIAN RUSSELL, which conjured up a picture of round arms, bovine eyes, and bee-stung mouth; ADA REHAN (titian hair and proud shoulders); MINNIE MADDERN, who was later Mrs. Fiske; RICHARD MANSFIELD; ROBERT BRUCE MANTELL. In October of this year Henry Irving with Ellen Terry and the Lyceum company invaded America. Irving's stock was booming in his own land where Prime Minister Gladstone had recently put out feelers: Would Mr. Irving accept a knighthood, if offered? Irving becomingly declined; it did him no harm, though, to have been made the offer. He opened in New York in *The Bells*, which he followed up with six more productions, beautifully mounted, and cast and directed with a finish new to this public. Every one was a success. Then he started out on a triumphant tour.

On November 5 Booth opened his own season in Boston. It was a fine engagement; all the same, that English visitor had made a difference. Disloyally the *New York Times* declared itself astonished "that Mr. Booth should lag so far behind other actors in enterprise and courage. . . . The example set by Mr. Irving ought not to be lost upon him altogether. Public taste is, we are convinced, growing beyond Mr. Booth's dull and slow methods."

Booth tried to avoid appearing in New York at the same time as Irving, which might look like rivalry. In the end their schedules did conflict, "but New York," Booth was sure, "is big enough for both and doubtless he will cut a broader swath than I." Irving was the rage. Irving was new, English, "interesting." Every new role of his was eagerly waited for. How would he do Hamlet?

Yet in the midst of the Irving furor and the talking down of the native product that went with it, someone who signed herself simply "Gwendolen" wrote to the Boston *Transcript* to ask: "With such an actor of our very own, why should we envy London its possession of Henry Irving?" Then Gwendolen

quoted from Mrs. Howe's poem "Hamlet at the Boston
Theater," written of Booth in 1858:

> And, beautiful as dreams of maidenhood
> That doubt defy,
> Young Hamlet, with his forehead grief-subdued,
> And visioning eye.

Father and daughter spent the summer of 1884 at Boothden.
Their red-roofed cottage, angular with dormers and by this
second summer overrun with ivy, was perched on a slope above
the Seaconnet River. Upriver northward lay Tiverton Heights
and to the south the glittering Atlantic. Westward, outside the
window of the room Booth used as his den, were the shining
farms and orderly meadows of Middletown and Portsmouth.

In his yacht, christened the *Edwina*, Booth cruised on the
river and into the ocean as far as West Island or even beyond.
The little yacht and a couple of rowboats were stored in a boat-
house and rolled to and from the river on a toylike marine railway with one tram car. Near the river's edge stood the repro-
duction of an old Norman mill built from a sketch he had
brought back from Europe. It made a landmark seen for miles,
and on foggy nights when he was out in the yacht, Edwina
climbed the spiral staircase that ran around the outside of the
mill and hung a lantern in an upper window. A sailcloth hammock with perpendicular ends and a flat bottom was set up in
the wide porch on the river-side of the cottage. This could be
closed at the sides and folded over at the top. Booth would lie
in it for hours, smoking and dozing. Edwina let him rest.

His lawns were as velvety and unblemished as any in the
county. About half the estate was used for farming. He had an
overseer, and Boothden's own eggs, butter, chickens, and
asparagus in season were sent him regularly when he was in
Boston. The surplus was sold. The costs outdid the profits, but
it was a constant source of pleasure to the son of a father who
had loved to dig in the red Maryland earth with his own hands.
As his associates among the gentlemen farmers of Rhode Island,
Booth had Ward McAllister and Cornelius Vanderbilt. So here

he was, with his mansion in Boston and his model farm at Newport. He had come a long way.

II

One good tour deserves another. This autumn of 1884 Irving and Terry made their second assault on the United States. Irving did Hamlet for the first time in New York. His melancholy prince, who had been originally influenced by Booth's in Manchester in 1861, had turned out a less poetic fellow than Booth's, but definitely "interesting," having his own astringent flavor, and he was received with applause and good words. Once again it was Irving here and Irving there and "have you seen Irving?"

Booth and Edwina were living congenially in Boston at 29 Chestnut Street and, possibly to compete with Irving, Booth was conning over several parts he hadn't played for years. He took Pescara, Sir Edward Mortimer, and Sir Giles Overreach out of mothballs, and doggedly reviewed Claude Melnotte and Ruy Blas, though these were young men's roles.

His Negro housewoman Julia, peering through doors left half-open, used to see him at work, watch him race his hands through his hair, which had broad streaks of gray in it, flip open the playbook, give a sharp glance, then bang the book shut, toss it on the table, nervously smooth its cover and begin to stalk up and down. If it were very late he studied up in his bedroom, where a crazy quilt Mrs. Anderson had made for him was spread over the bed, and a cloth that had been Anderson's and used to lie on their big table at the "Ranch" was on the night table. For Anderson, dear Davy, was dead after a long illness.

Booth acted in New York in January, 1885. A dispatch sent the Boston *Gazette* reported dourly "there is not much that is new to say of Mr. Booth, except that he has grown stouter and grayer, and that there are signs of thinness in his hair."

All along the road this spring his houses were excellent, though, as he was getting a guarantee regardless of the box office, he could only guess at the receipts. If Irving had hurt him, it was hard to see just how. Although blunt comparisons in Irving's favor cropped out in print, Booth's power to draw had never been stronger. In spite of his gray hair many people thought his acting showed a new life and vigor over what it had been for the past ten years.

All this was true. Yet looking back afterward, Winter, the dean now of New York critics and a friend of both actors, saw clearly that Booth's triumph in Germany had been his zenith, and that with Henry Irving's success in America Booth's decline began. Imperceptible at first, the movement was in progress. "Booth's star," said Winter, "had passed its meridian and was beginning to descend."

Edwina was to be married in May to Ignatius Grossmann, a Hungarian. Grossmann had taught languages in a New England college and then become a stock broker. His entry into the Booths' world was through his actor-brother Maurice, who played under the name of Maurice Neville. Booth wrote to Edwina on April 7: "Darling, I do not, I cannot allow my mind to dwell on the fact that we must be parted. The pain of it will be enough when it comes, yet I am confident—like a bitter draught—it will have a wholesome effect."

And next day, after hearing from her: "Darling, if Ignatius and I were both absent from you at the same time it might tax you sorely to provide us both with love-letters. Perhaps he'd be jealous if he read mine."

The engraved announcements by Mr. Edwin Booth that his daughter Edwina had been married on May 16, 1885, were issued from 29 Chestnut Street, where the marriage took place. The irreproachable correctness of his daughter's wedding may have partly made up to Booth for the occasions in his family when the marriage knot had been tied late or not at all.

And now he was really alone. "My darling," he wrote to Edwina, a bride of eight days, "I can't tell you just how I feel —the separation has been a wrench to my nerves; but when in the midst of my selfishness the thought comes of your happiness and the good that will come to you, I cease to grieve."

The happy couple had landed in England. He had gone to New York to see them sail, then brought himself back to Boston alone. "Now that you are safe over the sea, and the worst (my coming home) is over, I am as jolly as a shoebrush. You must think of me as not at all lonesome."

At night in his den he read and wrote late by the light of a green-shaded lamp, while the large, handsome house fell quiet around him. He was used to sitting alone at night and this helped the illusion that his daughter lay asleep upstairs.

Dr. Horace Furness was publishing a special edition of Shakespeare with erudite notes on the plays and had asked Booth to give his ideas on *Othello* and *The Merchant*. Booth wrote out what thoughts he had, advancing them with confidence and timidity mixed—" 'tis absurd for me to say this to you, who know more of Shakespeare in a moment than I've learned in thirty years." For he had never lived down, never would live down, his awe of learning. What were his poor player's intuitions compared to the lore of a scholar like Furness with a caravan of degrees after his name?

In June Booth went down to New York to help his mother and Rosalie move from Joseph's in Long Branch to a house in the city on West Twenty-third Street. At forty-five Joe was optimistically enrolling in New York University to go on with his study of medicine, dropped years before.

Recently old Mrs. Booth had fallen and broken her leg, a disaster at her age, and now in New York was a chair-ridden invalid. Booth wheeled her through the new rooms. Here at least there would be more "pass" for her to watch from the window and neighbors to wave at the heavy old face that nodded slowly back.

At Newport this summer he was flooded with guests, deliberately invited to keep himself busy, and yet in spite of them he sometimes slept clear through the sparkling summer mornings until time for lunch, and after dinner he slept again, slept fast and woke unrefreshed. Perhaps he had overdone the company. Even writing letters was harder than usual, and he had been fitted with pince-nez for reading and writing and found them a trial—"the *big D* glasses," they kept falling off. He began to wire his answers to letters except to Edwina to whom he always wrote, though less often than formerly until in a fright she cabled asking how he was. The tide of summer turned at last and at the end of August he could tell the one most in his thoughts: "I am counting the days between us now —not the weeks or months any more. Today next month I hope to have you here."

Earlier in August he had visited Barrett in Cohasset, Massachusetts. Barrett and his wife laughed a great deal together, Booth discovered, and Barrett and his children did sports and romped half the day over the tawny Cohasset rocks. The visitor, drawn temporarily into the family circle, found it "very happy, and they have a cozy little home here."

In the bosom of his home Barrett was relaxed and loving. But the fire that is never quenched burned in him still, and one afternoon as he and Booth sat gossiping with friends, Barrett said intensely that he would be willing to act without making any money *for fifty years* if by then he would be considered the head of his profession. Booth, who had been skimming the paper while the others talked, laid it down, lifted off his new pince-nez and, arching his brows with the relief, asked: "Well, Larry, after you get this leadership, what do you think it's worth?"

Barrett snapped back: "You ought to know. You have it."

Booth shook his head. "Leadership has its thorns."

The brooding Barrett's fingers itched to feel those thorns.

The more remarkable then that he should have proposed to Booth what he did during this visit. Why, he suggested, shouldn't he and Booth make a series of tours together, employing a strong company and with himself in charge of the business details Booth found unbearable? It would be the theatrical partnership of Booth and Barrett, but in casting and billing he, Barrett, would take second place.

Booth's support had been so outstandingly bad lately that the press accused him of shirking comparison with first-rate actors.

And his productions looked dingy, especially after Irving's. "Wretched stage setting, slop-shop costumes!" barked the press. His last manager, R. M. Field of Boston, had done really disgracefully by him in the season just over. It was partly Booth's own fault. Making his arrangements with managers beforehand he could never learn to protect or assert himself. He would be utterly confused and afterward at a loss about what had been decided on or what he had consented to.

Now Barrett, whose standards of production were as high as his own used to be, offered to relieve him of all this. Booth agreed tentatively to an arrangement with Barrett still a year off. Before Edwina's marriage he had been hoping that he could soon slow down and act less each season, taking "huge lumps of loaf" between engagements, until in a few years he could blessedly retire. But with his daughter's leaving home the scheme of his life changed. He supposed now that his future would be spent in work as long as his harness lasted—"I give no thought to it."

On October 22 his mother died of pneumonia at three in the morning. Booth reached New York four hours later, and it came over him that this was not the first time he had arrived too late. Turning back the sheet, he stared down at her face, become young again and blissful, with a sort of envy. "To such a weary sufferer," he wrote to Barrett, to whom he had grown much closer in the last weeks, "the end was a blessing, and to all who love her a sense of relief has buoyed—rather than depressed us."

His chief care was for the spinster Rosalie, who had had her share in all the Booth troubles, none of the Booth triumphs. After John's death she and Joe had been their mother's favorites —so Asia thought with a touch of bitterness. But Rosalie was of no use now to anyone. Booth heard her sigh just audibly and murmur: "I wish I was gone too."

"Poor, poor soul! I must now arrange something for her," and he asked kind Mrs. Anderson to keep an eye on Rose. "See her when you can conveniently, but do not treat her as a child —that's what she has chafed under all her life."

They buried Mrs. Booth beside her husband in Greenmount Cemetery. The family hurried away before the grave was covered over to avoid the crowd that lurked curiously outside, avid for a glimpse of any activity, any turning of the earth in the lot where John Wilkes' crumbling body lay.

III

Edwin Booth's Boston neighbors showed friendly interest, not curiosity, in his comings and goings. Charles Copeland, watching him draw near down Park Street, felt a throb of hero worship. Dr. Bartol, his neighbor on Chestnut Street, used to see him walking home from rehearsal. One day a shelf of snow slid off one of the steep Beacon Hill roofs onto the actor's head and shoulders. Booth didn't even raise his hand to brush it off but marched along powdered all over, "steady as an engine on the track," writes Bartol. "He seemed to find a stage in the street and in the world, and never to have left the tragic play behind."

Bartol knew Booth slightly. "I've led a useless life," the actor said to the clergyman once, and waved away Bartol's amazed protest.

Tom Aldrich, living on Mount Vernon Street with his wife, twin sons, and a setter dog, saw more of Booth now than he had in years. On his way home one night he noticed a light burning in the study at 29 Chestnut Street and tapped on the window. At the second tap the front door flew open and out plunged Booth, gripping a cocked revolver. His hair was on end; his eyes were distracted. "Hello, Ned," said Aldrich coolly. "Going hunting? I'll lend you Trip."

Sitting by his study lamp, Booth was at work on a new sort of thing for him. Laurence Hutton with Brander Matthews was bringing out a collection of short biographies of British and American actors and actresses. Booth had been asked to write about his father. Irving was to do Edmund Kean, but at the last minute he begged off and Booth undertook Kean, his father's arch rival. Lawrence Barrett was already doing Booth. "Treat me gently," Booth begged. He dreaded the drudgery of composition himself, put it off and off until there was almost no time left, then sat down without premeditation and worked all night.

Hutton and Matthews were amused, delighted. Booth's pocket biographies gave almost no biographical facts. Booth simply set down his crowding, vivid impressions of his father and Kean, with very few dates and no punctuation to speak of. But in imagination, taste, and flair his writing was on a different level from the rest sent in. He wrote as he acted, by inspiration. And he had his own sources of knowledge, outside the libraries.

He was too young to have met Kean. His essay on this wonderful actor had been inspired by the few stories his father had told him and by his contemplation of Kean's death mask on his study wall as he sat for nights on end smoking until dawn, communing with the mighty dead, alternately poring over the memoirs of actors and looking up sympathetically into their portraits and masks hung all about him: at Thomas Betterton's face, at "the beautiful features of Garrick" in their marvelous mobility. "Old Macklin and George Frederick Cooke gaze at me with hard immobile features. . . . From them I turn to the noble front of Kemble, . . . and then to his sister Siddons, . . . the feline loveliness of Rachel. . . . In the uncanny cast of the head of the dead Kean, which hangs above his portrait opposite my desk, I discover the comic as well as the tragic element . . . the distorted face . . . wasted by disease and suffering . . . his dead weird beauty."

This autumn of 1885 Booth left Boston for the road as usual. Now even the grandchildren of men and women who had seen the young Booth were being brought, as part of their education, to catch the last output of the great actor's powers—all many of them remembered were his bright, dark eyes.

Booth was looking forward to his own first grandchild, looking forward with dread because Edwina, her confinement imminent, was down with a dangerous gastric illness. She and her husband were in Boston, and Booth, absolutely racked with anxiety, was detained in New York by the endless indecisions and procrastinations of Mrs. Anderson, who was unable to decide what sort of gravestone she wanted for dear Davy, for which Booth had promised to pay. He couldn't bring himself to abandon the fussy, forlorn old lady to wrestle alone with her gloomy problem, though almost daily wires from his son-in-law, giving the latest bulletins on Edwina's condition, increased his worry.

By the time he reached Boston his daughter's life was despaired of. A little girl was born. The mother's life hung by a thread. Booth was hammering out his essay on Kean, writing until daybreak. Every day or evening Aldrich, "dear old Tom," stopped in to chat with him, "as he did once before—many years ago—when what I then thought the greatest calamity that could befall me, kept me housed for many weeks."

Edwina pulled slowly out of danger. And Booth wrote in strange condolence to William Winter, whose son had just died: "As I sat by what I believed would be Edwina's deathbed, the thought of her dear mother was always present, and I thanked God for her early death,—which spared her the sufferings she would have endured, in the misfortunes that so frequently have befallen me.

"I cannot grieve at death. It seems to me the greatest boon the Almighty has granted us. Consequently I cannot appreciate the grief of those who mourn the loss of loved ones, particularly if they go early from this hell of misery to which we have been doomed.

"Why do not you," he demanded of Winter, "look at this miserable little life, with all its ups and downs, as I do? At the very worst, 'tis but a scratch, a temporary ill, to be soon cured by that dear old doctor, Death—who gives us a life more healthful and enduring than all the physicians, temporal or spiritual, can give."

In New York again in April, 1886, he costarred splendidly with Tommaso Salvini in some special performances at the Academy of Music. Salvini played the Ghost to his Hamlet and King Lear to his Edgar. Their greatest joint triumph was

Othello, with Salvini as the Moor, his son Alessandro as Cassio (the two Italians played in their native language), and Booth as Iago. Copeland saw the *Othello* when they brought it to Boston in May: "It shines now in my memory as the greatest acting I have ever seen."

The poet Coleridge had said of Kean's acting that it was like reading Shakespeare by flashes of lightning, for Kean's brilliant spurts were pieced out with dull, dark intervals. But "when Salvini played Othello and Booth Iago," writes Copeland, "there were no flashes because there were no periods of darkness. It was like reading Shakespeare by a mighty fire that rose and fell with the passion of the scene."

Ever since he was in England last, Booth had been bothered with dizziness and an increasing tendency to stumble and fall. The great fear was of course that this would happen onstage, and his doctor vainly warned him not to smoke so much. Acting with Barrett recently, he had reeled, almost fallen, then staggered several yards, which was enough to start the fantastic story, spawned by the Boston *Home Journal*, that Barrett, resentful of Booth's ability, was pandering to his "inherited weakness" and had slipped "some potion into his claret" as they dined together before the play. "The cause," said the *Journal*, "is a jealous ambition on the part of this modern Iago, to whom Booth is enacting Cassio by being made drunk, Roderigo by putting money in his purse, and Othello by being utterly undone."

Worse was to come. On April 28, two nights after Booth's opening with Salvini in New York, he had most unluckily fallen flat onstage. He was acting Iago and it was in the scene of Othello's first raging—

> Villain, be sure thou prove my love a whore,
> Be sure of it.

Salvini's business was to hurl Iago to the floor, pretend to trample on him, then jerk him up. Yanked onto his legs, Booth took a couple of unsteady steps and dropped heavily backward, crashing through the brass guard rail of the footlights and putting out three of the gas jets. He would have plunged into the orchestra if some of the musicians hadn't shoved him back. He lay with his head hanging down limp toward the audience until Salvini rushed forward and almost lifted him to his feet before his clothes caught fire.

There was an awful silence. Then commenced the soft, contemptuous hisses and one or two groans and a rustle of taffeta as ladies here and there rose and swished out. A wooden-faced attendant appeared from the wing and relit the gas jets. The play went on and for the next few scenes Booth seemed to be himself again. But in the last act, during Othello's death, he began to mumble and sank into a chair, his head lolling to one side, his legs stuck out. A crowd of supers gathered mercifully around him. He was not drunk, as the papers insisted. He had felt another touch, a feathery brush, of a vertigo that portended worse things.

He was ill, he pleaded. He had rehearsed half the afternoon, gone home exhausted and smoked himself dizzy, had been told by his doctor not to act that night, but had had himself driven to the theater and during the performance had lain down every moment he was offstage. He pleaded in vain. Next morning the headline was HISTORY REPEATS ITSELF! "Never was Edwin Booth seen to worse advantage," grieved a Brooklyn paper. "An idol was shattered. . . . When the audience left the Academy it had Edwin Booth's secret, and denials will no longer keep it hidden."

The New York *World* interviewed an eyewitness "well known in Wall Street and in social circles." This gentleman, who had occupied one of the front boxes, bragged that he "could tell at a glance there was something wrong with Booth. He marched on the stage and stood for a moment leering at the actors . . . his head wabbled from side to side like a sick baby's. And when he began to talk in a husky voice, mumbling his lines, I knew he was drunk."

It did no good for friends like Bispham to print letters protesting that for twenty years Booth had almost never accepted more than a glass of beer and never a drop before acting. The public preferred to think he had got drunk to brace himself for the ordeal of acting with Salvini because Salvini "hogged the stage." "He is rich and lazy," sneered one of the papers, "so rich that he cares for no more money, so lazy that he won't rehearse."

Barrett was one of those who defended his friend publicly and Booth wrote to thank him: "Have suffered intensely since my 'accident.' Bless you for your generous defence."

He begged Edwina, whose happiness in her baby was dimmed by the scandal, not to mind what she read: "The slander is on the wing, and I must live it down, as I have done before."

And to Hutton on May 4: "My misery is not yet ended— every day some ugly reference to my misfortune appears and I am heartsick."

In Boston he tripped and pitched headlong again, but, mercifully, he was behind the scenes. He bitterly regretted that his essays on Kean and his father, which were ready for the press, were not to be published until fall. "Their appearance just now would help my cause, for in each of them I refer to the brutal censure of sick actors, or whenever an accident befalls them, while other brain-workers are excused on the ground of overwork and nervous prostration."

Of his father Booth had written: "Although his eccentricities were invariably attributed to the effect of alcohol, the charge was mainly false. . . . His vagaries were due solely to his peculiarly sensitive temperament. How often has the desire to hide myself almost mastered my own will, when, mentally or physically unfit, duty has compelled me to entertain an audience."

IV

Booth spent the last week of August, 1886, at Boothden with the Grossmanns, a devoted couple, and their baby. He was in a "down" mood; it was not, could not be, like the days he and Edwina used to pass alone. He was not happy there. He hurried away.

Meanwhile, Barrett in New York was actively lining up the first of his new partner's tours under his management. Barrett was not free to go along himself, not until next year. But he drew aside one of the young actresses he had picked for the company and urged her while on the road to set the pace for the others by "being herself" with Mr. Booth, by not being afraid of him, for on his "contented mind," said Barrett, "my own business future depends."

Kitty Molony's first chance came a week later in Bay City, Michigan. A handful of the actors were eating supper in the hotel after the play and glanced up to see Booth walk past the dining-room door alone, walking slowly and bowing gravely in at their gay table. In that polite smile and those grave eyes was an expression—could it be of loneliness? Was it possible Edwin Booth was lonely? Ignoring the etiquette that frowned on a star breaking bread with his support, Kitty sent Arthur Chase, the company manager, running after Booth to ask: Would he join them? They held their breaths, and then the greatest star of them all, looking shy but grateful, entered the dining room, piloted by Chase, and sat down at the company table to eat his plain supper. "I thank you all," he murmured when he had finished.

At her first introduction to him—timid on her side, reserved and dignified on his—at rehearsal in New York, Kitty had seen in Mr. Booth's face "that something," she writes, "that makes a face unmortal, and its painter immortal."

This closer glimpse of him as a human being was altogether too much for her. It was in the air to be "insane on" Booth. Emma Vaders, the company's leading lady, an intense little creature crammed with talent, was the next to fall. A third girl, Ida Rock, buried her face in Kitty's lap and moaned: "He's so sweet." Arthur Chase threw up his hands. He "pitied" Mr. Booth.

It was in the air. When they played in Kalamazoo at the end of September, and Booth lay resting in his hotel room before the show, his door opened abruptly and a gaunt giantess of a woman marched in and over to the bed. She stared down at him. He stared up fascinated into her hard face. He couldn't speak; he was trembling all over. Gloomily the woman bent down and kissed him on the mouth. Her mission accomplished, she tramped out again. In a freezing sweat Booth leaped up after her and locked the door. Never in his life had he been so terrified.

"Perhaps she was an old maid," piped one of the girls in the company to whom he was telling the story. No, he said, he had seen her wedding ring.

Barrett, having chosen this company with great care, wrote to learn Booth's opinion of it. Booth hedged: "You put me in a delicate position." The truth was he liked them all personally but, with the exception of Miss Vaders, "not as actors. . . . The leading young men seem to lack 'character' and force. . . . Royle, Harte, amount to nix."

Edwin Milton Royle (Tubal, Guildenstern) was the future author of the play *The Squaw Man* and the father of Selena Royle, the actress. Then there were John T. Malone (Claudius, Banquo) "and other poor sticks who smile and whine in tawdry fakements through their dreary scenes. . . . I am sorry for all of 'em for they are all so attentive and earnest."

This was today's generation. Yesterday's was headed by Charlie Barron, the virile but decayed player of second parts to the star, "who has really," said Booth, "acted Othello excellently; he *belches* here and there somewhat harshly, but not often," and dear old Mrs. ("Mama") Baker, the character woman, who "as Regan looks antique enough to spank old Lear; the Fool's line about making 'thy daughters thy mothers,' is not, in her case, at all inappropriate."

Business on this tour was already so good that Barrett, sprouting with plans away in New York, not only decided to extend the route west as far as California, which meant Booth would be trekking until spring, he was also arranging a second, much longer tour for next season when he could go too.

Even the remote prospect made Booth groan. " 'Thou torturest me, Tubal! My dear boy, I have barely set my foot upon the road when you appal me (one or two p's?) by your proposition to prolong the agony another weary year! . . . I have that unhappy disposition to agonize over coming events, and even now I am weary of the possible next season's labor. Not the labor of acting but of travel and digesting the wretched stuff one is compelled to gorge in these handsome hotels . . . my belly revolts . . . oh! to begin, before I've had a chance to ascertain if I can possibly endure the present, to arrange a future agony quite demoralizes me."

The chef at the Palmer House in Chicago, who was from Delmonico's, almost wept because Booth ate so little. And "Ah, Misser Boo," cried the Swiss waiter, "Madame Modjeska is like you. She do not eat, but she smoke all time—cigarettes."

They played in St. Louis, Cleveland, then in New York for four weeks. In her New York dressing room Kitty Molony broke her hand mirror and half as a joke let Booth know about it. She hadn't dreamed that her idol, "so balanced, so calm," could be superstitious, but to her astonishment a look of perfect despair flooded his face and he wailed: "Something will happen! To me—to the theater—to you! No—it is to *me!*"

Next morning he was flat on his back with what he dispiritedly called "belly trouble" and the theater stood dark ten days. He was still in bed on November 13, his fifty-third birthday, and he scribbled a line to Millie, his grandchild, who had begun to creep about. His head ached, he told her, and his fifty-three eyes were quite dim. "You and I eat just the same kind of food —plain milk mostly, only you take it from a bottle, which I've given up; it's a bad habit."

Propped up in bed he read the papers through his sliding pince-nez. A writer named Howard published an article sniping at his age. "Joe Howard today says I am a faded wraith of Hamlet. Joe loveth not Ned."

Joe hated Ned, whatever his reasons, and did his utmost to demolish him: "Rich, abundantly able to make illustrious the profession he does not adorn, and so meagrely equipped in all intellectual garnishings as to make it an absolute mental impossibility for him to discuss with any man of culture even the whys and wherefores of the things he does upon the stage.

. . . What is Booth's reputation today? That of a man content to work for money and money alone."

To their surprise and joy Booth's actors found their salaries paid during his illness—out of his own pocket, and he wrote to protest to Barrett the high rate of interest Barrett was currently paying him on a personal loan. "It is unfair and piggish to accept it." His bank accounts, he admitted cheerfully, were "fearfully muddled. Damn figgers, anyhow. 'I am ill at these numbers!' "

Back at the theater he spoke seriously to Kitty about the broken mirror. "You must not mind, now. It might have been my daughter. It might have been fatal."

Something prompted the young girl to answer firmly: "You will not be ill again this season, Mr. Booth." And instantly Booth's face cleared.

In Boston the huge Boston Theater, which many stars had trouble filling, was so packed for a performance of Booth's faded wraith that the orchestra had to be moved up onto the apron. He stayed with the Grossmanns, who were at 29 Chestnut Street. Edwina, expecting a second baby, was not feeling well, and Booth's head still ached. "Tho' the papers praise me," he admitted in a note to Barrett, "I have done some pretty bad work—notably with Lear, last night, whose wits were really wild with a hellish 'pain upon my forehead here.' "

The younger members of the company, not yet hardened to the life of the road, pitied Booth for the relentless timetable that dragged him away from his family five days before Christmas. They played in Syracuse on Christmas Day, after which it was one-night stands to Philadelphia, where they stayed two weeks, then struck out south and west. On January 17 they were in Baltimore. The bustling Barrett had been sure he could persuade Booth to act in the Capitol, but the easygoing Booth had taken his stand. "Nothing could induce me to act in Washington." He had declined an official invitation signed by President Chester Arthur. "This may be mere sentiment in me, but 'tis a strong one and will hold till my 'silver cord is broken.' I cannot, will not go there."

Already the travel, which was simply a lark to the girls and young men who sang round-songs and raced one another on the station platforms for exercise, was wearing on Booth as it had never done before, especially at night when the noise and motion kept him awake. To Barrett from Memphis he wailed that "the trip here was to me a fearful one! not a wink of sleep. . . . I thought I would go mad &, seriously, I believe such experience would soon—if oft repeated—put me in an asylum —or in a box; then to act with nerves prostrated, a raging headache and 'sick to me stummic'! Great *gord!*"

On his own initiative he had decided to drop three scheduled plays: *Richard III*, *Brutus*, and *Don Caesar de Bazan*. He had tried *Richard*, in St. Louis, where dear, warmhearted Kitty had acted one of the little princes, a part not suited to her. Even before the tour started, Booth had led her aside during rehearsal and with a melting, "Would it break your heart if—" made it clear he was withdrawing her from Osric in *Hamlet*. When it turned out she had been promised Lazarillo, another boy's part, in *Don Caesar* and the small but difficult role of Lucretia, victim of Tarquin's lust, in *Brutus*, and had had expensive costumes made, Booth explained to Barrett that cost what it might he must finish this tour without these vehicles. He couldn't bear to hurt Kitty's feelings. "She could not possibly do Lucretia or Lazarillo. . . . In my paternal weakness I concluded to omit the plays rather than break her aspiring heart by casting others for them."

In return for their thoughtfulness on that lonely night in Bay City, he invited Kitty, Emma Vaders, and Ida Rock to be his guests at meals in his private car, the David Garrick. Mama Baker, Mrs. Foster, the heavy woman, and Arthur Chase were asked too. Chase held the hat while the ladies drew lots every day for places. The longest slip meant the seat at Booth's right. Still very conscious of the Iago scandal, they stealthily took note that not a drop of alcohol was served at his table, nothing except milk and bottled water. They were fiercely, protectively partisan. Once the talk turned to the London Lyceum, how H. L. Bateman had got ahead of Booth in signing the lease of it, "and," interposed Mama Baker in her chesty tones, "he engaged an unknown provincial actor whose name was *Henry Irving*."

Then Mrs. Foster, eloquently: "Had *you* taken the Lyceum, Mr. Booth, there WOULD NOT HAVE BEEN A HENRY IRVING!"

"I dare say," Booth quietly acknowledged, "Irving would have had a harder, a longer, climb of it. . . . He might perhaps have taken a thornier path, but it would have led him where he is today, of course."

Another time Kitty put her foot in it, asking unthinkingly: "How many brothers and sisters did you have, Mr. Booth?"

The minute she spoke she could have bitten her tongue out. Booth only said stolidly: "I'll name them—you count them for me! Junius Brutus—after my father, of course—Rosalie, Henry, Mary, Frederick, Elizabeth—I come in here —Asia, Joe—how many is that?"

"Nine, Mr. Booth."

But he had left out one name.

They played in New Orleans. Booth's dressing-room window looked into a brothel next door. The faded Hamlet caught flashes of brunette good looks, heard the scrape of fiddles. Then far west they went into Texas, finally into California in March, 1887. Booth found his room at San Francisco's Palace Hotel jammed with camellias of red, white, and pink. Maidenhair ferns were pinned up and down the lace curtains, and a pillow of camellias said "Booth" and "Welcome" in purple violets. Two black-bordered cards showed all this was from the mother and sister of a young actor, Samuel Piercy, who had been Booth's leading man in Boston a few seasons earlier during a smallpox scare. Booth and Edwina had been inoculated but Piercy caught smallpox and died. Booth had been kind to him, extraordinarily kind.

The San Francisco engagement promised brilliantly, but for

Kitty and Arthur Chase there was a shadow over it, a gray shadow. Even friendly critics had begun to go for Booth's gray hair in *Hamlet*. The box office at the Baldwin Theater was sold out. Expectation was on tiptoe. After Barrett in a whole string of letters had advanced every reason except the real one why his star ought to wear a wig in *Hamlet* for the opening, he sent word to Chase to do what he could. Chase begged Kitty to do what *she* could—Booth's "paternal weakness" for her had not been overlooked.

Making several false starts and with palpitating delicacy she got the idea across. Booth demanded: "You think a wig may please those—I entertain?"

"Only a few."

"Hamlet! It's diabolical, a wig for Hamlet! If they don't like my Hamlet—let them stay away!"

His voice was grim, amused, a little sad. He wore the wig.

San Francisco hadn't forgotten her dark-haired favorite. His reception on opening night held up the play for five stunning minutes. But Booth was not well, was feeling dizzy again, and lonely too, he wrote to Barrett from his hotel room. "Have had a lonely sort of feeling, off and on, all the time I've been here; perhaps I'm tired. . . . I am still very anxious about Edwina —she must, surely, have gone past her time."

He included in this engagement a single performance of *Othello* in which he played the Moor. To be taken in Mr. Booth's arms and kissed by him in the love scenes was heaven to Emma Vaders as Desdemona, "and of course he knew it," exclaimed Kitty, yearning from a box.

They started east again, acting as they went. In the privacy of the David Garrick, as it sped past the breath-taking scenery of Wyoming and Colorado, the company's domestic intimacy with Booth deepened. He had appeared one day with his arms full of rolled-up socks that needed darning, and he gazed bashfully at the pining Kitty, Emma, and Ida. Could they, would they? Kitty jumped for the socks and divided her spoils. As the tour neared its end, the high and exquisite romance of it made the three young actresses count the days left and ache over the weeks gone. None of the three had been re-engaged for next fall.

Their last night of all was in New Bedford, Massachusetts, where they gave *Richelieu* to one of those mysteriously cold and sodden houses that the most successful tours occasionally stumble on. It was a disappointing windup and Booth was piqued. At Richelieu's line about "dull tiers of lifeless gapers" he winked offstage at Royle who had just made his exit as Huguet, then stalked down to the front and willfully turning his back on the house began to make horrible faces at the others. When the Curse of Rome, his tour de force, got hardly a ripple of the applause he was used to, he let himself go and finished the performance in a caricature of his usual acting so savagely funny that the helpless cast was in torture not to laugh. Chase allowed afterward he hadn't realized Mr. Booth "could be so full of the Old Nick." But he would never have done it if the play had been Shakespeare, said Booth almost fiercely.

Somehow for him as well as for the three girls this ending of a tour meant more than usual because these eight months had been "not the happiest point of my *life*," he told them wistfully, "another time was that, but it was the happiest season of my *career*." Everything, he mused, had hinged on that first evening when stage etiquette had been breached. "Had I been so foolish as not to accept your invitation to your first supper, this season would have been like all of them."

The girls and Chase stood around him in the echoing railway station as they had often done before, but this time to say good-by. They clung to his hand. Kitty burst into tears. He mounted the step of the moving train and waved back, smiling faintly.

CHAPTER 15

The Vulture Hours

To-morrow, and to-morrow, and to-morrow,
Creeps in this petty pace from day to day.
> Macbeth, *Act V, scene 5*

 EDWINA's second child was a boy, born on April 9, 1887. She and her husband had taken a house of their own on Beacon Street in Boston. Booth planned to sell the Chestnut Street house, which had got too large, then go back to New York to live by himself in an apartment. He would be traveling a great deal. "I hope, dear," he wrote to Edwina, "that you will enjoy many, many happy years in your charming little home." And to Barrett: "I shall never again attempt to 'set up my everlasting rest' outside of Mount Auburn, where I had my house prepared some 24 years ago; a cool, brick apartment that just fits my carcase."

It made him blue as indigo to walk through 29 Chestnut Street and see the stripped rooms, once so cozy. Had he allowed it to, his simmering depression could have swelled into a wild and bitter grief. But that way madness lay. "Let me shun that," he wrote.

Julia, his housekeeper, looked on while he packed his books. Her black face hung in gloomy folds. "Yes, Julia," he said, "this is the third time I've tried to make a home and failed, but still there's a little home always ready for me at Mount Auburn."

Most of this July he spent cruising up the coast into bracing Maine waters on the *Oneida*, a yacht belonging to his friend E. C. Benedict. Barrett was on board, so were those other good fellows Aldrich, Hutton, and Bispham. Booth's depression lifted a little as he broached a plan to them. It was a cherished plan, vaguely conceived as in memory of his father, to found in New York a really first-class club, which would be chiefly for actors but—and this was very important—also open to some eminent men in other lines: a social gathering place where all could get acquainted, where the insularity of "the profession" could be rubbed off and the nonprofessionals come to know actors as artists and gentlemen. For he could never be quite unconscious of the special quality of his own acceptance (Barrett's too) on equal terms by the very men he was talking with and others like them, educated men. The club he proposed would be "a beacon to incite emulation in the 'poor player' to lift up *himself* to a higher social grade than the Bohemian level."

"Call it 'The Players'!" Aldrich put in enthusiastically.

Definite plans for it had to be postponed while Booth and Barrett set off in September on their first tour together. Barrett had daringly insisted on doubling their prices, arguing that when the public saw them both it saw twice as much as usual and would willingly pay twice as much. Booth had been doubtful—"it would be a great risk and very unpleasant to come down." But Barrett had been right, of course.

When they steamed into Chicago in October they found Richard Mansfield creating a sensation there in *Dr. Jekyll and Mr. Hyde*. Already faint signs pointed to the thirty-three-year-old Mansfield as the coming tragedian. If a future leader in the field could be said to be emerging, it was Mansfield. Booth had no chance to see the play, but he took time to write his congratulations to the rising actor on his dual performance, "of which I have heard such glowing accounts."

This year the name of the stars' railway car was the Junius Brutus Booth. Booth and Barrett occupied it together. They looked a modern Brutus and Cassius to the life (the "noble Brutus," the "lean and hungry" Cassius) as they went for their walk every afternoon, sedately pacing the station platform in fur-collared overcoats.

The reporters' first question was always: "How do Mr. Booth and Mr. Barrett get along?" It seemed as if the alliance had brought out the best qualities in both men. At forty-nine Barrett had at last accepted the fact of Booth's superior gift. His ambition now was to be the second greatest American actor, and he slipped ungrudgingly into second place, giving himself second billing, secondary roles, the second-best dressing room. In their joint curtain calls he sometimes flung his arm lovingly around his partner's neck as he led him offstage and when he spoke the name "Edwin" his voice had a dramatic, solemn tone as though to convey the uniqueness of their relationship. He did every bit of the drudgery of booking, hiring, rehearsing, and keeping the machinery of the tour running smoothly.

"Barrett is in the seventh heaven," Booth told Edwina. "He works like a horse."

On his side, Booth luxuriated in being taken care of. All he had to do was act, then hold out his hand for his share of the profits. He was spared all decisions, and he sank comfortably into the habit of saying to his partner: "Tell me what you want me to do and I'll do it."

For the first time in years he had good support. However, critics must criticize and now they complained that the partners' repertoire was tiresomely limited. "Impossible not to recall here Henry Irving's splendid energy in preparing a new bill for us every night," grumbled the New York *Press*. "A clock-beating art is held out to us. Mr. Booth as Iago, Mr. Barrett as Othello. Mr. Booth as Othello, Mr. Barrett as Iago. Tick, tick, tick."

And yells of rage were heard from other stars, who had a hard time competing with Booth and Barrett when the two appeared separately and who were utterly destroyed when they played together. Any theater honored by a visit from "the combine" could count on standing room only, while the other houses in town stood three-quarters empty. Booth and Barrett appealed to the conservative, well-to-do element in every community, which could safely bring its young daughters and give the girls the satin programs for their memory books. The double prices charged actually seemed to draw rather than repel audiences, as Barrett had shrewdly guessed they would. People saved for weeks to see the famous team, and those luckless smaller stars who played a city just before or after Booth and Barrett almost lost their shirts.

When the first Booth-Barrett tour was over in the spring of 1888, an actor named Milton Nobles fumed furiously in the New York *Dramatic Mirror* that it had "swooped down upon the profession at large after the manner of a cyclone or a stroke of paralysis. Throughout the country—particularly, the one- and two-night stands—they simply killed the business for six or eight weeks in the midst of the season."

They nearly killed themselves. This was a much more strenuous tour than last season's, with Barrett often scheduling two shows a day, "like a traveling vaudeville," said Edwin Royle, who was in the company again. Very often now Booth held back his best, stinting the one-night stands, husbanding his powers for the large cities. Topeka or Elmira, whose unspoiled citizens flocked open-mouthed along the railway tracks when the Booth-Barrett special pulled in, definitely did not see the same quality of acting by Booth as Chicago or Pittsburgh. But they got their money's worth from the other partner, for Barrett never stinted onstage. "Mr. Booth can act when he wants to," observed the critic Nym Crinkle, who took away with his left hand the praise he gave with his right, "and Mr. Barrett always wants to."

II

Booth's club for actors was taking bodily form, fourteen bodily forms: On January 7, 1888, The Players was incorporated by himself and thirteen others, each a notable man in his line: they included Barrett, Jefferson, John Drew, Augustin Daly, and among the nontheatricals Bispham, Mark Twain, and General William Tecumseh Sherman.

The Booth-Barrett caravan was on the road when Bispham let Booth know he had been elected president. Booth was flattered, yet he could wish a man had been chosen "of a more positive nature . . . I shall make a sorry figure-head, a mere dummy, in the chair." The vice-president was Augustin Daly. Hutton and Bispham each had positions, and ever vigilant to protect his partner's pride, Booth reminded Bispham: "I do hope that Barrett was not forgotten, but that he was made a director as well as yourself."

Part of his dream was to buy a fine building, stuff it with furniture, and present it to The Players as his gift for their clubhouse. He had commissioned Bispham to look around for a place, having in mind some spacious old brownstone for about $80,000, but when Bispham reported finding just such a house in an exclusive neighborhood for $150,000 Booth wired him to accept.

Briefly in New York again on May 21, Booth and Barrett took part in a benefit for Lester Wallack, the representative in his generation of one of the great theatrical families of the country. Lester Wallack and his father, James William Wallack, called "the elder Wallack" (whom the elder Booth had flown at with a knife), had given their name to a succession of New York playhouses. The younger Wallack had been a butterfly of an actor, a specialist in elegantly comic and jauntily romantic costume parts, Doricourt in *She Stoops*, Puff in *The Critic*, Mercutio, Don Caesar de Bazan, Claude Melnotte. Now he was sixty-eight, jaunty, arthritic, elegant, and destitute.

A benefit at New York's Metropolitan Opera House had been organized to relieve the old actor's poverty. *Hamlet* was chosen and Booth invited to do the Prince. It was an all-star cast, with Frank Mayo as the King, John Gilbert as Polonius, Joseph Jefferson and William Florence as the Gravediggers. The Ophelia was Helena Modjeska; the Queen, Gertrude Kellogg; the Player Queen, Rose Coghlan. Stars who shone in their own right like E. L. Davenport, Minnie Maddern, Ferdinand Gottschalk, and May Robson had traveled half across the country to be supers and "walking ladies and gentlemen" for this performance. Many bought new costumes to be worn this one night, then laid away as souvenirs.

Everyone dressed quickly and flocked into the greenroom. Only Jefferson loitered in his street clothes, he didn't come on until the last act. The white-coated grips delighted in banging their flats into chattering groups to show these stars they thought them no better than anybody else. The volunteer orchestra began to tune up; it was led by twenty-six-year-old Walter Damrosch. When the play started the illustrious supers, careless of appearances, strayed all over the stage chasing the limelight. The audience interestedly picked them out. Both wings were so cluttered with performers anxious not to miss anything that the principals had to fight their way to the entrances.

Booth's black figure was the one seen most often worming through the crowd, arms thrusting like a swimmer's. He had taken no pains this time to hide his age. His Hamlet, gray-haired and lined, looked much older than Frank Mayo's King. Ten minutes after he opened his mouth his age was forgotten. "Mr. Booth never acted so brilliantly," applauded the *Herald*, "never with so much fire and feeling. . . . He dominated the stage, not alone by his genius, but by the courtesy of those around him. He was, as never before in his career, the star of stars."

If he hadn't been pledged to act in this benefit he would have begged off. Five days earlier his sister Asia had died in England of heart disease at fifty-two. Since Booth had seen her last, her adored first-born son Edwin Booth Clarke, who trained at Annapolis, had been lost at sea. Because there was no witness to his death, the mother had hoped on. She found some help for her trials in religion, yet the gloom and confusion of several of her recent letters had made Booth, after reading one of them, sigh to Hutton, who knew her well: "Poor girl! I fear she's 'off her head' seriously." Her husband brought her body home. She was buried at Greenmount with a Catholic service.

Just before her death she had secretly entrusted a small black book to Benjamin Farjeon, the English husband of Maggie Jefferson, being fearful that if it fell into John Clarke's hands he would tear it to pieces. The book had a lock and key and on the cover the stamped initials *J.W.B.* Asia had set down in it all she could remember of her younger brother—touching, human glimpses to be given to the public when the time came, if it ever did, for others to look with clear eyes at Johnny.

Down in Baltimore for Asia's funeral, Booth called on his old schoolmistress, Susan Hyde, and found her mortally ill, then two weeks later he learned she had died. "My dear old school-marm. . . . She was *woman* all through; in the true sense of that word: gentle in manner, soft in heart and low in her estimation of her worth: excellent things in woman!" He was writing to Barrett from the Hotel Vendome in Boston. "Bye-the-bye, how do your glands? Think of Bassanio and keep 'em down; no old fogy next season, mind you!" For Barrett had broken out with peculiar swellings of the face, which made him look mumpish, and had had to leave the company before work was over to undergo treatment.

"All but I are taking their ease for the summer," Booth told Winter a few weeks later when the tour had ended. "I am homeless and hang up at hotels here and there."

Jefferson wanted him for a visit at Buzzards Bay on Cape Cod. Wherever Jefferson was there would be "bushels of children and grandchildren, all so congenial and jolly." Booth always felt well at the Jeffersons' and stayed as long as he decently could; a visit to Joe "lifts me high up . . . his delicious company . . . his charming family circle."

On one of these visits Jefferson read Dickens aloud to them all. Booth had heard Dickens in person give one of his famous public readings from his own works and thought he was terrible, but Jefferson read with exquisite funniness the Crummles episode from *Nicholas Nickleby:*

"The theatrical profession!" said Mr. Vincent Crummles. "I am in the theatrical profession myself, my wife is in the theatrical profession, my children are in the theatrical profession. I had a dog that lived and died in it."

It was not so jolly at the hotel in Narragansett Pier where Booth spent part of July to be near Edwina and his own grandchildren. He seldom went to Boothden any more. The Grossmanns didn't care to live there, and the pretty estate was often deserted except for the staff. Now and then while he was at Narragansett he took the steamer across the Bay and drove out to inspect his property, staying only a few hours.

Barrett's lumps were still with him; they worried the doctors. However, treatment at Sulphur Springs had made them softer and he was able to set off on the old round with Booth in the middle of September. As before, they raked in the dollars, paid out with their strength. "These two actors have made money," said the Kansas City *Star*, "but they are for the present nearly worn out."

Just before they started Lester Wallack died, having had only four months to enjoy the spoils from his benefit. They were in St. Paul when William Warren of the Boston Museum, whose Boston debut Booth had seen with his father in 1846, died on September 21. Booth himself verged on fifty-five. And in a flash the milestone came, was passed. They were playing in New York on his birthday. Gifts gamboled in: flowers and fruit, and a portrait of Edwina from herself, and silk handkerchiefs from Barrett—"I must have had a hundred dozen silk handkerchiefs given me at various times." But in the midst of the celebrating he suffered an irreparable loss. He believed it was at Delmonico's he had dropped a dear little penknife Mollie had given him in the year of Edwina's birth, but the waiters searched in vain for it. "I never missed anything so much."

The house Booth had bought for The Players was at 16 Gramercy Park. He was reserving the third floor for himself. It would be his home. There he would live without paying rent, and if he liked, was free to lease the other of the two bedrooms on the floor to Barrett whenever his partner was staying in town—"I don't want to be there alone all the while." The architect Stanford White was doing over the house, and the costs would be about double what Booth originally intended, but he had given the order to go ahead. He was hard at it himself, excitedly plotting where to put furniture and hang pictures, and he selected Shakespearian quotations to appear in each room. To Hutton: "What think you of this as a motto for the grill—Let's '*mouth* it, as many of our Players do'? & for the *Toilet*—'Nature her custom holds, let shame say what it will'?"

Gramercy Park had an iron fence to keep out the public. It was a sacred rectangle with private houses on all four sides, and only the residents had keys to the Park gate. When these good burghers heard that a club for actors was to open among them, the hair on the back of their necks rose. Later, though, as they learned the quality of the members, they calmed down, and still on their guard, turned cordial to the extent that Booth could shyly boast: "The Players is already popular with the very best sort of folk."

Already the club was his darling, his pride. The money he had poured into it and the remarkable collection of theatrical relics and portraits he planned to give, and to which he was devotedly adding, had been accumulated by his own labors, were in a sense part of him, so that Jefferson, second president of The Players, was able to say after Booth's death that "it was not his wealth only, but it was himself that he gave."

Membership was small, and a residue of actors not asked to join aired the opinion that Booth was trying to buy his way into society by founding The Players. "Let's wait and see," sniffed the *Dramatic Mirror*, "of what mortal sort of use Mr. Booth's club is going to be to the profession. The actors . . . don't need any gilded halls and hammered brass grill rooms to make 'em acquainted or better their condition."

The clubhouse was thrown open at midnight on New Year's Eve, 1888. Booth stood on a dais in the main hall, in front of

the ornate marble fireplace with its carven masks of Comedy
and Tragedy, facing all the members. Not he but another Booth
seemed to dominate them: Junius Brutus in portrait stared with
thrusting gaze from the wall over the mantel. Booth handed
over to Daly as vice-president the deed conveying the house
and furnishings. Barrett importantly read aloud a letter from
Edwina and a poem composed for the evening by the Boston
poet Thomas Parsons. Edwina had sent a laurel wreath with a
card inscribed "Hamlet, king, father . . ." and when Barrett
reached a particular line of the poem—

Tragedian, take the crown!

the wreath was passed up to Booth, who tried to respond, got
stuck three times, cleared his throat, looked desperately embarrassed, dabbed with his handkerchief at his lips and finally
yielded with a faint: "I think I can say no more."

As the clock tolled twelve he stooped to the new fireplace
to light the Yule log, also sent by Edwina. Then he held high
a loving cup, which had belonged to William Warren, been
bequeathed by Warren to Jefferson and presented by Jefferson
to The Players. He tipped wine into it from a flagon that had
been his father's, drank ritually, and started the cup passing
from hand to hand in the flame-lit circle of gentlemen all,
while outside the city bells pealed in the New Year.

III

By noon next day several members had ordered lunch in
The Players grillroom. Others were reading in deep chairs in
the library as though the club had been running a year. To
Edwina, Booth couldn't help pluming himself: "Several of the
best men of New York are here, and it will, no doubt, be the
rendezvous of the choicest."

Having gone to bed at five and got up at one, both he and
Barrett were wan but jubilant. "All believe, as I do, that this
will be of more real benefit to the actor than anything ever done
in the world."

He could hardly wait to be in residence. He and Barrett

moved into their neighboring rooms on the third floor and began going down together to meals in the grill, where the waiter
who served them remembered that "Mr. Booth was gentle and
unassuming, Mr. Barrett decidedly loud and pretentious." Several times he carried their trays upstairs, and the two gentlemen's bedrooms, he noted, were furnished characteristically:
Mr. Barrett's with a "showy bed of oxidized silver," while Mr.
Booth's bed was a "simple affair of dull brass."

The papers having a great deal to say about the new club,
Booth's name naturally appeared in them over and over. Not so
Barrett's, but "no matter what the reporters say or omit in
their mention of us," Booth quickly forestalled his sensitive
partner, "the truth will be known and the truth is that without your influence I could never have done so much for the
Club. . . . I need your back-bone. If you should ever lose
interest in it I shall 'flop.' "

They were away on the road again, were in Baltimore when
Rosalie Booth slipped out from under the load of her ingrained
and hopeless melancholy and died on January 15, 1889, at sixty-
five. Her burial was at Greenmount; there was an Episcopal
service. Only two were left out of all the brood old Junius
Brutus had fathered by his second wife. Richard, the unwanted
first wife's son, had dropped out of sight years before. During
this spring Joseph in New York finally took his medical degree
and was made attending physician at the Northern Dispensary
on Christopher Street. He was forty-nine.

The incessant travel was a dreadful drain on Booth this season. He felt jounced and harried in spite of the cushions Barrett provided in the shape of private railway cars with beds
and bathtubs, and sybaritic hotel suites. He couldn't adjust
himself, couldn't relax—"I am aweary, aweary. . . ."

In Rochester on April 3 they were driving to the theater for
Othello when he began to feel, not ill exactly, but indescrib-
ably odd. At the stage entrance the doorman, an old-timer,
greeted them and when Booth tried to answer he could not.
He could not speak. Still he gave no sign to Barrett, but had
himself dressed as Iago and tottered on, hoping for a miracle.

None came. Facing the audience, the best he could force out was uncouth sounds. "What's the matter with Mr. Booth?" whispered Roderigo desperately into the wing.

And the hovering Barrett called: "Go for a doctor!"

The curtain was lowered. A doctor from across the street examined Booth and announced he had had a slight stroke. Then Barrett, knocked all of a heap by the verdict and close to tears at the sad appeal in his partner's eyes as Booth lay speechless on a couch, lost his head completely, rushed before the curtain and dismissed the huge audience in a voice filled with agony. "We fear," said Barrett, "that this is the beginning of the end. The world has probably heard for the last time the voice of the greatest actor who speaks the English language."

EDWIN BOOTH DYING! warned the newspapers. The editors had spent a busy night delving in their morgues for summaries of Booth's life. About the time the public read this news, and looking up from it, had begun to speak of the great actor in the past tense—individuals reminding themselves when they had seen him last—Booth was already talking and laughing with the relieved and red-eyed Barrett. His seizure had left him almost as swiftly as it had come. The tour was suspended while he went back to New York to be overhauled by a specialist who was less alarming than the doctor in Rochester, used the term "nervous prostration," and advised, first, rest, then a much lighter schedule, urging on Booth what all the doctors had urged unsuccessfully, *to smoke less.*

The story hinted at in some of the papers was that Barrett had been driving Booth unmercifully, exploiting his partner's genius and pitifully failing strength for his own aggrandizement. Even Edwina, whom the ominous headlines had sent hurrying north from Florida, wondered if Barrett wasn't working her father too hard. "You must not allow yourself to suppose," Booth corrected her, severely for him, ". . . that I am a mere tool in the hands of others. I do not consider it very complimentary to have my over-anxious friends blame others for leading me by the nose."

About his health he had no illusions, and sent a line to Barrett from The Players: "I have received my second warning, and we can't tell when I'll get notice to quit." His first warning had been the fit of vertigo while he was acting Iago with Salvini. Iago, it seemed, was his unlucky role.

He implored Barrett to let them both go slower next season, cut out some of the one-night stands and the two shows on Saturday. "Less $, of course, but I believe more life for both of us. . . . Darling, we are getting old."

Barrett had apologized for his outburst in front of the curtain, was tormenting himself that he had said too much. "Of course, my dear boy," Booth comforted him, "you could not avoid letting your very heart out, with all its fears, that doleful night. . . . God bless you, my dear friend, for your deep affection for me which is reciprocated fully—tho' I don't say much about it."

He was back with the tour by the middle of April. They played in San Francisco, the third time in three years that Booth had acted here, and business was not quite so good as usual. He and Barrett put the slackness down to the high prices (though the same prices had been gladly paid a year before) and to its being the end of May, when the best people were already out of town. Between performances they took easy walks in the park above the ocean, their carriage following. The California scenery was striking as ever, yet somehow it had lost its charm for Booth. San Francisco was the city of his youth. To be here now only made him homesick for his room at The Players.

This was a quiet brown room. East Twentieth Street below was noisy and public, but three floors above in his own bed-sitting room ("my nest among the tree-tops of Gramercy") Booth could be as quiet and private as he pleased, and so he was during this summer after he and Barrett had worked their way east again and brought the fatiguing season to a close.

The life of the club was languid through July and August, and the few members that drifted in and out in no way infringed on his seclusion. It was even a little lonely living on the third floor without Barrett, who was off taking treatments for the glandular disease that had its ups and downs but would not leave him, and on the whole was rather worse.

"Dear old Lumpy. . . ." Booth wrote to him. "Dear old Glanders. . . ." He wrote often and affectionately. "I have missed you very much altho' you won't believe it. I've not had a very jolly summer thus far. I agonized at the Pier for Edwina's sake and have promised to see her there again."

Much though he longed for his daughter and grandchildren, and hot and down-at-the-heel though he found New York in summer, he preferred being here on his own to enduring the formal resort life of Narragansett. On very sultry nights he ate his supper on the veranda of the grill, which gave onto a court, and later upstairs walked softly down the short hall to Barrett's vacant bedroom, where the silver bed shone in the moonlight, and lingered a few minutes by the open window to catch the breeze off the little back garden. Returning, he stationed himself beside his own window—a still figure reclining on a sofa, so nearly perfectly quiet he could hardly be distinguished in the darkening room—while the church clocks chimed from near and far, their strokes emphasizing the desertedness of the city so late in these summer nights.

Sometimes he dozed. Sometimes his mind seethed—"vulture thoughts," he called them—and he stared out with desperate wakefulness at Gramercy Park, whose trees were bathed in the light of a moon more remote and silvery than the low-hanging California moon. One o'clock struck, and after a long interval, two, then three. Often he heard four strike, and he looked expectantly for the gradual paling of the sky in the east; watched the slow taking shape of objects in his room; heard the clatter of milk carts, the imperative whistles bidding others to work. He called these his "vulture hours."

IV

Someone had quoted of Booth in print Samuel Johnson's line,

Superfluous lags the veteran on the stage,

and Booth took to calling himself "old Superfluous Lags" to his friends. It hurt, though. September marked his fortieth year in the profession. He celebrated by opening an engagement in Louisville. Barrett was not with him, though he had arranged the tour. Better from his treatments, at least on the surface, Barrett was rehearsing a new play in Chicago and had engaged Helena Modjeska to star with Booth at fifteen hundred dollars a week. Booth got three thousand, and his name was billed first. To Joseph Haworth, an actor who dropped by to see him, he spoke of his youth in California: "I could *act* then, had all the enthusiasm of youth—rosy hopes, great ambitions, and so forth; yet I couldn't convince the people I was a good actor. I am now old and they are paying five and ten dollars a seat, and I cannot act at all."

He and Modjeska had moved on to New York and were playing at the Broadway Theater when on November 11 the *Herald* dropped what Booth described as "a load of filth out of a clear sky."

It ran a headline on the first page of its news section:

MODJESKA'S GRIEVANCE

The Great Polish Actress Said to Be Unwilling
to Play with Edwin Booth for Personal Reasons

A scurrilous article unwound itself. Madame Modjeska, said the writer, frankly took no interest in the Booth-Barrett company outside of pocketing her salary. Neither she nor her husband, the Count Bozenta, would even speak to Barrett—"the arrogant little fellow," Bozenta was supposed to have called him. Booth, on his side, was reputedly jealous of her press notices. But the lady's "Personal Reasons" for seeking a release from her contract were the "ungentlemanly and unchivalrous" advances Mr. Booth had made her. This writer had interviewed Booth at The Players only the night before, and his account of the interview was broken into by piquant headings:

MR. BOOTH DENIES IT
TOO OLD FOR LOVE MAKING

"I asked Mr. Booth plainly if he had ever conducted himself in such a way as to give offence to Madame Modjeska. 'My dear sir,' Mr. Booth replied, knocking the ashes from his cigar, 'my dear fellow, Madame Modjeska and I are old enough to have grandchildren. My love-making days off the stage are over.'"

To Barrett, Booth explained that he had "foolishly let the dirty dog (Pierce he calls himself) see me because I thought to shield the lady's name. . . . The cur was in drink . . . but assured me that not a word of what he termed the 'poppycock' story should be printed."

Booth's lawyer, as he had done when the McVickers spread slander, advised his client to be patient; to keep dignified silence; not to sue. What was one more filthy reporter tearing at him? "This I must expect till the grass is rank above me."

The Booth-Modjeska alliance was an idea of Barrett's inspired by the sparkling team of Irving and Terry. But it was conceived too late. Both stars had seen their best days, and business at the Broadway was only fair. The lovely Modjeska at forty-five was, as far as looks went, past playing girlish parts like Ophelia and Julie in *Richelieu*, and Booth had had trouble this season deciding which of his well-worn vehicles to pit against the fresher attractions at other houses. He admitted to Barrett that in New York especially he felt stale, "*stale* in the reiterance of the same old plays. I feel it here more than elsewhere."

Barrett had wanted to revive *Richard III*, but Booth objected not only because of Mansfield's recent success as Richard but also because of his sumptuous new production of the play soon to be launched in New York. "*Richard III* with no appropriate scenery & in the face of what is promised by Mansfield, whose 'mount' as well as his performance in Boston, has been highly lauded by the papers here, would, it seems to me, be in the very worst taste possible & do me no good."

Otis Skinner, engaged as leading man in Barrett's place, was horrified to see how much Booth had deteriorated physically since 1880, when they had last acted together. For Booth to act these days with the force Skinner remembered, one of his support must set the pace for him, "give him the note," and this was very often up to Skinner as Macduff or Horatio. It would be the call of the bugle to the veteran war horse: in a flash Booth would respond, the old spell and power surging into his voice. The old fire blazed, but only for a moment, only to die down. "My flickering spark should be coaxed and husbanded." And again: "The vigor that I occasionally manifest is nervous force merely, which, like a stimulant, leaves me in a collapsed condition."

He was reporting to Barrett. Matinee days were the worst. "Yesterday I acted Richelieu—barely able to force through it . . . and in the evening I suffered tortures throughout Macbeth. The vertigo which afflicts me & the lack of physical strength are apparent to all."

Yet he was better off than Barrett, whose glands were worse again. Barrett's face was pathetically swollen, and he was fearfully sensitive about it. His throat hurt. His speech was affected, so were his nerves. He had a hysterical feeling almost all the time now, he confided to Booth. He had canceled the engagements of his new play, and before the year was out, sailed for Germany to try the waters at a spa. "The symptoms he describes are those which I am told are very serious," Booth wrote sadly to Edwina. "I do not think he will ever act again, even if he lives. This is *entre nous*. He is not hopeful now."

And to Barrett: "I have the best hopes . . . keep up yours. . . . Think of *nothing* but getting well. Follow the doctors' directions to the letter."

One of Booth's admirers had got the habit of popping to his feet in the theater whenever Booth took a call and encouraging the audience: "That's right. Call him out again! Call him out again! He won't be with you long." Possibly with the same thought, the art committee of The Players asked Booth in January, 1890, to sit for his portrait to John Singer Sargent.

"Buy some sandpaper and sandpaper your soul," Tom Aldrich warned him before the sittings began. Sargent had the reputation of exposing the secret selves of those he painted.

Irving had sat to him in London, had hated the result, and would never let it be shown. "Very good, but mean about the chin at present," Ellen Terry called Irving's portrait before it was finished. "There sat Henry and there by his side the picture, and I could scarce tell one from t'other."

Sargent had observed his new subject. He placed Booth in a characteristic pose: standing, gracious and meditative, with head inclined a little, as though listening, one foot forward a step, and both thumbs hooked in the trouser pockets. Just so had he seen Booth stand at The Players with his friends, deep in the conversations of which his own part was chiefly a silent encouragement. Booth even caught himself like this onstage, especially as Hamlet. The framed portrait was hung above the mantel in the club reading room. The figure seemed rather too tall, the legs were too slim and finickingly drawn, but with the grave, beautiful face even Aldrich was satisfied.

It was thus he looked . . .

Aldrich wrote, and ended his poem "Sargent's Portrait of Edwin Booth at 'The Players' " with an invocation:

> O Cruel Time,
> Whose breath sweeps mortal things away,
>   Spare long this image of his prime,
> That others standing in the place
>   Where save as ghosts we come no more,
> May know what sweet, majestic face
>   The gentle Prince of Players wore.

V

"I shall thank God from the very dregs of my soul when I get through this awful tour." Booth was writing from Chicago on March 20, 1890, to Barrett, who was in Paris waiting for the German baths to open. "My health (at night) is excellent, but all day I am utterly down, derry down."

The road this time had led him through Boston, Philadelphia, and Baltimore. In Boston at the end of January his hotel room had overlooked the Common, thick with pigeons, and one of the birds, a white one, had perched on his window sill every morning for just as long as he sat at the desk writing letters. Rain or shine, it visited him faithfully. "I wonder who it is— or was!"—this was to Bispham.

The tenant of a house in Dorchester, a good carriage drive out, answered her bell to find on her doorstep an oldish man who asked if he might see the house, explaining that he had lived there once. He gave no name, and the woman didn't then identify him. They went upstairs, where the caller disappeared inside a bedroom and shut the door. He slipped out again a few minutes later, saying only that his wife, whom he loved very much, had died in that room.

From Philadelphia in February Booth wrote again to tell Bispham that business there was great, " 'Tis remarkable how the old nag draws in his decadence! Perhaps 'tis his last 'spurt' on the home stretch."

The prospect for Baltimore had looked equally fine, but when he arrived business turned out "wretched, the worst engagement I ever played in my native city." Of course it was Lent and the weather was vile, which were two possible reasons why, though they were reasons he would have laughed at even two years earlier.

A fair number of people still traveled from Washington to see him act, and some spent the night afterward at the Mount Vernon Hotel, where he was staying. Coming home on Friday after the play, he had to stalk the gauntlet across the lobby to the elevator between a double line of women and girls. Then there were two sisters, seventeen and twenty, from a good Baltimore family, who ventured into his hotel and sent up their cards. They had got a "crush" on him. Booth had them in, giggling and nudging, and asked sternly what they were there for. "Oh," chirped the seventeen-year-old, "we saw you play last night and came to make your acquaintance."

Too old to be attracted, too tired and depressed to be lenient or amused, Booth gave the sisters a terrific calling down, warning them of the danger in running after actors. He held up the little cards between thumb and forefinger like something obscene, and pretending to assume the names on them were fictitious, said harshly: "If I knew your right names I should certainly tell your parents."

So to Chicago, where on March 19 he made two recordings for Edwina on the phonograph, wondrous new invention of Thomas A. Edison. Booth recited into the huge earlike horn Othello's address to the senators and Hamlet's "To be, or not to be," finding it hard to speak with full feeling in cold blood.

He was in Detroit when he wrote to Edwina, who had congratulated him on a critic's praise (the enthusiastic notices could be counted now): "Yes, it is indeed most gratifying to feel that age has not rendered my work stale and tiresome. . . . But as for the compensation? Nothing of fame or fortune can compensate for the spiritual suffering. . . . To pass life in a sort of dream, where 'Nothing is but what is not,' a loneliness in the very midst of a constant crowd, as it were, is not a desirable condition of existence, especially when the body also has to share the 'penalty of *greatness*.' "

Indianapolis, Vincennes, Decatur. . . . "Dear old Pal," Booth exhorted Barrett, "dear old Party. . . ." His letters were crammed with urgings to "get well *soon*," to "take *care* of yourself."

Barrett answered cheerfully, and Booth in turn grew cheerful: "Mightily rejoiceth your antique Pal at ye good knews frō thee!"

Of his own health he sighed that "any attempt at exercise only intensifies my exhaustion." Skinner used to call for him before their entrances in his dressing room hazy with smoke. Booth would lay down his cigar, try to stand, then, sick with dizziness, would reel and stumble, and it would be minutes before he could negotiate the trip to the wing on Skinner's arm. Back in November when Skinner played Macduff for the first time, he had been so nervous in the fight he had almost brained Booth with a terrific wallop on the crown of the head, which Booth's guard was too feeble to parry. Booth's wig and cap of chain mail saved him from concussion. He had staggered, whispered, "Go on," and afterward smiled over the near thing, but Skinner was in a frenzy.

When he was not acting, Booth was resting. He and Modjeska were perfectly friendly, but they hardly ever met except onstage. Between the acts Madame Modjeska sat in her dressing room, a Japanese kimono flung around her costume, brooding over a lapboard on which she played solitaire with cards not much bigger than thumbnails. Curls of perfumed cigarette smoke floated from her half-open door, while out of Booth's poured acrid clouds from his chain of cigars.

After the performance each went his way: Booth to his hotel room or more often on these grueling stretches of one-night stands to his Pullman drawing room, where he sat in a daze, too dull and empty to read or write letters. Outside the window hills and fields picked up speed in the same night-dimmed landscape his train had been passing for forty years. And the train whistle wailed, as though it feared the darkness, and underneath the wheels ground along the track, and he heard the syncopated chuffing of the locomotive, which seemed to say: "And *so* to bed, and *so* to bed, and *so* to bed."

VI

Barrett was home and actually seemed better, but Booth had sciatica badly this autumn of 1890. Getting out of bed in the morning, he couldn't walk at first without clutching two chairs. He was noticed hobbling through the streets leaning on a cane, which set the reporters buzzing. To scotch the stories of their failing health he and Barrett took themselves to the theater as spectators, sitting in a front box to see the comedian Francis Wilson, who after touching off each of his jokes looked up for the famous pair's reaction. Barrett would have jumped to his feet, be pacing the box and guffawing, but Booth stayed seated where he was with a tiny, sad, set smile, showing his amusement only by a twitch of the chest.

Wilson often ran across him at The Players. "*I* used to enjoy acting comedy," Booth confided softly, "especially farce. Oh, I went through it all. I went through it all."

Wilson had a photograph of the tragedian and begged to have it signed. "Certainly," said Booth, but he never got around to it.

It lay on his desk with the corners curling, and at last he admitted what was delaying him was the Shakespearian quotation Wilson wanted. "I'm just too lazy to look it up or think it up. If you'll provide it, I'll write it gladly—anything." Wilson, anxious to make sure of his souvenir, hastily thought of something, which Booth obediently copied.

On November 3 Booth and Barrett began their winter's stint in Baltimore. The decline in Booth's powers since the spring was obvious. He stumbled over words, left out lines and sometimes confused the play with another, transposing whole speeches. To Edwina he admitted that this season for the first time ever he had toiled through several performances "without my usual clear mental grasp of the character, and always with an uncertainty of gait and a *thinness* of voice, to my own ear, at least."

And to William Winter: "I don't know what's to become of me. I grow weaker all the time, and if I can't play the parts well I must leave the stage."

Very gently Winter advised him to do just that. Booth didn't really want the advice, not this advice, not yet. There was still in him a dogged vitality and as the weeks wore on his acting incredibly improved. "Here I am!' he greeted Bispham from Philadelphia. "On deck still, and feel much steadier than I've been yet this season. I am better in every way."

Again to Edwina from Boston after *Macbeth:* "Tonight I acted and felt throughout the play just as ever I did at my best. Not a stagger, not a sign of feebleness."

Nym Crinkle thought Booth and Barrett should both get off

the stage—"mummified actors . . . who are enduring by reason of packed spice and frankincense, that keep them in an unchangeable and antiseptic condition."

The unusually short tour wound up in Providence in December. Barrett played without his partner until March 2, 1891, when they began anew at the Broadway Theater in New York. They did *The Merchant* and *Julius Caesar*. Barrett's Bassanio was painfully mature. As for Booth—he should retire, said the *Times*. Barrett's Cassius was as good as ever. Not so Booth's Brutus, and those who loved him went once, then, shocked and disappointed, stayed away. On March 8 a venomous attack by Nym Crinkle appeared in *The World*. "Nowhere," jibed Nym Crinkle, "but at a public funeral and a public performance of Shakespeare do we parade the relics of departed worth."

He denounced the "tottering Mr. Booth . . . whose work was marked and marred by a careless feebleness." As Shylock, even Booth's make-up was slovenly, while as Brutus he seemed to go to sleep onstage, standing with his eyes shut and starting when his cue sounded. Nym Crinkle painted a cruel picture of how the wheel had come full circle. Booth was in the position of Forrest thirty years before when, old and half-paralyzed, Forrest was being forced off the stage by the buoyant young Booth. But "Mr. Booth's frame," taunted Nym Crinkle, "is not paralyzed. His interest is. He is not careworn, he is careless." And Nym Crinkle asked "if it be not better indeed to stop than to mar his own record by the want of *anima* to sustain it?"

Edwina, sick at heart, wrote to her father. In his answer he came as near scolding her as he ever did: " 'Tis childish to be so crushed by such vile wretches, with whom no reputation is sacred. . . . The public man (or woman) must bear the scorn, and stand unshaken by it, as I have done. . . . I have long since ceased to read 'theatrical news,' and have succeeded in letting my 'dear friends' know that I avoid such rot, and that it is brutal to mention it to me."

On Wednesday, March 18, Booth and Barrett were announced for *Richelieu*. On Wednesday morning Barrett seemed bouncing, and in the suite he had taken at the Windsor Hotel, needing more space than his bedroom at The Players, he was vivaciously occupied with the scene designer's drawings for a new play. In the evening they arrived early at the theater, had been there an hour or so when someone asked Booth to step into his partner's dressing room because Mr. Barrett was feeling ill.

Barrett had gone straight to his room and still in his hat and overcoat had sat down, tilted his chair back against the wall, let his head droop and covered his face with his hands. He had momentarily given way and had been crying when Booth came in. Booth leaned over and tried to coax him to go home, but Barrett refused. Controlling himself, he went to his make-up table to paint his still swollen face, dressed himself for De Mauprat, a young man's part, and the play began. Paradoxically, Booth felt better this night than he had in weeks, and Adam Badeau, who was in the house, was amazed at his force. But Barrett kept pushing himself until the third act, when the regular business gave him a chance to bend over the bed on which Richelieu was lying. Then very low he whispered: "I can't go on."

He had only a few more lines before his exit. He got himself offstage and another actor finished the play for him. He was put to bed at the Windsor. Booth saw him next day burning with fever. It hurt him to talk but be gasped out: "Don't come near me, Edwin! My disease may be infectious. You must be very careful."

He had caught no more than a heavy cold, but his two doctors feared pneumonia and with reason, for it set in almost immediately and in his debilitated condition, weakened by his chronic disease, was almost sure to be fatal. His wife was telegraphed for. Their family doctor had broken it to her long ago that her husband's glandular trouble was incurable and his days were numbered, but she had kept this to herself, though expecting for more than a year to be called to his side at any moment.

On Thursday night a substitute played Macduff. The third

night, Friday, Barrett's name was removed from the playbill. Booth was worried, but not alarmed. He was joyfully preoccupied with his own improvement ("Sure it is, I am as one renewed since two days past"), and after the performance he sent Theodore Bromley, their manager, to the hotel to inquire "how Lawrence was getting on."

Booth was sitting in the grill at The Players eating his supper of bread and milk when Bromley returned and said flatly and seriously: "Mr. Barrett has gone."

"Where to?" asked Booth, whose first thought was that Mrs. Barrett had taken her husband home. But Barrett was dead.

CHAPTER 16

A Scratch, A Temporary Ill

> *Good-night, sweet prince,*
> *And flights of angels sing thee to thy rest!*
> Hamlet, *Act V, scene 2*

 A LITTLE world within a world was set rocking by Barrett's death. Booth's room at The Players was like the office of a state official with its in-and-out-flowing streams of callers, as with Bromley's help he canceled engagements and adjusted broken contracts. On Monday, March 23, 1891, Barrett's body was taken to Cohasset, where, less than a week after his last performance, he was buried within earshot of the ocean waves.

In New York the weather was muggy, cloudy, and gloomy, adding to Booth's gloom. Used to disaster and constantly on the lookout for it, he was not so much shocked by Barrett's sudden going as fearfully depressed. Later in the week he was on his way out of the club when he met a boy rushing in with a package. He knew what it was and instructed: "Take it up-stairs"—meaning to The Players library on the second floor—"and unwrap it." But the boy climbed all three flights up to Booth's apartment, stripped the wrappings off a death mask of Barrett and set it on the center table. When Booth came home the first thing he saw in the darkened room was Barrett's face gleaming at him.

For the sake of the company he finished out the engagement at the Broadway Theater; there was only a week left. They played one more week at the Brooklyn Academy of Music, which ended Booth's part of the season, and after which the others, who had expected to continue through the spring with Barrett, were thrown out of work. "Mr. Booth," said a critic, "has gone weariedly and wearisomely through the final weeks of his season here . . . delivering the blank verse of Shakespeare blankly indeed, and presenting so weak a sight as to be pitiful."

The last performance in Brooklyn was a matinee of *Hamlet* on April 4. Somehow the public knew by instinct what Booth refused to know, that this performance was likely to be, not only his last of the season, but his farewell to the stage for good. Very early in the morning an enormous crowd of ticket seekers, conspicuous for the number of white-haired men and women in it and for the dozens of children clinging to their hands, formed outside the Brooklyn Academy. The curtain rose. Never had Barrett's eye and hand been more wanted.

"The players went shivering around complaining of the cold," objected the *Brooklyn Eagle*, "when leaves were green all over the trees, while in the graveyard the property man had neglected to give the digger any earth to throw out of the pit and the dummy that was supposed to represent Ophelia's body and was not a bit like it was deposited in a pit about a foot and a half deep."

Costumes and scenery were shabby and old, the company was apathetic, and the central figure, alas, was all these things. Booth's voice was so faint it could hardly be caught; most of the soliloquies went for nothing. Only in the interview with Ophelia and the business of hurling the recorder from him was there some of the old contagious excitement. Yet his reading when it could be heard and the mysterious melancholy were still beautiful. The art of a lifetime came to the support of fading nature. David Belasco, leaning forward in the audience, as were many others, in his eagerness to catch some touch of genius, remembered of the "To be or not to be" that "the familiar words seemed to come from Booth's lips for the first time, to utter thoughts then first formulated."

But this *Hamlet* could never have run a hundred nights. The audience let its star walk off in silence after his great points, only clapping decorously at the finish of each act. The reviews were not so much cruel as regretful. As the *Eagle* expressed it, "The framework of the great creation was there, but the whole performance seemed to be palsied."

At the end, however, there was stamping and bravoing as the house showed its true affection. Booth murmured a little speech. He had always claimed to be indignant at the snobbery of the public toward actors and the condescension implied by applause. Yet these, his last, words to an audience were in the traditional vein of the player who lives to please, must please to live: "Ladies and Gentlemen, I thank you for your great kindness. I hope that this is not the last time I shall have the honor of appearing before you. . . . I hope that my health and strength may be improved so that I can serve you better, and I shall always try to deserve the favor you have shown."

He dressed immediately, as he always did, and was among the first ready to leave. The instant he stepped through the stage door the actors still inside heard ringing cheers and hurrying after him they saw Montague Place billowing with people. Faces were at all the windows, and on the scaffolding of a building opposite, which was being repaired, men and boys had found a foothold on every plank. There was a mighty waving of hats and handkerchiefs. Police on horseback forced a passage for Booth to his carriage. Those near enough to see his face thought he seemed much moved. But those farther away could only see him lift his hat, look up and all around as if scanning the pit and galleries, then bow and climb into the carriage, which moved off slowly down a cleared lane.

Manager Bromley declared in the press that Mr. Booth planned to rest for a whole year, not, however, to retire. And this really was Booth's plan. Again, though, the public sensed differently. Saddened by his last performance, it began to think of him and the papers to refer to him as a figure on the shelf whose career was definitely over. "Booth at 58 is older than many a man of 70," one critic pronounced, and again the actor's life story was lugged out and summarized.

Booth in the meantime was at Narragansett with Edwina and her husband and his two grandchildren, little Mildred and Edwin, "my pets." He broke the visit by one to Jefferson at Crow's Nest, the house Jefferson had built in Buzzards Bay. It was right on the water, a roomy, luxurious place with a stained-glass "art window" on either side of the front door. One window had a picture of William Warren as Touchstone, the other of Booth as Hamlet. Along with the rollicking Jefferson tribe, Booth went to a Fourth of July celebration at which Grover Cleveland was guest of honor. Three people were needed to help Booth out of the carriage and across the lawn. They sat eating ice cream and watching fireworks burst and gaudily disintegrate over the black water, and a reporter in the background noted that Booth was "moody and silent."

Not so Jefferson, who talked ten to the dozen while his face radiated cheer; the lines in it were all laughter lines. Off the stage he had half a dozen hobbies, spent satisfying hours painting in oils, and had started a garden, explaining that all old people should have one—"it's so full of hope."

To match Jefferson's painting Booth had a gift for sculpture, discovered many years ago in Launt Thompson's studio. But he had made no use of it. He had a talent for writing, never developed. And now all impulse to create had left him. One thing, though, he had achieved in these last years: a serenity, a calm relaxing of his hold on life, as sublime in its way as Jefferson's joy in living. As they strolled with wonderful slowness along the beach together—Comedy and Tragedy personified—Booth turned his eyes away from the sea to sweep the desolate strand, and then "with a strange and prophetic kind of poetry," so said Jefferson later, "he likened it to his own failing health, the falling leaves, the withered sea-weed, the dying grass on the shore, and the ebbing tide that was fast receding from us."

And to Jefferson—who since Anderson's, and now Barrett's, death was becoming the friend of his bosom, for they were members of the same vagabond brotherhood with a bond stronger and richer than the one binding Booth to his gentlemen friends—to him Booth spoke quietly of his approaching death. He seemed hopeful and pleased at the approach. "I'm ready to go."

Then they spoke of the scrambling, climbing, sliding fortunes of actors, of the intrigues and savageries of their profession, and Booth said: "Joe, I've come to that part of my life when I can even rejoice at the success of my enemies."

II

For the first time in years there was no autumn season beginning. There were no rehearsals, no responsibilities. He had let go. And suddenly he looked much older. He had always dressed scrupulously and well, now he grew careless. Someone saw him on the street holding his little grandson by the hand, a striking-looking old man, sloppily dressed, clean-shaven, with heavy black eyebrows and soft whitening hair that flowed down under his straw hat nearly to his shoulders.

Sitting across from him in front of the fire at The Players, William Winter advised him to travel. "I've been traveling all my life," said Booth. "What I want now is to stay in one place with things I like around me. . . . Here is my bed, and here is the fire, and here are my books, and here *you* come to see me." Then he added: "I suppose I shall wear out here."

From the walls everywhere his face looked down at him in paint and marble, lighting the heavily curtained rooms and dim corridors. He saw himself young, dark-haired, debonair; in middle age; in character as Hamlet, Richelieu, and Iago; and he protested when Francis Wilson wanted to give The Players still another portait. "Please don't! Even now I can't go anywhere in the house without bumping into a Booth."

And there were his trophies: the Hundred Nights of Hamlet

medal; the gold and silver laurel wreaths he had won in Germany. There were portraits of his father; there was the framed playbill of his first appearance as Tressel. Upstairs and downstairs and flocking on the walls alongside the stairs were pictures, posters, memorabilia of the theatrical world, of professional ancestors from Richard Burbage down: the death mask of Kean, the painting of Rachel in her "feline loveliness," dozens of likenesses covering every practicable inch of the murky wall space. In glass cases were crowns, swords, quills, canes, bits of tarnished cloth, every sort of stage property proudly exhibited like jewels of great price, for they had been worn and handled by the great ones of the profession. A new member of The Players, Richard Harding Davis, exclaimed when he saw the display: "Why, I have an interesting relic I'd like to give the club, the playbill used at Ford's Theater in Washington on the night Lincoln was—" He stopped, but too late, for Booth had thrown up his hands and left the room.

The Players was Booth's home, and he was starved for domesticity. He showed excessive interest in the running of the club, never missing a directors' meeting, feeling it "outrageous" when one of the Dalys, Augustin or his brother Joseph, skipped several meetings—if he did it again Booth meant to take steps. He soberly studied the list of candidates for membership, voting against any suspected lightweights or rowdies, annoyed and hurt when they were occasionally elected in spite of him.

He sat at the long reading table downstairs in the room where Sargent's portrait of him, looking much more than two years younger, presided from above the mantel. Whenever he was observed coming in, a deferential murmur rippled through the room. He moved haltingly from member to member, speaking a word to each. Most stood until he was seated, and men who wore their hats in the house snatched them off. Usually he appeared in the grill about noon for a late breakfast, sitting down wearily at his special table. His old-fashioned dark suit looked as though he had slept in it, his stand-up collar was twitched to one side. He would order twice as much food as he could eat, then pick at it—his little joke. "It encourages the kitchen staff and besides it sends up the club's receipts."

On Saturdays about midnight the grill was hilarious with the after-theater crowd, and he often slipped downstairs to join in. There might be Wilson, John Drew, Otis Skinner, and Maurice Barrymore, whose little son John, with a round face and Dutch haircut, had been introduced to Booth. After he had listened awhile, Booth's mournful eyes would lighten, the crow's feet at their corners would deepen and lift; he would cock an eyebrow; the miracle of a smile would almost, though never quite, break on his lips, and the younger men would settle themselves to hear his soft, fatigued voice launch a train of funny stories.

Shakespeare's birthday, April 23, was Ladies' Day, the one day of the year when women were allowed in. It was Booth's favorite day to stay upstairs. Once Wilson induced him to make a grand entrance down the broad stairway across the lounge and into the twittering throng. Every woman in the place headed straight for him until he clung for rescue to Wilson's arm and muttered: "For God's sake, don't leave me!"

As time passed, he ventured down less often. On fine days he still descended sedately in the diminutive elevator, installed especially for him, and shuffled out to make the circuit of Gramercy Park. Sometimes he stopped for a pass or two at marbles with the neighborhood boys, one of whom was young Noble MacCracken, whom the years to come metamorphosed from a small boy "knuckling down" on the street corner into the tall president of Vassar College. To Dr. MacCracken the recurring figure of the tragedian in his slow promenade was a feature of his boyhood: "Mr. Booth was habitually sad, and I recall my father saying that he bore his family's tragedy all the time."

But for longer and longer periods Booth hibernated upstairs, where from his sofa by the window he could see the greenery of the park below, then the skeleton boughs, then snow, then green again. His room was a bachelor's room—dusty, a little gloomy, needing flowers or a lighted fire to bring it to life. It was oppressive with darkly gleaming furniture, with photographs, curios and peculiar keepsakes, not one of which would he willingly part with. Laurence Hutton was forever badgering him to sign a list specifically bequeathing his precious things to his friends, but he showed no eagerness to do the signing.

Perhaps he should have. Fifteen years after his death Edwina, who was going abroad to live, had to clear out her cellar of some of her father's personal effects, and they were sold at public auction. David Belasco, Julia Marlowe, and other theater people bought a few mementoes, but the general public showed little interest and the auctioneer almost wept over the small prices. Richard III's crown went for twelve dollars, the great mace to Belasco for eighteen dollars, the royal coat with fleurs-de-lis and lions woven in gold thread to a costumer for twelve dollars. Most of the costumes were let go piecemeal to different buyers. Richelieu's surplice of rare old lace collected at odd times by Booth was knocked down for nineteen dollars. Booth's personal tobacco box went to Belasco for eight dollars.

One old-time theatergoer could bear it no longer. He choked and broke away from the listless bidding, saying that "it reminds me of the Roman soldiers shaking dice for the clothes in the story of the Crucifixion."

Booth's room was divided by a fretwork arch and draw curtain that shut off the alcove where his bed was. The brass bed, which had a tester and curtains, was spread with the crazy quilt Mrs. Anderson had made him. On the bureau in the alcove were two small photographs, one of his mother, stern and sad in old age, and one of his grandchildren. To the left of the bed in the most retired position in the room was the picture of John Wilkes from which Edwin had never parted. Wilson caught sight of it during one of his calls, couldn't keep his eyes off it and was about to say something when he met Booth's eye, and Booth shook his head.

On the center table under the chandelier in the main section of the room lay a bronze cast of Booth's hand holding Edwina's baby hand. To the right of the fireplace leered three skulls, all used in *Hamlet*. Many years back one of them had rested on the shoulders of Lovett, the horse thief, and on one Booth had written: "The rest is silence," followed by his signature.

His desk stood against the wall, neatly piled with sheets of the club writing paper embossed with masks of Comedy and Tragedy. Above the desk was a portrait of his father and just below the portrait he had fixed appropriately a panel hewn out of the wood of the giant cherry tree from the farm in Maryland. On the wall nearest the window hung the most remarkable picture in the room, of Mary Devlin.

Years after Booth's death one of the distinguished guests to be taken on the grand tour of The Players was the Scottish playwright J. M. Barrie. The taciturn Scott gloomed through the building saying nothing but "Ah," until he arrived at Booth's room, which had become "the Booth Room," a dehumanized shrine where visitors instinctively dropped their voices. Barrie stopped under Mary's picture, still living, still fresh in the shrinelike atmosphere, and stood gazing up at it, sinking his eyes into it. "A verra byutiful face," he said earnestly to Wilson, who was showing him around. "A verra byutiful face."

In his room, with his things reinforcing him, Booth consented to pose for one more portrait, a drawing in black and white. The artist had trouble persuading him to sit in a handsome antique chair instead of his particular Victorian armchair upholstered in rep. Booth gave in at last—he always gave in now —and it came to light that he was partial to the rep-covered chair because it had stood in Jefferson's parlor in Richmond when Mary Devlin was living at Jefferson's. The chair was associated with his courtship. After his marriage he had asked Jefferson for it, and ever since it had had a place in his home— "I *would* have liked to have it in the portrait for Mollie's sake." Then he spoke very lovingly about Mary Devlin.

The Richmond-born sculptor Edward Valentine stopped in to see him. They spoke of Mary, looking at her picture, and the sculptor ventured: "I will describe her to you. She had black hair, grayish eyes, and a very white skin. Is that a description of her?"

"No," said Booth. "Her hair was brown, and her complexion was not so white."

Then Valentine spoke of the sad expression in Mary's eyes and Booth confirmed it: "I have seen her sitting with such an expression of eye that I thought she was dead."

He missed Barrett. More than once as he chatted with some caller, a horse-drawn truck rumbling by on Twentieth Street made vibrate the strings of the automatic harp that still hung on the door of Barrett's bedroom down the hall. "There comes poor Lawrence now," Booth would whisper with macabre humor.

Very often his caller was Winter, who was much given to lachrymose prophecies and alarmed comparisons of the past with the present, in favor of the past. Winter's reputation as a critic had begun to dim slightly. He feared and hated the turn toward realism and "rank, deadly pessimism" the drama was taking. He was contemptuous of Boucicault's sordid plays. He despised Ibsen, championed recently by George Bernard Shaw, and he moaned to Booth that the days of idealism in the drama were passing. Booth agreed, but mildly. He was outside the combat. When he talked of the past it was of personal things. Sometimes a biting word about the self-seekers he had known broke through his hard-won detachment. Once he mused aloud to Winter: "I was always of a boyish spirit, but there was an air of melancholy about me that made me seem more serious than I really was."

Francis Wilson, instead of indulging Booth's nostalgia, would prime him with the latest gossip and Booth was grateful: "You make me think I'm still of the present." It was hard for others to include him in the swim, either in their talk or thought; his productive years were so plainly over. When he went to the theater as one of the audience, it failed to stir him. He was too depleted mentally and physically to want to act. He had nothing left to give the public. For ten years he had longed for leisure. Now that he had it, the letdown and sameness of his life depressed him into an almost comatose indifference. Wilson discovered late one day that Booth had forgotten to eat anything. He had taken no food since the night before and complained in a puzzled way of feeling weak.

"Mr. Booth, if you don't eat how can you expect to live?" clucked the little comedian as he steered Booth down to the grill.

Booth looked straight at him. "It doesn't matter much, Wilson."

III

He sat propped in a chair on the lawn at Narragansett this summer of 1892 and watched his grandchildren's tireless racings and stumblings. Sometimes he loosed an unconscious sigh. He never complained of the children's noise, though at meals he might whimsically reprove them for shrill voices by quoting King Lear:

Her voice was ever soft,
Gentle and low, an excellent thing in woman.

His son-in-law took a snapshot of him seated on the porch: the old man with the untidy white hair and tragic eyes, the drooping lips, the pinched throat, the tired angle of the head and of the shoulders as they rested against the high chair back. There were other pictures snapped, some so unfair to Booth that Edwina would never allow them to be published. He was ill this summer and she nursed him. "Daughter, you make me like to be sick," he said more than once, reaching up out of the bed to hold her hand.

He would allow no one to help him in dressing or in any of his small occupations, though his hand sometimes refused to do his will and moved sharply the wrong way. Still more mystifying were the gaps in his consciousness, lost moments when he seemed to drop asleep. Often when he exerted himself to fix his mind on some definite thing, it buckled under him like drunken legs. He tried to explain this to Bispham, writing on

August 14; it was his last long letter to this old friend: "Many days have faded into weeks since I have written you, but not since my many attempts to do so, dear boy; they have been many and frequent, but all failures, desperate. . . . All my efforts have been senseless, and even now it is with difficulty I manage to scribble in desperation this bungling scrawl."

In October the Grossmanns spent some weeks in the resort town of Lakewood, New Jersey, and Booth went with them. "The most striking figure this fall among the guests at the Laurel House," burbled a reporter, "is that of a feeble, tottering old man with a pale and wonderfully sad face, who makes his way feebly through the corridors with the assistance of a heavy oaken cane. You would hardly know that it was Edwin Booth unless he raised those surprisingly lustrous and melancholy eyes . . . which remain unchanged."

They were not quite unchanged, though. A strange expression had entered them, a pained and worried look as if he asked himself: "What am I doing here?"

This was something new, the reporter was told. Mr. Booth had only had this look since his illness in the summer. The really extraordinary thing was his appearance of age. It was hard to believe he wasn't yet fifty-nine. The reporter inquired if Mr. Booth ever talked or seemed to think of acting again. No, never—"He doesn't think of anything more than he can help," Grossmann told the newspaper man.

Every day Booth joined the male guests in the hotel smoking room. He took the air on the veranda, seated in one of the ranged rocking chairs, and struggling to his feet each time his daughter came up to him. He played careful games with his lively grandchildren—played sitting down, for he was so weak that the little boy had once accidentally knocked him flat. It was Grossmann, smart in a nautical jacket and white trousers, who first interviewed anyone from outside who asked to see his father-in-law. He and Edwina would read a recommended book first, then turn it over to Booth if it were light enough.

Booth often drove around the lake with the Grossmanns and sometimes walked alone into the village, a shambling figure in a black frock coat and waistcoat and a black bow cravat, his tousled white hair thrown back from his forehead as if by constant combings with the fingers. The village people had grown used to him, only strangers stopped to stare. On rare days he pushed on as far as the lake bordered with dark pines under a wintry sky and rested there, leaning on his cane. The melancholy spot seemed to have a charm for him.

As the grandfather's clock in The Players intoned midnight, ushering in November 13, 1892, one of "the boys" down at the billiard table remembered this was the founder's fifty-ninth birthday. The building was canvassed, and the seventy-five or so members in it all signed their names to a round robin of good wishes, which was carried up to the third floor. Enthusiasm was dampened, however, when the bearer brought back word that Mr. Booth was sleeping and couldn't be disturbed.

Again it was Founder's Night, December 31. The New Year had been banged and tootled in, and inside the mellow fastness of The Players a toast had been drunk to Booth who, supported under both elbows, crept across the hall to the elevator, hesitated at the elevator door, turned himself around to face the members and waved and smiled. This was the last time many of them saw him.

Edwina had taken her children south. Without her near him he felt alone indeed, yet try as he would it was the end of January when he finally brought himself to write. "My darling daughter: Every day for the last month I have determined to write, but time has passed, and my girl still neglected. Try to forgive me, and I'll do better after this."

Unaccountably, three more weeks slipped by before he wrote again on February 19—"it seems much longer, quite three months; and I can offer no better reason for my neglect than sheer laziness. . . . So it has been day after day until now, when I find myself overwhelmed by a heap of unanswered letters."

He was too jaded and dazed to cope with the heap. Several people at once had sent pictures of him for his autograph. He had laid them aside, and when he turned back to them had got them all mixed up. So kind Harry Magonigle persuaded him to sign them all, and then Magonigle wrote to the senders asking them to describe their precious special photos. Then Bispham and Magonigle took over the answering of letters while Booth dozed on his sofa, absolutely overpowered by his strange inertia. "I can't account for it, except my lack of exercise. I do nothing but snooze all day, and see very few to talk to, except the doctors."

He had three doctors now who applied electricity, which was disagreeable. Still, he felt better after it. Their visit was the high point of his day. He had been outdoors only twice since Edwina's going. Magonigle sat with him every evening, staying to the very end to put him to bed and turn out the light. There were no more wakeful vulture hours. He went to bed at half past eight and slept heavily. "Every now and then," he wrote to Edwina on February 26, "I receive your welcome letters, darling, which make me very happy in my gloomy club-room; for I seldom go out or downstairs, keeping upstairs nearly all the time. Have been only to Daly's, and shall go again there to see the 'Twelfth Night' on Tuesday."

But the performance, with Ada Rehan as a flame-headed, hoydenish Viola, merely tired Booth and gave him no pleasure. "I don't feel yet the least desire for the stage, although my two visits have set all the managers and agents after me for engagements, of course. . . . There is a great Italian actress here, a Mlle. Duse, the greatest yet, they say. I shall see her in a few nights."

Then, lo, it was March, a dull, cold month with snow every day or the threat of snow. Booth had four doctors now. He sat down determinedly to write to Edwina in the late afternoon on March 4, a dismal Sunday: "Another day is about gone, and Sunday night is creeping ahead of me, and no letter mailed for you yet. . . . I can't account for it."

Scrawls from his grandchildren lay on his desk mutely reproaching him for his lack of response. But he could not, simply could not summon up strength to answer them. "I can't muster energy enough . . . but only silently wish them all sorts of good things, to share with darling mama, with my loving thoughts." This one letter had occupied his whole day, with frequent stops to collect himself. "I'll soon do better. . . . I can't scribble even half that I hoped for today."

He found it difficult to organize the simplest phrase, even to spell. "I don't know what is the cause. I certainly am much better than I was, in all respects, until I attempt to write, when all my wits seem to go astray, and my nerves get beyond control."

He was writing now on March 15. "Several days have gone by without my having had energy to write more than a telegram to you. . . . After breakfast I take a paper and lie on my sofa, where I get most sunlight, till about 3:30 or 4 o'clock, when I dine a little, and after go to Carryl's or Bispham's, or to the play, in order to get a vain hope for an interest in the theatre. My deafness is so much increased that I don't hear a word that is spoken on the stage. . . . I won't promise any more, but I'll try to finish this badly begun letter in the morning. . . .

"March 16. Good morning, my little ones! Only 'tis nearly evening again; the way I let time slip away is a caution to babies. . . . 'tis now nearly tomorrow evening ahead, and I'm just about awake, and have only just scratched a few lines addressed to my good little 'Babes in the Woods' 'way down South, where 'tis nice and warm, amongst the birds and flowers. Here 'tis just as cold as winter still. I'm really cold and shivering while I try to write."

IV

But as the northern spring grew milder Booth was able to get out occasionally. Badeau called, discovered him ready to leave for a walk, and offered to go with him. On the sidewalk Booth gripped Badeau's arm nervously. It took Badeau, who was in his spry prime at over sixty, a half an hour to help his old friend toddle around the Park and back to the clubhouse.

Things went better when they sat peacefully upstairs and talked of old days. Badeau had come to know Booth when he was dazzling New York for the first time; when his beauty and health had been so much a part of him, he had been so young, so poetic, so romantic, that Badeau found it sad beyond words to see him in his decadence, "to see his powers crumble and waste away; to see him decrepit, weary, worn, who had been alive with expression, captivating in bearing, majestic, terrible, tender, by turns."

"Only his eyes," said Badeau, "retained their marvelous beauty, like a lamp burning in a deserted temple, or the soul looking out through the windows of that body it was soon to leave."

Presiding as usual at a club directors' meeting, Booth seemed to be thinking of something else. The others deferentially recalled his attention to the matter under discussion.

Edwina and her husband were back in New York and on April 3 they took Booth with them to see Alessandro Salvini, son of Tommaso, in *Don Caesar de Bazan* at the Manhattan Opera House. Don Caesar had been one of Booth's roles. It was pitiable, wrote a lurking journalist, to watch the man, who so short a time before had been the first star of them all, inch across the lobby through the parting in the crowd, his eyes glassy with the strain of walking as his daughter and son-in-law almost lifted him along between them to a box on the ground floor. On April 11 he saw Daniel Frohman's production of *The Guardsman* at the New York Lyceum, but he seemed not to enjoy it much, nor could Edwina, who was too conscious of the effort it was costing her father to sit through the performance. This was the last time he was in a theater.

On Tuesday, April 17, he woke up with a headache. However, he dined at the Grossmanns' and, though feeble, seemed bright and spoke in his murmurous voice of how happy he was still to be able to get out to see them. Later in his room he read himself to sleep with a volume of William Winter's poems. When Magonigle stole in next morning to wake him he was unconscious, the book lying open. He had had a brain hemorrhage. His face was contorted down one side, only a streak of the whites showed under the eyelids; his right arm and side were paralyzed.

Edwina stationed herself by his bed. Twice in the long weeks to come her father recognized her and spoke to her distinctly; for the most part his speech was thick and wandering. He could keep down only milk at first and drank four glasses a day with relish. Later he grew stronger, all except his mind. When by June it looked as though he would live on indefinitely, the Grossmanns planned to move him to Narragansett, but on June 3 he had a relapse. The daily bulletin posted downstairs in The Players read: "Mr. Booth has gradually grown weaker during the past twenty-four hours, and there is now very little hope left of even a partial recovery."

EDWIN BOOTH DYING! Booth's gallant life story appeared in news columns side by side with a description, sparing nothing, of how he looked as he lay on his deathbed. Every few hours another bulletin went up in The Players: "About the same." "No change."

A knot of reporters had taken up positions in front of the Park and passed the time talking while they waited for Dr. St. Clair Smith to wave a handkerchief from the third-floor window as the signal that all was over. All except his devoted daughter already accepted Booth's death so completely that it was hard to believe he still breathed, even though weakly; that his relaxing body gave out a warmth, however feeble; that he had human wants and a will grown more imperious for the short time left it. Yet so he had, and he indicated fretfully that the shouts and peals of summer laughter of the children playing in the Park disturbed him.

Edwina brought his grandchildren up to the bed to say good-by. "How are you, dear Grandpa?" called little Edwin.

Booth was drifting off, facing out to sea, when the child's voice arrested him, and for a last moment the world he was taking leave of surged up in front of him, solid and clear, and he called back boyishly: "How are you yourself, old fellow?"

By June 6, three days after his relapse, a glance at his sunken face showed that he had not many hours. He lay on his back, his left arm crooked over his head and his paralyzed right arm rigid by his side. Every few minutes his breath seemed to be snatched away; he reached after it in drawn-out gasps. Dr. Smith and two nurses were with him. In the outer part of the room were Grossmann, Magonigle, Bispham, and Charles Carryl, who represented The Players. Edwina sat in the alcove by her father's bed. His waning presence, unseeing and unhearing, was still a companion to her, and she was grateful for every moment left.

During the evening a hard shower with thunder and lightning sprang up, but by midnight the rain had subsided, and the air was cool and fresh. It was after one in the morning of June 7, 1893, when without warning all the lights in the building and on the street below went out. Edwina cried: "Don't let father die in the dark!"

Then the lights flashed on again and almost in the same moment, with everyone in the room moving up swiftly to stand beside his bed, Booth died. So slight was the change in him that it was "like the passing of a shadow," said Dr. Smith. The doctor held his handkerchief outside the window and shook it gently, and the reporters streamed off, leaving the street deserted.

Down in the grill a group of the junior actors, E. H. Sothern with three friends, was sitting around a table. They were exclaiming loudly over the behavior of the lights when they heard Magonigle say behind them: "Hush, Mr. Booth is dead."

The face from which the spirit had departed looked at peace again. At eight in the morning a death mask was made of Booth by the man who had done the mask of Barrett.

Booth's funeral was held two days later at the Little Church Around the Corner, which was crowded with theater people, subdued and solemn. In the double line of honorary pallbearers were Aldrich, Bispham, and Furness, but the most conspicuous was Jefferson, who seemed aged and sad. All eyes rested on him and the thought in everyone's mind was: When he follows Booth the old order changes.

As Booth's coffin was being carried out of the church after the Episcopal service to the sonorous "Dead March" from *Saul*—in this same moment by an eerie coincidence three stories of Ford's Theater in Washington, where Lincoln had been shot by John Wilkes Booth and which had since been made into government offices, collapsed with a splintering roar, killing over twenty persons.

Booth's body was taken immediately to the Boston train. In New York the flags of two theaters—and only two, Daly's and Palmer's—fluttered at half-mast as he left the city for the last time. "There goes the greatest American actor," sighed one of the profession as the cortege drove through Boston late in the afternoon.

The sun was setting as a slow procession of family and friends toiled on foot up the slope inside Mount Auburn Cemetery in Cambridge. Several hundred strangers watched from a distance. Edwina and her uncle Joseph stood together as the coffin, with a spray of evergreen laid on it by Julia Ward Howe, was lowered into the grave, bringing Booth to rest beside Mary Devlin.

After the clergyman finished speaking, even after the grave was filled, many in the group around it lingered, thoughtful for a moment, while the sun dropped behind the Belmont Hills.

Notes on Sources

DURING Edwin Booth's lifetime and just after his death several books were published that have been invaluable to his later biographers. Chief among these standard sources are Asia Booth Clarke's books about her family; William Winter's *Life and Art of Edwin Booth*, The Macmillan Company, 1893; and Edwina Booth Grossmann's *Edwin Booth: Recollections by his daughter and letters to her and to his friends*, The Century Company, 1894.

William Winter's several volumes of reminiscences are studded with anecdotes about Booth; and in the last twenty years have appeared four up-to-date books, each with its special value. *Darling of Misfortune*, by Richard Lockridge, The Century Company, 1932, is an exceedingly readable biography and covers new ground. Its detailed information on the rise and fall of Booth's Theater is of immense interest. Stanley Kimmel's *The Mad Booths of Maryland*, Bobbs-Merrill, 1940, is an absorbing and really monumental work on the entire Booth family, providing much new material, particularly on the background and family life and relationships of the Booths, and the adventures of Edwin and Junius Jr. in California. The chapters on John Wilkes Booth are perhaps the most definitive that have yet been written about Edwin's unhappy brother. Otis Skinner's *The Last Tragedian*, Dodd, Mead, is interesting for the selection of Booth's own letters that it presents and for Skinner's memories of the great actor, and equally interesting is Katherine Goodale's charming reminiscential *Behind the*

Scenes with Edwin Booth, Houghton Mifflin Company, 1931, which brings the tragedian to life in a wonderfully vivid way.

The present biography is indebted for facts to all these sources. It is indebted also to a number of persons who had some contact with Edwin Booth in life and have contributed to the author their particular anecdotes and fresh, individual impressions. The innumerable reviews and newspaper articles consulted are not listed here; they are available to any student. Grateful thanks for access to the letters and papers of Edwin Booth, many of them never before published, are due to The Players, the Theatre Collection of the Museum of the City of New York, the New York Public Library Manuscript and Theatre Collections, the Harvard Theatre Collection, the Princeton University Library, and the Valentine Museum of Richmond, Virginia. Special thanks goes to the distinguished actress Miss Helen Menken for permission to read her collection of Booth family letters, and thanks goes also to Miss May Davenport Seymour, Curator of the Theatre and Music Collections of the Museum of the City of New York; to Mrs. Marguerite McAneny, Custodian of the William Seymour Theatre Collection, and Mr. Alexander Clark, Curator of Manuscripts, at Princeton University Library; to Dr. William Van Lennep and Miss Mary Reardon of the Harvard Theater Collection; to Mr. George Freedley, Librarian in Charge of the Theatre Collection, Mr. Robert W. Hill, Keeper of Manuscripts, and Mr. Edward Morrison of the Manuscript Division, at the New York Public Library; and to Mr. Pat Carroll at The Players.

The courtesy of Mr. Edwin Booth Grossmann, the grandson of Edwin Booth, in approving the use of certain hitherto unpublished excerpts from family letters, is most gratefully acknowledged.

Acknowledgment is due to G. P. Putnam's Sons for permission to quote from *The Unlocked Book, a Memoir of John Wilkes Booth by his sister Asia Booth Clarke*, with a Foreword by Eleanor Farjeon; and also from *Ellen Terry's Memoirs*. Direct quotations from *The Unlocked Book* include all con-

versations between Asia Booth Clarke and her brother John
Wilkes in Chapters 4, 5, 7 and 8; the gypsy's prediction to
John Wilkes in Chapter 4, and in the same chapter John Wilkes'
warning to Asia about her husband, "Always bear in mind
you're a professional stepping-stone"; John Wilkes' description
to Asia in Chapter 5 of John Brown's execution; Asia's opinion
that Edwin "trembled for his own laurels" and the Southerner's
exclamation overheard by her that "*Our Wilkes* looks like a
young god!" both quoted in Chapter 7; and in Chapter 8,
Asia's realization about her brother beginning "I knew then
that my hero was a spy, a blockade-runner, a rebel . . . ,"
John Wilkes' request to Asia's children to "remember me, babies, in your prayers," John S. Clarke's demand for a divorce
"which would be *his* only salvation now," Asia's remark that
her husband considered all the Booths "Iagos" and "loathed
their secretiveness," the letters to Asia from Edwin Booth and
Effie Germon and Asia's comment on Effie Germon's letter,
Edwin's denial of any connection with "Claud Burroughs,"
the conversations between Asia and the detective and between
Asia and Mr. Hemphill, and several statements by Asia occa-
sioned by Lincoln's assassination, beginning "If Wilkes Booth
was mad . . . ," "There is no solidity in Love . . . ," and
"Those who have passed through such an ordeal. . . ." Material in Chapter 8 given as from the pen of Charles Warwick
has also been quoted from *The Unlocked Book*. From *Ellen
Terry's Memoirs* have been quoted directly all descriptive comments by Miss Terry on Edwin Booth and on Henry Irving,
which appear in Chapters 11, 12 and 15.

Material from *Footlights and Spotlights*, by Otis Skinner,
copyright 1924, 1951, is used by special permission of the publishers, The Bobbs-Merrill Company, Inc. It includes Skinner's
description in Chapter 9 of Booth's Othello as being human,
poetic and lovely, "very much like Booth himself"; also the
incident in Chapter 10 of Booth's burning the contents of John
Wilkes' trunk, which was originally told to Otis Skinner by
Garrie Davidson. The version of the incident given in this
book has been adapted from Davidson's account in *Footlights
and Spotlights,* and all conversation occurring in it is quoted

directly from *Footlights and Spotlights*. The incident in Chapter 15 of Skinner's accidentally striking Booth on the head during *Macbeth* has also been adapted from Otis Skinner's account in *Footlights and Spotlights*.

From *Mad Folk of the Theatre*, by Otis Skinner, copyright 1928, and used by special permission of the publishers, The Bobbs-Merrill Company, Inc., are taken the anecdote in Chapter 1 of Junius Brutus Booth begging his audience to "shut up," and promising it "in ten minutes . . . the God damnedest Lear you ever saw in your lives," and the excerpt quoted in Chapter 1 from Mr. Booth's letter to a friend beginning "Your loving communication has been just delivered," and ending ". . . Steamboat about to go."

Mrs. Katherine Goodale (Kitty Molony) has graciously given permission for quotations from *Behind the Scenes with Edwin Booth*. The description in Chapter 14 of Booth's tour in 1886–1887 with the "David Garrick" company owes much to Mrs. Goodale's first-hand account. All conversations involving Kitty Molony and members of the David Garrick company are quoted directly from Mrs. Goodale's book. The explanation in Chapter 10 of how Booth grew seven feet tall when he delivered the Curse of Rome, and the episode in Chapter 13 of the American woman in Germany who shied off from kissing Booth, were originally described in *Behind the Scenes with Edwin Booth*. Mrs. Goodale's book is also the source of Booth's exclamation in Chapter 11 about his near escape from Mark Gray's bullet "My caul saved me! Second sight—premonition—warning! . . ."

All statements by Edward H. House and excerpts from correspondence between House and Edwin Booth, as well as all remarks by Charles Reade and excerpts from a reminiscential conversation between Reade and Booth, are quoted from "Edwin Booth in London," by E. H. House, from *Century Magazine*, copyright 1897, Century Company, and are reprinted by permission of Appleton-Century-Crofts, Inc. This material is found in Chapter 12.

The account in Chapter 4 of Booth's first meeting with Mary Devlin and of the complication in their courtship when she almost became engaged to another man is based on the article by Anne M. Fauntleroy, "The Romance of Mary Devlin Booth," *Ladies' Home Journal*, September, 1904. Booth's words written to his mother that he had seen and acted with a young woman who much impressed him, and Mary's confession that she "was inspired" and could "act forever" with Booth and later that they were "all in all to each other," are quoted directly from this article and are reprinted by special permission of the *Ladies' Home Journal*, copyright 1932, The Curtis Publishing Company.

Miss Mildred Howells and Mr. John Mead Howells have given kind permission to quote in Chapter 9 from William Dean Howells' *Literary Friends and Acquaintance*, Harper, 1900, in retelling the famous "It's Lincoln's hand!" story, involving Booth and James Lorimer Graham.

Otis Skinner's description in Chapter 11 of Booth and his second wife backstage, beginning "She would attend to all the robing and make-up . . . ," is reprinted by permission of Dodd, Mead & Company from *The Last Tragedian*, by Otis Skinner, copyright 1939, by Dodd, Mead & Company, Inc.

Grateful acknowledgment is made of permission by the respective publishers to quote from the following other sources:

The Cowells in America, edited by M. Willson Disher, Oxford University Press, 1934, for Mrs. Sam Cowell's description in Chapter 5 of seeing Booth as Brutus and Petruchio.

Vagrant Memories, by William Winter, The George H. Doran Company, 1915, for the anecdote in Chapter 2 about Junius Brutus Booth diving under the bed to escape from Thomas R. Gould, for the anecdote in Chapter 8 of John McCullough telling Edwin Forrest that John Wilkes Booth was supposed to have shot Lincoln, for Booth's words to a clergyman in Chapter 10, "There is no door in my theater through which God cannot see," and for Booth's words to Winter in Chapter 16, "Here is my bed, and here is the fire, and here are my books, and here *you* come to see me. I suppose I shall wear out here."

Autobiographical Sketch of Mrs. John Drew, Scribner's,

1899, for Mrs. Drew's comments in Chapter 1 on Junius Brutus Booth when he crowed like a rooster during *Hamlet*.

The Melancholy Tale of 'Me,' by Edward H. Sothern, Scribner's, 1916, for Sothern's description of Booth's Hamlet in Chapter 11 beginning "His genius shone like a good deed. . . ."

Joseph Jefferson, by Francis Wilson, Scribner's, 1906, for Jefferson's description of young Booth in Chapter 4 beginning "There was a gentleness and sweetness of manner in him . . ." and for Jefferson's instructions to Mary Devlin in the same chapter, "Tomorrow, Mary, you'll rehearse Juliet to the Romeo of a new and rising tragedian," for Jefferson's statement to The Players after Booth's death quoted in Chapter 15 that "It was not his wealth only, but it was himself that he gave," and for Jefferson's account in Chapter 16 of how Booth compared his own failing health to the desolate landscape as they strolled on the beach at Buzzards Bay.

"A Group of Players," by Laurence Hutton, *Harper's New Monthly Magazine,* January, 1898, for Hutton's description in Chapter 10 of standing in the wing watching Booth act Richelieu, for several excerpts from Booth's letters to Hutton quoted in Chapter 12, for Manager Bromley's announcement "Mr. Barrett has gone" and Booth's query "Where to?" quoted at the end of Chapter 15, for Booth's instructions in Chapter 16 to an errand boy to "take [Barrett's death mask] upstairs and unwrap it," and for Booth's explanation in Chapter 16 that he would have liked to have the rep-covered chair in the picture "for Mollie's sake."

"Edwin Booth as I Knew Him," by Edwin Milton Royle, *Harper's Magazine,* May, 1916, for Booth's comment on Robert Browning's affectation, his conversation with Tennyson, and Mrs. Florence Irving's letter to him, all quoted in Chapter 12, for Booth's exclamation on the German Prince Karl's death quoted in Chapter 13, and for the exhortation to the audience by one of Booth's admirers quoted in Chapter 15 beginning "That's right, call him out again! . . ."

Family Circle, by Cornelia Otis Skinner, Houghton Mifflin

Company, 1948, for Booth's advice to Otis Skinner in Chapter 11 beginning "Young man, I've been watching you and you're killing yourself. . . ."

Reminiscences of a Dramatic Critic, by Henry Austin Clapp, Houghton Mifflin Company, 1902, for the description of Booth in Chapter 4 as being "crude with the promise-crammed crudity of genius . . . ," and for Charles Fechter's confusion of "whet" and "wet" quoted in Chapter 10.

Reminiscences, by Julia Ward Howe, Houghton Mifflin Company, 1899, for Booth's words to Mrs. Howe in Chapter 4 about "little Mary Devlin" in "several *heavy* parts," for Mrs. Howe's description in Chapter 4 of Booth's and Mary Devlin's performance together in *Romeo and Juliet* beginning "Few who saw it will ever forget it . . . ," and for her description in Chapter 6 of Booth following the casket at Mary's funeral.

John Wilkes Booth, by Francis Wilson, Houghton Mifflin Company, 1929, for the line from Booth's letter to Junius in Chapter 4, "I don't think John will startle the world, but he is improving fast and looks beautiful," for John Wilkes' warning to John S. Clarke in Chapter 7 beginning "Never again, if you value your life, speak to me so . . . ," and for Colonel Conger's description in Chapter 8 of John Wilkes trapped in the burning barn.

Francis Wilson's Life of Himself, Houghton Mifflin Company, 1924, for the discussion in Chapter 14 between Booth and Lawrence Barrett on the leadership of their profession, for Booth's reminiscence to Wilson in Chapter 15 beginning "*I* used to enjoy acting comedy . . ." and his rueful explanation of why he had not signed his photograph for Wilson, for the quotation in Chapter 16 of Booth's several remarks to Wilson —about not being able to "go anywhere in the house without bumping into a Booth," "For God's sake, don't leave me," "You make me think I'm still of the present"—and finally for J. M. Barrie's comment on seeing Mary Devlin's picture at The Players: "A verra byutiful face."

Special mention should be made of *Crowding Memories*, by Mrs. Thomas Bailey Aldrich (Lilian Woodman), Houghton

Mifflin Company, 1920. On Mrs. Aldrich's unique account is based the description in Chapters 5 and 6 of the Woodman sisters' first meeting and subsequent intimacy with the Booths. All conversation and correspondence that involves both the Woodmans and the Booths is quoted directly from this book, as are also Mary Devlin's exclamation at the theater, "Oh, I've said the wrong line and Edwin is saying it"; her request to her maid to "take me upstairs and put me to bed, I feel as if I should never be warm again"; Mrs. Stoddard's letter to Mary about Booth's drinking and Mary's reply to Mrs. Stoddard; the telegram from Dr. Miller to the stage manager at the Winter Garden; the words quoted in Chapter 8 of Booth's Negro dresser beginning "Oh, Massa Edwin, the President has been shot . . . ," Mrs. Booth's prayer after hearing of John Wilkes Booth's crime, "O God, if this be true, let him not live to be hanged," and Launt Thompson's words to Mrs. Booth when he escorted her to the Philadelphia train beginning "You will need now all your courage."

Acknowledgment of brief quotation is also made to the authors and publishers of the following sources:

Edwin Booth, by Charles Townsend Copeland, Small, Maynard and Company, 1901, for Copeland's descriptions of Booth walking down Park Street and of Booth's and Salvini's acting in *Othello*, quoted in Chapter 14.

With Walt Whitman in Camden, Volume I, by Horace Traubel, Small, Maynard and Company, 1906, for Whitman's thoughts on Booth in Chapter 11 beginning "Edwin had everything but guts. . . ."

"Edwin Booth's Opinion of the Players of His Day," by Edgar Beecher Bronson, *Theatre Magazine*, May, 1910, for Booth's letter to Robertson about trying "strong names" quoted in Chapter 10 and beginning ". . . all these half-baked stars. . . ."

Shakespeare on the Stage, by William Winter, Moffat, Yard and Company, 1911, for Edwin Forrest's acid comments on the performances of Booth and Cushman in *Macbeth* quoted in Chapter 5, and for Booth's statement to Winter in Chapter 8 beginning "All my life I have thought of dreadful things that might happen to me. . . ."

Shakespeare on the Stage, Second Series, by William Winter, Moffat, Yard and Company, 1915, for Winter's description of Booth as King Lear quoted in Chapter 11 and beginning "I remember him—indeed, who that saw him could ever forget. . . ."

Other Days, by William Winter, Moffat, Yard and Company, 1908, for Booth's words "It is the last recall" spoken at John Brougham's grave and quoted in Chapter 11, and for Barrett's admission "I can't go on" during his last performance, and his warning in his last illness beginning "Don't come near me, Edwin . . . ," both quoted in Chapter 15.

Life and Art of Richard Mansfield, by William Winter, Moffat, Yard and Company, 1910, for Booth's comment to Winter that Irving's Hamlet had "rather a lot of red silk pocket handkerchief in it," and Irving's verdict that Booth was "a magnificent reader," both quoted in Chapter 12.

"Two Great Othellos," by Clara Morris, *Munsey's Magazine,* November, 1909, for Clara Morris' description of Salvini's Othello in Chapter 10.

Life on the Stage, by Clara Morris, McClure, Phillips and Company, 1901, for Mr. Ellsler's opinion quoted in Chapter 5 that John Wilkes "has more of the old man's power in one performance than Edwin can show in a year . . . ," for John Wilkes' famous comment quoted in Chapter 7 that Edwin "*is* Hamlet, melancholy and all," and for Clara Morris' statement about John Wilkes after the assassination quoted in Chapter 8 and beginning "He was so young, so bright, so gay. . . ."

Julia Ward Howe, by Laura E. Richards and Maud Howe Elliott, Houghton Mifflin Company, 1916, for Senator Charles Sumner's assertion "I have outlived my interest in individuals" and Mrs. Howe's comment that "fortunately God Almighty had not . . . got so far," quoted in Chapter 6.

"The Eloquence of Silence," by Julia Marlowe, *Green Book Magazine,* March, 1913, for Julia Marlowe's description of seeing Booth as Iago quoted in Chapter 12.

"Edwin Booth in Old California Days," *The Green Book Album*, June, 1911, for J. J. McCloskey's reminiscences about Edwin Booth in Chapter 3 and the elder Booth's angry instructions to Edwin during their first rehearsal in San Francisco.

"A Conversation with Joseph Haworth," *Arena*, January, 1901, for Booth's remark to Haworth in Chapter 15 beginning "I could *act* then, had all the enthusiasm of youth. . . ."

The Life of Thomas Bailey Aldrich, by Ferris Greenslet, Houghton Mifflin Company, 1908, for Aldrich's joke to Booth in Chapter 14: "Hello, Ned! Going hunting? I'll lend you Trip!"

"Edwin Booth and Ole Bull," by R. Ogden Doremus, *Critic*, March, 1906, for Mary McVicker's protest beginning "Please don't ask Edwin to read *Manfred* . . ." quoted in Chapter 9.

Sketches of Tudor Hall and the Booth Family, by Ella V. Mahoney, Tudor Hall, May, 1925, for the remark attributed to John Wilkes in Chapter 8 beginning: "If I hadn't been very courageous, I'd have given up right there . . . ," and for the old Baltimore woman's exclamation "How beautiful was Asia! How handsome John Wilkes Booth!" quoted in Chapter 11.

The request for tickets from Boston Corbett to Edwin Booth, from which a line is quoted in Chapter 11, is in the possession of The Peale Museum, Baltimore, Maryland. The diary of John Wilkes Booth and the letters from Mrs. Mary Ann Booth to John Wilkes, from which quotation is made in Chapter 8, are in the possession of the Judge Advocate General's Office, Washington, D.C., and are quoted with the permission of that Office.

Index